Operational Level

Paper P1

Performance Operations

EXAM PRACTICE KIT

CIMA

PUBLISHING

KAPLAN

PUBLISHING

Published by: Kaplan Publishing UK

Unit 2 The Business Centre, Molly Millars Lane, Wokingham, Berkshire RG41 2QZ

Acknowledgements

We are grateful to the Chartered Institute of Management Accountants for permission to reproduce past examination questions. The answers to CIMA Exams have been prepared by Kaplan Publishing, except in the case of the CIMA November 2010 and subsequent CIMA Exam answers where the official CIMA answers have been reproduced.

British Library Cataloguing in Publication Data
A catalogue record for this book is available from the British Library

ISBN: 978 0 85732 755 0

Printed and bound in Great Britain.

CONTENTS

Key features in this edition

In addition to providing a wide ranging bank of real past exam questions, we have also included in this edition:

- Paper specific information and advice on **exam technique**.

- Our **recommended approach** to make your revision for this particular subject as effective as possible.

  This includes step by step guidance on how best to use our Kaplan material (Complete Text, Kaplancards and Exam Kit) at this stage in your studies.

- Enhanced **tutorial answers** packed with specific key answer tips, technical tutorial notes and exam technique tips from our experienced tutors.

- **Examiner's comments** reproduced from the Post Exam Guide with the kind permission of CIMA.

You will find a wealth of other resources to help you with your studies on the following sites:

www.EN-gage.co.uk

www.cimaglobal.com

INDEX TO QUESTIONS AND ANSWERS

INTRODUCTION

This new Paper P1 (introduced in 2010) has changed considerably from the old Paper P1, which was predominantly concerned with costing and budgeting methodologies - some 80% of the syllabus weighting was concerned with those areas but now it is 40%.

Areas have been introduced into the new paper P1 from the old Paper P2, covering project appraisal (25%) and uncertainty in analysis (15%). The balance of the paper covers managing short term finance, which was in Paper P7 of the old syllabus.

The direction of the new paper has therefore a much broader view of performance, dealing with details of capital budgeting and treasury management issues. The rather narrow technical approach used in the previous syllabus has been replaced, with the student now required to understand the wider aspects of financial operations. Students should ensure that they cover any deficiencies in their basic costing knowledge, since this new Paper P1 will not spend as much time on this area.

KEY TO THE INDEX

PAPER ENHANCEMENTS

We have added the following enhancements to the answers in this exam kit:

Key answer tips

Many answers include key answer tips to help your understanding of each question.

Tutorial note

Many answers include more tutorial notes to explain some of the technical points in more detail.

Top tutor tips

For selected questions, we "walk through the answer" giving guidance on how to approach the questions with helpful 'tips from a top tutor', together with technical tutor notes.

These answers are indicated with the "footsteps" icon in the index.

ANALYSIS OF PAST EXAM PAPERS

The table below summarises the key topics that have been tested in the syllabus examinations to date.

Section A will feature questions on many syllabus areas, but the following table illustrates the topics that have been examined in section B and C.

Where a question has a number in brackets it indicates that the topic appeared more than once in that question and the number in brackets explains how many times it appeared.

	Pilot	May 10	Sept 10	Nov 10	Mar 11	May 11	Sept 11	Nov 11	Mar 12	May 12	Sept 12
Traditional costing									B		
Modern production environment		B	B								
Throughput accounting							B				
Activity Based and Environmental Costing				C	C			B	B x 2		
Variance analysis	C									C	
Advanced variances		C	C			C	C	C	C	B	C
Budgeting	B	B x 2	B x 2	B	B	B	B	B		B	B
Forecasting	B										
Risk and uncertainty	B	B	B	B x 2	B x 2	B	B	B x 2	B	B	B
Investment appraisal	C	C	C	C	C	B/C	B/C	C	C	B/C	B/C
Overall working capital				B							
Inventory		B	B							B	B
Cash control								B	B		
Receivables	B	B	B	B	B	B		B	B		B x 2
Payables											
Short-term finance/investments				B	B x 2	B x 2	B x 2			B	

Key:

B	This topic appeared as a five mark question in section B of the exam
C	This topic appeared as a twenty five mark question in section C of the exam
B/C	This topic appeared as both a five mark question in section B of the exam and as a twenty five mark question in section C of the exam
B x 2	This topic appeared as two five mark questions in section B of the exam

EXAM TECHNIQUE

- Use the allocated **20 minutes reading and planning time** at the beginning of the exam:
  - read the questions and examination requirements carefully, and
  - begin planning your answers.

  See the Paper Specific Information for advice on how to use this time for this paper.

- **Divide the time** you spend on questions in proportion to the marks on offer:
  - there are 1.8 minutes available per mark in the examination
  - within that, try to allow time at the end of each question to review your answer and address any obvious issues

  Whatever happens, always keep your eye on the clock and **do not over run on any part of any question!**

- Spend the last **five minutes** of the examination reading through your answers, and **making any additions or corrections**.

- If you **get completely stuck** with a question:
  - leave space in your answer book, and
  - **return to it later.** Remember that there is no negative marking, so in Section A questions that offer a multiple choice, you should guess at an answer rather than leaving it out completely.

- Stick to the question and **tailor your answer** to what you are asked.
  - pay particular attention to the verbs in the question.

- If you do not understand what a question is asking, **state your assumptions**.

  Even if you do not answer in precisely the way the examiner hoped, you should be given some credit, if your assumptions are reasonable.

- You should do everything you can to make things easy for the marker.

  The marker will find it easier to identify the points you have made if your **answers are legible**.

- **Written questions**. Your answer should have:
  - a clear structure
  - a brief introduction, a main section and a conclusion.

  Be concise.

  It is better to write a little about a lot of different points than a great deal about one or two points.

- **Computations**:

  It is essential to include all your workings in your answers.

  Many computational questions require the use of a standard format:

  e.g. income tax computations, corporation tax computations and capital gains.

  Be sure you know these formats thoroughly before the exam and use the layouts that you see in the answers given in this book and in model answers.

- **Reports, memos and other documents**:

  Some questions ask you to present your answer in the form of a report, a memo, a letter or other document.

  Make sure that you use the correct format – there could be easy marks to gain here.

PAPER SPECIFIC INFORMATION

THE EXAM

FORMAT OF THE EXAM

		Number of marks
Section A :	A variety of compulsory objective test questions, each worth between two and four marks. Mini scenarios may be given, to which a group of questions relate.	20
Section B:	Six compulsory short answer questions, each worth five marks. A short scenario may be given, to which some or all questions relate.	30
Section C:	One or two compulsory questions. Short scenarios may be given, to which questions relate.	50
		————
		100
		————

Total time allowed: 3 hours plus 20 minutes reading and planning time.

SYLLABUS STRUCTURE

		Weighting
A	**Cost accounting systems**	30%
B	**Forecasting and budgeting techniques**	10%
C	**Project appraisal**	25%
D	**Dealing with uncertainty in analysis**	15%
E	**Managing short term finance**	20%

PASS MARK

The pass mark for all CIMA Qualification examination papers is 50%.

READING AND PLANNING TIME

Remember that all three hour paper based examinations have an additional 20 minutes reading and planning time.

KAPLAN GUIDANCE

As all questions are compulsory, there are no decisions to be made about choice of questions, other than in which order you would like to tackle them.

Therefore, in relation to P1, we recommend that you take the following approach with your reading and planning time:

- **Skim through sections B and C** assessing the level of difficulty of each question.

- **For section C, write down** on the question paper next to the mark allocation **the amount of time you should spend on each part.** Do this for each part of every question.

- **Decide the order** in which you think you will attempt each question:

   This is a personal choice and you have time on the revision phase to try out different approaches, for example, if you sit mock exams.

   A common approach is to tackle the question you think is the easiest and you are most comfortable with first.

   Others may prefer to tackle the longest questions first, or conversely leave them to the last.

   Psychologists believe that you usually perform at your best on the second and third question you attempt, once you have settled into the exam, so not tackling the bigger Section C questions first may be advisable.

   It is usual however that student tackle their least favourite topic and/or the most difficult question in their opinion last.

   Whatever you approach, you must make sure that you leave enough time to attempt all questions fully and be very strict with yourself in timing each question.

- **For each question** in turn, read the requirements and then the detail of the question carefully.

   Always read the requirement first as this enables you to **focus on the detail of the question with the specific task in mind**.

   For computational questions:

   Highlight key numbers / information and key words in the question, scribble notes to yourself on the question paper to remember key points in your answer.

   Jot down proformas required if applicable.

   For written questions:

   Plan your beginning, middle and end and the key areas to be addressed and your use of titles and sub-titles to enhance your answer.

- You should not use this time to read **section A**. There will be too much to read and you will achieve little form this.

For all questions:

Spot the easy marks to be gained in a question and parts which can be performed independently of the rest of the question. For example, writing down due dates of payment of tax, due dates for making elections, laying out basic proformas correctly.

Make sure that you do these parts first when you tackle the question.

Don't go overboard in terms of planning time on any one question – you need a good measure of the whole paper and a plan for all of the questions at the end of the 20 minutes.

By covering all questions you can often help yourself as you may find that facts in one question may remind you of things you should put into your answer relating to a different question.

- With your plan of attack in mind, **start answering your chosen question** with your plan to hand, as soon as you are allowed to start.

DETAILED SYLLABUS

The detailed syllabus and study guide written by the CIMA can be found at:

www.cimaglobal.com

KAPLAN'S RECOMMENDED REVISION APPROACH

QUESTION PRACTICE IS THE KEY TO SUCCESS

Success in professional examinations relies upon you acquiring a firm grasp of the required knowledge at the tuition phase. In order to be able to do the questions, knowledge is essential.

However, the difference between success and failure often hinges on your exam technique on the day and making the most of the revision phase of your studies.

The **Kaplan Complete Text** is the starting point, designed to provide the underpinning knowledge to tackle all questions. However, in the revision phase, pouring over text books is not the answer.

Kaplan Online fixed tests help you consolidate your knowledge and understanding and are a useful tool to check whether you can remember key topic areas.

Kaplancards and Revision Notes are designed to help you quickly revise a topic area, however you then need to practice questions. There is a need to progress to full exam standard questions as soon as possible, and to tie your exam technique and technical knowledge together.

The importance of question practice cannot be over-emphasised.

The recommended approach below is designed by expert tutors in the field, in conjunction with their knowledge of the examiner and their recent real exams.

The approach taken for the fundamental papers is to revise by topic area. However, with the professional stage papers, a multi topic approach is required to answer the scenario based questions.

You need to practice as many questions as possible in the time you have left.

OUR AIM

Our aim is to get you to the stage where you can attempt exam standard questions confidently, to time, in a closed book environment, with no supplementary help (i.e. to simulate the real examination experience).

Practising your exam technique on real past examination questions, in timed conditions, is also vitally important for you to assess your progress and identify areas of weakness that may need more attention in the final run up to the examination.

In order to achieve this we recognise that initially you may feel the need to practice some questions with open book help and exceed the required time.

The approach below shows you which questions you should use to build up to coping with exam standard question practice, and references to the sources of information available should you need to revisit a topic area in more detail.

Remember that in the real examination, all you have to do is:

- attempt all questions required by the exam

- only spend the allotted time on each question, and

- get them at least 50% right!

Try and practice this approach on every question you attempt from now to the real exam.

EXAMINER COMMENTS

From looking at the post-exam guidance, the common mistakes are as follows :

- misallocation of time;

- running out of time ;

- showing signs of spending too much time on an earlier questions and clearly rushing the answer to a subsequent question;

- Not relating the answer to the scenario / context of the question.

Good exam technique is vital.

THE KAPLAN PAPER P1 REVISION PLAN

Stage 1: Assess areas of strengths and weaknesses

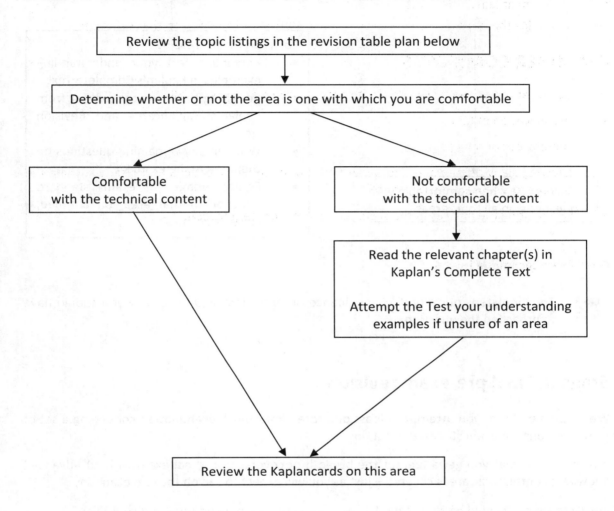

Stage 2: Practice questions

Follow the order of revision of topics as recommended in the revision table plan below and attempt the questions in the order suggested.

Try to avoid referring to text books and notes and the model answer until you have completed your attempt.

Try to answer the question in the allotted time.

Review your attempt with the model answer and assess how much of the answer you achieved in the allocated exam time.

Fill in the self-assessment box below and decide on your best course of action.

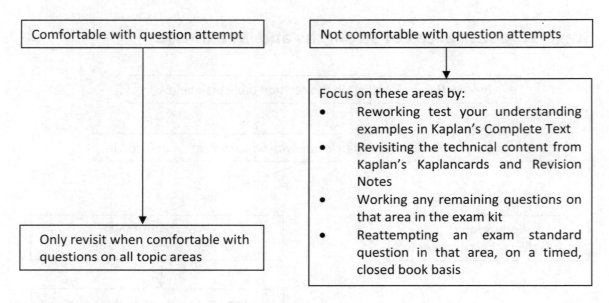

| Comfortable with question attempt | Not comfortable with question attempts |

Focus on these areas by:
- Reworking test your understanding examples in Kaplan's Complete Text
- Revisiting the technical content from Kaplan's Kaplancards and Revision Notes
- Working any remaining questions on that area in the exam kit
- Reattempting an exam standard question in that area, on a timed, closed book basis

Only revisit when comfortable with questions on all topic areas

Note that:

 The "footsteps questions" give guidance on exam technique and how you should have approached the question.

Stage 3: Final pre-exam revision

We recommend that you **attempt at least one three hour mock examination** containing a set of previously unseen exam standard questions.

It is important that you get a feel for the breadth of coverage of a real exam without advanced knowledge of the topic areas covered – just as you will expect to see on the real exam day.

Ideally this mock should be sat in timed, closed book, real exam conditions and could be:

- a mock examination offered by your tuition provider, and/or

- the pilot paper which can be found on www.cimaglobal.com

THE DETAILED REVISION PLAN

Topic	Complete Text Chapter	Questions to attempt	Tutor guidance	Date attempted	Self assessment
Traditional costing	2	199 273	A lot of this chapter should be familiar to students. The subject matter will form the basis of other questions on areas such as throughput and activity based accounting. Break even principles have been popular in past exams so it is important that you are comfortable with that area.		
Production systems	3	197 203	The areas in this chapter should be no more than a five mark discursive question. Key areas are JIT and TQM.		
Throughput accounting	4	204 209	Throughput accounting is reasonably straight forward provided you understand the basics of costing from chapter 2 and how to calculate throughput. It is a popular question for students in the exam, but, as the question choice suggests, it is more likely to be examined in section A or B than in section C.		
Activity based and environmental costing	5	198 207 274	Any long form question on ABC is likely to start with an absorption costing calculation so ensure you are happy with chapter 2 before proceeding onto this topic. It will be important that you understand environmental costing terminology.		

Topic	Complete Text Chapter	Questions to attempt	Tutor guidance	Date attempted	Self assessment
Variances	6 to 8	217 219 279 281 283	Variances are a regularly examined area. You need to be comfortable with the basics (Q277), but at this level questions are likely to include either planning variances (Q283) or mix and yield/quantity variances (Q219).		
Budgeting	9 to 11	205 223 229 286	The discursive elements of budgeting as well as forecasting and functional budgets are likely to be limited to sections A and B. Cash budgets (a topic covered again in chapter 17) can become a compulsory section C question. They have a standard technique that you should get comfortable with (see the walkthrough in question 286).		
Uncertainty and risk	12	237 238 240 244 290	In this area you need to be comfortable with drawing decision trees. The topic is very popular in section B and you need to ensure you are comfortable with all of the different risk attitudes and associated decision making techniques. The topic is less likely to appear in section C, but Q290 has a walkthrough that may be worth a read so that some technique points are developed for use in this section.		

Topic	Complete Text Chapter	Questions to attempt	Tutor guidance	Date attempted	Self assessment
Basic investment appraisal	13	246 248	It is vital that you master all the techniques on this chapter before proceeding to the next chapter. This chapter (and in particular basic NPV techniques) will give you the skills to pick up the easier marks in the tough questions that follow. Practice as many section A questions as possible to fine tune the techniques that will be required in chapter 14. Replacement analysis and sensitivity analysis have appeared in both section B and section C in past exams.		
Advanced investment appraisal	14	291 293 297 302	In dealing with these advanced questions it will be important that you have a proforma that you set up very early in your answer and that you can deal well with areas such as tax depreciation. To date, this topic has appeared in every exam and you should aim to cover as many questions in this area as possible until you are consistently passing them.		

Topic	Complete Text Chapter	Questions to attempt	Tutor guidance	Date attempted	Self assessment
Working capital management	15-18	251 254 261 262 305	The key here is to understand the balance between profitability (which can come from having a high working capital balance) and liquidity (which comes from keeping working capital low). Question 305 covers all of these areas very well and contains a tutor walkthrough, although section C questions on this area are not as common as some other areas.		
Short-term finance and investments	19	265 268 272	This is mainly a discursive area that should be a straightforward way to finish your revision.		

Note that not all of the questions are referred to in the programme above. We have recommended an approach to build up from the basic to exam standard questions.

We have not recommended any **section A** questions as you should attempt as many of these as possible. You should set yourself regular 10 question tests from random chapters. It is better to do, say, every fifth question rather than every question in order as this will test your adaptability better. When you attempt section A questions make sure that you audit the answer – determine why you got it wrong, spot the 'trick' that threw you off, and try to learn from the experience so that you do not repeat the mistake in the future. You will see that in the real exam a lot of the section A questions are similar to those contained in this exam kit. Therefore the more you attempt as part of your revision, the higher your recognition rate will be on the day of the exam. You may find that you are attempting questions on the day (albeit with different numbers) which are very similar to ones that you practiced as part of your revision. Prior to the exam, and when you have revised the entire syllabus, you should attempt the past exam sections contained at the end of section A.

The remaining questions are available in the kit for extra practice for those who require more question on some areas.

MATHS TABLES AND FORMULAE

PRESENT VALUE TABLE

Present value of $1, that is $(1+r)^{-n}$ where r = interest rate; n = number of periods until payment or receipt.

Periods	Interest rates (r)									
(n)	1%	2%	3%	4%	5%	6%	7%	8%	9%	10%
1	0.990	0.980	0.971	0.962	0.952	0.943	0.935	0.926	0.917	0.909
2	0.980	0.961	0.943	0.925	0.907	0.890	0.873	0.857	0.842	0.826
3	0.971	0.942	0.915	0.889	0.864	0.840	0.816	0.794	0.772	0.751
4	0.961	0.924	0.888	0.855	0.823	0.792	0.763	0.735	0.708	0.683
5	0.951	0.906	0.863	0.822	0.784	0.747	0.713	0.681	0.650	0.621
6	0.942	0.888	0.837	0.790	0.746	0705	0.666	0.630	0.596	0.564
7	0.933	0.871	0.813	0.760	0.711	0.665	0.623	0.583	0.547	0.513
8	0.923	0.853	0.789	0.731	0.677	0.627	0.582	0.540	0.502	0.467
9	0.914	0.837	0.766	0.703	0.645	0.592	0.544	0.500	0.460	0.424
10	0.905	0.820	0.744	0.676	0.614	0.558	0.508	0.463	0.422	0.386
11	0.896	0.804	0.722	0.650	0.585	0.527	0.475	0.429	0.388	0.350
12	0.887	0.788	0.701	0.625	0.557	0.497	0.444	0.397	0.356	0.319
13	0.879	0.773	0.681	0.601	0.530	0.469	0.415	0.368	0.326	0.290
14	0.870	0.758	0.661	0.577	0.505	0.442	0.388	0.340	0.299	0.263
15	0.861	0.743	0.642	0.555	0.481	0.417	0.362	0.315	0.275	0.239
16	0.853	0.728	0.623	0.534	0.458	0.394	0.339	0.292	0.252	0.218
17	0.844	0.714	0.605	0.513	0.436	0.371	0.317	0.270	0.231	0.198
18	0.836	0.700	0.587	0.494	0.416	0.350	0.296	0.250	0.212	0.180
19	0.828	0.686	0.570	0.475	0.396	0.331	0.277	0.232	0.194	0.164
20	0.820	0.673	0.554	0.456	0.377	0.312	0.258	0.215	0.178	0.149

Periods	Interest rates (r)									
(n)	11%	12%	13%	14%	15%	16%	17%	18%	19%	20%
1	0.901	0.893	0.885	0.877	0.870	0.862	0.855	0.847	0.840	0.833
2	0.812	0.797	0.783	0.769	0.756	0.743	0.731	0.718	0.706	0.694
3	0.731	0.712	0.693	0.675	0.658	0.641	0.624	0.609	0.593	0.579
4	0.659	0.636	0.613	0.592	0.572	0.552	0.534	0.516	0.499	0.482
5	0.593	0.567	0.543	0.519	0.497	0.476	0.456	0.437	0.419	0.402
6	0.535	0.507	0.480	0.456	0.432	0.410	0.390	0.370	0.352	0.335
7	0.482	0.452	0.425	0.400	0.376	0.354	0.333	0.314	0.296	0.279
8	0.434	0.404	0.376	0.351	0.327	0.305	0.285	0.266	0.249	0.233
9	0.391	0.361	0.333	0.308	0.284	0.263	0.243	0.225	0.209	0.194
10	0.352	0.322	0.295	0.270	0.247	0.227	0.208	0.191	0.176	0.162
11	0.317	0.287	0.261	0.237	0.215	0.195	0.178	0.162	0.148	0.135
12	0.286	0.257	0.231	0.208	0.187	0.168	0.152	0.137	0.124	0.112
13	0.258	0.229	0.204	0.182	0.163	0.145	0.130	0.116	0.104	0.093
14	0.232	0.205	0.181	0.160	0.141	0.125	0.111	0.099	0.088	0.078
15	0.209	0.183	0.160	0.140	0.123	0.108	0.095	0.084	0.079	0.065
16	0.188	0.163	0.141	0.123	0.107	0.093	0.081	0.071	0.062	0.054
17	0.170	0.146	0.125	0.108	0.093	0.080	0.069	0.060	0.052	0.045
18	0.153	0.130	0.111	0.095	0.081	0.069	0.059	0.051	0.044	0.038
19	0.138	0.116	0.098	0.083	0.070	0.060	0.051	0.043	0.037	0.031
20	0.124	0.104	0.087	0.073	0.061	0.051	0.043	0.037	0.031	0.026

Cumulative present value of $1 per annum, Receivable or Payable at the end of each year for n years $\dfrac{1-(1+r)^{-n}}{r}$

Periods	Interest rates (r)									
(n)	1%	2%	3%	4%	5%	6%	7%	8%	9%	10%
1	0.990	0.980	0.971	0.962	0.952	0.943	0.935	0.926	0.917	0.909
2	1.970	1.942	1.913	1.886	1.859	1.833	1.808	1.783	1.759	1.736
3	2.941	2.884	2.829	2.775	2.723	2.673	2.624	2.577	2.531	2.487
4	3.902	3.808	3.717	3.630	3.546	3.465	3.387	3.312	3.240	3.170
5	4.853	4.713	4.580	4.452	4.329	4.212	4.100	3.993	3.890	3.791
6	5.795	5.601	5.417	5.242	5.076	4.917	4.767	4.623	4.486	4.355
7	6.728	6.472	6.230	6.002	5.786	5.582	5.389	5.206	5.033	4.868
8	7.652	7.325	7.020	6.733	6.463	6.210	5.971	5.747	5.535	5.335
9	8.566	8.162	7.786	7.435	7.108	6.802	6.515	6.247	5.995	5.759
10	9.471	8.983	8.530	8.111	7.722	7.360	7.024	6.710	6.418	6.145
11	10.368	9.787	9.253	8.760	8.306	7.887	7.499	7.139	6.805	6.495
12	11.255	10.575	9.954	9.385	8.863	8.384	7.943	7.536	7.161	6.814
13	12.134	11.348	10.635	9.986	9.394	8.853	8.358	7.904	7.487	7.103
14	13.004	12.106	11.296	10.563	9.899	9.295	8.745	8.244	7.786	7.367
15	13.865	12.849	11.938	11.118	10.380	9.712	9.108	8.559	8.061	7.606
16	14.718	13.578	12.561	11.652	10.838	10.106	9.447	8.851	8.313	7.824
17	15.562	14.292	13.166	12.166	11.274	10.477	9.763	9.122	8.544	8.022
18	16.398	14.992	13.754	12.659	11.690	10.828	10.059	9.372	8.756	8.201
19	17.226	15.679	14.324	13.134	12.085	11.158	10.336	9.604	8.950	8.365
20	18.046	16.351	14.878	13.590	12.462	11.470	10.594	9.818	9.129	8.514

Periods	Interest rates (r)									
(n)	11%	12%	13%	14%	15%	16%	17%	18%	19%	20%
1	0.901	0.893	0.885	0.877	0.870	0.862	0.855	0.847	0.840	0.833
2	1.713	1.690	1.668	1.647	1.626	1.605	1.585	1.566	1.547	1.528
3	2.444	2.402	2.361	2.322	2.283	2.246	2.210	2.174	2.140	2.106
4	3.102	3.037	2.974	2.914	2.855	2.798	2.743	2.690	2.639	2.589
5	3.696	3.605	3.517	3.433	3.352	3.274	3.199	3.127	3.058	2.991
6	4.231	4.111	3.998	3.889	3.784	3.685	3.589	3.498	3.410	3.326
7	4.712	4.564	4.423	4.288	4.160	4.039	3.922	3.812	3.706	3.605
8	5.146	4.968	4.799	4.639	4.487	4.344	4.207	4.078	3.954	3.837
9	5.537	5.328	5.132	4.946	4.772	4.607	4.451	4.303	4.163	4.031
10	5.889	5.650	5.426	5.216	5.019	4.833	4.659	4.494	4.339	4.192
11	6.207	5.938	5.687	5.453	5.234	5.029	4.836	4.656	4.486	4.327
12	6.492	6.194	5.918	5.660	5.421	5.197	4.988	7.793	4.611	4.439
13	6.750	6.424	6.122	5.842	5.583	5.342	5.118	4.910	4.715	4.533
14	6.982	6.628	6.302	6.002	5.724	5.468	5.229	5.008	4.802	4.611
15	7.191	6.811	6.462	6.142	5.847	5.575	5.324	5.092	4.876	4.675
16	7.379	6.974	6.604	6.265	5.954	5.668	5.405	5.162	4.938	4.730
17	7.549	7.120	6.729	6.373	6.047	5.749	5.475	5.222	4.990	4.775
18	7.702	7.250	6.840	6.467	6.128	5.818	5.534	5.273	5.033	4.812
19	7.839	7.366	6.938	6.550	6.198	5.877	5.584	5.316	5.070	4.843
20	7.963	7.469	7.025	6.623	6.259	5.929	5.628	5.353	5.101	4.870

FORMULAE

PROBABILITY

$A \cup B$ = **A or B**.
$A \cap B$ = **A and B** (overlap).

$P(B \mid A)$ = probability of B, **given** A.

Rules of Addition

If A and B are mutually exclusive:
$$P(A \cup B) = P(A) + P(B)$$

If A and B are **not** mutually exclusive:
$$P(A \cup B) = P(A) + P(B) - P(A \cap B)$$

Rules of Multiplication

If A and B are *independent*:
$$P(A \cap B) = P(A) * P(B)$$

If A and B are **not** *independent*:
$$P(A \cap B) = P(A) * P(B \mid A)$$

$E(X) = \sum (\text{probability} * \text{payoff})$

DESCRIPTIVE STATISTICS

Arithmetic Mean

$$\bar{x} = \frac{\sum x}{n} \qquad \bar{x} = \frac{\sum fx}{\sum f} \quad \text{(frequency distribution)}$$

Standard Deviation

$$SD = \sqrt{\frac{\sum(x - \bar{x})^2}{n}} \qquad SD = \sqrt{\frac{\sum fx^2}{\sum f} - \bar{x}^2} \quad \text{(frequency distribution)}$$

INDEX NUMBERS

Price relative = $100 * P_1/P_0$

Quantity relative = $100 * Q_1/Q_0$

Price:
$$\frac{\sum w * \left(\dfrac{P_1}{P_0} \right)}{\sum w} \times 100$$

Quantity:
$$\frac{\sum w * \left(\dfrac{Q_1}{Q_0} \right)}{\sum w} \times 100$$

TIME SERIES

Additive Model   Series = Trend + Seasonal + Random

Multiplicative Model   Series = Trend * Seasonal * Random

FINANCIAL MATHEMATICS

Compound Interest (Values and Sums)

Future Value S, of a sum of X, invested for n periods, compounded at $r\%$ interest

$S = X[1 + r]^n$

Annuity

Present value of an annuity of £1 per annum receivable or payable for n years, commencing in one year, discounted at $r\%$ per annum:

$$PV = \frac{1}{r}\left(1 - \frac{1}{[1+r]^n}\right)$$

Perpetuity

Present value of £1 per annum, payable or receivable in perpetuity, commencing in one year, discounted at $r\%$ per annum:

$$PV = \frac{1}{r}$$

LEARNING CURVE

$Y_x = aX^b$

where:

Y_x = the cumulative average time per unit to produce X units;

a = the time required to produce the first unit of output;

X = the cumulative number of units;

b = the index of learning.

The exponent b is defined as the log of the learning curve improvement rate divided by log 2.

INVENTORY MANAGEMENT

Economic Order Quantity

$$EOQ = \sqrt{\frac{2C_oD}{C_h}}$$

where: C_o = cost of placing an order

C_h = cost of holding one unit in inventory for one year

D = annual demand

Section 1

SECTION A-TYPE QUESTIONS

All questions in this section carry two marks each, unless otherwise stated.

COST ACCOUNTING SYSTEMS

1   A business reported a marginal costing profit of $45,000 last period. Its inventory values for the period were as follows:

	$
Opening inventory	16,000
Closing inventory	20,800

If the business had used absorption costing, the inventory values would have been as follows:

	$
Opening inventory	28,000
Closing inventory	36,400

What would have been the reported profit using absorption costing?

A $41,400

B $48,600

C $57,000

D $60,600

2   A company has a budget to produce 5,000 units of Product B in December. The budget for December shows that, for Product B, the opening inventory will be 400 units and the closing inventory will be 900 units. The monthly budgeted production cost data for Product B for December is as follows:

Variable direct costs per unit	$6.00
Variable production overhead costs per unit	$3.50
Total fixed production overhead costs	$29,500

The company absorbs overheads on the basis of the budgeted number of units produced.

The budgeted profit for Product B for December, using **absorption costing**, is:

A $2,950 lower than it would be using marginal costing

B $2,950 greater than it would be using marginal costing

C $4,700 lower than it would be using marginal costing

D $4,700 greater than it would be using marginal costing.

3   A company operates a standard absorption costing system. The budgeted fixed
     production overheads for the company for the latest year were $330,000 and budgeted
     output was 220,000 units. At the end of the company's financial year the total of the
     fixed production overheads debited to the Fixed Production Overhead Control Account
     was $260,000 and the actual output achieved was 200,000 units.

     The under / over absorption of overheads was

     A $40,000 over absorbed

     B $40,000 under absorbed

     C $70,000 over absorbed

     D $70,000 under absorbed

4   Company B uses a throughput accounting system. The details of product X per unit are as
     follows:

     Selling price   €50
     Material cost   €16
     Conversion costs   €20
     Time on bottleneck resource   8 minutes

     The return per hour for product X is:

     A   €105

     B   €225

     C   €255

     D   €375

5   A company produces two products, S and T, which pass through two production
     processes, X and Y. The time taken to make each product in each process is:

	Product S	Product T
Process X	5 mins	7.5 mins
Process Y	18 mins	12 mins

     The company operates a 15-hour day and have an average downtime each day of:

Process X	1.5 hours
Process Y	1.0 hours

     The costs and revenue for each unit of each product are:

	Product S	Product T
	$	$
Direct materials	20.00	20.00
Direct labour	18.00	14.00
Variable overhead	4.00	4.00
Fixed costs	5.00	4.00
Total cost	47.00	42.00
Selling price	$95.00	$85.00

Sales demand restricts the output of S and T to 50 and 80 units a day respectively.

(a) **Identify** which of the processes is the bottleneck process. **(2 marks)**

(b) **Determine** the daily production plan that would maximise the throughput contribution. **(3 marks)**

(Total: 5 marks)

6 **What is defined as 'an activity within an organisation which has a lower capacity than preceding or subsequent activities, thereby limiting throughput'?**

A   Bottleneck

B   Constraint

C   Limiting factor

D   Restraint

7 **A company can produce many types of product but is currently restricted by the number of labour hours available on a particular machine. At present this limitation is set at 12,000 hours per annum. One type of product requires materials costing $5 which are then converted to a final product that sells for $12. Each unit of this product takes 45 minutes to produce on the machine. The conversion costs for the factory are estimated to be $144,000 per annum.**

Calculate the throughput accounting ratio for this product and state the significance of the result. **(3 marks)**

The following data relate to Questions 8 and 9.

A manufacturing company recorded the following costs in October for Product X:

	$
Direct materials	20,000
Direct labour	6,300
Variable production overhead	4,700
Fixed production overhead	19,750
Variable selling costs	4,500
Fixed distribution costs	16,800
Total costs incurred for Product X	72,050

During October 4,000 units of Product X were produced but only 3,600 units were sold. At the beginning of October there was no inventory.

8 **The value of the inventory of Product X at the end of October using marginal costing was:**

A $3,080

B $3,100

C $3,550

D $5,075

9   The value of the inventory of Product X at the end of October using throughput accounting was:

A $630

B $1,080

C $1,100

D $2,000

The following data relate to Questions 10 and 11.

The following data relate to a manufacturing company. At the beginning of August there was no inventory. During August 2,000 units of Product X were produced, but only 1,750 units were sold. The financial data for Product X for August were as follows:

	$
Materials	40,000
Labour	12,600
Variable production overheads	9,400
Fixed production overheads	22,500
Variable selling costs	6,000
Fixed selling costs	19,300
Total costs for X for August	109,800

10   The value of inventory of X at 31 August using a marginal costing approach is:

A $6,575

B $7,750

C $8,500

D $10,562

11   The value of inventory of X at 31 August using a throughput accounting approach is:

A $5,000

B $6,175

C $6,575

D $13,725

The following data relate to Questions 12 to 14.

SM makes two products, Z1 and Z2. Its machines can only work on one product at a time. The two products are worked on in two departments by differing grades of labour. The labour requirements for the two products are as follows:

	Minutes per unit of product	
	Z1	Z2
Department 1	12	16
Department 2	20	15

The current selling prices and costs for the two products are shown below:

	Z1	Z2
	$ per unit	$ per unit
Selling price	50.00	65.00
Direct materials	10.00	15.00
Direct labour	10.40	6.20
Variable overheads	6.40	9.20
Fixed overheads	12.80	18.40
Profit per unit	10.40	16.20

There is currently a shortage of labour and the maximum times available each day in Departments 1 and 2 are 480 minutes and 840 minutes, respectively.

As part of the budget-setting process, SM needs to know the optimum output levels. All output is sold.

12   Calculate the maximum number of each product that could be produced each day, and identify the limiting factor/bottleneck.   (3 marks)

13   Using traditional contribution analysis, calculate the 'profit-maximising' output each day, and the contribution at this level of output.   (3 marks)

14   Using a throughput approach, calculate the 'throughput-maximising' output each day, and the 'throughput contribution' at this level of output.   (3 marks)

15   A business manufactures a single product which sells for $45 per unit. The budgeted data for the latest period are as follows:

Production and sales volume	2,000 units
	$
Material cost	13,500
Direct labour cost	11,800
Production overhead	32,400
Non-production overhead	21,900

Actual production volume and costs were as budgeted for the period but the actual sales volume achieved was 1,800 units. There was no inventory at the beginning of the period. **Calculate** the profit for the period using:

(a)   absorption costing   (2 marks)

(b)   marginal costing   (2 marks)

(c)   throughput accounting.   (2 marks)

(Total: 6 marks)

16   A company has budgeted breakeven sales revenue of $800,000 and fixed costs of $320,000 for the next period.

The sales revenue needed to achieve a profit of $50,000 in the period would be:

A $850,000

B $925,000

C $1,120,000

D $1,200,000

17   A food-processing company operates an activity based costing (ABC) system. Which of the following would be classified as a facility-sustaining activity?

(i)   General staff administration

(ii)   Plant management

(iii) Technical support for individual products and services

(iv)   Updating of product specification database

(v)   Property management

A   (i) and (ii)

B   (i), (ii) and (v)

C   (ii), (iii) and (iv)

D   (ii), (iii), (iv) and (v)

E   All of them

18   P operates an activity based costing (ABC) system to attribute its overhead costs to cost objects.

In its budget for the year ending 31 August 20X6, the company expected to place a total of 2,895 purchase orders at a total cost of $110,010. This activity and its related costs were budgeted to occur at a constant rate throughout the budget year, which is divided into 13 four-week periods.

During the four-week period ended 30 June 20X6, a total of 210 purchase orders were placed at a cost of $7,650.

The over-recovery of these costs for the four-week period was:

A $330

B $350

C $370

D $390

19 **Which of the following statements are correct?**

(i)   A cost driver is any factor that causes a change in the cost of an activity.

(ii) For long-term variable overhead costs, the cost driver will be the volume of activity.

(iii) Traditional absorption costing tends to under-allocate overhead costs to low-volume products.

A   (i) and (iii) only

B   (ii) and (iii) only

C   (i) and (ii) only

D   (i), (ii) and (iii)

The following data relate to Questions 20 and 21.

DRP has recently introduced an Activity Based Costing system. It manufactures three products:

	Product D	Product R	Product P
Budgeted annual production (units)	100,000	100,000	50,000
Batch size (units)	100	50	25
Machine set-ups per batch	3	4	6
Purchase orders per batch	2	1	1
Processing time per unit (minutes)	2	3	3

Three cost pools have been identified. Their budgeted costs for 20X4 are as follows:

Machine set-up costs $150,000

Purchasing of materials $70,000

Processing $80,000

20 **Calculate the annual budgeted number of:**

(a)   batches

(b)   machine set-ups

(c)   purchase orders

(d)   processing minutes.   **(4 marks)**

21 **Calculate the budgeted overhead unit cost for Product R for inclusion in the budget for 20X4.**   **(4 marks)**

22 **Explain in less than 50 words, why the costs absorbed by a product using an activity based costing approach could be higher than those absorbed if a traditional labour-based absorption system were used, and identify TWO implications of this for management.**
                                                                          (4 marks)

23 **Which of the following statements about JIT is correct?**

A JIT protects an organisation against risks of disruption in the supply chain.

B A narrow geographical spread in a business makes JIT more difficult to apply.

C With JIT, there is a risk that stocks could become obsolete.

D JIT is more difficult to implement when it is not easy to predict patterns of demand.

24 **Which feature distinguishes backflush accounting from other systems?**

A Costs are attached when output is completed or sold.

B Cost records reflect the flow of work through the production process.

C Entries are not made until the customer pays for goods purchased.

D Material entries are made when the material is received and moved.

25 **Which of the following are aspects of a successful JIT system?**

(i) Demand-driven production

(ii) Savings in total machine set-up time

(iii) Grouping machines or workers by product or component rather than by the type of work performed

A (i) only

B (i) and (ii) only

C (i) and (iii) only

D (ii) and (iii) only

26 **T uses a standard labour hour rate to charge its overheads to its clients' work. During the last annual reporting period production overheads were under-absorbed by $19,250. The anticipated standard labour hours for the period were 38,000 hours while the standard hours actually charged to clients were 38,500. The actual production overheads incurred in the period were $481,250.**

The budgeted production overheads for the period were:

A $456,000

B $462,000

C $475,000

D None of the above

27 **In the context of quality costs, training costs and reworking costs are classified as:**

	Training costs	Reworking costs
A	internal failure costs	external failure costs
B	prevention costs	external failure costs
C	external failure costs	internal failure costs
D	prevention costs	internal failure costs

28   **Summary results for Y Limited for March are shown below:**

	$000	*Units*
Sales revenue	820	
Variable production costs	300	
Variable selling costs	105	
Fixed production costs	180	
Fixed selling costs	110	
Production in March		1,000
Opening inventory		0
Closing inventory		150

Using *marginal costing*, the profit for March was:

A $170,000

B $185,750

C $197,000

D $229,250

29   **Two CIMA definitions follow:**

(1)   A system that converts a production schedule into a listing of the materials and components required to meet that schedule so that adequate inventory levels are maintained and items are available when needed.

(2)   An accounting-oriented information system, generally software-driven, which aids in identifying and planning the enterprise-wide resources needed to resource, make, account for and deliver customer orders.

Which of the following pairs of terms matches the definitions?

	Definition 1	*Definition 2*
A	Material requirements planning	Enterprise resource planning
B	Manufacturing resource planning	Material requirements planning
C	Material requirements planning	Manufacturing resource planning
D	Manufacturing resource planning	Enterprise resource planning

30   **Which of the following statements is/are true?**

(i)   Computer-integrated manufacturing (CIM) brings together advanced manufacturing technology and modern quality control into a single computerised coherent system.

(ii)   Flexible manufacturing systems (FMS) are simple systems with low levels of automation that offer great flexibility through a skilled workforce working in teams.

(iii)   Electronic data interchange (EDI) is primarily designed to allow the operating units in an organisation to communicate immediately and automatically with the sales and purchasing functions within the organisation.

A   (i) only

B   (i) and (ii) only

C   (i) and (iii) only

D   (ii) and (iii) only

31 Definition 1: 'A system that converts a production schedule into a listing of materials and components required to meet the schedule so that items are available when needed.'

Definition 2: 'An accounting system that focuses on ways by which the maximum return per unit of bottleneck activity can be achieved.'

Which of the following pairs of terms correctly matches definitions 1 and 2 above?

	Definition 1	*Definition 2*
A	Manufacturing resources planning (MRP2)	Backflush accounting
B	Material requirements planning (MRP1)	Throughput accounting
C	Material requirements planning (MRP1)	Theory of constraints
D	Supply chain management	Throughput accounting

32 **Which of the following statements is/are true?**

(i) Enterprise Resource Planning (ERP) systems use complex computer systems, usually comprehensive databases, to provide plans for every aspect of a business.

(ii) Flexible Manufacturing Systems (FMS) are simple systems with low levels of automation that offer great flexibility through a skilled workforce working in teams.

(iii) Just-in-time (JIT) purchasing requires the purchasing of large quantities of inventory items so that they are available immediately when they are needed in the production process.

A   (i) only

B   (i) and (ii) only

C   (i) and (iii) only

D   (ii) and (iii) only

33 **Overheads will always be over-absorbed when:**

A   actual output is higher than budgeted output

B   actual overheads incurred are higher than the amount absorbed

C   actual overheads incurred are lower than the amount absorbed

D   budgeted overheads are lower than the overheads absorbed.

34 **Which of the following definitions are correct?**

(i) Just-in-time (JIT) systems are designed to produce or procure products or components as they are required for a customer or for use, rather than for inventory.

(ii) Flexible manufacturing systems (FMS) are integrated, computer-controlled production systems, capable of producing any of a range of parts and of switching quickly and economically between them.

(iii) Material requirements planning (MRP) systems are computer-based systems that integrate all aspects of a business so that the planning and scheduling of production ensures components are available when needed.

A   (i) only

B   (i) and (ii) only

C   (i) and (iii) only

D   (ii) and (iii) only

35   WTD Ltd produces a single product. The management currently uses marginal costing but is considering using absorption costing in the future.

The budgeted fixed production overheads for the period are $500,000. The budgeted output for the period is 2,000 units. There were 800 units of opening inventory at the beginning of the period and 500 units of closing inventory at the end of the period.

If absorption costing principles were applied, the profit for the period compared to the marginal costing profit would be:

A $75,000 higher

B $75,000 lower

C $125,000 higher

D $125,000 lower

36   S Ltd manufactures three products, A, B and C. The products use a series of different machines but there is a common machine, P, that is a bottleneck.

The selling price and standard cost for each product for the forthcoming year is as follows:

	A	B	C
	$	$	$
Selling price	200	150	150
Direct materials	41	20	30
Conversion costs	55	40	66
Machine P – minutes	12	10	7

Calculate the return per hour for each of the products.   **(4 marks)**

37   X Ltd has two production departments, Assembly and Finishing, and two service departments, Stores and Maintenance.

Stores provides the following service to the production departments: 60% to Assembly and 40% to Finishing.

Maintenance provides the following service to the production and service departments: 40% to Assembly, 45% to Finishing and 15% to Stores.

The budgeted information for the year is as follows:

Budgeted fixed production overheads
        Assembly $100,000
        Finishing $150,000
        Stores $50,000
        Maintenance $40,000

Budgeted output   100,000 units

At the end of the year after apportioning the service department overheads, the total fixed production overheads debited to the Assembly department's fixed production overhead control account were $180,000.

The actual output achieved was 120,000 units.

Calculate the under-/over-absorption of fixed production overheads for the Assembly department. **(4 marks)**

STANDARD COSTING

38 The materials price variance for the month of January was $2,000 (F) and the usage variance was $450 (F). The standard material usage per unit is 6 kg, and the standard material price is $3.00 per kg. 600 units were produced in the period and there was no change in inventory levels during the period.

Material purchases in the period were:

A 2,000 kg

B 2,933 kg

C 3,450 kg

D 3,600 kg

The following data relate to Questions 39 and 40.

X40 is one of many items produced by the manufacturing division. Its standard cost is based on estimated production of 10,000 units per month. The standard cost schedule for one unit of X40 shows that 2 hours of direct labour are required at $15 per labour hour. The variable overhead rate is $6 per direct labour hour. During April, 11,000 units were produced; 24,000 direct labour hours were worked and charged; $336,000 was spent on direct labour; and $180,000 was spent on variable overheads.

39 The direct labour rate variance for April is:

A $20,000 Favourable

B $22,000 Favourable

C $24,000 Adverse

D $24,000 Favourable

40 The variable overhead efficiency variance for April is:

A $12,000 Adverse

B $12,000 Favourable

C $15,000 Adverse

D $15,000 Favourable

41   Which of the following best describes a basic standard?

A   A standard set at an ideal level, which makes no allowance for normal losses, waste and machine downtime.

B   A standard which assumes an efficient level of operation, but which includes allowances for factors such as normal loss, waste and machine downtime.

C   A standard which is kept unchanged over a period of time.

D   A standard which is based on current price levels.

The following data relate to Questions 42 and 43.

X Ltd operates a standard costing system and absorbs fixed overheads on the basis of machine hours. Details of budgeted and actual figures are as follows:

	Budget	*Actual*
Fixed overheads	$2,500,000	$2,010,000
Output	500,000 units	440,000 units
Machine hours	1,000,000 hours	900,000 hours

42   The fixed overhead expenditure variance is

A $190,000 favourable

B $250,000 adverse

C $300,000 adverse

D $490,000 favourable

43   The fixed overhead volume variance is

A $190,000 favourable

B $250,000 adverse

C $300,000 adverse

D $490,000 favourable)

44   Y has set the current budget for operating costs for its delivery vehicles, using the formula described below. Analysis has shown that the relationship between miles driven and total monthly vehicle operating costs is described in the following formula:

$$y = \$800 + \$0.0002x^2$$

where

y is the total monthly operating cost of the vehicles, and

x is the number of miles driven each month

The budget for vehicle operating costs needs to be adjusted for expected inflation in vehicle operating costs of 3%, which is not included in the relationship shown above.

The delivery mileage for September was 4,100 miles, and the total actual vehicle operating costs for September were $5,000.

The total vehicle operating cost variance for September was closest to:

A $713 Adverse

B $737 Adverse

C $777 Adverse

D $838 Adverse

45   **The CIMA official definition of the 'variable production overhead efficiency variance' is set out below with two blank sections.**

'Measures the difference between the variable overhead cost budget flexed on _____ and the variable overhead cost absorbed by _____ .'

Which combination of phrases correctly completes the definition?

	Blank 1	Blank 2
A	actual labour hours	budgeted output
B	standard labour hours	budgeted output
C	actual labour hours	output produced
D	standard labour hours	output produced

46   **P has the following budget and actual data:**

Budget fixed overhead cost $170,000
Budget production (units)   42,500
Actual fixed overhead cost $182,000
Actual production (units)   40,000

The fixed overhead volume variance is:

A $7,500 (A)

B $10,000 (A)

C $10,000 (F)

D $7,500 (F)

47   **R uses a standard costing system and has the following labour cost standard in relation to one of its products:**

10 hours skilled labour at $9.50 per hour = $95.00

During March 20X9, 6,200 of these products were made which was 250 units less than budgeted. The labour cost incurred was $596,412 and the number of direct labour hours worked was 62,890. The direct labour variances for the month were:

	Rate	Efficiency
A	$1,043 (F)	$8,900 (A)
B	$7,412 (F)	$8,455 (A)
C	$1,043 (F)	$8,455 (A)
D	$7,412 (F)	$8,900 (A)

48 L uses a standard costing system. The standard cost card for one of its products shows that the product should use 6 kgs of material P per finished unit, and that the standard price per kg is $6.75. L values its inventory of materials at standard prices.

During November 20X1, when the budgeted production level was 2,000 units, 2,192 units were made. The actual quantity of material P used was 13,050 kgs and material L inventories were reduced by 500 kgs. The cost of the material L which was purchased was $72,900.

The material price and usage variances for November 20X1 were:

	Price	Usage
A	15,185.50 (F)	450.00 (F)
B	11,812.50 (F)	688.50 (F)
C	15,187.50 (F)	450.00 (A)
D	11,812.50 (F)	688.50 (A)

The following data relate to Questions 49 and 50.

Trafalgar budgets to produce 10,000 units of product D12, each requiring 45 minutes of labour. Labour is charged at $20 per hour, and variable overheads at $15 per labour hour. During September, 11,000 units were produced. 8,000 hours of labour were paid at a total cost of $168,000. Variable overheads in September amounted to $132,000.

49 What is the labour efficiency variance for September?

    A $5,000 Adverse

    B $5,000 Favourable

    C $5,250 Favourable

    D $10,000 Adverse

50 What is the variable overhead expenditure variance for September?

    A $3,750 Favourable

    B $,125 Favourable

    C $12,000 Adverse

    D $12,000 Favourable

51 Operation B, in a factory, has a standard time of 15 minutes. The standard rate of pay for operatives is $10 per hour. The budget for a period was based on carrying out the operation 350 times. It was subsequently realised that the standard time for Operation B included in the budget did not incorporate expected time savings from the use of new machinery from the start of the period. The standard time should have been reduced to 12 minutes.

Operation B was actually carried out 370 times in the period in a total of 80 hours. The operatives were paid $850.

The operational labour efficiency variance was:

A $60 adverse

B $75 favourable

C $100 adverse

D $125 adverse

52   The fixed overhead volume variance is defined as:

A   the difference between the budgeted value of the fixed overheads and the standard fixed overheads absorbed by actual production

B   the difference between the standard fixed overhead cost specified for the production achieved, and the actual fixed overhead cost incurred

C   the difference between budgeted and actual fixed overhead expenditure

D   the difference between the standard fixed overhead cost specified in the original budget and the same volume of fixed overheads, but at the actual prices incurred

53   A company operates a standard absorption costing system. The following fixed production overhead data are available for the latest period:

Budgeted Output	300,000 units
Budgeted Fixed Production Overhead	$1,500,000
Actual Fixed Production Overhead	$1,950,000
Fixed Production Overhead Total Variance	$150,000 adverse

The actual level of production for the period was nearest to:

A   277,000 units

B   324,000 units

C   360,000 units

D   420,000 units

The following data relate to Questions 54 and 55.

Z sells PCs that it purchases through a regional distributor. An extract from its budget for the 4-week period ended 28 March 20X8 shows that it planned to sell 600 PCs at a unit price of $500, which would give a contribution to sales ratio of 25%.

Actual sales were 642 PCs at an average selling price of $465. The actual contribution to sales ratio averaged 20%.

54   The sales price variance (to the nearest $1) was:

A $22,470   (F)

B $1,470   (A)

C $1,470   (F)

D $22,470   (A)

55 **The sales volume contribution variance (to the nearest $1) was:**

A $5,050 (F)

B $5,150 (F)

C $5,250 (F)

D $5,350 (F)

The following data relate to Questions 56 and 57.

SW manufactures a product known as the TRD100 by mixing two materials. The standard material cost per unit of the TRD100 is as follows:

				$
Material X	12 litres	@	$2.50	30
Material Y	18 litres	@	$3.00	54

In October 20X3, the actual mix used was 984 litres of X and 1,230 litres of Y. The actual output was 72 units of TRD100.

---

56 **Calculate the total material mix variance for October 20X3.** **(3 marks)**

57 **Calculate the total material yield variance for October 20X3.** **(3 marks)**

The following data relate to Questions 58 and 59.

A cleaning material, X2, is manufactured by mixing three materials. Standard cost details of the product are as follows.

Cost per batch of 10 litres of X2

				$
Material C	6 litres	@	$3	18
Material D	3 litres	@	$1	3
Material E	1 litre	@	$5	5
	——			——
	10			26
	——			——

In the latest period, the actual mix used was 200 litres of C, 75 litres of D and 25 litres of E. The output achieved was 280 litres of cleaning material X2.

---

58 **Using the average valuation basis, calculate the material mix variance for each material and in total.** **(4 marks)**

59 **Calculate the total material yield variance.**

60   **A company has a process in which the standard mix for producing 9 litres of output is as follows:**

	$
4.0 litres of D at $9 per litre	36.00
3.5 litres of E at $5 per litre	17.50
2.5 litres of F at $2 per litre	5.00
	58.50

A standard loss of 10% of inputs is expected to occur. The actual inputs for the latest period were:

	$
4,300 litres of D at $9.00 per litre	38,700
3,600 litres of E at $5.50 per litre	19,800
2,100 litres of F at $2.20 per litre	4,620
	63,120

Actual output for this period was 9,100 litres.

Calculate:

(a)   the total materials mix variance   **(2 marks)**

(b)   the total materials yield variance.   **(2 marks)**

(Total: 4 marks)

61   **Which of the following events would help to explain an adverse material usage variance?**

(i)   The standard allowance for material wastage was set too high.

(ii)   Material purchased was of a lower quality than standard.

(iii) Lower grade and less experienced employees were used than standard.

(iv)   More material was purchased than budgeted for the period because output was higher than budgeted.

A   (i), (ii) and (iii) only

B   (ii), (iii) and (iv) only

C   (ii) and (iii) only

D   (ii) and (iv) only

62   **Which of the following is the most likely to result in an adverse variable overhead efficiency variance?**

A   Higher bonus payments to employees than standard

B   Less experienced employees were used than standard

C   The use of more expensive, higher quality materials than standard

D   Machine power costs per hour were higher than standard

63 **PQR Ltd operates a standard absorption costing system. Details of budgeted and actual figures are as follows:**

	Budget	Actual
Sales volume (units)	100,000	110,000
Selling price per unit	$10	$9.50
Variable cost per unit	$5	$5.25
Total cost per unit	$8	$8.30

(i) **Calculate** the sales price variance. **(2 marks)**

(ii) **Calculate** the sales volume profit variance. **(2 marks)**

(Total: 4 marks)

The following data relate to Questions 64 to 66.

The following data relate to Product Z and its raw material content for September:

Budget

Output   11,000 units of Z

Standard materials content   3 kg per unit at $4.00 per kg

Actual

Output   10,000 units of Z

Materials purchased and used   32,000 kg at $4.80 per kg

It has now been agreed that the standard price for the raw material purchased in September should have been $5 per kg.

64 **The materials planning price variance for September was:**

A $6,000 Adverse

B $30,000 Adverse

C $32,000 Adverse

D $33,000 Adverse

65 **The materials operational usage variance for September was:**

A $8,000 Adverse

B $9,600 Adverse

C $9,600 Favourable

D $10,000 Adverse

66 **The materials operational price variance for September was:**

A $6,000 Adverse

B $6,400 Favourable

C $30,000 Adverse

D $32,000 Adverse

67 **A company manufactures a fruit flavoured drink concentrate by mixing two liquids (X and Y). The standard cost card for ten litres of the drink concentrate is:**

			$
Liquid X	5 litres	@ $16 per litre	80
Liquid Y	6 litres	@ $25 per litre	150
	11 litres		230

The company does not hold any inventory. During the last period the company produced 4,800 litres of the drink concentrate. This was 200 litres below the budgeted output. The company purchased 2,200 litres of X for $18 per litre and 2,750 litres of Y for $21 per litre.

The materials mix variance for the period was:

A $150 adverse

B $450 adverse

C $6,480 favourable

D $6,900 favourable

The following data relate to Questions 68 and 69.

A company has a process in which three inputs are mixed together to produce Product S. The standard mix of inputs to produce 90 kg of Product S is shown below:

	$
50 kg of ingredient P at $75 per kg	3,750
30 kg of ingredient Q at $100 per kg	3,000
20 kg of ingredient R at $125 per kg	2,500
	9,250

During March 2,000 kg of ingredients were used to produce 1,910 kg of Product S. Details of the inputs are as follows:

	$
1,030 kg of ingredient P at $70 per kg	72,100
560 kg of ingredient Q at $106 per kg	59,360
410 kg of ingredient R at $135 per kg	55,350
	186,810

68 **Calculate the materials mix variance for March.** (3 marks)

69 **Calculate the materials yield variance for March.** (3 marks)

The following data relate to Questions 70 and 71.

Q plc uses standard costing. The details for April were as follows:

Budgeted output	15,000	units
Budgeted labour hours	60,000	hours
Budgeted labour cost	$540,000	
Actual output	14,650	units
Actual labour hours paid	61,500	hours
Productive labour hours	56,000	hours
Actual labour cost	$522,750	

70 **Calculate the idle time variance for April.**

71 **Calculate the labour efficiency variance for April.**

The following data relate to Questions 72 to 74.

A company uses standard absorption costing. The following information was recorded by the company for October:

	Budget	Actual
Output and sales (units)	8,700	8,200
Selling price per unit	£26	£31
Variable cost per unit	£10	£10
Total fixed overheads	$34,800	$37,000

72 **The sales price variance for October was:**

    A $38,500 Favourable

    B $41,000 Favourable

    C $41,000 Adverse

    D $65,600 Adverse

73 **The sales volume profit variance for October was:**

    A $6,000 Adverse

    B $6,000 Favourable

    C $8,000 Adverse

    D $8,000 Favourable

74 **The fixed overhead volume variance for October was:**

    A $2,000 Adverse

    B $2,200 Adverse

    C $2,200 Favourable

    D $4,200 Adverse

75 **The production volume ratio in a period was 95%.**

Which statement will always be true?

A   Actual hours worked exceeded the budgeted hours

B   Actual hours worked exceeded the standard hours of output

C   Budgeted hours exceeded the standard hours of output

D   Budgeted output was less than the actual output

76 **PP Ltd operates a standard absorption costing system. The following information has been extracted from the standard cost card for one of its products:**

Budgeted production	1,500 units
Direct material cost: 7 kg × $4.10	$28.70 per unit

Actual results for the period were as follows:

Production	1,600 units
Direct material (purchased and used): 12,000 kg	$52,200

It has subsequently been noted that, owing to a change in economic conditions, the best price that the material could have been purchased for was $4.50 per kg during the period.

(a)   **Calculate** the material price planning variance.

(b)   **Calculate** the operational material usage variance.   **(4 marks)**

77 **SS Ltd operates a standard marginal costing system. An extract from the standard cost card for the labour costs of one of its products is as follows:**

Labour cost	
5 hours × $12	$60

Actual results for the period were as follows:

Production	11,500 units
Labour rate variance	$45,000 adverse
Labour efficiency variance	$30,000 adverse

Calculate the actual rate paid per direct labour hour.   **(4 marks)**

BUDGETING

78 **Which of the following can be identified as purposes of budgeting?**

(i)   Communication

(ii)   Authorisation

(iii)   Sales maximisation

(iv)   Co-ordination

A   (ii) and (iv) only

B   (i) and (ii) only

C   (i), (ii) and (iv) only

D   All of them

79   **An incremental budgeting system is:**

A   a system which budgets only for the extra costs associated with a particular plan

B   a system which budgets for the variable manufacturing costs only

C   a system which prepares budgets only after the manager responsible has justified the continuation of the relevant activity

D   a system which prepares budgets by adjusting the previous year's values by expected changes in volumes of activity and price/inflation effects.

80   **EFG uses an Activity Based Budgeting system. It manufactures three products, budgeted details of which are set out below:**

	Product E	Product F	Product G
Budgeted annual production (units)	75,000	120,000	60,000
Batch size (units)	200	60	30
Machine set-ups per batch	5	3	9
Purchase orders per batch	4	2	2
Processing time per unit (minutes)	3	4	4

Three cost pools have been identified. Their budgeted costs for the year ending 30 September 20X3 are as follows:

Machine set-up costs	$180,000
Purchasing of materials	$95,000
Processing	$110,000

Calculate the budgeted machine set-up cost per unit of product F.   **(3 marks)**

The following data relate to Questions 81 and 82.

A division of LMN operates a fleet of minibuses that carries people and packages for other divisions.

In the year ended 31 October 20X3, it carried 4,420 people and 30,500 kgs of packages. It incurred costs of $850,000.

The division has found that 60% of its total costs are variable, and that 50% of these vary with the number of people and the other 50% varies with the weight of the packages.

The company is now preparing its budget for the three months ending 31 January 20X4 using an incremental budgeting approach. In this period it expects:

•   All prices to be 2% higher than the average paid in the year ended 31 October 20X3.

•   Efficiency levels to be unchanged.

•   Activity levels to be:

   −   1,150 people

   −   8,100 kgs of packages.

81   The budgeted people-related cost (to the nearest $100) for the three months ending 31 January 20X4 is:

A $55,300

B $6,400

C $66,300

D $67,700

82   The budgeted package-related cost (to the nearest $100) for the three months ending 31 January 20X4 is:

A $56,400

B $57,600

C $67,800

D $69,000

83   The following details relate to product X in two accounting periods:

Number of units	500	800
	$/unit	$/unit
Direct materials	2.00	2.00
Direct labour	1.50	1.50
Production overhead	2.50	1.75
Other overhead	1.00	0.625
	7.00	5.875

The fixed cost per period and variable cost per unit are:

	Period fixed cost	Variable cost/unit
	$	$
A	1,000	1.125
B	1,000	4.00
C	1,500	3.50
D	1,500	4.00

84   PP Ltd is preparing the production and material purchases budgets for one of their products, the SUPERX, for the forthcoming year.

The following information is available:

SUPERX

Sales demand (units)	30,000
Material usage per unit	7 kgs
Estimated opening inventory	3,500 units
Required closing inventory	35% higher than opening inventory

How many units of the SUPERX will need to be produced?

A   28,775

B   30,000

C   31,225

D   38,225

85   **The following cost per unit details have been extracted from a production overhead cost budget:**

Output (units)	6,000	10,000
Production overhead ($/unit)	3.20	3.00

The budget cost allowance for production overhead for an activity level of 7,350 units is:

A $20,505

B $21,765

C $22,845

D $23,515

86   **Which of the following definitions best describes 'Zero-Based Budgeting'?**

A   A method of budgeting where an attempt is made to make the expenditure under each cost heading as close to zero as possible.

B   A method of budgeting whereby all activities are re-evaluated each time a budget is formulated.

C   A method of budgeting that recognises the difference between the behaviour of fixed and variable costs with respect to changes in output and the budget is designed to change appropriately with such fluctuations.

D   A method of budgeting where the sum of revenues and expenditures in each budget centre must equal zero.

87   **The overhead costs of RP have been found to be accurately represented by the formula:**

$$y = \$10,000 + \$0.25x$$

where y is the monthly cost and x represents the activity level measured as the number of orders.

Monthly activity levels of orders may be estimated using a combined regression analysis and time series model:

$$a = 100,000 + 30b$$

where a represents the de-seasonalised monthly activity level and b represents the month number.

In month 240, the seasonal index value is 108.

Calculate the overhead cost for RP for month 240 to the nearest $1,000.   **(3 marks)**

The following data relate to Questions 88 and 89.

H is forecasting its sales for next year using a combination of time series and regression analysis models. An analysis of past sales units has produced the following equation for the quarterly sales trend:

$$y = 26x + 8,850$$

where the value of x represents the quarterly accounting period and the value of y represents the quarterly sales trend in units. Quarter 1 of next year will have a value for x of 25.

The quarterly seasonal variations have been measured using the multiplicative (proportional) model and are:

Quarter 1   − 15%

Quarter 2   − 5%

Quarter 3   + 5%

Quarter 4   + 15%

Production is planned to occur at a constant rate throughout the year.

The company does not hold inventories at the end of any year.

88   **The difference between the budgeted sales for quarter 1 and quarter 4 next year are:**

    A   78 units

    B   2,850 units

    C   2,862 units

    D   2,940 units

89   **The number of units to be produced in each quarter of next year will be nearest to:**

    A   9,454 units

    B   9,493 units

    C   9,532 units

    D   9,543 units

90   **Monthly sales of product R follow a linear trend of y = 9.72 + 5.816x, where y is the number of units sold and x is the number of the month. Monthly deviations from the trend follow an additive model.**

    The forecast number of units of product R to be sold in month 23, which has a seasonal factor of plus 6.5 is, to the nearest whole unit:

    A   134

    B   137

    C   143

    D   150

91 **Nile is preparing its sales budget . Estimated sales are 120,000 units if the Summer is rainy, and 80,000 units if the Summer is dry. The probability of a dry Summer is 0.4.**

What is the expected value for sales volume?

A   96,000 units

B   100,000 units

C   104,000 units

D   120,000 units

92 **The budgeted total costs for two levels of output are as shown below:**

Output	25,000 units	40,000 units
Total cost	$143,500	$194,000

Within this range of output it is known that the variable cost per unit is constant but fixed costs rise by $10,000 when output exceeds 35,000 units. **Calculate for a budgeted output of 36,000 units:**

(i) the variable cost per unit and (ii) the total fixed costs.   **(3 marks)**

93 **Which of the following best describes 'budgetary slack'?**

A   The difference between what has been set as a budgetary objective and what has been achieved for the period.

B   The demotivating impact of a budgetary target that has been set too high.

C   The deliberate over-estimation of expenditure and/or under-estimation of revenues in the budgetary planning process.

D   Accumulated favourable variances reported against a specific item of budgeted expenditure.

94 **A company is preparing its maintenance budget. The number of machine hours and maintenance costs for the past six months have been as follows:**

Month	Machine hours	$
1	10,364	35,319
2	12,212	39,477
3	8,631	31,420
4	9,460	33,285
5	8,480	31,080
6	10,126	34,784

The budget cost allowance for an activity level of 9,340 machine hours, before any adjustment for price changes, is nearest to:

A $21,000

B $30,200

C $33,000

D $34,000

95 Z plc has found that it can estimate future sales using time series analysis and regression techniques. The following trend equation has been derived:

$$y = 25,000 + 6,500x$$

where

      y is the total sales units per quarter

      x is the time period reference number

Z has also derived the following set of seasonal variation index values for each quarter using a multiplicative (proportional) model:

Quarter 1	70
Quarter 2	90
Quarter 3	150
Quarter 4	90

Using the above model, **calculate** the forecast for sales units for the third quarter of year 7, assuming that the first quarter of year 1 is time period reference number 1.

96 A company is preparing its cash budget for February using the following data. One line in the cash budget is for purchases of a raw material, J. The opening inventory of J in January is expected to be 1,075 units. The price of J is expected to be $8 per unit. The company pays for purchases at the end of the month following delivery.

One unit of J is required in the production of each unit of Product 2, and J is only used in this product. Monthly sales of Product 2 are expected to be:

January	4,000 units
February	5,000 units
March	6,000 units

The opening inventory of Product 2 in January is expected to be 1,200 units.

The company implements the following inventory policies. At the end of each month the following amounts are held:

      Raw materials: 25% of the requirement for the following month's production

      Finished goods: 30% of the following month's sales

Calculate the value for purchases of J to be included in the cash budget for February.

(4 marks)

The following data relate to Questions 97 and 98.

K makes many products, one of which is Product Z. K is considering adopting an activity-based costing approach for setting its budget, in place of the current practice of absorbing overheads using direct labour hours. The main budget categories and cost driver details for the whole company for October are set out below, excluding direct material costs:

Budget category	$	Cost driver details
Direct labour	128,000	8,000 direct labour hours
Set-up costs	22,000	88 set-ups each month
Quality testing costs*	34,000	40 tests each month
Other overhead costs	32,000	Absorbed by direct labour hours

* A quality test is performed after every 75 units produced

The following data for Product Z is provided:

Direct materials	Budgeted cost of $21.50 per unit
Direct labour	Budgeted at 0.3 hours per unit
Batch size	30 units
Set-ups	2 set-ups per batch
Budgeted volume for October	150 units

97   Calculate the budgeted unit cost of Product Z for October assuming that a direct labour-based absorption method was used for all overheads.

98   Calculate the budgeted unit cost of Product Z for October using an activity-based costing approach.   (3 marks)

99   If the budgeted fixed costs increase, the gradient of the line plotted on the budgeted Profit/Volume (P/V) chart will:

A   increase

B   decrease

C   not change

D   become curvi-linear

100   XYZ Ltd is preparing the production budget for the next period. The total costs of production are a semi-variable cost. The following cost information has been collected in connection with production:

Volume (units)	Cost
4,500	$29,000
6,500	$33,000

The estimated total production costs for a production volume of 5,750 units is nearest to

A $29,200

B $30,000

C $31,500

D $32,500

101 A company uses time series and regression techniques to forecast future sales. It has derived a seasonal variation index to use with the multiplicative (proportional) seasonal variation model. The index values for the first three quarters are as follows:

Quarter	Index value
Q1	80
Q2	80
Q3	110

The index value for the fourth quarter (Q4) is:

A   −270

B   −269

C   110

D   130

102 RF Ltd is about to launch a new product in June 2007. The company has commissioned some market research to assist in sales forecasting. The resulting research and analysis established the following equation:

$Y = A x^{0.6}$

Where Y is the cumulative sales units, A is the sales units in month 1, x is the month number.
June 2007 is Month 1. Sales in June 2007 will be 1,500 units.

Calculate the forecast sales volume for each of the months June, July and August 2007 and for that three month period in total.   **(4 marks)**

103 A company has the following budgeted sales figures:

Month 1	$90,000
Month 2	$105,000
Month 3	$120,000
Month 4	$108,000

80% of sales are on credit and the remainder are paid in cash. Credit customers paying within one month are given a discount of 1.5%. Credit customers normally pay within the following time frame:

Within 1 month   40% of credit sales

Within 2 months   70% of credit sales

Within 3 months   98% of credit sales

There is an expectation that 2% of credit sales will become irrecoverable (bad) debts.

Outstanding receivables at the beginning of month 1 includes $6,000 expected to be received in month 4.

Calculate the total receipts expected in month 4.   **(4 marks)**

104 **D plc operates a retail business. Purchases are sold at cost plus 25%. The management team is preparing the cash budget and has gathered the following data:**

1   The budgeted sales are as follows:

Month	$000
July	100
August	90
September	125
October	140

2   It is management policy to hold inventory at the end of each month which is sufficient to meet sales demand in the next half month. Sales are budgeted to occur evenly during each month.

3   Creditors are paid one month after the purchase has been made.

Calculate the entries for 'purchases' that will be shown in the cash budget for:

(i)   August

(ii)   September

(iii)   October

(3 marks)

105 **S plc produces and sells three products, X, Y and Z. It has contracts to supply products X and Y, which will utilise all of the specific materials that are available to make these two products during the next period. The revenue these contracts will generate and the contribution to sales (C/S) ratios of products X and Y are as follows:**

	Product X	Product Y
Revenue	$10 million	$20 million
C/S ratio	15%	10%

Product Z has a C/S ratio of 25%.

The total fixed costs of S plc are £5.5 million during the next period and management has budgeted to earn a profit of $2 million.

Calculate the revenue that needs to be generated by Product Z for S plc to achieve the budgeted profit.   **(3 marks)**

106 **A master budget comprises the:**

A   budgeted income statement and budgeted cash flow only

B   budgeted income statement and budgeted balance sheet only

C   budgeted income statement and budgeted capital expenditure only

D   budgeted income statement, budgeted balance sheet and budgeted cash flow only

JD Ltd manufactures plastic components for the car industry. The following budgeted information is available for three of its key plastic components:

	W	X	Y
	$ per unit	$ per unit	$ per unit
Selling price	200	183	175
Direct material	50	40	35
Direct labour	30	35	30
Units produced and sold	10,000	15,000	18,000

The total number of activities for each of the three products for the period is as follows:

Number of purchase requisitions	1,200	1,800	2,000
Number of set ups	240	260	300

Overhead costs have been analysed as follows:

Receiving/inspecting quality assurance	$1,400,000
Production scheduling/machine set up	$1,200,000

Calculate the budgeted profit per unit for each of the three products using activity-based budgeting.

(4 marks)

108 **JB has budgeted production for the next budget year of 36,000 units. Each unit of production requires 4 labour hours and the budgeted labour rate is $12 per hour excluding overtime. Idle time is expected to be 10% of total hours available i.e. including idle time. Due to labour shortages it is expected that 20% of the hours paid, including idle time, will be paid at an overtime rate of time and a half.**

Required:

Calculate the labour cost budget for the year.

(3 marks)

109 **GS has budgeted sales for the next two years of 24,000 units per annum spread evenly throughout both years. The estimated opening inventory of finished goods at the start of the next year is 500 units but GS now wants to maintain inventory of finished goods equivalent to one month's sales.**

Each unit uses 2kg of material. The estimated opening raw material inventory at the start of the next year is 300kg but GS now wants to hold sufficient raw material inventory at the end of each month to cover the following month's production.

The change in the policy for inventory holding for both raw materials and finished goods will take effect in the first month of next year and will apply for the next two years.

The budgeted material cost is $12 per kg.

Required:

Calculate the material purchases budget for the next year in $.

(3 marks)

110   A company is preparing its annual budget and is estimating the number of units of Product A that it will sell in each quarter of Year 2. Past experience has shown that the trend for sales of the product is represented by the following relationship:

y = a + bx where

y = number of sales units in the quarter

a = 10,000 units

b = 3,000 units

x = the quarter number where 1 = quarter 1 of Year 1

Actual sales of Product A in Year 1 were affected by seasonal variations and were as follows:

Quarter 1:   14,000 units

Quarter 2:   18,000 units

Quarter 3:   18,000 units

Quarter 4:   20,000 units

Required:

Calculate the expected sales of Product A (in units) for each quarter of Year 2, after adjusting for seasonal variations using the additive model.   **(4 marks)**

111   DB's latest estimate for trade payables outstanding at the end of this year is 45 days. Estimated purchases for this year are $474,500. DB is preparing the budget for next year and estimates that purchases will increase by 10%.

The trade payables amount, in $, outstanding at the end of next year is estimated to be the same as at the end of this year.

Required:

Calculate the budgeted trade payable days at the end of next year.   **(3 marks)**

112   PJ has budgeted sales for the next two years of 144,000 units per annum spread evenly throughout each year. The estimated closing inventory at the end of this year is 6,500 units. PJ wants to change its inventory policy so that it holds inventory equivalent to one month's sales. The change in inventory policy will take place at the beginning of next year and will apply for the next two years.

Each unit produced requires 2 hours of direct labour. The budgeted direct labour rate per hour is $15. It is anticipated that 80% of production will be paid at the budgeted rate and the remainder will be paid at the overtime rate of time and a half. PJ treats overtime costs as part of direct labour costs.

Required:

Calculate the direct labour cost budget for the next year.   **(3 marks)**

FINANCIAL INFORMATION FOR LONG-TERM DECISION MAKING

113 A company is evaluating a new product proposal. The proposed product selling price is $220 per unit and the variable costs are $55 per unit. The incremental cash fixed costs for the product will be $190,000 per annum. The discounted cash flow calculations results in a positive NPV:

		Cash flow $	Discount rate	Present value $
Year 0	Initial outlay	(2,000,000)	1.000	(2,000,000)
Year 1–6	Annual cash flow	450,000	4.623	2,080,350
Year 6	Sale of assets	75,000	0.630	47,250
Net present value				127,600

What is the percentage change in selling price that would result in the project having a net present value of zero?

A   3.2%

B   4.6%

C   5.9%

D   7.0%

114 The details of an investment project are as follows:

Cost of asset bought at the start of the project	$80,000
Annual cash inflow	$25,000
Cost of capital, after tax	5% each year
Life of the project	8 years

Corporation tax is 25% and is paid in equal quarterly instalments in the 6th and 9th months of the year in which the profit was earned and in the 1st and 3rd months of the following year.

Writing down allowances of 20% reducing balance will be claimed each year.

(Assume the asset is bought on the first day of the tax year and that the company's other projects generate healthy profits.)

The present value of the cash flows that occur in the second year of the project is:

A $17,006

B $19,053

C $20,271

D $25,940

The following data relate to Questions 115 and 116.

A company is considering investing in a project that would have a four-year life span. The investment would involve an immediate cash outflow of $250,000 and have a zero residual value. In each of the four years, 6,000 units would be produced and sold. The contribution per unit, based on current prices, is $12. The company has an annual cost of capital of 10%. It is expected that the inflation rate will be 4% in each of the next four years.

---

115 **The net present value of the project (to the nearest $100) is:**

    A $800

    B $1,300

    C $1,800

    D $2,300

116 **If the annual inflation rate is now projected to be 6%, the maximum monetary cost of capital for this project to remain viable is (to the nearest 0.5%):**

    A   11.0%

    B   11.5%

    C   12.0%

    D   12.5%

117 **B Company is deciding whether to launch a new product. The initial outlay for the product is $60,000. The forecast possible annual cash inflows and their associated probabilities are shown below:**

	Probability	Year 1	Year 2	Year 3
Optimistic	0.25	$35,000	$40,000	$32,000
Most likely	0.55	$20,000	$26,000	$28,000
Pessimistic	0.20	$18,000	$24,000	$22,000

The company's cost of capital is 8% per annum.

Assume the cash inflows are received at the end of the year and that the cash inflows for each year are independent.

The expected net present value for the product is:

    A   ($500)

    B $8,634

    C $10,189

    D $12,348

The following data relate to Questions 118 and 119.

A company is considering investing in a manufacturing project that would have a three-year life span. The investment would involve an immediate cash outflow of $50,000 and have a zero residual value. In each of the three years, 4,000 units would be produced and sold. The contribution per unit, based on current prices, is $5. The company has an annual cost of capital of 8%. It is expected that the inflation rate will be 3% in each of the next three years.

118 **The net present value of the project (to the nearest $500) is:**

    A $4,500

    B $5,000

    C $5,500

    D $6,000

119 If the annual inflation rate is now projected to be 4%, the maximum monetary cost of capital for this project to remain viable is (to the nearest 0.5%):

A   13.0%

B   13.5%

C   14.0%

D   14.5%

The following data relate to Questions 120 and 121.

A company is carrying out sensitivity analysis on an investment project. The initial DCF analysis, at a cost of capital of 10%, is as follows:

Year	Item	Cash flow $	DF @ 10%	PV $
0	Cost of machine	(50,000)	1.000	(50,000)
1	Net cash flow from sales	22,000	0.909	19,998
2	Net cash flow from sales	22,000	0.826	18,172
3	Net cash flow from sales	10,000	0.751	7,510
3	Residual value of the machine	10,000	0.751	7,510
	NPV			+ 3,190

The investment is in a machine that will make a product, Product Q. Product Q will sell for $40 per unit, and will have a variable cost of $10 per unit. Annual sales will be 1,000 units in years 1 and 2, and 600 units in year 3. Additional fixed cost expenditure on cash items will be $8,000 each year.

The residual value of the machine will be 20% of the initial cost of the machine.

120 To the nearest 0.1%, by how much could the selling price per unit of the product fall short of the expected $40 without the project ceasing to be viable, given no change in any of the other cash flow estimates?

A   3.6%

B   6.0%

C   6.1%

D   7.0%

121 To the nearest $1,000, what is the maximum amount that the machine can cost, without the project ceasing to be viable, given no change in any of the other cash flow estimates?

A $53,000

B $54,000

C $55,000

D $56,000

122 **A project has a net present value of $320,000.**

The sales revenues for the project have a total pre-discounted value of $900,000 and a total present value of $630,000 after tax.

The sensitivity of the investment to changes in the value of sales is closest to:

A $310,000

B $580,000

C   51%

D   36%

The following data relate to Questions 123 and 124.

An education authority is considering the implementation of a CCTV (closed circuit television) security system in one of its schools.

Details of the proposed project are as follows:

Life of project	5 years
Initial cost	$75,000
Annual savings:	
Labour costs	$20,000
Other costs	$5,000
Cost of capital	15% per annum

---

123 **Calculate the internal rate of return for this project.**

124 **Calculate the percentage change in the annual labour cost savings that could occur before the project ceased to be viable.** **(3 marks)**

The following data relate to Questions 125 and 126.

CC Company is considering an investment of $300,000 which will earn a contribution of $40,000 each year for 10 years at today's prices. The contribution will rise at the rate of 6% per year because of inflation. The company's cost of money is 11% per annum.

---

125 **Calculate the company's real cost of capital.**

126 **Calculate the net present value of the project.**

127 The management accountant of Bar Company has estimated that the cash flows for Project X would be as follows:

Year	Investment $	Running costs $	Savings $
0	(120,000)		
1		(80,000)	150,000
2		(100,000)	160,000
3		(120,000)	170,000
4		(150,000)	180,000

The project has a positive NPV of $22,900 when discounted at the company's cost of capital, which is 20% per annum.

On reviewing the cost estimates, the management accountant decides that the running costs will in fact be 20% higher each year than originally estimated, although savings will be higher too.

Calculate the minimum percentage that annual savings must be higher than originally estimated for the project to remain viable. **(4 marks)**

128 JAH Company is about to invest $400,000 in machinery and other capital equipment for a new product venture. Cash flows for the first three years are estimated as follows

Year	$000
1	210
2	240
3	320

JAH Company requires a 17% return for projects of this type. The above cash flows do not include expenditure on an advertising campaign, which will be incurred in equal annual amounts at the beginning of years 1, 2 and 3.

Ignoring any residual values of the capital equipment, **calculate** the maximum annual amount that can be spent on advertising, to the nearest $000. **(3 marks)**

129 X Company takes on a five-year lease of a building for which it pays $27,200 as a lump sum payment. X Company then sub-lets the building for five years at a fixed annual rent, with the rent payable annually in arrears.

Calculate the annual rental charge, if the rent is set at a level that will earn a DCF yield of 17% for X Company.

130 A company is evaluating a new product proposal. The proposed product selling price is $180 per unit and the variable costs are $60 per unit. The incremental cash fixed costs for the product will be $160,000 per annum. The discounted cash flow calculation results in a positive NPV:

		Cash flow $	Discount rate	Present value $
Year 0	Initial outlay	(1,000,000)	1.000	(1,000,000)
Years 1–5	Annual cash flow	320,000	3.791	1,213,120
Year 5	Working capital released	50,000	0.621	31,050
Net present value				244,170

What is the percentage change in selling price that would result in the project having a net present value of zero? **(4 marks)**

131 A company is considering investing in a project that requires an initial outflow of $500,000 and will generate expected cash inflows in terms of today's $ of $130,000 over each of the next four years. The company's monetary cost of capital is 7% and inflation is predicted to be 4% over the next four years.

Calculate the company's real cost of capital and the net present value of the project. **(4 marks)**

132 The details of an investment project are:

Life of the project 10 years
Cost of asset bought at the start of the project $100,000
Annual cash inflow $20,000
Cost of capital, after tax 8% each year

Corporation tax is 30% and is paid in equal quarterly instalments in the 7th and 10th months of the year in which the profit was earned and in the 1st and 4th months of the following year.

Writing down allowances of 25% reducing balance will be claimed each year.

(Assume the asset is bought on the first day of the tax year and that the company's other projects generate healthy profits.)

(Round all cash flows to the nearest $ and discount end of year cash flows.)

Calculate the present value of the cash flows that occur in the second year of the project. **(4 marks)**

133 An investment project that requires an initial investment of $500,000 has a residual value of $130,000 at the end of five years. The project's cash flows have been discounted at the company's cost of capital of 12% and the resulting net present value is $140,500. The profitability index of the project is closest to:

A 0.02

B 0.54

C 0.28

D 0.26

134 CC Company is considering an investment of $300,000 which will earn a contribution of $40,000 each year for 10 years at today's prices. The contribution will rise at the rate of 6% per year because of inflation. The company's cost of money is 11% per annum.

Calculate the net present value of the project. **(4 marks)**

135 A company has determined that the net present value of an investment project is $12,304 when using a 10% discount rate and $(3,216) when using a discount rate of 15%.

Calculate the internal rate of return of the project to the nearest 1%.

136 A five-year project has a net present value of $160,000 when it is discounted at 12%. The project includes an annual cash outflow of $50,000 for each of the five years. No tax is payable on projects of this type.

The percentage increase in the value of this annual cash outflow that would make the project no longer financially viable is closest to:

A   64%

B   89%

C   113%

D   156%

The following data relate to Questions 137 and 138.

An investment project with no residual value has a net present value of $87,980 when it is discounted using a cost of capital of 10%. The annual cash flows are as follows:

Year	$
0	(200,000)
1	80,000
2	90,000
3	100,000
4	60,000
5	40,000

137 Calculate the Accounting Rate of Return (ARR) of the project using the average investment value basis.   (2 marks)

138 Calculate the Internal Rate of Return (IRR) of the project.   (3 marks)

The following data relate to Questions 139 to 141.

M plc is evaluating three possible investment projects and uses a 10% discount rate to determine their net present values.

Investment	A	B	C
	$000	$000	$000
Initial investment	400	450	350
Incremental cash flows			
Year 1	100	130	50
Year 2	120	130	110
Year 3	140	130	130
Year 4	120	130	150
Year 5*	100	150	100
Net present value	39	55	48

* Includes $20,000 residual value for each investment project.

139 Calculate the payback period of investment A.

140 Calculate the discounted payback period of investment B.   (3 marks)

141   Calculate the Internal Rate of Return (IRR) of investment C.   **(3 marks)**

142   X is considering the following five investments:

Investment	J	K	L	M	N
	$000	$000	$000	$000	$000
Initial investment	400	350	450	500	600
Net present value	125	105	140	160	190

Investments J and L are mutually exclusive; all of the investments are divisible and none of them may be invested in more than once.

The optimum investment plan for X assuming that the funding available is limited to $1m is:

A $400,000 in J plus $600,000 in N

B $400,000 in M plus $600,000 in N

C $500,000 in M plus $500,000 in N

D $350,000 in K plus $600,000 in N plus $50,000 in M.

143   **A company is considering an investment of $400,000 in new machinery. The machinery is expected to yield incremental profits over the next five years as follows:**

Year	Profit ($)
1	175,000
2	225,000
3	340,000
4	165,000
5	125,000

Thereafter, no incremental profits are expected and the machinery will be sold. It is company policy to depreciate machinery on a straight line basis over the life of the asset. The machinery is expected to have a value of $50,000 at the end of year 5.

Calculate the payback period of the investment in this machinery to the nearest 0.1 years.

144   **An investment company is considering the purchase of a commercial building at a cost of $0.85m. The property would be rented immediately to tenants at an annual rent of $80,000 payable in arrears in perpetuity.**

Calculate the net present value of the investment assuming that the investment company's cost of capital is 8% per annum.

Ignore taxation and inflation.

THE TREATMENT OF UNCERTAINTY IN DECISION MAKING

The following data relate to Questions 145 and 146.

X Company can choose from five mutually exclusive projects. The projects will each last for one year only and their net cash inflows will be determined by the prevailing market conditions. The forecast annual cash inflows and their associated probabilities are shown below.

Market conditions	Poor	Good	Excellent
Probability	0.20	0.50	0.30
	$000	$000	$000
Project L	500	470	550
Project M	400	550	570
Project N	450	400	475
Project O	360	400	420
Project P	600	500	425

145 Based on the expected value of the net cash inflows, which project should be undertaken?

A L

B M

C N

D P

146 The value of perfect information about the state of the market is:

A Nil

B $5,000

C $26,000

D $40,000

The following data relate to Questions 147 and 148.

P Company currently sells 90,000 units of product Y per annum. At this level of sales and output, the selling price and variable cost per unit are $50 and $21 respectively. The annual fixed costs are $1,200,000. The management team is considering lowering the selling price per unit to $45.

The estimated levels of demand at the new price, and the probabilities of them occurring, are:

Selling price of $45

Demand	Probability
100,000 units	0.45
120,000 units	0.55

It is thought that at either of the higher sales and production levels, the variable cost per unit, and the probability of it occurring, will be as follows:

Variable cost (per unit)	Probability
$20	0.40
$18	0.60

147 **Calculate the probability that lowering the selling price to $45 per unit would increase profit.** **(4 marks)**

148 **Calculate the expected value of the company profit if the selling price is reduced to $45 per unit.** **(4 marks)**

149 **The daily demand for a perishable product has the following probability distribution:**

Demand (units)	Probability
100	0.25
200	0.40
300	0.35

Each item costs $4 and is sold for $8. Unsold items are thrown away at the end of the day.

If orders must be placed before the daily demand is known, **calculate** how many units should be purchased at the beginning of each day in order to maximise expected profit?

(4 marks)

150 **A company has estimated the selling prices and variable costs of one of its products as follows:**

Selling price per unit		Variable cost per unit	
$	Probability	$	Probability
40	0.30	20	0.55
50	0.45	30	0.25
60	0.25	40	0.20

Given that the company will be able to supply 1,000 units of its product each week irrespective of the selling price, and that selling price and variable cost per unit are independent of each other, **calculate** the probability that the weekly contribution will exceed $20,000.

(4 marks)

The following data relate to Questions 151 and 152.

A company expects to sell 1,000 units per month of a new product but there is uncertainty as to both the unit selling price and the unit variable cost of the product. The following estimates of selling price, variable costs and their related probabilities have been made:

Selling price		Unit variable cost	
$ per unit	Probability	$ per unit	Probability
20	25%	8	20%
25	40%	10	50%
30	35%	12	30%

There are specific fixed costs of $5,000 per month expected for the new product.

151 **The expected value of monthly contribution is:**

A $5,890

B $10,300

C $10,890

D $15,300

152 **The probability of monthly contribution from this new product exceeding $13,500 is:**

A   24.5%

B   30.5%

C   63.0%

D   92.5%

153 **A baker is trying to decide the number of batches of a particular type of bread that he should bake each day. Daily demand ranges from 10 batches to 12 batches. Each batch of bread that is baked and sold yields a positive contribution of $50, but each batch of bread baked that is not sold yields a negative contribution of $20.**

Assuming the baker adopts the *minimax regret* decision rule, **calculate** the number of batches of bread that he should bake each day. You must justify your answer.   **(4 marks)**

MANAGING SHORT-TERM FINANCE

154 **If an entity regularly fails to pay its suppliers by the normal due dates, it may lead to a number of problems:**

(i)   having insufficient cash to settle trade payables

(ii)   difficulty in obtaining credit from new suppliers

(iii)   reduction in credit rating

(iv)   settlement of trade receivables may be delayed.

Which TWO of the above could arise as a result of exceeding suppliers' trade credit terms?

A   (i) and (ii)

B   (i) and (iii)

C   (ii) and (iii)

D   (iii) and (iv)

155   **A conservative policy for financing working capital is one where short-term finance is used to fund:**

A   all of the fluctuating current assets, but no part of the permanent current assets

B   all of the fluctuating current assets and part of the permanent current assets

C   part of the fluctuating current assets and part of the permanent current assets

D   part of the fluctuating current assets, but no part of the permanent current assets

156   **ABC has produced the following sales forecast:**

	$000
January	750
February	760
March	770
April	780
May	790
June	800

Currently 20% of customers pay in cash. Of the credit customers (excluding those who become irrecoverable debts), 60% pay in one month, 30% pay in two months and 10% in three months. Irrecoverable debts are 2%. This payment pattern is expected to continue.

What are the forecast cash receipts in April?   **(3 marks)**

157   **If the current ratio for a company is equal to its acid test (that is, the quick ratio), then:**

A   the current ratio must be greater than one

B   the company does not carry any inventory

C   trade receivables plus cash is greater than trade payables minus inventory

D   working capital is positive

158   **In October, a company made credit purchases of $18,000 and credit sales of $24,000. All sales are made on the basis of cost plus 25%. By how much will working capital increase in October as a result of these transactions?**

159   **The following items have been extracted from a company's budget for next month:**

	$
Sales on credit	240,000
Expected increase in inventory next month	20,000
Expected decrease in trade receivables next month	12,000

What is the budgeted receipt from trade receivables next month?   **(3 marks)**

160 DY had a balance outstanding on trade receivables at 30 September 20X6 of $68,000. Forecast credit sales for the next six months are $250,000 and customers are expected to return goods with a sales value of $2,500.

Based on past experience, within the next six months DY expects to collect $252,100 cash and to write off as irrecoverable debts 5% of the balance outstanding at 30 September 20X6.

Calculate DY's forecast trade receivables days outstanding at 31 March 20X7.   **(4 marks)**

161 A company has annual sales of $40 million, annual cost of sales of $30 million and makes annual purchases of $15 million. Its balance sheet includes among assets and liabilities the following:

Trade receivables $4 million
Trade payables $3 million
Inventory $8 million

What is its cash conversion cycle?

A   206.5 days

B   60.8 days

C   36.5 days

D   97.3 days

162 XYZ's annual sales are $100m of which 95% are made on credit. Receivables at the beginning of the year were $10 million and at the end of the year total receivables were $12 million. 10% of receivables were non-trade related.

What is XYZ's average collection period?

A   36.5 days

B   40 days

C   38 days

D   46 days

163 DY's trade receivables balance at 1 April 2006 was $22,000. DY's income statement showed revenue from credit sales of $290,510 during the year ended 31 March 2007.

DY's trade receivables at 31 March 2007 were 49 days.

Assume DY's sales occur evenly throughout the year and that all balances outstanding at 1 April 2006 have been received.

Also, it should be assumed all sales are on credit, there were no irrecoverable debts and no trade discount was given.

How much cash did DY receive from its customers during the year to 31 March 2007?

A $268,510

B $273,510

C $312,510

D $351,510

164   **The following items were extracted from a company's budget for next month:**

	$
Purchases on credit	360,000
Expected decrease in inventory during the month	12,000
Expected increase in trade payables during the month	15,000

What is the budgeted payment to trade creditors for the month?

A $333,000

B $345,000

C $357,000

D $375,000

165   **The trial balance of EH at 31 October 2007 showed trade receivables of $82,000 before adjustments.**

On 1 November 2007 EH discovered that one of its customers had ceased trading and was very unlikely to pay any of its outstanding balance of $12,250.

On the same date EH carried out an assessment of the collectability of its other trade receivable balances. Using its knowledge of its customers and past experience EH determined that the remaining trade receivables had suffered a 3% impairment at 31 October 2007.

What is EH's balance of trade receivables, as at 31 October 2007?

A $66,202

B $67,290

C $67,657

D $79,540

166   **EV had inventory days outstanding of 60 days and trade payables outstanding of 50 days at 31 October 2007.**

EV's inventory balance at 1 November 2006 was $56,000 and trade payables were $42,000 at that date. EV's cost of goods sold comprises purchased goods cost only. During the year to 31 October 2007, EV's cost of goods sold was $350,000.

Assume purchases and sales accrue evenly throughout the year and use a 365-day year. Further assume that there were no goods returned to suppliers and EV claimed no discounts.

Calculate how much EV paid to its credit suppliers during the year to 31 October 2007.

(4 marks)

167 DX had the following balances in its trial balance at 30 September 20X6:

Trial balance extract at 30 September 20X6

	$000	$000
Revenue		2,400
Cost of sales	1,400	
Inventories	360	
Trade receivables	290	
Trade payables		190
Cash and cash equivalents	95	

Calculate the length of DX's working capital cycle at 30 September 20X6.   **(4 marks)**

168 An enterprise commenced business on 1 April 20X2. Revenue in April 20X2 was $20,000, but this is expected to increase at 2% a month. Credit sales amount to 60% of total sales. The credit period allowed is one month. Irrecoverable debts are expected to be 3% of credit sales, but other customers are expected to pay on time. Cash sales represent the other 40% of revenue.

How much cash is expected to be received in May 20X2?   **(3 marks)**

169 Which of the following is LEAST likely to characterise overtrading?

    A   Increased borrowing

    B   Increased cash balances

    C   Increased turnover

    D   Reduced working capital

170 An aged creditors analysis (aged trade payables analysis) is:

    A   a listing of trade payables by date of invoicing

    B   a listing of trade payables with whom you are in arrears

    C   the proportion of purchases by value which are overdue

    D   a breakdown of trade payables according to length of time elapsing since the purchase was made

171 FGH requires a rate of return of 12.85% each year.

Two of FGH's suppliers, P and Q, are offering the following terms for immediate cash settlement:

Supplier	Cash settlement discount	Normal settlement period
P	1%	1 month
Q	2%	2 months

Which of the discounts should be accepted to achieve the required rate of return?

    A   The discounts offered by both P and Q

    B   The discount offered by P only

    C   The discount offered by Q only

    D   Neither of them

172 WM's major supplier, INT, supplies electrical tools and is one of the largest companies in the industry, with international operations. Deliveries from INT are currently made monthly, and are constant throughout the year. Delivery and invoicing both occur in the last week of each month.

Details of the credit terms offered by INT are as follows:

Normal credit period	Cash discount	Average monthly purchases
40 days	2% for settlement in 10 days	$100,000

WM always takes advantage of the cash discount from INT.

Calculate the annual rate of interest (to two decimal places) implied in the cash discount offered by INT. Assume a 365-day year. **(3 marks)**

173 What are the three main services provided by a without recourse factor? **(3 marks)**

174 Invoice discounting normally involves:

A   offering a cash discount for early settlement of invoices

B   selling an invoice to a discount house at a profit

C   selling an individual invoice for cash to a factor organisation at a discount

D   writing off an invoice, partly or in total, as an irrecoverable debt

175 XYZ has $1 million to invest for one year. It can lock it away at a fixed rate of 7% for the full year, or invest at 6.5% for a three-month term, speculating on an increase in interest rates. Assume the rate available increases to 7.5% after three months and XYZ invests at this rate for the rest of the year.

By how much is XYZ better off from its gamble on interest rates?

A $2,500

B $12,836

C $73,414

D $3,414

176 After a bill of exchange has been accepted, there are a number of possible actions that the drawer could take.

Which ONE of the following is NOT a possible course of action?

A   Ask the customer for immediate payment

B   Discount the bill with a bank

C   Hold the bill until the due date and then present it for payment

D   Use the bill to settle a trade payable

177 The bank accepts the instrument drawn upon it by its customer, and then sells it into a secondary market at a discount, including a commission, passing the proceeds to its client. The bank then pays the bill at face value. Which description best describes this instrument?

    A   A letter of credit

    B   A forfaiting agreement

    C   An acceptance credit

    D   A commercial bill

178 Which of the following most appropriately describes forfaiting?

    A   It is a method of providing medium-term export finance

    B   It provides short-term finance for purchasing fixed assets which are denominated in a foreign currency

    C   It provides long-term finance to importers

    D   It is the forced surrender of a share due to the failure to make a payment on a partly paid share

179 List FOUR forms of short-term finance generally available to small entities. **(4 marks)**

180 AL's customers all pay their accounts at the end of 30 days. To try and improve its cash flow, AL is considering offering all customers a 15% discount for payment within 14 days.

Calculate the implied annual (interest) cost to AL of offering the discount, using compound interest methodology and assuming a 365-day year. **(3 marks)**

181 An entity's working capital financing policy is to finance working capital using short-term financing to fund all the fluctuating current assets as well as some of the permanent part of the current assets.

The above policy is an example of:

    A   an aggressive policy

    B   a conservative policy

    C   a short-term policy

    D   a moderate policy

182 BE has been offering 60-day payment terms to its customers, but now wants to improve its cash flow. BE is proposing to offer a 1.5% discount for payment within 20 days.

Assume a 365-day year and an invoice value of $1,000.

What is the effective annual interest rate that BE will incur for this action? **(4 marks)**

183 The trade receivables ledger account for customer C shows the following entries:

		Debits	Credits
		$	$
Balance brought forward		0	
10 June X6	Invoice 201	345	
19 June X6	Invoice 225	520	
27 June X6	Invoice 241	150	
3 July X6	Receipt 1009 – Inv 201		200
10 July X6	Invoice 311	233	
4 August X6	Receipt 1122 – Inv 225		520
6 August X6	Invoice 392	197	
18 August X6	Invoice 420	231	
30 August X6	Receipt 1310 – Inv 311		233
7 September X6	Invoice 556	319	
21 September X6	Receipt 1501 – Inv 392		197
30 September X6	Balance	845	

Prepare an aged analysis showing the outstanding balance on a monthly basis for customer C at 30 September 20X6. **(4 marks)**

184 DR has the following balances under current assets and current liabilities:

Current assets	$
Inventory	50,000
Trade receivables	70,000
Bank	10,000

Current liabilities	$
Trade payables	88,000
Interest payable	7,000

DR's quick ratio is

A 0.80 : 1

B 0.84 : 1

C 0.91 : 1

D 1.37 : 1

185 SK sells bathroom fittings throughout the country in which it operates. In order to obtain the best price, it has decided to purchase all its annual demand of 10,000 shower units from a single supplier. RR has offered to provide the required number of showers each year under an exclusive long-term contract.

Demand for shower units is at a constant rate all year. The cost to SK of holding one shower unit in inventory for one year is $4 plus 3% of the purchase price.

RR is located only a few miles from the SK main showroom. It has offered to supply each shower unit at $400 with a transport charge of $200 per delivery. It has guaranteed such a regular and prompt delivery service that SK believes it will not be necessary to hold any safety inventory (that is, buffer inventory) if it uses RR as its supplier.

Using the economic order quantity model (EOQ model), **calculate** the optimal order size, assuming that RR is chosen as the sole supplier of shower units for SK. **(3 marks)**

186 Which of the following would be LEAST likely to arise from the introduction of a Just-in-Time inventory ordering system?

    A   Lower inventory holding costs

    B   Less risk of inventory shortages

    C   More frequent deliveries

    D   Increased dependence on suppliers

187 Which of the following is LEAST relevant to the simple economic order quantity (EOQ) model for inventory?

    A   Safety stock

    B   Annual demand

    C   Holding costs

    D   Order costs

188 PB uses 2,500 units of component X per year. Its production director has calculated that the cost of placing and processing a purchase order for component X is $185, and the cost of holding one unit of component X for a year is $25.

What is the economic order quantity (EOQ) for component X and, assuming a 52-week year, what is the average frequency at which purchase orders should be placed?

	EOQ	Frequency of orders
A	136 units	3 weeks
B	136 units	6 weeks
C	192 units	4 weeks
D	192 units	5 weeks

189 Calculate the economic order quantity (EOQ) for the following item of inventory:

- quantity required per year 32,000 items
- order costs are $15 per order
- inventory holding costs are estimated at 3% of inventory value per year
- each unit currently costs $40.

190 The economic order quantity formula includes the cost of placing an order. However, the Management Accountant is unsure which of the following items would usually be included in 'cost of placing an order':

    (i)   administrative costs

    (ii)   postage

    (iii)   quality control cost

    (iv)   unit cost of products

    (v)   storekeeper's salary.

SECTION A-TYPE QUESTIONS : **SECTION 1**

Which THREE of the above would be regarded as part of the cost of placing an order?

    A   (i), (ii) and (iii) only

    B   (i), (iv) and (v) only

    C   (ii), (iii) and (iv) only

    D   (i), (ii) and (v) only

191   **DS uses the Economic Order Quantity (EOQ) model. Demand for DS's product is 95,000 units per annum. Demand is evenly distributed throughout the year. The cost of placing an order is $15 and the cost of holding a unit of inventory for a year is $3.**

    How many orders should DS make in a year?   **(3 marks)**

192   **A bond with a coupon rate of 7% is redeemable in eight years' time for $100. Its current purchase price is $82. What is the percentage yield to maturity?**   **(4 marks)**

193   **CX purchased $10,000 of unquoted bonds when they were issued by Z. CX now wishes to sell the bonds to B. The bonds have a coupon rate of 7% and will repay their face value at the end of five years. Similar bonds have a yield to maturity of 10%.**

    Calculate the current market price for the bonds.   **(3 marks)**

194   **A bond has a current market price of $83. It will repay its face value of $100 in 7 years' time and has a coupon rate of 4%.**

    If the bond is purchased at $83 and held, what is its yield to maturity?   **(4 marks)**

195   **DK is considering investing in government bonds. The current price of a $100 bond with 10 years to maturity is $88. The bonds have a coupon rate of 6% and repay face value of $100 at the end of the 10 years.**

    Calculate the yield to maturity.   **(4 marks)**

MARCH 2012 EXAM

196   **A decision maker who makes decisions using the expected value criterion would be classified as:**

    A   Risk averse

    B   Risk seeking

    C   Risk neutral

    D   Risk spreading   **(2 marks)**

197   **A company's management is considering investing in a project with an expected life of 4 years. It has a positive net present value of $180,000 when cash flows are discounted at 8% per annum. The project's cash flows include a cash outflow of $100,000 for each of the four years. No tax is payable on projects of this type.**

The percentage increase in the annual cash outflow that would cause the company's management to reject the project from a financial perspective is, to the nearest 0.1%:

A   54.3%

B   45.0%

C   55.6%

D   184.0%   **(2 marks)**

198   **PT provides expert quality assurance services on a consultancy basis. The management of the company is unsure whether to price the services it offers at the Deluxe, High, Standard or Low fee level. There is uncertainty regarding the mix of staff that would be available to provide each of the services. As the staff are on different pay scales the mix of staff would affect the variable costs of each service.**

The table below details the annual contribution earned from each of the possible outcomes.

Staffing mix	Fee level			
	Deluxe	High	Standard	Low
X	$135,000	$140,000	$137,500	$120,000
Y	$150,000	$160,000	$165,000	$160,000
Z	$165,000	$180,000	$192,500	$200,000

If PT applies the minimax regret criterion, the fee level it will choose is:

A   Deluxe

B   High

C   Standard

D   Low   **(2 marks)**

The following data relate to Questions 199 and 200.

FP is a retailer of office products. For one particular model of calculator there is an annual demand of 26,000 units. Demand is predictable and spread evenly throughout the year. Supplies are received 2 weeks after placing the order and no buffer inventory is required.

The calculators cost $14 each. Ordering costs are $160 per order. The annual cost of holding one calculator in inventory is estimated to be 10% of the purchase cost.

199   **The economic order quantity (EOQ) for this model of calculator will be:**

A   2,438 units

B   771 units

C   67 units

D   2,060 units   **(2 marks)**

200 FP has decided not to use the EOQ and has decided to order 2,600 calculators each time an order is placed. The total ordering and holding costs per annum will be:

A $5,240

B $19,800

C $208,014

D $3,420 **(2 marks)**

201 **State** THREE ways that an accepted bill of exchange can be used by the holder. **(3 marks)**

202 **A company is considering investing $50,000 in a project which will yield $5,670 per annum in perpetuity. The company's cost of capital is 9% per annum.**

Calculate the net present value of the project. **(3 marks)**

203 **PL currently earns an annual contribution of $2,880,000 from the sale of 90,000 units of product B. Fixed costs are $800,000 per annum.**

The management of PL is considering reducing the selling price per unit to $48. The estimated levels of demand at the revised selling price and the probabilities of them occurring are as follows:

Selling price of $48

Demand	Probability
100,000 units	0·40
120,000 units	0·60

The estimated variable costs per unit at either of the higher levels of demand and the probabilities of them occurring are as follows:

Variable cost (per unit)	Probability
$21	0·25
$19	0·75

The level of demand and the variable cost per unit are independent of each other.

Required:

Calculate the probability that the profit will increase from its current level if the selling price is reduced to $48. **(4 marks)**

(Total: 20 marks)

MAY 2012 EXAM

204 **The term 'budgetary slack' refers to the:**

A   Lead time between the preparation of the functional budgets and the approval of the master budget by senior management

B   Difference between the budgeted output and the actual output

C   Difference between budgeted capacity utilisation and full capacity

D   Intentional over estimation of costs and/or under estimation of revenue in a budget

(2 marks)

205 **Which of the following would NOT be associated with a company that is overtrading?**

A   A dramatic reduction in sales revenue

B   A rapid increase in the outstanding overdraft amount

C   A rapid increase in the volume of inventory

D   A rapid increase in sales revenue   **(2 marks)**

206 **A company has recorded the following activity levels and distribution costs for the previous three quarters:**

Quarter	Volume Units	Total cost $
1	64,000	200,000
2	80,000	240,000
3	100,000	290,000

What will be the distribution costs in quarter 4 if the expected level of activity is 85,000 units? You should assume that the cost behaviour pattern in the previous three quarters will continue in quarter 4.

A $252,500

B $255,000

C $254,303

D $253,963   **(2 marks)**

207 **A company has annual sales revenues of $48 million. The company earns a constant gross margin of 40% on sales. All sales and purchases are on credit and are evenly distributed over the year.**

The following are maintained at a constant level throughout the year:

Inventory $8 million

Trade receivables $10 million

Trade payables $5 million

The company's cash operating cycle to the nearest day is:

A   99 days

B   114 days

C   89 days

D   73 days   **(2 marks)**

208   **A company is considering factoring as a way of managing its trade receivables. It currently has a balance outstanding on trade receivables of $250,000. It has annual sales revenue of $1,500,000 which occurs evenly throughout the year. Trade receivables are expected to continue at the same level for the next year.**

The factor will advance 80% of invoiced sales and will charge interest at a rate of 10% per annum.

The interest charge for next year payable to the factor will be:

A $25,000

B $150,000

C $20,000

D $120,000   **(2 marks)**

209   **A supplier has offered CB an early settlement discount of 3% if payment is made within 20 days of the invoice date. CB currently takes 58 days to pay this supplier.**

Calculate, to the nearest 0.1%, the effective annual interest rate to CB of the early settlement discount. You should assume a 365 day year and use a compound interest methodology.   **(3 marks)**

210   **A company has recently carried out a post-completion audit at the end of Year 2 of a project that had an original investment of $100,000. It is concerned that the estimated cash flows are not going to be achieved.**

The cash flows that were forecast when the investment decision was originally taken were as follows:

	$
Year 1	60,000
Year 2	80,000
Year 3	(70,000)
Year 4	80,000
Year 5	60,000

The data from the post-completion audit show that the net cash outflow in Year 3 will be $90,000 and the cash inflows in Years 4 and 5 will be $60,000 and $40,000 respectively. You should assume that all cash flows with the exception of the original investment will arise at the end of the year.

The company's cost of capital is 12% per annum.

Required:

Demonstrate, using calculations, whether or not the project should be abandoned immediately. You should assume that there will be no additional costs associated with abandoning the project. **(3 marks)**

211 **RT is preparing the production budget for Product R and the material purchases budget for Material T for next year. Each unit of Product R requires 6 kg of Material T.**

The estimated inventory at the beginning of next year for Product R is 6,000 units and the company wants to decrease the inventory held by 10% by the end of next year.

The estimated inventory at the beginning of next year for Material T is 60,000 kg and due to problems with the material supplier the closing inventory at the end of next year is to be increased to 75,000 kg.

The budgeted sales of Product R for next year are 80,000 units.

Required:

(i) **Calculate** the production budget for Product R for next year.

(ii) **Calculate** the material purchases budget for Material T for next year. **(4 marks)**

(Total: 20 marks)

SEPTEMBER 2012 EXAM

212 **A company commenced business on 1 August. Total sales revenue in August was $200,000 and is expected to increase at a rate of 2% per month. Credit sales represent 60% of total sales revenue and the remaining 40% is cash sales. The credit period allowed is one month. Bad debts are expected to be 3% of credit sales but the remaining credit sales customers are expected to pay on time.**

The estimated receipts in September from cash and credit sales are:

A $195,552

B $196,400

C $198,000

D $201,600 **(2 marks)**

213 **A company operates a throughput accounting system. The details per unit of Product C are:**

Selling price	$28.50
Material cost	$9.25
Labour cost	$6.75
Overhead costs	$6.00
Time on bottleneck resource	7.8 minutes

The throughput contribution per hour for Product C is:

A $50.00

B $122.85

C $121.15

D $148.08 **(2 marks)**

214   The following details have been extracted from the accounts payable records of RS.

Invoices paid in the month of purchase	15% of total value
Invoices paid in the first month after purchase	65% of total value
Invoices paid in the second month after purchase	20% of total value

The pattern of payments is expected to continue in the future and has been used to produce RS's cash budget for October to December.

Purchases for October to December are budgeted as follows:

October	$280,000
November	$250,000
December	$300,000

A settlement discount of 5% is taken on invoices paid in the month of purchase.

The amount budgeted to be paid to suppliers in December is:

A $264,500

B $261,250

C $250,325

D $263,500 **(2 marks)**

215   The fixed production overhead volume variance can be defined as

A   the difference between the budgeted fixed production overhead cost and the standard fixed production overhead cost absorbed by actual production.

B   the difference between the standard fixed production overhead cost absorbed by actual production and the actual fixed overhead cost incurred.

C   the difference between the budgeted and actual fixed production overhead cost.

D   the difference between the budgeted fixed production overhead cost and the budgeted production at the actual absorption rate incurred. **(2 marks)**

216   A master budget comprises the

A   budgeted income statement and budgeted cash flow statement only.

B   budgeted income statement and budgeted balance sheet only.

C   budgeted income statement and budgeted capital expenditure only.

D   budgeted income statement, budgeted balance sheet and budgeted cash flow statement only. **(2 marks)**

217 **LM operates a parcel delivery service. Last year its employees delivered 15,120 parcels and travelled 120,960 kilometres. Total costs were $194,400.**

LM has estimated that 70% of its total costs are variable with activity and that 60% of these costs vary with the number of parcels and the remainder vary with the distance travelled.

LM is preparing its budget for the forthcoming year using an incremental budgeting approach and has produced the following estimates:

- All costs will be 3% higher than the previous year due to inflation

- Efficiency will remain unchanged

- A total of 18,360 parcels will be delivered and 128,800 kilometres will be travelled.

Required:

Calculate the following costs to be included in the forthcoming year's budget:

(i) the total variable costs related to the number of parcels delivered.

(ii) the total variable costs related to the distance travelled. **(3 marks)**

218 **A capital investment project has the following estimated cash flows and present values:**

Year		Cash flow $	Discount factor @ 12%	Present value $
0	Initial investment	(200,000)	1.000	(200,000)
1-5	Contribution per annum	108,000	3.605	389,340
1-5	Fixed costs per annum	(30,000)	3.605	(108,150)
5	Residual value	30,000	0.567	17,010

Required:

Calculate the sensitivity of the investment decision to a change in the annual contribution.

(3 marks)

219 **DB manufactures and sells e-readers. The standard labour cost per unit of the product is $7. Each unit takes 0.5 hours to produce at a labour rate of $14 per hour. The budgeted production for August was 20,000 units.**

The Production Director subsequently reviewed the market conditions that had been experienced during August and determined that market labour rates were $17.50 per hour. The actual production was 22,000 units. Actual labour hours worked were 11,400 hours at $15.50 per hour.

Required:

Calculate the following variances for August:

(i) The labour rate planning variance

(ii) The labour rate operational variance

(iii) The labour efficiency operational variance **(4 marks)**

(Total: 20 marks)

Section 2

SECTION B-TYPE QUESTIONS

COST ACCOUNTING SYSTEMS

220 MARGINAL COST PROFIT AND CASH FLOW

Briefly discuss the assertion that marginal costing profits are a better indicator of cash flow than absorption costing profits. **(5 marks)**

221 BACKFLUSH ACCOUNTING (SEPT 10)

Explain why a backflush cost accounting system may be considered more appropriate than a traditional cost accounting system, in a company that operates a just-in-time production and purchasing system. **(5 marks)**

222 ACTIVITY BASED COSTING (MAR 12)

KY makes several products including Product W. KY is considering adopting an activity-based approach for setting its budget. The company's production activities, budgeted activity costs and cost drivers for next year are given below:

Activity	$	Cost driver	Cost driver quantity
Set-up costs	200,000	No. of set-ups	800
Inspection/quality control	120,000	No. of quality tests	400
Stores receiving	252,000	No. of purchase requisitions	1,800

Machines are reset after each batch. Quality tests are carried out after every second batch.

The budgeted data for Product W for next year are:

Direct materials	$2·50 per unit
Direct labour	0·03 hours per unit @ $18 per hour
Batch size	150 units
Number of purchase requisitions	80
Budgeted production	15,000 units

Calculate, using activity-based costing, the budgeted total production cost per unit for Product W. **(5 marks)**

223 ABSORPTION COSTING (MAR 12)

The following details have been extracted from KL's budget:

Selling price per unit	$140
Variable production costs per unit	$45
Fixed production costs per unit	$32

The budgeted fixed production cost per unit was based on a normal capacity of 11,000 units per month.

Actual details for the months of January and February are given below:

	January	February
Production volume (units)	10,000	11,500
Sales volume (units)	9,800	11,200
Selling price per unit	$135	$140
Variable production cost per unit	$45	$45
Total fixed production costs	$350,000	$340,000

There was no closing inventory at the end of December.

Required:

(i)   **Calculate** the actual profit for January and February using absorption costing. You should assume that any under / over absorption of fixed overheads is debited / credited to the Income Statement each month.   **(3 marks)**

The actual profit figure for the month of January using marginal costing was $532,000.

(ii)   **Explain,** using appropriate calculations, why there is a difference between the actual profit figures for January using marginal costing and using absorption costing.

(2 marks)

(Total: 5 marks)

224 IMPROVING THE THROUGHPUT ACCOUNTING RATIO

Management considers that the throughput accounting (TA) ratio for product C in relation to the labour-intensive packing process is unacceptably low. **Explain** three actions that could be considered to improve the TA ratio.   **(5 marks)**

225 ABC AND PROFITABILITY

Explain the circumstances in which the use of activity based costing is likely to result in more meaningful information about product costs and profitability.   **(5 marks)**

226 MANUFACTURING RESOURCE PLANNING SYSTEM (MAY 07)

Briefly explain the role of a Manufacturing Resource Planning System in supporting a standard costing system.   **(5 marks)**

227   JUST-IN-TIME (MAY 07)

Briefly explain the main differences between the traditional manufacturing environment and a just-in-time manufacturing environment.   **(5 marks)**

228   THROUGHPUT ACCOUNTING (SEPT 11)

A company manufactures two products A and B. The budget statement below was produced using a traditional absorption costing approach. It shows the profit per unit for each product based on the estimated sales demand for the period.

	Product A	Product B
	$	$
Selling price per unit	46	62
Production costs per unit:		
Material costs	18	16
Labour costs	4	10
Overhead costs	8	12
Profit per unit	16	24

Additional information:

	Product A	Product B
Estimated sales demand (units)	6,000	8,000
Machine hours per unit	0.5	0.8

It has now become apparent that the machine which is used to produce both products has a maximum capacity of 8,000 hours and the estimated sales demand cannot be met in full. Total production costs for the period, excluding direct material cost, are $248,000.   No inventories are held of either product.

Required:

(i)   **Calculate** the return per machine hour for each product if a throughput accounting approach is used.   **(2 marks)**

(ii) **Calculate** the profit for the period, using a throughput accounting approach, assuming the company prioritises Product B.   **(3 marks)**

(Total: 5 marks)

229   MRP AND ABB (MAY 10)

A medium-sized manufacturing company, which operates in the electronics industry, has employed a firm of consultants to carry out a review of the company's planning and control systems. The company presently uses a traditional incremental budgeting system and the inventory management system is based on economic order quantities (EOQ) and reorder levels. The company's normal production patterns have changed significantly over the previous few years as a result of increasing demand for customised products. This has resulted in shorter production runs and difficulties with production and resource planning.

The consultants have recommended the implementation of activity based budgeting and a manufacturing resource planning system to improve planning and resource management.

(a) **Explain** how a manufacturing resource planning system would improve the planning of purchases and production for the company. **(5 marks)**

(b) **Explain** the benefits for the company that could occur following the introduction of an activity based budgeting system. **(5 marks)**

230 TOTAL QUALITY MANAGEMENT (MAY 08)

Describe THREE key features that are present in any organisation that is successfully focused on Total Quality Management (TQM). **(5 marks)**

231 ENVIRONMENTAL COSTING (NOV 11)

Explain THREE benefits that a company could gain from using environmental costing.
(5 marks)

232 ENVIRONMENTAL COSTS (MAR 12)

Environmental costs can be categorised as 'environmental internal failure costs' and 'environmental external failure costs'.

Required:

Explain what is meant by both of these categories giving TWO examples of each type of environmental cost. **(5 marks)**

233 MARGINAL COSTING AND THROUGHPUT ACCOUNTING (MAY 06)

Compare and contrast marginal costing and throughput accounting. **(5 marks)**

STANDARD COSTING

234 FIXED OVERHEAD VOLUME VARIANCE

Explain the meaning of the fixed production overhead volume variance and discuss briefly its usefulness to management. **(5 marks)**

235 DIAGNOSTIC RELATED GROUPS

Explain how the use of diagnostic related groups enables standard costing to be applied in the healthcare industry. **(5 marks)**

236 MIX AND YIELD VARIANCES

Explain the meaning of the materials mix and yield variances and discuss briefly any limitations in their usefulness. **(5 marks)**

237 LABOUR RATE VARIANCE

State FIVE possible causes of an adverse labour rate variance. **(5 marks)**

238 LABOUR VARIANCES (NOV 05)

A management consulting company had budgeted the staff requirements for a particular job as follows:

	$
40 hours of senior consultant at $100 per hour	4,000
60 hours of junior consultant at $60 per hour	3,600
	———
Budgeted staff cost for job	7,600
	———

The actual hours recorded were:

	$
50 hours of senior consultant at $100 per hour	5,000
55 hours of junior consultant at $60 per hour	3,300
	———
Actual staff cost for job	8,300
	———

The junior consultant reported that for 10 hours of the 55 hours recorded there was no work that she could do.

Calculate the following variances:

- idle time variance
- labour mix variance
- labour efficiency variance. **(5 marks)**

239 PLANNING AND OPERATING VARIANCES (MAY 07)

A company uses variance analysis to monitor the performance of the team of workers which assembles Product M. Details of the budgeted and actual performance of the team for last period were as follows:

	Budget	*Actual*
Output of product M	600 units	680 units
Wage rate	$30 per hour	$32 per hour
Labour hours	900 hours	1,070 hours

It has now been established that the standard wage rate should have been $31.20 per hour.

(i) **Calculate** the labour rate planning variance and calculate the operational labour efficiency variance.

(ii) **Explain** the major benefit of analysing variances into planning and operational components. **(5 marks)**

240 INVESTIGATION OF VARIANCES (MAY 07)

Briefly explain three factors that should be considered before deciding to investigate a variance. **(5 marks)**

241 FG (MAY 12)

FG, an ink manufacturer, produces black ink by mixing three chemicals.

The standard material costs per litre of black ink are as follows:

			$
0.50 litres of Chemical A	@	$0.60 per litre	0.30
0.30 litres of Chemical B	@	$1.40 per litre	0.42
0.25 litres of Chemical C	@	$1.00 per litre	0.25
1.05			0.97

Actual data for April were as follows:

Output of black ink (000s litres)　　　　　3,300

Raw materials used	Quantity (000s litres)	Cost ($000)
Chemical A	2,144	1,120
Chemical B	824	1,040
Chemical C	792	620

Required:

Calculate the following variances for April:

(i)　　The total material mix variance　　　　　　　　　　　　　　**(3 marks)**

(ii)　　The total material yield variance　　　　　　　　　　　　　**(2 marks)**

(Total: 5 marks)

242 HOSPITAL CARE (MAY 06)

The standard cost schedule for hospital care for a minor surgical procedure is shown below. Staff: patient ratio is 0.75:1

	$
Nursing costs: 2 days × 0.75 × $320 per day	480
Space and food costs: 2 days × $175 per day	350
Drugs and specific materials	115
Hospital overheads: 2 days × $110 per day	220
Total standard cost	**1,165**

The actual data for the hospital care for one patient having the minor surgical procedure showed that the patient stayed in hospital for three days. The cost of the drugs and specific materials for this patient was $320. There were 0.9 nurses per patient on duty during the time that the patient was in hospital. The daily rates for nursing pay, space and food, and hospital overheads were as expected.

Prepare a statement that reconciles the standard cost with the actual costs of hospital care for this patient. The statement should contain FIVE variances that will give useful information to the manager who is reviewing the cost of hospital care for minor surgical procedures.　　　　　　　　　　　　　　　　　　　　　**(5 marks)**

243 MODERN BUSINESS ENVIRONMENT (MAY 07)

Briefly discuss THREE reasons why standard costing may not be appropriate in a modern business environment. **(5 marks)**

244 BENCHMARKING

Explain benchmarking and how it can be used to improve an organisation's performance. **(5 marks)**

BUDGETING

245 XY (SEPT 10)

XY, a not-for-profit charity organisation which is funded by public donations, is concerned that it is not making the best use of its available funds. It has carried out a review of its budgeting system and is considering replacing the current system with a zero-based budgeting system.

Explain the potential advantages AND disadvantages for the charity of a zero-based budgeting system.. **(5 marks)**

246 PRODUCTION COST BUDGET (MAY 10)

The production budgets for quarters 1 and 2 for a manufacturing company are as follows:

	Quarter 1	Quarter 2
Production (Units)	15,000	20,000
Budgeted production costs	$	$
Direct materials	180,000	240,000
Production labour	155,000	195,000
Production overheads	210,000	240,000

The cost structure, which is expected to continue unchanged in quarter 3, is as follows:

(i) The variable cost elements are linear and vary in direct proportion to volume.

(ii) There is a bulk purchase discount of 5% on materials if orders exceed $250,000 per quarter. The discount will apply to the purchase of all materials in that quarter.

(iii) The company operates a JIT system for material purchases.

(iv) Fixed production overheads will increase by $20,000 per quarter at production output levels in excess of 22,000 units in a quarter.

The budgeted production volume for quarter 3 is 23,000 units.

Prepare the production cost budget for quarter 3. **(5 marks)**

247 BUDGET SETTING PROCESS (NOV 10)

Explain the stages in the budget setting process for a company that uses a zero-based budgeting system. **(5 marks)**

248   ZBB (MAY 09)

(a)   **Explain** how "zero based budgeting" can overcome the problems that are associated with "incremental budgeting".   **(5 marks)**

(b)   A management consulting company had set the budget for the staff requirements for a particular job as follows:

	£
50 hours of senior consultant at £120 per hour	6,000
90 hours of junior consultant at £80 per hour	7,200
Budgeted staff cost for job	13,200

The actual hours recorded were:

	£
60 hours of senior consultant at £130 per hour	7,800
90 hours of junior consultant at £75 per hour	6,750
Actual staff cost for job	14,550

The junior consultant reported that for 10 hours of the 90 hours he recorded there was no work that he could do.

(i)   **Calculate** the following variances:

- Idle time variance
- Labour mix variance   **(3 marks)**

(ii)   **Explain** the worth, or otherwise, of this company calculating the labour mix variance in this situation.   **(2 marks)**

(Total for sub-question (b) = 5 marks)

(c)   **Explain** the importance to management, for planning and control purposes, of the differing definitions of "variable" costs offered by traditional costing methods and activity based costing.   **(5 marks)**

(d)   A company budgeted to produce 400 units of a product in a period. The standard cost card of the product showed that the standard cost of the material used to manufacture each unit of the product was 6 kg costing £12 per kg.

The actual results for the period were that 380 units were produced from 2,500 kg of material which had cost £29,000.

It has now been realised that the standard material content per unit should have been 6.75 kg.

Calculate

- the materials usage planning variance
- the operational materials price variance
- the operational materials usage variance   **(5 marks)**

249   INCREMENTAL BUDGETING (SEPT 12)

Explain the limitations of incremental budgeting.   **(5 marks)**

250 MCDONALDIZATION AND BUDGETS (NOV 05)

UV Limited is a catering company that provides meals for large events. It has a range of standard meals at fixed prices. It also provides meals to meet the exact requirements of a customer and prices for this service are negotiated individually with each customer.

Discuss how a 'McDonaldization' approach to service delivery would impact on budget preparation and control within UV Limited. **(5 marks)**

251 QR (SEPT 10)

QR uses an activity based budgeting (ABB) system to budget product costs. It manufactures two products, product Q and product R. The budget details for these two products for the forthcoming period are as follows:

	Product Q	Product R
Budgeted production (units)	80,000	120,000
Number of machine set ups per batch	4	2
Batch size (units)	5,000	4,000

The total budgeted cost of setting up the machines is $74,400.

Required:

(i) **Calculate** the budgeted machine set up cost per unit of product Q. **(3 marks)**

(ii) **State** TWO potential benefits of using an activity based budgeting system. **(2 marks)**

(Total: 5 marks)

252 DECISION PACKAGES (MAR 11)

'A zero-based budgeting system involves establishing decision packages that are then ranked in order of their relative importance in meeting the organisation's objectives'.

Required:

Explain the above statement and the difficulties that a not-for-profit organisation may experience when trying to rank decision packages. **(5 marks)**

253 BUDGET CONFLICTS (MAY 11)

"Different budgets should be used for different purposes. The budget used for planning purposes should be different from the budget used to set performance targets."

Required:

Explain the above statement and the conflicts that may arise when a single budget is used for both purposes. **(5 marks)**

254 BUDGET PARTICIPATION (SEPT 11)

Explain the advantages of management participation in budget setting and the potential problems that may arise in the use of the resulting budget as a control mechanism.

(5 marks)

255 X PLC (NOV 06)

X plc manufactures specialist insulating products that are used in both residential and commercial buildings. One of the products, Product W, is made using two different raw materials and two types of labour. The company operates a standard absorption costing system and is now preparing its budgets for the next four quarters. The following information has been identified for Product W:

Sales

Selling price	$220 per unit

Sales demand

Quarter 1	2,250 units
Quarter 2	2,050 units
Quarter 3	1,650 units
Quarter 4	2,050 units
Quarter 5	1,250 units
Quarter 6	2,050 units

Costs

Materials

A	5 kgs per unit @ $4 per kg
B	3 kgs per unit @ $7 per kg

Labour

Skilled	4 hours per unit @ $15 per hour
Semi-skilled	6 hours per unit @ $9 per hour
Annual overheads	$280,000
	40% of these overheads are fixed and the remainder varies with total labour hours. Fixed overheads are absorbed on a unit basis.

Inventory holding policy

Closing inventory of finished goods	30% of the following quarter's sales demand
Closing inventory of materials	45% of the following quarter's materials usage

The management team is concerned that X plc has recently faced increasing competition in the marketplace for Product W. As a consequence there have been issues concerning the availability and costs of the specialised materials and employees needed to manufacture Product W, and there is concern that these might cause problems in the current budget-setting process.

(a) **Prepare** the following budgets for each quarter for X plc:

   (i)   Production budget in units

   (ii) Raw material purchases budget in kgs and value for Material B.   **(5 marks)**

(b) X plc has just been informed that Material A may be in short supply during the year for which it is preparing budgets. **Discuss** the impact this will have on budget preparation and other areas of X plc.   **(5 marks)**

(c)   X plc currently uses incremental budgeting. **Explain** how Zero-Based Budgeting could overcome the problems that might be faced as a result of the continued use of the current system.   **(5 marks)**

(d)   **Briefly explain** how linear regression analysis can be used to forecast sales and briefly discuss whether it would be a suitable method for X plc to use.   **(5 marks)**

(Total: 20 marks)

256   TIME SERIES IN FORECASTING

Describe the strengths and weaknesses of using time series analysis to prepare forecasts.
(5 marks)

257   BUDGETARY CONTROL (NOV 11)

Explain THREE benefits that organisations gain from using budgetary planning and control systems.   **(5 marks)**

258   CENTRALISED PURCHASING (MAY 12)

A company currently operates from a number of different locations which have their own purchasing departments. Senior management are now considering whether to change to a system where all purchasing is carried out by a centralised purchasing department.

Explain the benefits that should result from the company using a centralised purchasing system.   **(5 marks)**

259   PROBLEMS IN CENTRALISED PURCHASING (SEPT 12)

Explain the disadvantages for a company of using a centralised purchasing system.
(5 marks)

260   TOP DOWN BUDGETING (MAY 12)

A company currently operates a 'top-down' budgeting system where senior managers impose budgets on departmental managers. It is now considering allowing departmental managers to participate in the setting of their own budgets.

Explain the arguments for and against the participation of departmental managers in the preparation of their budgets.   **(5 marks)**

THE TREATMENT OF UNCERTAINTY IN DECISION MAKING

261 GT (NOV 11)

GT is considering building a restaurant in a new retail park.

It can build either a small restaurant or a large restaurant. Since there are strict local planning regulations, once GT has committed to the size of restaurant it cannot be extended later.

Past experience suggests that there is a 60% chance that demand will be high and a 40% chance that demand will be low. Estimates of the net present values of the future cash flows for GT associated with each size of restaurant are as follows:

	Demand	
Size of restaurant	Low	High
	$	$
Small	800,000	1,200,000
Large	(1,000,000)	2,000,000

Required:

(i) **Demonstrate**, using a decision tree, which course of action GT should pursue.

(3 marks)

GT could commission a market research survey that will give an accurate prediction of the level of demand.

Required:

(ii) **Calculate** the maximum price that GT should pay for the market research survey.

(2 marks)

(Total: 5 marks)

262 DECISION TREE (SEPT 11)

A company is considering whether to develop an overseas market for its products. The cost of developing the new market is estimated to be $250,000. There is a 70% probability that the development of the new market will succeed and a 30% probability that the development of the new market will fail and no further expenditure will be incurred.

If the market development is successful the profit from the new market will depend on prevailing exchange rates. There is a 50% chance that exchange rates will be in line with expectations and a profit of $500,000 will be made. There is a 20% chance that exchange rates will be favourable and a profit of $630,000 will be made and a 30% chance that exchange rates will be adverse and a profit of $100,000 will be made.

The profit figures stated are before taking account of the development costs of $250,000.

Required:

Demonstrate, using a decision tree, whether the company should develop an overseas market for its products.   **(5 marks)**

263 NEW PRODUCT (NOV 11)

A company is planning to launch a new product. The price at which it can sell the product will be determined by the number of other entrants into the market. The possible selling prices and variable costs and their respective associated probabilities are as follows:

Selling price per unit		Variable cost per unit	
$	Probability	$	Probability
80	0.25	40	0.20
100	0.30	60	0.55
120	0.45	80	0.25

Selling price and variable cost per unit are independent of each other.

Required:

(i) **Calculate** the probability of the contribution being greater than $39 per unit.

(3 marks)

(ii) **Calculate** the expected value of the contribution per unit. **(2 marks)**

(Total: 5 marks)

264 RISK ATTITUDES (MAR 11)

A company uses a third party delivery service to deliver goods to customers. The current average cost per delivery is $12.50. The company is trying to decide whether to establish an in-house delivery service. A number of factors could affect the average total cost per delivery for the in-house delivery service. The table below shows the possible average total costs and the probability of each one occurring:

Average total cost	Probability
$10.50	0.05
$10.70	0.10
$11.00	0.08
$12.10	0.12
$12.50	0.14
$12.60	0.16
$14.20	0.12
$15.60	0.18
$15.80	0.05

The expected value of the average total cost, based on the probability distribution above, is $13.

Required:

Explain the decision that the company manager is likely to make, based on the probability distribution and the current delivery cost of $12.50 per delivery, if the manager is:

(i) Risk neutral

(ii) Risk averse

(iii) Risk seeking **(5 marks)**

265 PERFECT INFORMATION (MAR 11)

A company has to decide which of three new mutually exclusive products to launch. The directors believe that demand for the products will vary depending on competitor reaction. There is a 30% chance that competitor reaction will be strong, a 20% chance that competitor reaction will be normal and a 50% chance that competitor reaction will be weak. The company uses expected value to make this type of decision.

The net present value for each of the possible outcomes is as follows:

Competitor reaction	Product A	Product B	Product C
	$000s	$000s	$000s
Strong	200	400	600
Normal	300	600	400
Weak	500	800	500

A market research company believes it can provide perfect information on potential competitor reaction in this market.

Required:

Calculate the maximum amount that should be paid for the information from the market research company. **(5 marks)**

266 CONSUMER DEMAND (MAY 11)

A company has to decide which of three mutually exclusive projects to invest in during the next year. The directors believe that the success of the projects will vary depending on consumer demand. There is a 20% chance that consumer demand will be above average; a 45% chance that consumer demand will be average and a 35% chance that consumer demand will be below average.

The net present value for each of the possible outcomes is as follows:

Consumer demand	Project A	Project B	Project C
	$000s	$000s	$000s
Above average	400	300	800
Average	500	400	600
Below average	700	600	300

A market research company believes it can provide perfect information on potential consumer demand in this market.

Required:

Calculate, on the basis of expected value, the maximum amount that should be paid for the information from the market research company. **(5 marks)**

267 CLOTHING RETAILER (MAY 12)

A clothing retailer is considering which of three mutually exclusive advertising packages to use when it launches its new range of autumn fashion. The sales revenue from the range will depend on customer reaction to the chosen advertising package. There is a 25% chance that customer reaction will be good; a 40% chance that customer reaction will be moderate and a 35% chance that customer reaction will be poor.

The contribution, net of advertising costs, for each of the possible outcomes is as follows:

Customer reaction	Package A $000s	Package B $000s	Package C $000s
Good	700	900	800
Moderate	600	500	400
Poor	400	300	500

A market research company believes it can provide perfect information on potential customer reaction to the range.

Required:

Calculate, on the basis of expected value, the maximum amount that should be paid for the information from the market research company. **(5 marks)**

268 ELECTRONIC GOODS (SEPT 12)

The manager of a retail store that sells electronic goods is deciding which of three credit agreements to offer to its customers. Past experience has shown that there are three possible reactions to each of the agreements. The profit will depend on customers' reaction to the agreement on offer.

The profit for each of the possible outcomes is as follows:

Customer reaction	Agreement A $	Agreement B $	Agreement C $
Strong	52,600	44,800	64,700
Moderate	43,700	36,200	41,600
Weak	38,200	34,500	33,100

Required:

(i) **Prepare** a regret matrix and use it to identify the agreement that the manager would select if the minimax regret criterion was used to make the decision. **(3 marks)**

(ii) **Describe** the attitude to risk of a manager that is risk averse. **(2 marks)**

(Total: 5 marks)

269 MAXIMIN AND MAXIMAX (NOV 10)

AP sells fruit in a market where the level of demand is uncertain. AP has to order the fruit before the demand level is known.

The payoff table below shows the profits AP can expect depending on the level of order that is placed and the level of demand that occurs.

Demand level	Level of order		
	High	Medium	Low
Good	$600	$300	$100
Average	$200	$400	$100
Poor	$(100)	$300	$200

Required:

(i) **Identify** which order level would be selected if AP applied:

    (a)   the maximin decision criterion

    (b)   the maximax decision criterion   **(2 marks)**

(ii) **Identify**, using a minimax regret table, the order level that would be selected if AP applied the minimax regret decision criterion.   **(3 marks)**

        (Total: 5 marks)

FINANCIAL INFORMATION FOR LONG TERM DECISION MAKING

270 TS (MAY 11)

TS operates a fleet of vehicles and is considering whether to replace the vehicles on a 1, 2 or 3 year cycle.

Each vehicle costs $25,000. The operating costs per vehicle for each year and the resale value at the end of each year are as follows:

	Year 1	Year 2	Year 3
	$	$	$
Operating costs	5,000	8,000	11,000
Resale value	18,000	15,000	5,000

The cost of capital is 6% per annum.

Required:

Calculate the optimum replacement cycle for the vehicles. You should assume that the initial investment is incurred at the beginning of year 1 and that all other cash flows arise at the end of the year.   **(5 marks)**

271 TWO ASSETS (SEPT 12)

A company's Financial Director is deciding whether to purchase or lease two assets:

Asset 1 has a ten year life with a zero residual value. It can be purchased for $120,000. If the asset is purchased it would be paid for in cash on the day the asset is acquired. Alternatively, it can be leased for ten payments of $18,000 per annum payable each year in advance.

Asset 2 has a five year life. It can be purchased for $51,000 and will have a residual value of $20,000 after five years. If the asset is purchased it would be paid for in cash on the day the asset is acquired. Alternatively, it can be leased for five payments of $10,000 per annum payable each year in arrears. If leased, the asset will remain the property of the lessor and will be returned at the end of the five year contract.

The cost of capital is 10% per annum. Ignore taxation.

Required:

Prepare calculations to show whether each of the assets should be purchased or leased.

(5 marks)

272 SENSITIVITY ANALYSIS (MAY 12)

A capital investment project has the following estimated cash flows and present values:

Year		Cash flow	DF @ 12%	Present value
		$		$
0	Initial investment	(100,000)	1.000	(100,000)
1-5	Contribution per annum	52,000	3.605	187,460
1-5	Fixed costs per annum	(25,000)	3.605	(90,125)
5	Residual value	20,000	0.567	11,340

Required:

(i) **Calculate** the sensitivity of the investment decision to a change in the annual fixed costs. **(3 marks)**

(ii) **State** TWO benefits to a company of using sensitivity analysis in investment appraisal. **(2 marks)**

(Total: 5 marks)

273 ST (SEPT 11)

ST needs to replace its fleet of delivery vans and is considering two alternative types of van as the replacement. One of the vans has an estimated life of 4 years whilst the other has an estimated life of 5 years. The vans will be required for the foreseeable future.

The estimated cash flows over the life of the van are given below:

Year	Van A	Van B
	$	$
0	(25,000)	(30,000)
1	(2,000)	(3,000)
2	(2,000)	(3,000)
3	(3,000)	(3,000)
4	5,000	(4,000)
5		6,000

The company's cost of capital is 8% per annum.

Required:

Demonstrate, by calculation, which of the two vans should be purchased. **(5 marks)**

274 SENSITIVITY AND UNCERTAINTY (MAR 12)

Explain why sensitivity analysis is useful when dealing with uncertainty in project appraisal. **(5 marks)**

MANAGING SHORT-TERM FINANCE

275 WCC (NOV 10)

An extract from WCC's trial balance at the end of its financial year is given below:

	$000
Sales revenue (80% on credit)	1,400
Cost of sales	1,215
Purchases of materials (95% on credit)	915
Inventories at end of year	
Raw materials	85
Finished goods	90
Trade receivables	185
Trade payables	125

Required:

Calculate the length of WCC's working capital cycle to the nearest 0.1 of a day. **(5 marks)**

276 JE (NOV 09)

The following is an extract from JE's financial statements for the years ended 30 September 2008 and 2009.

	As at September X8	As at September X9
Balance Sheet extracts	$000	$000
Trade receivables	250	390
Inventories	160	200
Bank and cash equivalents	90	10
Trade payables	300	500
Bank overdraft	0	100

Income Statement extracts		
Revenue (all credit sales)	2,250	3,150
Cost of sales*	1,910	2,800
Gross Profit	340	350

*there are no purchases for cash

Required:

Calculate five relevant working capital and efficiency ratios for JE for the two years ended 30 September 2008 and 2009. **(5 marks)**

277   HL (MAY 09)

HL has been trading profitably, but has recently been accused of overtrading.

Required:

(i)   **Define** the meaning of overtrading, and explain what is likely to happen if HL is overtrading. **(3 marks)**

(ii)   **Identify** actions that HL could take to correct the problems of overtrading.   **(2 marks)**

(Total: 5 marks)

278   DISCOUNTS (MAR 12)

TJ allows credit to customers provided that they have satisfactory trade references. Customers however are exceeding credit terms and taking on average 55 days to pay. In an effort to reduce the level of trade receivables, TJ is considering offering a 2% discount to customers paying within 20 days.

Required:

(i)   **Calculate,** to the nearest 0·1%, the effective annual interest rate to TJ of offering this discount. You should assume a 365 day year and use compound interest methodology. **(3 marks)**

(ii)   **State** TWO methods, other than asking for trade references, that TJ could use to assess the credit worthiness of new customers. **(2 marks)**

(Total: 5 marks)

279   CREDIT LIMITS (NOV 11)

Discuss TWO sources of information that a company could use when setting credit limits for customers. **(5 marks)**

280   WITHOUT RECOURSE FACTORING (MAR 11)

A company is considering the use of without recourse factoring to manage its trade receivables. It currently has a balance outstanding on trade receivables of $180,000 and annual sales revenue of $1,095,000. It anticipates that this level of sales revenue and trade receivables will continue for at least the next year. It estimates that the use of the factoring company will result in a reduction in credit control costs of $20,000 per annum.

The factoring company will charge a fee of 2.5% of invoiced sales. It will give an advance of 90% of invoiced sales and charge interest at a rate of 12% per annum.

Required:

(i) **Calculate** the annual cost of factoring net of credit control cost savings. **(3 marks)**

The company currently finances its accounts receivables with a bank overdraft at an interest rate of 15% per annum.

(ii) **Calculate** whether there is a financial benefit from using the factor. You should ignore bad debts. **(2 marks)**

(Total: 5 marks)

281 FACTORING (MAY 11)

Discuss the advantages AND disadvantages of factoring as a method of managing trade receivables. **(5 marks)**

282 AGED RECEIVABLES ANALYSIS (MAY 10)

The trade receivable ledger account for customer J from 1 January to 30 April 2010 shows the following:

All figures in $		Debit	Credit	Balance
01-Jan-2010	Balance b/fwd			125
10-Jan-2010	Invoice No. 234	181		306
12-Jan-2010	Invoice No. 263	92		398
18-Jan-2010	Invoice No. 297	287		685
23-Jan-2010	Receipt No. 85 (Balance b/fwd + Inv No.263)		217	468
09-Feb-2010	Invoice No. 328	294		762
13-Feb-2010	Credit Note No.167 (Inv No. 234)		63	699
05-Mar-2010	Invoice No. 365	135		834
15-Mar-2010	Invoice No. 379	232		1,066
18-Mar-2010	Receipt No. 102 (Inv No. 297)		287	779
25-Mar-2010	Invoice No. 391	71		850
01-Apr-2010	Receipt No. 126 (Inv No. 328)		294	556
24-Apr-2010	Invoice No. 438	145		701

Required:

(i) **Prepare** an age analysis of trade receivables, for customer J, at 30 April 2010 showing the outstanding balance analysed by month. **(3 marks)**

(ii) **State** two benefits of preparing an age analysis of trade receivables. **(2 marks)**

(Total: 5 marks)

283   CREDIT TERMS (SEPT 12)

GH is a manufacturer of leather goods. The company has recently won a contract to supply CD, a major department store chain, with a range of products. The contract will require significant investment in non-current assets and working capital. GH will raise a loan from its bank for the investment in non-current assets but is considering alternative methods of reducing the required investment in working capital. These methods include offering early settlement discounts and debt factoring.

CD's normal credit term from its suppliers is 90 days. GH is considering offering an early settlement discount of 3% for payments received within ten days in order to reduce the working capital requirement.

Required:

(a)   (i)   **Calculate,** to the nearest 0.1%, the effective annual interest rate to GH of the early settlement discount. You should assume a 365 day year and use a compound interest methodology.   **(3 marks)**

(ii)   **State** TWO disadvantages to GH of using a bank loan to finance the additional working capital.   **(2 marks)**

(b)   **Explain** the advantages and disadvantages to GH of using debt factoring to finance the additional working capital.   **(5 marks)**

(Total: 10 marks)

284   EOQ (SEPT 10)

BB manufactures a range of electronic products. The supplier of component Y has informed BB that it will offer a quantity discount of 1.0% if BB places an order of 10,000 components or more at any one time.

Details of component Y are as follows:

Cost per component before discount $2.00

Annual purchases   150,000 components

Ordering costs $360 per order

Holding costs $3.00 per component per annum

Required:

(i)   **Calculate** the total annual cost of holding and ordering inventory of component Y using the economic order quantity and ignoring the quantity discount.   **(2 marks)**

(ii)   **Calculate** whether there is a financial benefit to BB from increasing the order size to 10,000 components in order to qualify for the 1.0% quantity discount.   **(3 marks)**

(Total: 5 marks)

285   INVENTORY LEVELS (MAY 10)

A company, which uses the EOQ inventory management model, purchases 64,000 units of raw materials per year. The purchase price of the raw material is $10 per unit. The cost of holding one unit in inventory is $1.20 per year. The cost of reordering and taking delivery is $150 per order regardless of the size of the order.

Assuming that usage is predictable and spread evenly throughout the year and that ordering and delivery are simultaneous, **calculate** for the raw material:

(i)   The total annual cost of holding and ordering inventory.   **(3 marks)**

Past experience has shown that the supplier of the raw material can be unreliable and that the delivery period can be between one week and three weeks. If the company wants to hold enough raw material to ensure that it never runs out, **calculate** for the raw material:

(ii)   The lowest inventory level at which raw material should be reordered.   **(2 marks)**

(Total: 5 marks)

286   CH (NOV 11)

CH is a building supplies company that sells products to trade and private customers.

Budget data for each of the six months to March are given below:

	Oct $000	Nov $000	Dec $000	Jan $000	Feb $000	March $000
Credit sales	250	250	250	260	260	280
Cash sales	60	60	65	75	80	90
Credit purchases	170	180	180	200	200	200
Other operating costs (excluding depreciation)	90	90	90	122	123	123

80% of the value of credit sales is received in the month after sale, 10% two months after sale and 8% three months after sale. The balance is written off as a bad debt.

75% of the value of credit purchases is paid in the month after purchase and the remaining 25% is paid two months after purchase.

All other operating costs are paid in the month they are incurred.

CH has placed an order for four new forklift trucks that will cost $25,000 each. The scheduled payment date is in February.

The cash balance at 1 January is estimated to be $15,000.

Required:

Prepare a cash budget for each of the THREE months of January, February and March.

(5 marks)

287   JL (MAR 12)

JL is preparing its cash budget for the next three quarters. The following data have been extracted from the operational budgets:

Sales revenue	Quarter 1	$500,000
	Quarter 2	$450,000
	Quarter 3	$480,000
Direct material purchases	Quarter 1	$138,000
	Quarter 2	$151,200
	Quarter 3	$115,600

Additional information is available as follows:

- JL sells 20% of its goods for cash. Of the remaining sales value, 70% is received within the same quarter as sale and 30% is received in the following quarter. It is estimated that trade receivables will be $125,000 at the beginning of Quarter 1. No bad debts are anticipated.

- 50% of payments for direct material purchases are made in the quarter of purchase, with the remaining 50% in the quarter following purchase. It is estimated that the amount owing for direct material purchases will be $60,000 at the beginning of Quarter 1.

- JL pays labour and overhead costs when they are incurred. It has been estimated that labour and overhead costs in total will be $303,600 per quarter. This figure includes depreciation of $19,600.

- JL expects to repay a loan of $100,000 in Quarter 3.

- The cash balance at the beginning of Quarter 1 is estimated to be $49,400 positive.

Required:

Prepare a cash budget for each of the THREE quarters. **(5 marks)**

288 BILLS OF EXCHANGE (MAY 09)

Bills of exchange are sometimes used for export transactions.

A bill of exchange with a face value of $1,000 has 91 days to maturity. The discount yield required by an investor, HG, is 7%. Assume a 365 day year.

Required:

(i) **Identify** THREE ways in which an accepted bill of exchange can be used by the holder.

(3 marks)

(ii) **Calculate** the maximum price HG should be willing to pay for the bill. **(2 marks)**

(Total: 5 marks)

289 TREASURY BILLS (MAR 11)

A company has surplus funds to invest for a period of 3 months. It is considering potential investment opportunities as follows:

Investment 1

Purchase treasury bills issued by the country's central bank. The treasury bills can be purchased now for a period of 91 days. The purchase price is $995 per $1,000.

Investment 2

Invest in a 30 day notice bank deposit account. The account will pay a variable rate of interest of 2.5% per annum, payable quarterly.

Required:

Explain the advantages AND disadvantages to the company of each of the investments.

Your answer should include relevant calculations. **(5 marks)**

290   COUPON RATE (MAR 11)

A bond has a coupon rate of 8% and will repay its nominal value of $100 when it matures in 6 years' time.

The bond's yield to maturity is 6.58%.

Required:

Explain why there may be a difference between a bond's coupon rate and its yield to maturity.   **(5 marks)**

291   RISK AND YIELD (NOV 06)

DH raised cash through an equity share issue to pay for a new factory it planned to construct. However, the factory contract has been delayed and payments are not expected to be required for three or four months. DH is going to invest its surplus funds until they are required.

One of the directors of DH has identified three possible investment opportunities:

(i)   Treasury bills issued by the central bank of DH's country. They could be purchased on 1 December 20X6 for a period of 91 days. The likely purchase price is $990 per $1,000.

(ii)   Equities quoted on DH's local stock exchange. The stock exchange has had a good record in recent months with the equity index increasing in value for 14 consecutive months. The director recommends that DH invests in three large multinational entities, each paying an annual dividend that provides an annual yield of 10% on the current share price.

(iii)   DH's bank would pay 3.5% per year on money placed in a deposit account with 30 days' notice.

Required:

As Assistant Management Accountant, you have been asked to **prepare notes** on the risk and effective yield of each of the above investment opportunities for use by the Management Accountant at the next board meeting.   **(5 marks)**

292   YIELD TO MATURITY (MAY 11)

A bond has a coupon rate of 6% and will repay its nominal value of $100 when it matures after four years.

The bond will be purchased today for $103 ex-interest and held until maturity.

Required:

Calculate, to 0.01%, the yield to maturity for the bond based on today's purchase price.   **(5 marks)**

293   EXPORT FINANCING (MAY 11)

Describe the following methods of export financing:

(i)   Bills of exchange

(ii)   Forfaiting

(iii)   Documentary credits   **(5 marks)**

294   OVERDRAFT (SEPT 11)

Explain the advantages AND disadvantages of an overdraft as a method of short-term finance for a company.   **(5 marks)**

295   INVESTMENT RISKS (SEPT 11)

When deciding where to invest short term cash surpluses, it is necessary to consider the following two types of risk:

(i)   Default risk

(ii)   Interest rate risk

Required:

Explain what is meant by each of the TWO types of risk listed above. Your answer should include an example of each type of risk.   **(5 marks)**

296   INVESTING CASH SURPLUSES (MAY 12)

Explain THREE factors that a company should consider before deciding how to invest short term cash surpluses.   **(5 marks)**

Section 3

SECTION C-TYPE QUESTIONS

COST ACCOUNTING SYSTEMS

297 RETAIL COMPANY (NOV 09) *Walk in the footsteps of a top tutor*

The management team of a retail company has produced the draft income statement and draft balance sheet as shown below.

Budgeted Income Statement for the year ending 31 December 2010

	£
Sales revenue	3,900,000
Cost of sales	2,600,000
Gross profit	1,300,000
Selling and administration costs	860,000
Operating profit	440,000

Budgeted Balance Sheet as at 31 December 2010

	£	£
Non-current assets		
Land	200,000	
Buildings	1,500,000	
Plant and machinery	1,250,000	
Accumulated depreciation	(910,000)	
		2,040,000
Current assets		
Inventory	182,280	
Receivables	501,000	
Cash	289,300	972,580
Current liabilities		
Payables (for goods for resale)		(428,980)
Total assets less current liabilities		2,583,600

Shareholders' funds

Share capital	380,000
Retained earnings	2,203,600
	2,583,600

(a) The team now thinks that its forecasts may have been too optimistic and would like to assess the impact of several independent changes (that would occur on 1 January 2010) on the draft budget statements:

(i) increase inventory to £200,000;

(ii) increase receivables days to 60 days;

(iii) reduce selling prices by 5%.

Required:

Identify the effect and then calculate the result of each of the *independent* changes on the items shown in the table below. Reproduce the table in your answer book and insert the figures that would appear for the items in the revised draft income statements and draft balance sheets as a result of the independent changes (i), (ii) and (iii). **(11 marks)**

	(i)	(ii)	(iii)
Operating profit			
Inventory			
Receivables			
Cash			
Payables			

The team is considering a proposal from a manufacturer who has offered to become the sole supplier to the company. The supplier would reduce the unit cost of sales by 20% in return for an annual fee of £600,000. Currently the cost of sales is wholly variable and 40% of the selling and administration costs vary with sales revenue.

Required:

(b) (i) **Calculate the current breakeven point (in £000).**

(ii) **Calculate the breakeven point in (£000) if the supplier's offer is accepted.**

(iii) **Discuss the advantages and disadvantages of this offer to the retail company.**
(10 marks)

(c) **Explain why the Beyond Budgeting model may be more appropriate than traditional budgeting in an organisation that has adopted Total Quality Management.** **(9 marks)**

(Total: 30 marks)

298   HIP, KNEE AND SHOULDER (NOV 10)

A healthcare company specialises in hip, knee and shoulder replacement operations, known as surgical procedures. As well as providing these surgical procedures the company offers pre operation and post operation in-patient care, in a fully equipped hospital, for those patients who will be undergoing the surgical procedures.

Surgeons are paid a fixed fee for each surgical procedure they perform and an additional amount for any follow-up consultations. Post procedure follow-up consultations are only undertaken if there are any complications in relation to the surgical procedure. There is no additional fee charged to patients for any follow up consultations. All other staff are paid annual salaries.

The company's existing costing system uses a single overhead rate, based on revenue, to charge the costs of support activities to the procedures. Concern has been raised about the inaccuracy of procedure costs and the company's accountant has initiated a project to implement an activity-based costing (ABC) system.

The project team has collected the following data on each of the procedures.

Procedure Information	Hip	Knee	Shoulder
Fee charged to patients per procedure	$8,000	$10,000	$6,000
Number of procedures per annum	600	800	400
Average time per procedure	2.0 hours	1.2 hours	1.5 hours
Number of procedures per theatre session	2	1	4
In-patient days per procedure	3	2	1
Surgeon's fee per procedure	$1,200	$1,800	$1,500
% of procedures with complications	8%	5%	10%
Surgeon's fee per follow up consultation	$300	$300	$300
Cost of medical supplies per procedure	$400	$200	$300

The project team has obtained the following information about the support activities.

Activity	Cost Driver	Overheads $000
Theatre preparation for each session	Number of theatre preparations	864
Operating theatre usage	Procedure time	1,449
Nursing and ancillary services	In-patient days	5,428
Administration	Sales revenue	1,216
Other overheads	Number of procedures	923

Required:

(a)   Calculate the profit per procedure for each of the three procedures, using the current basis for charging the costs of support activities to procedures.   **(5 marks)**

(b)   Calculate the profit per procedure for each of the three procedures using activity-based costing.   **(13 marks)**

(c)   Discuss the ways in which the information obtained by the project team may be of benefit to the management of the company.   **(7 marks)**

(Total: 25 marks)

299 RJ (MAY 07)

RJ produces and sells two high performance motor cars: Car X and Car Y. The company operates a standard absorption costing system. The company's budgeted operating statement for the year ending 30 June 2008 and supporting information is given below:

Operating statement year ending 30 June 2008

	Car X $000	Car Y $000	Total $000
Sales	52,500	105,000	157,500
Production cost of sales	40,000	82,250	122,250
Gross profit	12,500	22,750	35,250
Administration costs			
Variable	6,300	12,600	18,900
Fixed	7,000	9,000	16,000
Profit/(loss)	(800)	1,150	350

The production cost of sales for each car was calculated using the following values:

	Car X Units	$000	Car Y Units	$000
Opening inventory	200	8,000	250	11,750
Production	1,100	44,000	1,600	75,200
Closing inventory	300	12,000	100	4,700
Cost of sales	1,000	40,000	1,750	82,250

Production costs

The production costs are made up of direct materials, direct labour, and fixed production overhead. The fixed production overhead is general production overhead (it is not product specific). The total budgeted fixed production overhead is $35,000,000 and is absorbed using a machine hour rate. It takes 200 machine hours to produce one Car X and 300 machine hours to produce one Car Y.

Administration costs

The fixed administration costs include the costs of specific marketing campaigns: $2,000,000 for Car X and $4,000,000 for Car Y.

Required:

(a) Produce the budgeted operating statement in a marginal costing format.   **(7 marks)**

(b) Reconcile the total budgeted absorption costing profit with the total budgeted marginal costing profit as shown in the statement you produced in part (a).

(5 marks)

The company is considering changing to an activity based costing system. The company has analysed the budgeted fixed production overheads and found that the costs for various activities are as follows:

	$000
Machining costs	7,000
Set up costs	12,000
Quality inspections	7,020
Stores receiving	3,480
Stores issues	5,500
	35,000

The analysis also revealed the following information:

	Car X	Car Y
Budgeted production (number of cars)	1,100	1,600
Cars per production run	10	40
Inspections per production run	20	80
Number of component deliveries during the year	492	900
Number of issues from stores	4,000	7,000

Required:

(c) **Calculate the budgeted production cost of one Car X and one Car Y using the activity based costing information provided above.** **(10 marks)**

(d) **Prepare a report to the Production Director of RJ which explains the potential benefits of using activity based budgeting for performance evaluation.** **(8 marks)**

(Total: 30 marks)

300 PHOTOCOPYING COMPANY (MAR 11)

A company sells and services photocopying machines. Its sales department sells the machines and consumables, including ink and paper, and its service department provides an after sales service to its customers. The after sales service includes planned maintenance of the machine and repairs in the event of a machine breakdown. Service department customers are charged an amount per copy that differs depending on the size of the machine.

The company's existing costing system uses a single overhead rate, based on total sales revenue from copy charges, to charge the cost of the Service Department's support activities to each size of machine. The Service Manager has suggested that the copy charge should more accurately reflect the costs involved. The company's accountant has decided to implement an activity-based costing system and has obtained the following information about the support activities of the service department:

Activity	Cost Driver	Overheads per annum $000
Customer account handling	Number of customers	126
Planned maintenance scheduling	Number of planned maintenance visits	480
Unplanned maintenance scheduling	Number of unplanned maintenance visits	147
Spare part procurement	Number of purchase orders	243
Other overheads	Number of machines	600
Total overheads		1,596

The following data have also been collected for each machine size:

	Small photocopiers	Medium photocopiers	Large photocopiers
Charge per copy	$0.03	$0.04	$0.05
Average number of copies per year per machine	60,000	120,000	180,000
Number of machines	300	800	500
Planned maintenance visits per machine per year	4	6	12
Unplanned maintenance visits per machine per year	1	1	2
Total number of purchase orders per year	500	1,200	1,000
Cost of parts per maintenance visit	$100	$300	$400
Labour cost per maintenance visit	$60	$80	$100

Each customer has a service contract for two machines on average.

Required:

(a) **Calculate the annual profit per machine for each of the three sizes of machine, using the current basis for charging the costs of support activities to machines.**

(4 marks)

(b) **Calculate the annual profit per machine for each of the three sizes of machine using activity-based costing.** (14 marks)

(c) **Explain the potential benefits to the company of using an activity-based costing system.** (7 marks)

(Total: 25 marks)

STANDARD COSTING

301 HB (MAY 12)

HB makes and sells a single product. The company operates a standard marginal costing system and a just-in-time purchasing and production system. No inventory of raw materials or finished goods is held.

Details of the budget and actual data for the previous period are given below.

Budget data

Standard production costs per unit:

		$
Direct material	8kg @ $10.80 per kg	86.40
Direct labour	1.25 hours @ $18.00 per hour	22.50
Variable overheads	1.25 hours @ $6.00 per direct labour hour	7.50

Standard selling price: $180 per unit

Budgeted fixed production overheads: $170,000

Budgeted production and sales: 10,000 units

Actual data

Direct material: 74,000 kg @ $11.20 per kg

Direct labour: 10,800 hours @ $19.00 per hour

Variable overheads: $70,000

Actual selling price: $184 per unit

Actual fixed production overheads: $168,000

Actual production and sales: 9,000 units

Required:

(a) **Prepare a statement using marginal costing principles that reconciles the budgeted profit and the actual profit. Your statement should show the variances in as much detail as possible.** (11 marks)

(b) (i) **Explain why the variances used to reconcile profit in a standard marginal costing system are different from those used in a standard absorption costing system.** (4 marks)

 (ii) **Calculate the variances that would be different and any additional variances that would be required if the reconciliation statement was prepared using standard absorption costing.**

 Note: Preparation of a revised statement is not required. (4 marks)

(c) **Explain the arguments for the use of traditional absorption costing rather than marginal costing for profit reporting and inventory valuation.** (6 marks)

(Total: 25 marks)

302 PRODUCT MANAGER (NOV 09) *Walk in the footsteps of a top tutor*

A company manufactures many different products. Each product has a Product Manager. The company's management information system produces cost reports for each of the products that are made.

An analysis of previous reports has revealed the following information for Product X:

Units produced	Average variable cost per unit	Total product-specific costs	Head office costs
	$	$000	$000
5,000	160	500	300
10,000	150	500	600
15,000	140	800	900
20,000	140	800	1,200
25,000	155	1,100	1,500
30,000	170	1,100	1,800

Required:

(a) **Explain, for each of the three costs in the above table, possible reasons for the cost/volume relationships.** (6 marks)

Budgeted and actual information for Product Y for the previous period was as follows:

	Budget	Actual
Output	80,000 units	76,000 units
Direct materials	480,000 kg	430,000 kg
Direct labour	200,000 hours	196,000 hours
	$	$
Direct materials	960,000	924,500
Direct labour	1,600,000	1,626,800
Fixed production overheads	640,000	590,000

The company uses standard absorption costing.

Required:

(b) **Produce a statement that reconciles the standard and actual total costs for the previous period's output and shows the variances in as much detail as possible.**

(11 marks)

(c) **It has now been realised that the standard price of the direct materials used to manufacture Product Y in the previous period should have been $2.10 per kg.**

(i) **Calculate the direct materials planning variance.**

(ii) **Calculate the operational direct materials price and usage variances.**

(4 marks)

(Total: 21 marks)

303 WESTERN EUROPE (MAY 10)

A company manufactures a range of industrial cleaning products from its automated factory in Western Europe. The company has recently introduced a just-in-time system for raw material purchases.

The company uses a standard absorption costing system for planning and control purposes although this system is now under review.

The following budget data relate to the production of one of its major products CP1 for April. The product is manufactured by mixing two raw materials ETH1 and RXY2.

	Quantity	Cost/kg	Cost
Raw material input			
ETH1	0.30kg	$18.00	$5.40
RXY2	0.70kg	$6.00	$4.20
Raw material cost per kg of input			$9.60
Yield			96%
Raw materials cost per kg of output			$10.00
Fixed production overheads per kg of output			$4.00
Total standard cost per kg of output			$14.00

Budget data for product CP1 for the period is detailed below:

- Sales – 72,000kg
- Production – 70,000kg
- Opening inventory – 2,000kg of CP1 (valued at $28,000)
- Selling price per kg – $20.00
- Fixed production overheads – $280,000

The fixed production overhead absorption rate is based on the budgeted number of kilograms produced.

Actual data for product CP1 for the period was as follows:

- Sales – 71,000kg
- Production – 69,000kg
- Selling price per kg – $20.30
- Fixed production overheads incurred – $278,000
- Cost per kg of ETH1 – $18.10
- Cost per kg of RXY2 – $5.80
- Input of ETH1 – 22,100kg
- Input of RXY2 – 47,900kg

Required:

(a)   **Produce a statement that reconciles the budgeted and actual profit for CP1 for April showing the variances in as much detail as possible.**   **(19 marks)**

(b)   **Discuss three reasons why the use of a standard costing system is considered inappropriate in a company that operates in an advanced manufacturing technology environment.**   **(6 marks)**

(Total: 25 marks)

304   PQ (SEPT 12)

PQ produces two products, Product B and Product C. The company uses a standard absorption costing system that absorbs overheads on the basis of direct labour hours. The company operates a just-in-time purchasing and production system and no inventory of raw materials or finished goods is held.

Standard selling prices are determined by adding a 100% mark-up to total production costs per unit.

The following budget and actual data relate to August.

Budget data:

	Product B	Product C
Production and sales	2,200 units	1,800 units
Standard production costs per unit:	$	$
Direct material ($5 per kg)	25.00	35.00
Direct labour ($7 per hour)	14.00	10.50
Variable overhead	3.00	2.25
Fixed overhead	8.00	6.00

Actual data:

	Product B	Product C
Production and sales	3,000 units	1,500 units
Selling price per unit	$110	$105

Production costs:

Direct material	$124,800 (25,600 kg)
Direct labour	$ 67,980 (9,140 hours)
Variable overheads	$ 14,300
Fixed overheads	$ 27,000

The company produces a monthly variance analysis report which has previously included the calculation of the sales volume profit variance. The new management accountant has decided to extend this analysis and replace the sales volume profit variance with the sales mix profit margin variance and the sales quantity profit variance.

Required:

(a) Prepare a statement that reconciles the budgeted gross profit and actual gross profit for August. The variances should be shown in as much detail as possible including the individual sales mix profit margin variances and the individual sales quantity profit variances. **(17 marks)**

(b) Explain the benefits to the company of separating the sales volume profit variance into the sales mix profit margin variance and the sales quantity profit variance. You should use the figures calculated in part (a) to illustrate your answer. **(4 marks)**

(c) Explain TWO reasons why a standard costing system may not be considered appropriate in a modern manufacturing environment. **(4 marks)**

(Total: 25 marks)

305 PRE-PREPARED MEALS (MAY 11) *Walk in the footsteps of a top tutor*

A company produces trays of pre-prepared meals that are sold to restaurants and food retailers. Three varieties of meals are sold: economy, premium and deluxe.

Extracts from the budget for last year are given below:

	Economy	Premium	Deluxe
Sales quantity (trays)	180,000	360,000	260,000
Selling price per tray	$2.80	$3.20	$4.49
Total sales revenue	$504,000	$1,152,000	$1,167,400
Direct material cost per tray	$1.00	$1.60	$2.20
Total direct material cost	$180,000	$576,000	$572,000
Direct labour cost per tray	$0.50	$0.50	$0.50
Total direct labour cost	$90,000	$180,000	$130,000

Overhead costs for the budget were estimated using the high-low method based on the total overhead costs for three previous years.

Output (trays)	720,000	680,000	840,000
Total overheads	$1,016,000	$992,000	$1,096,000

Actual results for last year were as follows:

	Economy	*Premium*	*Deluxe*
Sales quantity (trays)	186,000	396,000	278,000
Selling price per tray	$2.82	$3.21	$4.50
Total sales revenue	$524,520	$1,271,160	$1,251,000
Direct material cost per tray	$1.10	$1.50	$2.10
Total direct material cost	$204,600	$594,000	$583,800
Direct labour cost per tray	$0.52	$0.54	$0.48
Total direct labour cost	$96,720	$213,840	$133,440
Variable overhead per tray	$0.64	$0.66	$0.63
Total variable overheads	$119,040	$261,360	$175,140

Actual fixed overheads: $546,000

The company operates a just-in-time system for purchasing and production and does not hold any inventory.

Ignore inflation.

Required:

(a) **Calculate, for the original budget, the budgeted fixed overhead costs, the budgeted variable overhead cost per tray and the budgeted total overheads costs.** **(3 marks)**

(b) **Prepare, for last year, a budget control statement on a marginal cost basis for the Premium product.**

The statement should show the original budget, the flexed budget and the total budget variances for sales revenue and each cost element. **(5 marks)**

(c) **Discuss the benefits of flexible budgeting for planning and control purposes.**

You should use the figures calculated in (b) above to illustrate your answer.

(6 marks)

(d) The company has previously calculated only a sales volume variance but has now decided that valuable management information will be provided by further analysis of this variance.

(i) **Calculate the sales quantity contribution variance.** **(3 marks)**

(ii) **Calculate the sales mix contribution variance.** **(3 marks)**

(e) **Explain why the analysis of the sales volume variance into the sales quantity and sales mix variances will provide valuable management information.**

Your answer should refer to the figures calculated in (d) above. **(5 marks)**

(Total: 25 marks)

306 TP (NOV 11)

TP makes wedding cakes that are sold to specialist retail outlets which decorate the cakes according to the customers' specific requirements. The standard cost per unit of its most popular cake is as follows:

		$
Direct material:		
Ingredient A	4 kg at $25 per kg	100
Ingredient B	3 kg at $22 per kg	66
Ingredient C	2 kg at $11.50 per kg	23
Direct labour	3 hours at $12 per hour	36
Variable overhead	3 hours at $8 per hour	24
Standard cost		249

The budgeted production for the period was 10,000 units.

Actual results for the period were as follows:

Production (units)		9,000
		$
Direct material:		
Ingredient A	35,000 kg	910,000
Ingredient B	28,000 kg	630,000
Ingredient C	27,000 kg	296,000
Direct labour	30,000 hours	385,000
Variable overhead		230,000

The general market prices at the time of purchase for Ingredient A and Ingredient B were $23 per kg and $20 per kg respectively.

TP operates a JIT purchasing system for ingredients and a JIT production system; therefore there was no inventory during the period.

Required:

(a) **Prepare a statement which reconciles the flexed budget material cost and the actual material cost. Your statement should include the material price planning variances, and the operational variances including material price, material mix and material yield.** **(12 marks)**

(b) **Discuss the usefulness of the planning and operational variances calculated in part (a) for TP's management.** **(5 marks)**

The budgeted selling price for the product is $400 per unit. Budgeted sales volume for the period was 10,000 units. Actual results for the period were as follows:

Sales volume	9,000 units
Sales revenue	$3,456,000

Required:

(c)   Calculate the total sales price variance and the total sales volume contribution variance.   **(4 marks)**

(d)   Explain the benefits that TP should gain from operating a JIT purchasing system for materials.   **(4 marks)**

(Total: 25 marks)

307   FA AND FB (NOV 08)   *Walk in the footsteps of a top tutor*

A company manufactures two types of fertilizer (FA and FB). The company uses a standard costing system for planning and control purposes. Standards are set annually but budgets and variance reports are prepared each period.

Chemicals

Three chemicals (C1, C2 and C3) are used to make the fertilizers. C2 and C3 can be input directly to the manufacturing process but C1 has to be treated before it can be used. The treatment results in a loss of 30% of the chemicals treated. There are no further losses in the manufacturing process.

Details of the standards for the chemicals are as follows:

	C1	C2	C3
Price per kg	$8	$15	$12
Treatment loss	30%		
Content of finished product:			
per unit of FA	0.20kg	0.15kg	Nil
per unit of FB	0.20kg	Nil	0.25kg

Inventory Policies

Chemicals: end of period holdings must be equal to 50% of the following period's requirements.

Treated C1 is used immediately. There are never any inventories of treated C1 at the start or end of any period.

Fertilizers: no finished products are to be held.

Period 1 Output and sales

	Budget	Actual
FA	40,000 units	38,000 units
FB	24,000 units	25,000 units

Periods 2 and 3 Sales budgets

	Period 2	Period 3
FA	40,000 units	44,000 units
FB	24,000 units	33,000 units

Required:

(a) During Period 1, the quantity of C1 used was 17,740 kg. Calculate for Period 1 for C1:

    (i)   the materials usage variance for the whole process

    (ii)   the treatment loss percentage   **(6 marks)**

(b) In Period 1, the company purchased and used 6,450 kg of C3. The cost of this purchase was $94,000. It has now been realised that the standard price of C3 should have been $14.50 per kg for Period 1.

    (i)   Calculate the planning variance, and the operational price and usage variances for C3 for Period 1.   **(7 marks)**

    (ii)   Explain two problems associated with the reporting of planning variances.

                                                           (3 marks)

(c) Prepare the Purchases Budget for C2 for Period 2.   **(5 marks)**

(d) 'Variance analysis presents results after the actual events have taken place and therefore it is of little use to management for planning and control purposes, particularly in a modern manufacturing environment'.

    Discuss the above statement.   **(9 marks)**

                                                    (Total: 30 marks)

308 HR (MAR 12)

HR is a paint manufacturer that produces a range of paints which it sells to trade and retail outlets.

The standard material cost for 100 litres of white paint is given below:

Raw Material	Volume (litres)	Standard cost per litre $	Standard cost $
A	28	1·40	39.20
B	27	1·20	32.40
C	8	3·65	29.20
D	42	2·60	109.20
	105		210.00

During February, HR produced 7,800 litres of white paint using the following raw materials:

Raw Material	Volume (litres)	Actual cost per litre $
A	2,800	1·50
B	2,700	1·30
C	1,000	4·00
D	1,900	2·50
	8,400	

There was no opening or closing inventory of raw materials.

Required:

(a) Prepare a statement that reconciles the standard material cost to the actual material cost for February. Your statement should include the individual material price variances, the individual material mix variances and the total material yield variance. **(10 marks)**

(b) State THREE factors that a company would need to consider before deciding whether to investigate a variance. **(3 marks)**

HR uses skilled staff to operate the machinery that converts the raw materials for the paint into the finished product. The standard direct labour hours for each 100 litres of white paint produced are as follows:

8 direct labour hours at $24 per hour

During February, 640 direct labour hours were worked at a total cost of $16,500.

It has now been realised that a new wage rate of $26 per hour had been agreed with the workers.

Required:

(c) Calculate the labour rate planning variance for February. **(2 marks)**

(d) Calculate the operational labour rate variance and the operational labour efficiency variance for February. **(4 marks)**

(e) Explain the importance of separating variances into their planning and operational components.

You should use the figures calculated in part (c) to illustrate your answer. **(6 marks)**

(Total: 25 marks)

BUDGETING

309 Q (MAY 08)

Q, a new company, is being established to manufacture and sell an electronic tracking device: the Trackit. The owners are excited about the future profits that the business will generate. They have forecast that sales will grow to 2,600 Trackits per month within five months and will be at that level for the remainder of the first year.

The owners will invest a total of $250,000 in cash on the first day of operations (that is the first day of Month 1). They will also transfer non-current assets into the company.

Extracts from the company's business plan are shown below.

Sales

The forecast sales for the first five months are:

Month	Trackits (units)
1	1,000
2	1,500
3	2,000
4	2,400
5	2,600

The selling price has been set at $140 per Trackit.

Sales receipts

Sales will be mainly through large retail outlets. The pattern for the receipt of payment is expected to be as follows:

Time of payment	% of sales value
Immediately	15*
One month later	25
Two months later	40
Three months later	15

The balance represents anticipated bad debts.

*A 4% discount will be given for immediate payment.

Production

The budget production volumes in units are:

Month 1	Month 2	Month 3	Month 4
1,450	1,650	2,120	2,460

Variable production cost

The budgeted variable production cost is $90 per unit, comprising:

	$
Direct materials	60
Direct wages	10
Variable production overheads	20
	___
Total variable cost	90
	___

Direct materials: Payment for purchases will be made in the month following receipt. There will be no opening inventory of materials in Month 1. It will be company policy to hold inventory at the end of each month equal to 20% at of the following month's production requirements. The direct materials cost includes the cost of an essential component that will be bought in from a specialist manufacturer.

Direct wages will be paid in the month in which the production occurs.

Variable production overheads: 65% will be paid in the month in which production occurs and the remainder will be paid one month later.

Fixed overhead costs

Fixed overheads are estimated at $840,000 per annum and are expected to be incurred in equal amounts each month. 60% of the fixed overhead costs will be paid in the month in which they are incurred and 15% in the following month. The balance represents depreciation of non-current assets.

Ignore VAT and Tax.

Required:

(a) Prepare a cash budget for each of the first three months and for that three-month period in total. **(14 marks)**

(b) There is some uncertainty about the cost of the specialist component (this is included in the direct material cost). It is thought that the cost of the component could range between $32 and $50 per Trackit. It is currently included in the cost estimates at $40 per Trackit.

Calculate the budgeted total net cash flow for the three-month period in total if the cost of the component was:

(i) $32

(ii) $50 **(6 marks)**

(c) Prepare a report for the owners of Q that offers advice about the profitability of their business and the situation revealed by the extracts from the business plan and your answers to (a) and (b) above. **(10 marks)**

(Total: 30 marks)

310 RF LTD (MAY 07) *Walk in the footsteps of a top tutor*

RF Ltd is a new company which plans to manufacture a specialist electrical component. The company founders will invest $16,250 on the first day of operations, that is, Month 1. They will also transfer fixed capital assets to the company.

The following information is available:

Sales

The forecast sales for the first four months are as follows:

Month	Number of components
1	1,500
2	1,750
3	2,000
4	2,100

The selling price has been set at $10 per component in the first four months.

Sales receipts

Time of payment	% of customers
Month of sale	20*
One month later	45
Two months later	25
Three months later	5

The balance represents anticipated bad debts.

*A 2% discount is given to customers for payment received in the month of sale.

Production

There will be no opening inventory of finished goods in Month 1 but after that it will be policy for the closing inventory to be equal to 20% of the following month's forecast sales.

Variable production cost

The variable production cost is expected to be $6.40 per component.

	$
Direct materials	1.90
Direct wages	3.30
Variable production overheads	1.20
	————
Total variable cost	6.40
	————

Notes:

Direct materials: 100% of the materials required for production will be purchased in the month of production. No inventory of materials will be held. Direct materials will be paid for in the month following purchase.

Direct wages will be paid in the month in which production occurs.

Variable production overheads: 60% will be paid in the month in which production occurs and the remainder will be paid one month later.

Fixed overhead costs

Fixed overhead costs are estimated at $75,000 per annum and are expected to be incurred in equal amounts each month. 60% of the fixed overhead costs will be paid in the month in which they are incurred and 30% in the following month. The balance represents depreciation of fixed assets.

Calculations are to be made to the nearest $1.

Ignore VAT and Tax.

Required:

(a) Prepare a cash budget for each of the first three months and in total.　　(15 marks)

(b) There is some uncertainty about the direct material cost. It is thought that the direct material cost per component could range between $1.50 and $2.20.

Calculate the budgeted total net cash flow for the three month period if the cost of the direct material is:

(i) $1.50 per component; or

(ii) $2.20 per component.　　(6 marks)

(c) Using your answers to part *(a)* and *(b)* above, discuss the benefits or otherwise of performing 'what if' analysis when preparing cash budgets.　　(9 marks)

(Total: 30 marks)

311　THIRTEEN WEEKS (MAY 09)

A company manufactures and sells a single product. Next year's budgeted profit (based on absorption costing) on the projected sales of 810,000 units is £1,611,000. In view of this figure the company is thinking of investing in new machinery at some time in the forthcoming year.

The company is preparing its cash budget for next year. The company divides the year into four periods, each of thirteen weeks. Sales and production will occur at even rates within each period. Details are as follows:

Sales budget (810,000 units)

The selling price is £30 per unit. All sales will be on credit and payment will be received five weeks after the date of sale. It is expected that 2% of all sales will become bad debts. The budgeted sales units are:

Period	1	2	3	4
Sales (units)	150,000	200,000	180,000	280,000

The product incurs variable selling costs of £1.60 per unit. These are paid in the period in which they are incurred.

Production budget (860,000 units)

Period	1	2	3	4
Production (units)	210,000	210,000	220,000	220,000
Production cost per unit	£	*Notes*		
Raw materials	9.50	Purchased on credit. Paid for four weeks after purchase.		
Production wages	8.20	Paid one week in arrears. These are variable costs.		
Production expenses	7.00	See below.		
	———			
	24.70			

Raw material inventory

The company wishes to increase inventory to six weeks of forward production by the end of Period 1 and then to seven weeks by the end of Period 2. Purchases will occur evenly throughout the periods.

Production expenses

The production expenses of £7.00 per unit are detailed below:

	£	*Notes*
Variable expenses	1.10	Paid in the period incurred
Depreciation	2.70	This is an annual fixed cost that is absorbed on a per unit basis by the budgeted production of 860,000 units
Fixed expenses	3.20	Absorbed on a per unit basis based on the annual production of 860,000 units. Paid in two equal instalments at the beginning of periods 1 and 3.

Long term borrowing

The company has a long term loan. The balance on this loan at the start of the year will be £10m. Interest on this loan is charged at 9% per annum on the amount outstanding at the start of the year and is to be paid in two equal instalments at the end of period 2 and at the end of period 4. The loan is "interest only": there are no capital repayments due.

Opening balances

	£	
Raw materials inventory	710,000	(all purchased at the current price)
Trade receivables (net of bad debts)	2,430,000	
Bank and cash	76,000	
Trade payables	612,000	
Unpaid wages	130,000	
Loan	10,000,000	

Required:

(a) Calculate, in units, the budgeted breakeven point and margin of safety for the next year. **(6 marks)**

(b) It is now thought that the price of raw materials could range from £7.50 to £11.50 for each unit produce. Produce a diagram that shows the sensitivity of the budgeted profit to changes in the price of the raw materials. **(4 marks)**

(c) Prepare, showing all cash flows, a cash budget for period 1 and a cash budget for period 2 (assume the price of raw materials is £9.50 for each unit produced).

(14 marks)

(d) Explain three areas from your cash budget which would cause problems for the company's management team. **(6 marks)**

(Total: 30 marks)

THE TREATMENT OF UNCERTAINTY IN DECISION MAKING

312 A BANK (MAY 08)

A bank is reviewing the bank account it offers to its business customers and the charges it makes for routine transactions (for example paying into the account, writing cheques, making electronic payments and transfers). Currently, the bank's charges to its business customers are £0.60 per routine transaction. The bank pays interest to the customer at 0.1% per year on any balance in the account.

According to the bank's records, there are currently one million business customers. Each customer makes one thousand routine transactions each year; 45% of business customers maintain an average balance of £2,000 in their account. The accounts of the other 55% of business customers are overdrawn with an average overdraft balance of £4,000. Interest on overdrawn accounts is charged at 20% per year.

In addition, the bank has a number of savings account customers which, together with the bank's business customers, result in a balance of net funds that are invested by the bank and yield an annual return by 3% per year.

The bank is concerned about a growing tendency for its competitors to provide routine transactions free of charge to their business customers. As a result the bank is considering two account options:

Account Option One

An account that charges the business customer a fixed fee of £10 per month, with no further charges for any routine transactions. Interest would be paid to the business customer at 0.5% per year on any balances in the account. The bank expects that if it adopts this charging structure, it will increase the number of business customers by 5% from its present level.

Account Option Two

An account that does not charge the customer for any routine transactions, but pays no interest on any balances in the account. The bank expects that if it adopts this charging structure, this will increase the number of business customers by 10% from its present level. The bank does not expect the profile of new business customers to be different from existing business customers in terms of the balances in their accounts or the number of routine transactions they make. Interest will continue to be charged at 20% per year on overdrawn accounts. The bank does not expect that either of these options will result in any changes to its existing staffing or other resources.

The bank also expects that if it takes no action and continues with its existing bank account that the number of business customers will fall by 20%.

Required:

(a)   Recommend which course of action the bank should take by preparing calculations to show the annual profits from:

    (i)   continuing with the existing bank account

    (ii)   each of the two account options described above.   **(12 marks)**

The bank is also reviewing its policy with regard to small loans. Currently, the bank charges an arrangement fee of £500 per loan and interest on the average loan balance. The profit the bank makes on the interest it charges is 5% of the average loan balance. The bank's records show that there are 200,000 small loans in issue at any one time. The average loan balance is £5,000.

Market research undertaken by the bank has shown that if it were to carry out an advertising campaign that specifically targeted the small loans market, the number of loans would increase, though the amount of the increase is uncertain. It is predicted that the advertising campaign may increase the number of loans in issue at any one time to 250,000, 280,000 or 300,000.

Furthermore, it is believed that the advertising campaign would increase the value of the loans. The amount of the increase is uncertain, but it is believed that the average loan balance may increase to £7,500; or that they may increase by £9,000; or that they may increase by £10,000.

The expected total cost of the advertising campaign and the associated administrative costs are £112 million.

Required:

(b)   (i)   Prepare a two-way data table that shows profit that would be earned by the bank for each of the NINE possible outcomes that are expected to arise as a result of the advertising campaign.   **(8 marks)**

(ii)   State any other factors the bank should consider before making its decision and advise the bank on whether or not it should carry out the advertising campaign.   (5 marks)

(Total: 25 marks)

313   H PRINTING (MAY 07)

H, a printing company, uses traditional absorption costing to report its monthly profits.

It is seeking to increase its business by winning work from new customers. It now has the opportunity to prepare a quotation for a large organisation that currently requires a new catalogue of its services.

A technical report on the resource requirements for the catalogues has been completed at a cost of $1,000 and its details are summarised below:

Production period

It is expected that the total time required to print and despatch the catalogue will be one week.

Material A

10,000 sheets of special printing paper will be required. This is a paper that is in regular use by H and the company has 3,400 sheets in inventory. These originally cost $1.40 per sheet but the current market price is $1.50 per sheet. The resale price of the sheets held in inventory is $1.20 per sheet.

Material B

This is a special ink that H will need to purchase at a cost of $8 per litre. 200 litres will be required for this catalogue but the supplier has a minimum order size of 250 litres. H does not foresee any other use for this ink, but will hold the surplus in inventory. H's inventory policy is to review slow moving items regularly. The cost of any inventory item that has not been used for more than six months is accounted for as an expense of the period in which that review occurs.

Direct labour

Sufficient people are already employed by H to print the catalogue, but some of the printing will require overtime working due to the availability of a particular machine that is used on other work.

The employees are normally paid $8 per hour, the order will require 150 hours of work and 50 of these hours will be in excess of the employees' normal working week. A rate of $10 per hour is paid for these overtime hours. Employees are paid using an hourly rate with a guaranteed minimum wage for their normal working week.

Supervision

An existing supervisor will take responsibility for the catalogue in addition to her existing duties. She is not currently fully employed and receives a salary of $500 per week.

Machinery

Two different types of machine will be required:

Machine A will print the catalogues. This is expected to take 20 hours of machine time. The running cost of machine A is $5 per hour. There is currently 30 hours of unused time on machine A per week that is being sold to other printers for $12 per hour.

Machine B will be used to cut and bind the catalogues. This machine is being used to full capacity in the normal working week and this is why there is a need to work overtime. The catalogue will require 25 machine hours and these have a running cost of $4 per hour.

Despatch

There will be a delivery cost of $400 to transport the catalogues to the customer.

Fixed overhead costs

H uses a traditional absorption costing system to attribute fixed overhead costs to its work. The absorption rate that it uses is $20 per direct labour hour.

Profit mark-up

H applies a 30% mark-up to its costs to determine its selling prices.

Required:

(a)   In order to assist the management of H in preparing its quotation, prepare a schedule showing the relevant costs for the production of the catalogues. State clearly your reason for including or excluding each value that has been provided in the above scenario.   **(15 marks)**

(b)   Explain how the use of relevant costs as the basis of setting a selling price may be appropriate for short-term pricing decisions but may be inappropriate for long-term pricing decisions. Your answer should also discuss the conflict between reporting profitability within a traditional absorption costing system and the use of relevant cost based pricing.   **(10 marks)**

(Total: 25 marks)

314   HEALTH CLINIC (MAY 06)   *Walk in the footsteps of a top tutor*

A health clinic is reviewing its plans for the next three years. It is a not-for-profit organisation but it has a financial responsibility to manage its costs and to ensure that it provides a value for money service to its clients. The health clinic uses the net present value technique to appraise the financial viability of delivering the service, but it also considers other non-financial factors before making any final decisions.

The present facilities, which incur an annual total cost of $300,000, are only sufficient to meet a low level of service provision, so the manager is considering investing in facilities to meet potential higher levels of demand. For the purpose of evaluating this decision the possible levels of demand for the health clinic's services have been simplified to high, medium or low.

The possible demand for the services in the first year and the level of demand that could follow that specific level in the next years, and their expected probabilities, are as follows:

Year 1	Probability	Years 2 and 3	Probability
Low	30%	Low	40%
		Medium	60%
		High	0%
Medium	50%	Low	30%
		Medium	40%
		High	30%
High	20%	Low	0%
		Medium	30%
		High	70%

The level of demand will be the same in years 2 and 3.

The manager is considering two alternative investments in facilities:

Facility A has the capacity to meet the low and medium levels of demand and requires an investment at the start of year 1 of $500,000. Thereafter it incurs annual fixed costs of $100,000 and annual variable costs depending on the level of operation. These annual variable costs are expected to be $150,000 at the low level of operation and $250,000 at the medium level of operation.

Facility B has the capacity to meet all levels of demand and requires an investment at the start of year 1 of $800,000. Thereafter it incurs annual fixed costs of $200,000 and annual variable costs depending on the level of operation. These annual variable costs are expected to be $100,000 at the low level of operation, $150,000 at the medium level of operation and $200,000 at the high level of operation.

Neither of these alternative investments has any residual value at the end of year 3.

If the facilities of the health clinic are insufficient to meet the level of service demand that occurs, the clinic must obtain additional facilities on a yearly contract basis at the following annual costs:

Level of service provision available internally	Level of service provision demanded	Annual cost of additional facilities
Low	Medium	$100,000
Low	High	$250,000
Medium	High	$150,000

These additional facilities are not under the direct control of the health clinic manager.

Note: All monetary values used throughout the question have been stated in terms of their present value. No further discounting is required.

Required:

(a) **Prepare a decision tree to illustrate the investment decision that needs to be made by the manager of the health clinic. (Numerical values are NOT required.) (6 marks)**

(b) **Advise the manager of the health clinic which investment decision should be undertaken on financial grounds.   (15 marks)**

(c) **Briefly discuss any non-financial factors that the manager should consider before making her final investment decision.   (4 marks)**

(Total: 25 marks)

FINANCIAL INFORMATION FOR LONG-TERM DECISION MAKING

315   REGIONAL AIRPORT (MAY 10) *Walk in the footsteps of a top tutor*

A small regional airport is modernising its facilities in anticipation of significant growth in the number of passengers using the airport. It is expected that the number of passengers will increase by 10% per annum as a result of a "low cost" airline opening new routes to and from the airport.

At present, the airport has only one food outlet selling sandwiches and other cold food and drinks. To improve the facilities available to customers, the management of the airport is considering opening a restaurant selling a range of hot food and drinks. The cost of fitting out the new restaurant, which will have to be fully refurbished after four years, is estimated to be $350,000. These assets are expected to have a residual value of $30,000 at the end of four years.

A firm of consultants carried out an extensive study in relation to this project at a cost of $30,000. The key findings from their report, regarding expected revenue and contribution from the restaurant, are as follows:

- Average revenue: $9.00 per customer
- Average variable cost: $5.00 per customer
- Demand in year 1: 500 customers per day

Future demand for the restaurant is expected to rise in line with passenger numbers.

The airport operates for 360 days per year.

Other relevant information from the consultants' report is listed below:

1   **Staffing of the new restaurant:**

- Number of employees (Years 1 and 2): 4
- Numbers employees (Years 3 and 4): 5
- Average salary per employee: $20,000 per annum

2   **Overheads**

- The annual budgeted fixed overhead of the airport which will be apportioned to the restaurant is $80,000.
- The annual overheads apportioned to the cold food outlet will be $30,000.
- The airport's overheads are expected to increase by the following annual amounts as a direct result of the opening of the restaurant:

  - Electricity: $40,000
  - Advertising: $20,000
  - Audit: $10,000

3   **Cold food outlet**

The average contribution from the sale of cold food is $2.50 per customer. If the restaurant is not opened it is expected that the cold food outlet will sell to 1,200 customers per day in the coming year and in subsequent years the customer numbers will rise in line with passenger numbers.

If the restaurant is opened, the consultants expect sales from the existing cold food outlet to initially reduce by 40% in year 1 and then to increase in line with passenger numbers.

The airport's Financial Director has provided the following taxation information:

- Tax depreciation: 25% reducing balance per annum.
- The first year's tax depreciation allowance is used against the first year's net cash inflows.
- Taxation rate: 30% of taxable profits. Half of the tax is payable in the year in which it arises, the balance is paid the following year.
- Any taxable losses resulting from this investment can be set against profits made by the airport company's other business activities since the airport company is profitable.
- The airport company uses a post-tax cost of capital of 8% per annum to evaluate projects of this type. Ignore inflation.

Required:

(a) **Calculate the net present value (NPV) of the restaurant project.** **(16 marks)**

(b) The Managing Director of a company has been presented with the details of three potential investment projects. He has very little experience of project appraisal and has asked you for help.

The project details are given below:

	Project A	Project B	Project C
Expected NPV	$150,000	$180,000	$180,000
Standard Deviation of Expected NPV	$10,000	$50,000	$30,000
IRR	12%	12%	10%

The three projects will require the same level of initial investment. The projects are mutually exclusive and therefore the Managing Director can only choose one of them.

Required:

Interpret the information for the Managing Director (your answer should include an explanation of the factors he should consider when deciding which project to undertake). **(9 marks)**

(Total: 25 marks)

316 GYMNASIUM (SEPT 10)

The management of a hotel is considering expanding its facilities by providing a gymnasium and spa for the use of guests. It is expected that the additional facilities will result in an increase in the occupancy rate of the hotel and in the rates that can be charged for each room.

The cost of refurbishing the space, which is currently used as a library for guests, and installing the spa is estimated to be $100,000. The cost of the gymnasium equipment is expected to be $50,000. The gymnasium and spa will need to be refurbished and the equipment replaced every four years. The equipment will be sold for $15,000 cash at the end of year 4. This amount includes the effect of inflation.

The hotel's accountants have produced a feasibility report at a cost of $10,000. The key findings from their report, regarding occupancy rates and room rates are as follows:

Current occupancy rate: 80%

Number of rooms available: 40

Current average room rate per night: $250

Occupancy rates, following the opening of the gymnasium and spa, are expected to rise to 82% and the average room rate by 5%, excluding the effect of inflation.

The hotel is open for 360 days per year.

Other relevant information from the accountants' report is listed below:

1   **Staffing of the gymnasium and spa**

    Number of employees : 4

    Average salary per employee: $30,000 per annum

2   **Overheads**

    The current budgeted overhead absorption rate for the hotel is $80 per square metre per annum. The area required for the gymnasium and spa is 400 square metres.

    The hotel's overheads are expected to increase by $42,000 directly as a result of opening the gymnasium and spa.

3   **Inflation**

    Inflation is expected to be at a rate of 4% per annum and will apply to sales revenue, overhead costs and staff costs. The rate of 4% will apply from Year 2 to each of the subsequent years of the project.

4   **Taxation**

    The hotel's accountants have provided the following taxation information:

    Tax depreciation available on all costs of refurbishing, installation and equipment: 25% reducing balance per annum.

    Taxation rate: 30% of taxable profits. Half of the tax is payable in the year in which it arises, the balance is paid the following year.

    Any losses resulting from this investment can be set against taxable profits made by the company's other business activities.

The company uses a post-tax money cost of capital of 12% per annum to evaluate projects of this type.

Required:

(a)   Calculate the net present value (NPV) of the gymnasium and spa project. **(16 marks)**

(b)   Calculate the post-tax money cost of capital at which the hotel would be indifferent to accepting / rejecting the project. **(4 marks)**

(c)   Discuss an alternative method for the treatment of inflation that would result in the same NPV.

      Your answer should consider the potential difficulties in using this method when taxation is involved in the project appraisal. **(5 marks)**

(Total: 25 marks)

317 SQ (NOV 07) *Walk in the footsteps of a top tutor*

SQ manufactures and sells a range of products. Details for one of the products, product Q, are shown below.

Existing production facility

The present production facility can continue to be used to produce up to 120,000 units of product Q each year. It is estimated that the facility can be used for a further five years but annual maintenance costs will rise substantially. An analysis of the latest costs is set out below:

	$ per unit
Direct materials	50
Direct labour	30
Variable production overhead	25
Fixed production overhead*	20
Variable selling and distribution overhead**	10

* The fixed production overhead costs are absorbed into product costs using an absorption rate which is 25% of prime cost. These fixed overhead costs are mainly central production facility costs that are not specific to any particular product or activity and would continue to be incurred regardless of the production method used by SQ. However, they also include facility maintenance costs (see above). In addition, SQ incurs annual fixed non-production costs of $24 million.

** These are selling and distribution costs which are not affected by the production method that is used for the product.

Proposed new production facility

The company is considering an investment of $4 million in a new production facility for product Q. The new facility is to be operational from 1 January 2008. It will have a life of five years and at the end of its life it will have a residual value of $0.4 million. It is expected that the facility will have significant benefits. Firstly it will increase SQ's production capacity for product Q by 30%, secondly it will reduce product Q's direct labour and variable production overhead costs by 20% per unit, and finally the savings in annual maintenance costs will be as follows:

Year	$000
2008	70
2009	80
2010	80
2011	110
2012	130

You have also obtained the following further information:

Demand

Currently SQ produces 120,000 units of product Q each year and these sell for $150 per unit. There is significant demand for the product and SQ estimates that it could sell more units if it had the capacity to produce them.

If the selling price remains unchanged, customer demand for 2008 and future years is estimated to be as shown in the following table:

Year	Customer demand (units)
2008	130,000
2009	140,000
2010	147,000
2011	154,000
2012	162,000

Cost structure

No changes are expected to either cost structure or to cost levels other than those referred to above.

Taxation

SQ pays corporation tax at the rate of 30% of its taxable profits. Half of this tax is payable in the year in which the profit is earned and the other half is payable one year later. If the investment in the new production facility goes ahead on 1 January 2008 (the first day of SQ's accounting year), it will qualify for tax depreciation at the rate of 25% per annum on a reducing balance basis.

Cost of capital

SQ's after-tax cost of capital is 12% per annum.

Required:

(a) (i)   **Calculate the Net Present Value (NPV) of the investment in the new facility.**

(14 marks)

      (ii)   **Explain two other factors that SQ should consider before making its decision.**

(4 marks)

(b)   A company is thinking of investing in a new project. The details are as follows:

Investment	$15,000
Time span	3 years
Annual cash inflows	$30,000
Annual cash outflows	$22,500
Cost of capital	10%
NPV @ 10%	$3,652.50

The project does not have a residual value. Ignore taxation.

      (i)   **Calculate the Internal Rate of Return (IRR) of the investment proposal.**

(3 marks)

      (ii)   **Calculate the sensitivity of the investment to changes in the annual cash inflows.**

(4 marks)

(Total: 25 marks)

318 HOTEL GROUP (NOV 09)

A hotel group is considering the purchase of a new hotel on 1 January 20X0, the first day of its next financial year. The building will cost $650,000 and the equipment and other furnishings are expected to cost $250,000, also at the start of 20X0. The equipment and other furnishings will qualify for tax depreciation at the rate of 20% per annum on a reducing balance basis. No tax depreciation is available on the cost of the building. The building will be sold at the end of 20X4 for $650,000 and the equipment will be sold for $100,000 at the same time.

Guest revenue

The hotel is expected to open to guests on 1 July 20X0 and guest revenue for the remainder of 20X0 is expected to be $130,000. The number of guests in future calendar years is expected to increase in accordance with the following index (20X0 = 100):

20X1	180
20X2	190
20X3	210
20X4	220

Guest related costs

Variable guest related costs, which vary in direct proportion to the number of guests, are expected to be $20,000 in 20X0. In addition, there are annual guest related fixed costs which are expected to be $40,000 in 20X0. These fixed costs are not affected by the number of guests or by the opening dates of the hotel.

Other fixed costs

In addition to the guest related costs identified above, the hotel expects to incur other fixed costs of $25,000 per year, at 20X0 prices.

Inflation

The hotel group expects that cost inflation (applying to all types of cost) will be in accordance with the following index (20X0 = 100):

20X1	104
20X2	105
20X3	107
20X4	110

The group has decided that it will increase its prices to guests and these will increase in accordance with the following index (20X0 = 100):

20X1	100
20X2	102
20X3	104
20X4	107

Taxation

The hotel will be liable to Corporation Tax on its profits at the rate of 30%, payable in two equal instalments; one in the year in which the profits are earned and one in the following year.

Cost of capital

The hotel group's post tax money cost of capital is 8% per annum.

Required:

(a)   Calculate the net present value of the cash flows arising from the investment and recommend to the hotel group whether or not to proceed with the purchase of the hotel.   **(14 marks)**

(b)   Calculate the sensitivity of the investment to a change in the value of "other fixed costs".   **(6 marks)**

(Total: 20 marks)

319   CAR MANUFACTURER (NOV 10)

A car manufacturer has been experiencing financial difficulties over the past few years. Sales have reduced significantly as a result of the worldwide economic recession. Costs have increased due to quality issues that led to a recall of some models of its cars.

Production volume last year was 50,000 cars and it is expected that this will increase by 4% per annum each year for the next five years.

The company directors are concerned to improve profitability and are considering two potential investment projects.

Project 1 – implement a new quality control process

The company has paid a consultant process engineer $50,000 to review the company's quality processes. The consultant recommended that the company implement a new quality control process. The new process will require a machine costing $20,000,000. The machine is expected to have a useful life of five years and no residual value.

It is estimated that raw material costs will be reduced by $62 per car and that both internal and external failure costs from quality failures will be reduced by 80%.

Estimated internal and external failure costs per year without the new process, based on last year's production volume of 50,000 cars, and their associated probabilities are shown below:

Internal Failure Costs		External Failure Costs	
$	Probability	$	Probability
300,000	50%	1,300,000	60%
500,000	30%	1,900,000	30%
700,000	20%	3,000,000	10%

Internal and external failure costs are expected to increase each year in line with the number of cars produced.

The company's accountant has calculated that this investment will result in a net present value (NPV) of $1,338,000 and an internal rate of return of 10.5%.

Project 2 – in-house component manufacturing

The company could invest in new machinery to enable in-house manufacturing of a component that is currently made by outside suppliers. The new machinery is expected to cost $15,000,000 and have a useful life of five years and no residual value. Additional working capital of $1,000,000 will also be required as a result of producing the component in-house.

The price paid to the current supplier is $370 per component. It is estimated that the in-house variable cost of production will be $260 per component. Each car requires one component. Fixed production costs, including machinery depreciation, are estimated to increase by $5,000,000 per annum as a result of manufacturing the component in-house.

Depreciation is calculated on a straight line basis.

Additional Information

The company is unable to raise enough capital to carry out both projects. The company will therefore have to choose between the two alternatives.

Taxation and inflation should be ignored.

The company uses a cost of capital of 8% per annum.

Required:

(a)   Calculate for Project 1 the relevant cash flows that the accountant should have used for year 1 when appraising the project.

All workings should be shown in $000.   **(6 marks)**

(b)   Calculate for Project 2:

(i)   the net present value (NPV)

(ii)   the internal rate of return (IRR)

All workings should be shown in $000.   **(10 marks)**

(c)   Advise the company directors which of the two investment projects should be undertaken.   **(4 marks)**

(d)   A company is considering two alternative investment projects both of which have a positive net present value. The projects have been ranked on the basis of both net present value (NPV) and internal rate of return (IRR). The result of the ranking is shown below:

	Project A	Project B
NPV	1st	2nd
IRR	2nd	1st

Discuss potential reasons why the conflict between the NPV and IRR ranking may have arisen.   **(5 marks)**

                                                                         (Total: 25 marks)

320 RESTAURANT (NOV 08 EXAM)

A restaurant company is considering further investment in order to increase its seating capacity. The company prepares its accounts to 31 December each year and, if accepted, the proposed investment would be made on 1 January 20X9 and will become operational immediately.

Based on the actual results for the year to date, the latest forecast income statement for the company for the year to 31 December 20X8 is as follows:

	£000	£000
Food sales	180	
Drink sales	150	330
Food costs	125	
Drink costs	70	
Staff costs	55	
Other costs *	45	295
Profit		35

*These other costs include rent, light & heat, power and administration overheads. 30% of these costs vary in proportion to the value of sales and the remainder are fixed costs.

The proposed investment

At present the restaurant is not able to exploit the growing demand from customers because it does not have sufficient seating capacity. The restaurant is considering the investment of £40,000 on 1 January 20X9. It is expected that this will increase the seating capacity of the restaurant by 30% compared to the present level. The lease of the current business premises ends at the end of 20Y2. At that time the £40,000 investment will have no residual value. Of this total investment, £30,000 will qualify for 100% tax depreciation in 20X9 and the remainder will qualify for 20% tax depreciation per year, commencing in 20X9, calculated on a reducing balance basis. Any balancing tax charge will be made or allowance will be available at the end of 20Y2.

Sales

It is expected that the additional sales of food and drink will be proportional to the seating capacity increase and that the mix of food sales and drink sales will not change.

Costs

It is expected that apart from the effects of inflation (see below):

Food costs and drink costs will continue to be the same percentages of food sales and drink sales as they are in the forecast income statement shown above.

Staff costs are step costs and are expected to increase by 20% from their forecast value for 20X8 if there is any capacity increase.

The variable element of other costs is expected to increase in proportion to the capacity increase; the fixed cost element is expected to increase by £10,000 if there is any capacity increase.

Inflation

Cost inflation is predicted to be 4% per annum for each of the years 20X9 to 20Y2 whereas selling prices are only expected to increase by 3% per annum during the same period.

Taxation

The company pays tax on its profits at 20%. This is payable one year after the profit is earned.

Cost of capital

The company's post tax money cost of capital for evaluating this investment is 8% per annum.

Required:

(a)   **Prepare calculations to show whether the investment is worthwhile assuming that the 30% increase in seating capacity is fully utilised and recommend whether the investment should proceed.**   **(14 marks)**

(b)   **Calculate and interpret the Internal Rate of Return (IRR) of the proposed investment.**   **(6 marks)**

(c)   **Calculate the sensitivity of your recommendation to changes in the percentage capacity utilisation.**   **(5 marks)**

(Total: 25 marks)

321   DP (MAY 12)

DP is considering whether to purchase a piece of land close to a major city airport. The land will be used to provide 600 car parking spaces. The cost of the land is $6,000,000 but further expenditure of $2,000,000 will be required immediately to develop the land to provide access roads and suitable surfacing for car parking. DP is planning to operate the car park for five years after which the land will be sold for $10,000,000 at Year 5 prices. A consultant has prepared a report detailing projected revenues and costs.

Revenues

It is estimated that the car park will operate at 75% capacity during each year of the project.

Car parking charges will depend on the prices being charged by competitors. There is a 40% chance that the price will be $60 per week, a 25% chance the price will be $50 per week and a 35% chance the price will be $70 per week.

DP expects that it will earn a contribution to sales ratio of 80%.

Fixed Operating Costs

DP will lease a number of vehicles to be used to transport passengers to and from the airport. It is expected that the lease costs will be $50,000 per annum.

Staff costs are estimated to be $350,000 per annum.

The company will hire a security system at a cost of $100,000 per annum.

Inflation

All of the values above, other than the amount for the sale of the land at the end of the five year period, have been expressed in terms of current prices. The vehicle leasing costs of $50,000 per annum will apply throughout the five years and is not subject to inflation.

Car parking charges and variable costs are expected to increase at a rate of 5% per annum starting in Year 1.

All fixed operating costs **excluding** the vehicle leasing costs are expected to increase at a rate of 4% per annum starting in Year 1.

Other Information

The company uses net present value based on the expected values of cash flow when evaluating projects of this type.

DP has a money cost of capital of 8% per annum.

DP's Financial Director has provided the following taxation information:

- Tax depreciation is not available on either the initial cost of the land or the development costs.
- Taxation rate: 30% of taxable profits. Half of the tax is payable in the year in which it arises, the balance is payable in the following year.

All cash flows apart from the initial investment of $8,000,000 should be assumed to occur at the end of the year.

Required:

(a)   **Evaluate the project from a financial perspective. You should use net present value as the basis of your evaluation and show your workings in $000.**   **(14 marks)**

(b)   **Calculate the internal rate of return (IRR) of the project.**   **(5 marks)**

(c)   The main reason why discounted cash flow methods of investment appraisal are considered theoretically superior is that they take account of the time value of money.

   Explain the THREE elements that determine the 'time value of money' and why it is important to take it into consideration when appraising investment projects.

   (6 marks)

   (Total: 25 marks)

322   BUS OPERATOR (MAR 11)

A bus operator has been experiencing a fall in passenger numbers over the past few years as a result of intense competition from other transport providers. The company directors are concerned to improve profit and are considering two possible alternatives.

Passenger volume last year was 20,000 passengers per day. The average fare was $2 per passenger per day and variable costs per passenger per day were $0.50. If no investment is made the current passenger volume, average fares and variable costs will remain the same on current routes for the next five years. The company operates a full service for 365 days of the year.

Project 1

The company hired a management consultant, at a cost of $50,000, to review the company's fare structure. The consultant recommended that the company reduce fares by 10% which will result in a 20% increase in passenger volume in the first year. In order to maintain this level of passenger numbers, fares will remain at the reduced rate for years 2 to 5.

The increase in passenger numbers will result in the need for four new buses costing $250,000 each. The new buses will be depreciated on a straight line basis over their useful life of 5 years. They will have no residual value at the end of their useful life. Other annual fixed costs, including advertising costs, will increase by $100,000 in the first year and will remain at that level for the life of the project. Variable costs will remain at $0.50 per passenger per day for the life of the project.

Project 2

Increase the number of buses to enable new routes to be opened. The new buses are expected to cost $5,000,000 in total and have a useful life of five years with no residual value. Fixed costs, including straight line depreciation, are expected to increase by $3,500,000 in the first year, as a result of opening the new routes. Fixed costs will remain at the higher level for the life of the project. Additional working capital of $1,000,000 will also be required.

The passenger numbers for year 1 on the new routes are predicted as follows:

Passenger numbers per day	Probability
6,000	50%
9,000	30%
12,000	20%

It is expected that passenger numbers will increase by 3% per annum for the following four years. The average fare per passenger for year 1 will be $2 and will remain at that level for the life of the project. Variable costs will remain at $0.50 per passenger per day for the life of the project.

Additional Information

Tax and inflation should be ignored. The company uses a cost of capital of 8% per annum.

Required:

(a) (i) Advise the management of the company which project should be undertaken based on a financial appraisal of the projects.

You should use net present value (NPV) to appraise the projects.   **(13 marks)**

(ii) Explain TWO other major factors that should be considered before a final decision is made.   **(4 marks)**

(b) Calculate the sensitivity of the choice between Project 1 and Project 2 to a change in passenger numbers for Project 2.   **(4 marks)**

(c) Company D is planning its capital investment programme for next year. It is considering four potential projects all of which have a positive net present value. The initial investment, internal rate of return (IRR) and net present value (NPV), based on a cost of capital of 12%, are given below for each project.

Project	Investment	NPV at 12%	IRR
	$000	$000	
A	50	13.6	12.6%
B	40	15.2	10.3%
C	20	10.2	13.1%
D	30	12.3	11.2%

Funding for the company is restricted to $110,000. The projects are independent and divisible i.e. part of a project can be undertaken.

Required:

Prioritise the projects and determine how much funding should be allocated to each project. **(4 marks)**

(Total: 25 marks)

323 GR (NOV 11)

GR is an outsourcing company that provides call centre services to a range of clients. As a result of technical advances in telecommunication equipment, the company's existing telephone system is out-dated and inefficient and needs to be replaced. A technical consultant, hired at a cost of $80,000, has prepared a report outlining two possible replacement systems. The details of each system are as follows:

	System 1	System 2
Initial investment	$600,000	$800,000
Estimated useful life	3 years	5 years
Residual value	$60,000	$50,000
Contribution per annum	$580,000	$600,000
Fixed maintenance costs per annum	$20,000	$40,000
Other fixed operating costs per annum	$360,000	$305,000

The maintenance costs are payable annually in advance. All other cash flows apart from the initial investment should be assumed to occur at the end of each year.

Depreciation has been calculated using the straight line method and has been included in other fixed operating costs.

The company uses a cost of capital of 12% per annum to evaluate projects of this type.

Required:

(a) **Prioritise the two systems using an annualised equivalent approach. You should ignore taxation and inflation. Your workings should be shown in $000.** **(12 marks)**

(b) **Explain the purpose of sensitivity analysis in investment appraisal.** **(4 marks)**

(c) **Calculate the sensitivity of your recommendation in part (a) to changes in the contribution generated by System 1.** **(4 marks)**

The company's financial director has provided the following taxation information:

- Tax depreciation: 25% of the reducing balance per annum, with a balancing adjustment in the year of disposal.

- Taxation rate: 30% of taxable profits. Half of the tax is payable in the year in which it arises, the balance is paid in the following year.

Required:

(d) **Calculate, for System 2, the tax depreciation and the resulting tax cash flows for each year. Your workings should be shown in $000.** **(5 marks)**

(Total: 25 marks)

324   EF (SEPT 12)

EF operates tourist attractions in major capital cities. The company is considering opening a new attraction in Eastern Europe.

The initial capital investment will be $120 million. EF plans to operate the attraction for five years after which it will be sold to another operator at an estimated price of $50 million at

Year 5 prices.

A market research survey has estimated the following visitor numbers and associated probabilities, revenue and operating costs:

Revenue and variable costs

Number of visitors per year	Probability
1.2 million	30%
0.8 million	50%
0.6 million	20%

It is expected that the number of visitors per year will remain constant for the life of the project.

The entrance fee for the attraction will be $40. Each visitor is expected to spend an average of $15 on souvenirs and $5 on refreshments.

The variable costs are estimated to be $25 per visitor. This includes the variable cost of operating the attraction and the cost of souvenirs and refreshments.

Fixed operating costs

The company will lease the land on which the attraction is to be situated at a cost of $500,000 per annum. The lease cost will remain the same throughout the life of the project.

Maintenance costs are estimated to be $200,000 per annum.

Inflation

All of the values above, other than the amount payable by the purchaser at the end of the five year period, have been expressed in terms of current prices. The lease cost of $500,000 per annum will apply throughout the life of the project and is not subject to inflation.

A general rate of inflation of 4% per annum is expected to apply to all revenues and costs, excluding the lease cost throughout the life of the project, starting in Year 1.

Other information

The company uses net present value based on the expected values of cash flow when evaluating projects of this type.

The company has a money cost of capital of 12% per annum.

The company's Financial Director has provided the following taxation information:

- The initial investment will qualify for tax depreciation at 25% of the reducing balance per annum with a balancing adjustment in the year of disposal.

- The first claim for tax deprecation will be made against the profits from Year 1.

- Taxation rate: 30% of taxable profits. Half of the tax is payable in the year in which it arises, the balance is payable in the following year.

All cash flows apart from the initial investment of $120 million should be assumed to occur at the end of the year.

Required:

(a) **Evaluate the project from a financial perspective. You should use net present value as the basis of your evaluation and show your workings in $000.** **(14 marks)**

(b) (i) **Calculate the internal rate of return (IRR) of the project.** **(4 marks)**

(ii) **Calculate the payback period for the project. You should assume for this purpose that all cash flows occur evenly throughout the year.** **(3 marks)**

(c) **Explain the difference between the real cost of capital and the money cost of capital. You should include a numerical example to illustrate your answer.** **(4 marks)**

(Total: 25 marks)

325 5G MOBILE PHONE (MAY 11)

A company is considering the launch of a new 5G mobile phone. Experience from the sale of previous models has shown that the expected life of the new model is four years and life cycle sales will total 25,000,000 units. Sales volumes over the life cycle of the product will follow the pattern shown below.

Year 1	20%
Year 2	40%
Year 3	30%
Year 4	10%

The company's research and development division, which has an annual budget of $35,000,000, has developed a prototype of the 5G phone. A further investment of $600,000,000 in a new manufacturing facility will be required at the start of year 1 to put the new model into production. It is expected that the new manufacturing facility will have a residual value of $100,000,000 at the end of four years.

The new model is to be marketed initially at a premium price of $300 per unit. The price will remain at $300 for the first year after which prices will be reduced by 20% per annum.

The 5G model will be produced exclusively in the new manufacturing facility. The total fixed manufacturing costs will be $300,000,000 per year excluding depreciation. It is also anticipated that a further $150,000,000 will be spent in each of years 1 and 2 and $100,000,000 in year 3, on further development and marketing of the new model. The variable cost per unit will be $125 and this is expected to remain the same throughout the life of the model.

It is estimated that the launch of the new model will result in a reduction in sales of the current 4G model of 2,000,000 units in the first year after which there will no longer be a market for the 4G model. It was never anticipated that there would be a market for the 4G model after this period. The contribution per unit of the 4G model is $100.

The company's financial director has provided the following taxation information:

- Tax depreciation: 25% reducing balance per annum.
- Taxation rate: 30% of taxable profits. Half of the tax is payable in the year in which it arises, the balance is paid in the following year.
- Any taxable losses resulting from this investment can be set against profits made by the company's other business activities.

The company uses a post-tax cost of capital of 8% per annum to evaluate projects of this type. Ignore inflation.

Required:

(a) Calculate the net present value (NPV) of the project.

Workings should be shown in $millions. (12 marks)

(b) (i) Calculate the internal rate of return (IRR) of the project.

(ii) Calculate the discounted payback period of the project. (5 marks)

(c) Discuss the reasons why a company may want to calculate the IRR and discounted payback period of a project even though NPV is the theoretically superior method of investment appraisal. (4 marks)

(d) Explain the benefits to a company of carrying out a post-completion audit of a project. (4 marks)

(Total: 25 marks)

326 OWN BRAND PRODUCTS (SEPT 11) *Walk in the footsteps of a top tutor*

A major retail company which sells its 'own brand' products is deciding whether to open new retail outlets in a rapidly expanding overseas market. Past experience from entering other overseas markets has shown that acceptance of the brand can depend on a number of factors and that sales in the first four years are a good indicator of the potential of the market for the future.

Year 1 sales will depend on how readily the brand is accepted. A consultancy firm, with experience of the overseas market, was employed at a cost of $0.5m to provide detailed information on the market and an estimate of the likelihood of the brand being accepted. The consultancy firm estimated that there is a 50% chance that the brand will be well received and sales in year 1 will be $450m, there is a 20% chance that the brand will be very well received and sales in year 1 will be $600m, and there is a 30% chance that the brand will not be well received and sales in year 1 will be $300m. Sales are then expected to increase by $100m each year, irrespective of sales in the first year.

An investment of $600m is required to develop and fit out the retail outlets. The costs will be depreciated on a straight line basis over the four year period. The development and fit out costs will be eligible for tax depreciation. It is expected that the retail outlets will have a residual value of $400m at the end of four years. The residual value will be treated for tax purposes as a balancing adjustment. There will also be a requirement for $60m of working capital.

The average contribution to sales ratio is expected to be 60%. Fixed costs relating to the retail outlets, including depreciation, are expected to be $150m per annum and will remain the same for the four year period. It is also anticipated that a further $50m will be spent in each of the four years on marketing the brand.

The company's financial director has provided the following taxation information:

- Tax depreciation: 25% reducing balance per annum.

- Taxation rate: 30% of taxable profits. Half of the tax is payable in the year in which it arises, the balance is paid in the following year.

- Any taxable losses resulting from this investment can be set against profits made by the company's other business activities.

The company uses a post-tax cost of capital of 8% per annum to evaluate projects of this type. Ignore inflation.

Required:

(a)   **Advise the directors of the company whether they should go ahead with the investment from a financial perspective.**

You should use net present value (NPV) as the basis of your evaluation. Workings should be shown in $millions ($m).   **(12 marks)**

(b)   (i)   **Calculate the sensitivity of the investment decision to a change in the level of annual fixed cost relating to the retail outlets i.e. not including the marketing costs.**   **(4 marks)**

         (ii)   **Explain the benefits of carrying out a sensitivity analysis before making investment decisions.**   **(3 marks)**

(c)   (i)   **Calculate the payback period of the project.**   **(2 marks)**

         (ii)   **Explain the reasons why a company's management may be interested in the payback period of a project. You should use the scenario given above to illustrate your answer.**   **(4 marks)**

                                                                                                     (Total: 25 marks)

327   MGC (MAR 12)

MGC is a private golf club that has seen a reduction in its membership over the past few years. In an attempt to attract new members and retain existing members, the golf club committee is considering building a golf driving range and an indoor swimming pool.

The project would require an initial expenditure of $600,000. The club has agreed to sell the driving range and swimming pool for $30,000 at the end of 5 years. The expenditure will qualify for tax depreciation.

The committee commissioned a market research survey at a cost of $40,000. The survey estimated the increase in members from current levels as a result of the project. The results were as follows:

Increase in members	Probability
1,000	0.30
700	0.50
500	0.20

It is believed that the number of members will remain the same for the life of the project. The contribution earned on membership fees received will be 55% of fee revenue in all years.

The following operating costs and revenues are expected for each year of the project. Their values for Year 1 are:

Membership fee income	$800 per member (payable at the end of each year)
Project specific overheads	$120,000 (this figure does not include depreciation)

An inflation rate of 4% per annum will apply to these revenues and costs from Year 2 and for the remainder of the project.

The club's accountants have provided the following information:

- Tax depreciation: 25% reducing balance per annum with a balancing adjustment in the year of disposal.

- Taxation rate: 30% of taxable profits. Half of the tax is payable in the year in which it arises, the balance is paid in the following year.

- Any losses resulting from this investment can be set against profits made by the company's other business activities.

The club uses a post-tax money cost of capital of 12% per annum to evaluate projects of this type.

Required:

(a)   (i)   **Evaluate the proposed expansion from a financial perspective. You should use net present value as the basis of your evaluation and show your workings in $000.**   **(12 marks)**

      (ii)   **Explain TWO non-financial factors that the club should consider before making a final decision.**   **(4 marks)**

(b)   **Calculate the internal rate of return (IRR) of the project.**   **(4 marks)**

(c)   (i)   **Calculate MGC's real cost of capital.**   **(2 marks)**

      (ii)   **Explain the way in which the real cost of capital may be used to calculate the net present value of a project when the cash flows are subject to inflation. Your answer should consider the potential difficulties in using this method when taxation is involved in the project appraisal.**   **(3 marks)**

(Total: 25 marks)

328   H (MAY 08 EXAM)

H is a well-established manufacturer of household products. It produces its accounts to 31 December each year.

The machinery that is currently being used to manufacture one of H's products will have to be scrapped on 31 December 20X8, because H can no longer obtain a safety certificate for it. H is considering investing $500,000 in new machinery on 1 January 20X9 in order to continue manufacturing this product. If the project does not go ahead, H will no longer be able to manufacture the product.

The new machinery will have sufficient production capacity to meet the expected sales demand levels for the next five years. It will have a life of five years, and at the end of that time it will be sold for $100,000. It will qualify for tax depreciation at the rate of 20% per annum on a reducing balance basis.

Sales revenues and production costs for the current year, which ends on 31 December 20X8, are predicted to be as follows:

	$000
Sales revenue	540
Production costs	
Variable production costs	240
Fixed overhead *	120
	360
Fixed non-production costs	80
Profit before tax	100

* Fixed production overhead cost includes $20,000 for depreciation of the existing machinery.

Sales

The following table of index numbers (20X8 = 100) shows the predicted levels of sales volume.

	20X9	20Y0	20Y1	20Y2	20Y3
Sales volume	103	105	109	107	110

Assume there are no changes in the selling price other than those caused by selling price inflation, which is expected to be 4% per year.

Costs

Production costs are not expected to change as a result of investing in the new machinery, but production cost inflation is expected to be 5% per year. Non-production cost inflation is expected to be 3% per year.

Taxation

H is liable to pay tax on its profits at the rate of 30%. Half of this is payable in the year in which the profit is earned and the remainder is payable in the following year.

H has a post tax money cost of capital of 14% per annum.

Required:

(a) Calculate the Net Present Value (NPV) of the project (to the nearest $000).

(15 marks)

(b) Calculate the post tax money cost of capital at which H would be indifferent to accepting/rejecting the project. (4 marks)

(c) Explain your treatment of inflation in your solution to part (a) above and describe an alternative method that would have provided the same NPV. (6 marks)

(Total: 25 marks)

MANAGING SHORT-TERM FINANCE

329 BF *Walk in the footsteps of a top tutor*

BF manufacturers a range of electrical products such as portable media players and laptop computers. It has annual credit sales of $72 million and makes a gross profit margin of 20%. Current assets consist of inventory and accounts receivable. Current liabilities consist of accounts payable and an overdraft with an average interest rate of 11% per year. The company gives 12 week's credit to its customers who are mainly large retailers. On the other hand, it is allowed, on average, only 4 week's credit by trade suppliers. It has an overall operating cycle of 15 weeks.

Other relevant information:

Current ratio of BF	1.2
Cost of long-term finance of BF	8%

Required:

(a) Discuss the key factors which determine the level of investment in current assets.

(6 marks)

(b) Discuss the ways in which factoring and invoice discounting can assist in the management of accounts receivable. **(6 marks)**

(c) Calculate the size of the overdraft of BF, the net working capital of the company and the total cost of financing its current assets. **(6 marks)**

(d) One of BF's products has had supplier problems in the past. Due to past delays in suppliers providing goods, BF has had to hold an inventory of raw materials, in order that the production could continue to operate smoothly. Due to recent improvements in supplier reliability, BF is re-examining its inventory holding policies and recalculating economic order quantities (EOQ).

- Item 'Z' costs BF $10.00 per unit.

- Expected annual production usage is 65,000 units.

- Procurement costs (cost of placing and processing one order) are $25.00.

- The cost of holding one unit for one year has been calculated as $3.00.

The supplier of item 'Z' has informed BF that if the order were 2,000 units or more at one time, a 2% discount would be given on the price of the goods.

Required:

(i) Calculate the total cost of inventory for the raw material when using the economic order quantity. **(4 marks)**

(ii) Determine whether accepting the discount offered by the supplier will minimise the total cost of inventory for the raw material. **(3 marks)**

(Total: 25 marks)

330 MISHA ARIF

Misha Arif will set up a new business as a sole trader on 1 January 20X3 making figurines based on characters from popular children's tales. Misha has past experience in running a small business and is aware of the importance of working capital management. He is in the process of planning the initial cash flows of the business in order to highlight areas that may cause problems for his new venture.

He estimates that there will not be any sales demand in the first month of operations, January 20X3, so production in that month will be used to build up inventories to satisfy the expected demand in February 20X3. Thereafter it is intended to schedule production in order to build up sufficient finished goods inventory at the end of each month to satisfy demand during the following month. Production will, however, need to be 5% higher than sales due to expected defects that will have to be scrapped. Defects are only discovered after the goods have been completed. The company will not hold inventories of raw materials or work in progress.

As the business is new, demand is uncertain, but Misha has estimated three possible levels of demanded units in 20X3 as follows:

	Low	Medium	High
Probability	(15%)	(80%)	(5%)
February	6,000	7,000	8,000
March	8,000	10,000	12,000
April	12,000	14,000	16,000
May	10,000	16,000	18,000
June	16,000	22,000	26,000

Demand for July 20X3 onwards is expected to be the same as June 20X3. The selling price will be set at $50 per unit and it is not expected that will change in the first year of production.

It is expected that 20% of the total sales value will be cash sales, mainly being retail customers making small purchases. The remaining 80% of sales will be made to large distributors on two months' credit. A 5% discount will, however, be offered to credit customers settling within one month. It is estimated that customers, representing half of credit sales by value, will take advantage of the discount while the remainder will take the full two months to pay.

Variable production costs (excluding costs of rejects) per unit are as follows:

	$
Labour	5
Materials	15
Variable overhead	10

Labour is paid in the month in which labour costs are incurred. Materials are paid one month in arrears and variable overheads are paid two months in arrears. Fixed production and administration overheads, including depreciation of $7,000 per month, are $105,000 per month and are payable in the same month as the expenditure is incurred.

Misha employed a firm of consultants to give him initial business advice. Their fee of $100,000 will be paid in February 20X3. Smelting machinery will be purchased on 1 January 20X3 for $800,000 payable in February 20X3.

Misha has $150,000 available for investment in the business, which he intends to pay into his bank account on 1 January 20X3 as the initial capital of the business. He suspects that this will be insufficient for his business plans, but would be wary of investing any more of his personal cash. The only asset Misha has is his house that is valued at $2,000,000, but he has an outstanding mortgage of $850,000 on this property. Misha believes that better management of working capital areas such as creditors, debtors and inventories would be a better way to solve what he believes will be a short-term problem for the business.

Required:

(a) Prepare a monthly cash budget for Misha Arif's business for the six month period ending 30 June 20X3. Calculations should be made on the basis of the expected values of sales. The cash budget should show the net cash inflow or outflow in each month and the cumulative cash surplus or deficit at the end of each month.

(15 marks)

(b) Explain how better working capital management might alleviate the initial cash flow problems that the new business will encounter. (5 marks)

(c) If better working capital policies were not employed, identify sources of short-term funding that may be used instead to help the business through its difficult early phase. (5 marks)

(Total: 25 marks)

Section 4

ANSWERS TO SECTION A-TYPE QUESTIONS

COST ACCOUNTING SYSTEMS

1   B

	$
Marginal costing profit	45,000
Less: fixed cost included in opening inventory (28,000 – 16,000)	(12,000)
Plus: fixed cost included in closing inventory (36,400 – 20,800)	15,600
Absorption costing profit	48,600

Alternative approach

Increase in inventory using marginal costing	$4,800
Increase in inventory using absorption costing	$8,400
Difference = fixed overhead absorbed in inventory	$3,600

Inventory is increasing so absorption costing profit is higher than marginal costing profit by the amount of fixed overhead absorbed.

Absorption costing profit = $45,000 + $3,600 = $48,600

2   B

The opening inventory was 400 units and the closing inventory was 900 units, therefore inventory has increased.

If production is greater than sales then absorption costing will show the higher profit.

Difference in profit: = Change in inventory × Fixed production cost per unit

= (900 – 400) × $29,500/5,000 units = $2,950

3   A

OAR = $330,000/220,000 = $1.50 per unit

	$
Overhead absorbed (200,000 units × $1.50)	300,000
Actual overhead	260,000
Over absorbed	40,000

4   C

$$\text{Return per minute} = \frac{\text{Selling price - material cost}}{\text{Time on bottleneck resource}}$$

$$= \frac{50 - 16}{8}$$

$$= €4.25$$

Return per hour   =   €4.25 × 60   = €255

5   (a)

	Product S		*Product T*

Throughput of process X per day

$13.5 \text{ hrs} \times \dfrac{60}{5} = 162.00$ $13.5 \text{ hrs} \times \dfrac{60}{7.5} = 108.00$

(Production time: 15 − 1.5 = 13.5 hours)

Throughput of process Y per day

$14 \text{ hrs} \times \dfrac{60}{18} = 46.67$ $14 \text{ hrs} \times \dfrac{60}{12} = 70.00$

(Production time: 15 − 1 = 14 hours)

Process Y is the bottleneck process because it limits the production of both products to figures that are less than sales demand.

(b)   Throughput contribution per hour of product S: $\dfrac{(\$95.00 - 20.00)}{18} \times 60 = \$250.00$

Throughput contribution per hour of product T: $\dfrac{(\$85.00 - 20.00)}{12} \times 60 = \$325.00$

The optimum production plan to maximise throughput contribution per day is to produce 70 units of product T.

6   A

This is the CIMA *Official Terminology* definition of a bottleneck. With a throughput accounting approach, the aim should be to reduce or remove bottlenecks, so as to increase throughput.

7

Return per factory hour = $\dfrac{\$12 - \$5}{0.75 \text{hrs}}$ = $9.333

Cost per factory hour = $144,000/12,000 = $12

TA ratio = 9.3333/12 = 0.778

A profitable product should have a ratio greater than 1. This product is making a loss as cost per hour is exceeding throughput per hour.

8   **B**

Using marginal costing inventory is valued at the variable production cost per unit

	$
Direct materials	20,000
Direct labour	6,300
Variable production overhead	4,700
Total variable cost	31,000

Inventory value = 400 units × 31,000/4,000 = $3,100

9   **D**

Using throughput accounting inventory is valued at material cost

Inventory value = 20,000/4,000 × 400 units = $2,000

10   **B**

The inventory will be valued at production cost, to be more precise at variable production cost.

Cost per unit = $\dfrac{\$40,000 + \$12,600 + \$9,400}{2,000\,\text{units}}$ = $31 per unit

No. of units in closing inventory = 2,000 − 1,750 = 250 units.

Therefore value of closing inventory = 250 units × $31 = $7,750.

11   **A**

Under throughput accounting, finished goods will be valued at direct material cost.

Cost per unit = $\dfrac{\$40,000}{2,000\,\text{units}}$ = $20 per unit

No. of units in closing inventory = 2,000 − 1,750 = 250 units.

Therefore value of closing inventory = 250 units × $20 = $5,000

12

	Z1	Z2
	Maximum production	*Maximum production*
Department 1	480 min/12 min = 40 units	480 min/16 min = 30 units
Department 2	840 min/20 min = 42 units	840 min/15 min = 56 units

Department 1 is the problem for both products. We can make 42 units of Z1 as far as Department 2 is concerned, but Department 1 is only able to process 40 units. Similarly for Z2, Department 2 can deal with 56 units, but Department 1 can only cope with 30. In both cases Department 1 is the bottleneck.

13

	Z1	Z2
	$	$
Selling price	50	65
Variable cost	26.80	30.40
Contribution	23.20	34.60
No. of bottleneck min per unit	12	16
Contribution per min	1.93	2.16
Priority	2nd	1st

The optimum plan is to concentrate on Z2. We will make the maximum, which is 30 units (from Question 31).

Contribution = 30 units × $34.60 per unit = $1,038.

14

	Z1	Z2
	$	$
Selling price	50	65
Direct material	10	15
Throughput	40	50
No. of bottleneck min per unit	12	16
Throughput per min	3.33	3.13
Priority	1st	2nd

The optimum plan is to concentrate on Z1. We will make the maximum, which is 40 units.

Throughput = 40 units × $40 per unit = $1,600.

15

(a) **Absorption costing**

Value of closing inventory = $(13,500 + 11,800 + 32,400) × 200/2,000 = $5,770

	$	$
Sales (1,800 × $45)		81,000
Cost of production	57,700	
Less closing inventory	5,770	
Cost of sales		51,930
Gross profit		29,070
Non-production overhead		21,900
Profit		7,170

(b)   **Marginal costing**

Value of closing inventory = $(13,500 + 11,800) \times 200/2,000 = $2,530$

	$	$
Sales		81,000
Variable cost of production	25,300	
Less closing inventory	2,530	
Cost of sales		22,770
Contribution		58,230
Fixed overhead		54,300
Profit		3,930

(c)   **Throughput accounting**

Value of closing inventory = $13,500 \times 200/2,000 = $1,350$

	$	$
Sales		81,000
Material costs	13,500	
Less closing inventory	1,350	
Cost of sales		12,150
Throughput		68,850
Operating expenses		66,100
Net profit		2,750

16   B

$$\text{Breakeven sales revenue} = \frac{\text{fixed costs}}{\text{C/S ratio}}$$

$$800,000 = \frac{\$320,000}{\text{C/S ratio}}$$

$$\text{C/S ratio} = \frac{\$320,000}{\$800,000} = 40\%$$

Sales revenue required to achieve a target profit of $50,000

$$= \frac{\$320,000 + 50,000}{40\%} = \underline{\$925,000}$$

17 B

Activity	Classification
(i)	Facility-sustaining
(ii)	Facility-sustaining
(iii)	Product-sustaining
(iv)	Product-sustaining
(v)	Facility-sustaining

18 A

$$\text{Cost driver rate} = \frac{\text{Budgeted cost of orders}}{\text{Budgeted number of orders}} = \frac{\$110,010}{2,895} = \$38 \text{ for each order}$$

	$
Cost recovered: 210 orders × $38	7,980
Actual costs incurred	7,650
Over-recovery of costs for four-week period	330

19 D

Statement (i) provides a definition of a cost driver. Cost drivers for long-term variable overhead costs will be the volume of a particular activity to which the cost driver relates, so Statement (ii) is correct. Statement (iii) is also correct. In traditional absorption costing, standard high-volume products receive a higher amount of overhead costs than with ABC. ABC allows for the unusually high costs of support activities for low-volume products (such as relatively higher set-up costs, order processing costs and so on).

20

(a)

Budgeted number of batches:

Product D (100,000/100)	=	1,000
Product R (100,000/50)	=	2,000
Product P (50,000/25)	=	2,000
		5,000

(b)

Budgeted machine set-ups:

Product D (1,000 × 3)	=	3,000
Product R (2,000 × 4)	=	8,000
Product P (2,000 × 6)	=	12,000
		23,000

(c)

Budgeted number of purchase orders:

Product D (1,000 × 2)	=	2,000
Product R (2,000 × 1)	=	2,000
Product P (2,000 × 1)	=	2,000
		6,000

(d)

Budgeted processing minutes:

Product D (100,000 × 2)	=	200,000
Product R (100,000 × 3)	=	300,000
Product P (50,000 × 3)	=	150,000
		650,000 minutes

21

Budgeted cost per set-up:

$$= \frac{\$150,000}{23,000} = \$6.52$$

Budgeted unit cost of R: $= \dfrac{\$6.52 \times 4}{50} = \$0.52$

Budgeted cost per order:

$$= \frac{\$70,000}{6,000} = \$11.67$$

Budgeted unit cost of R: $= \dfrac{\$11.67 \times 1}{50} = \$0.23$

Budgeted processing cost per minute:

$= \dfrac{\$80,000}{650,000} = \$0.12$ Budgeted unit cost of R $= \$0.12 \times 3 = \$0.36$

Total budgeted unit cost of R is:

		$
Set-up costs	=	0.52
Purchasing costs	=	0.23
Processing costs	=	0.36
Total cost	=	1.11 per unit

22   ABC

Costs could be higher under ABC if:

- a product is produced in small batches
- there is production complexity not represented in direct labour hours.

Management may choose to increase batch sizes and/or increase selling prices in order to cover the extra product costs.

23   D

Statements A, B and C are incorrect. JIT makes an organisation more vulnerable to disruptions in the supply chain, because there are no buffer inventories as protection against a breakdown in supply. JIT is easier to implement when an organisation operates within a narrow geographical area, and close to its suppliers. (At Toyota, where JIT originated, manufacturing operations were initially carried out within a 50 kilometre radius.) With little or no inventories, the risk of inventory obsolescence should not exist.

Statement D is correct. When demand is difficult to predict, it becomes more difficult to operate a demand-driven operation.

24   A

Instead of building up product costs sequentially from start to finish of production, backflush accounting calculates product costs retrospectively, at the end of each accounting period, when goods are completed or sold.

25   C

Item (ii) is not an aspect of JIT. There will be more small production runs and so more time spent on machine set-up. Total machine set up time will therefore rise rather than decline if JIT is introduced. Producing only in response to demand, and organising work into work cells, with each cell producing an entire product or job (and so reducing material movements), are characteristic features of JIT.

26   A

	$
Actual overhead incurred	481,250
Less under-absorbed overhead	19,250
Overhead absorbed	462,000

Overhead absorbed = Actual standard hours charged × OAR

So OAR = overhead absorbed/actual standard hours charged = $462,000/38,500 = $12

OAR = Budgeted overheads/budgeted labour hours

So budgeted overheads = OAR × budgeted labour hours = $12 × 38,000 = $456,000

27   D

Training should prevent future failure costs. Reworking costs are an internal failure cost.

28   A

	$000	$000
Sales revenue		820
Variable cost of sales		
Opening inventory	0	
Variable production costs	300	
	300	
Less closing inventory	45	
		255
		565
Variable selling costs		105
Contribution		460
Fixed costs		
Production	180	
Selling	110	
		290
Profit		170

Working

The closing inventory is valued at cost. As it is a marginal costing system the inventory is valued at variable cost, i.e. $300,000/1,000 units = $300 per unit. The closing inventory is 150 units, therefore the closing inventory value is $300/unit × 150 units = $45,000.

29   A

These are the official CIMA definitions for MRP and ERP respectively.

30   A

Option (i) is true.

Option (ii) is false. Flexible manufacturing systems may not be simple and may have a substantial degree of automation.

Option (iii) is false. EDI is most often used to allow communication with outside businesses, with customers and suppliers.

31   B

Definition 1 is of an MRP1 system and definition 2 is of throughput accounting.

32   A

(i) is correct. An FMS is a highly automated, complex, computerised production system so (ii) is incorrect. JIT purchases inventory as required so (iii) is incorrect.

33   C

Option A may lead to over-absorption but this will depend on the extent to which actual overhead costs differ from budget. Option B describes under-absorption. Option D refers to budgeted overheads, which are used to calculate the OAR but otherwise not used in the calculation of under-/over-absorption.

34   B

(i) and (ii) are the correct definitions. An MRP system is a computer system for production, planning, purchasing and inventory control. It does not integrate all aspects of a business.

35   B

OAR = $500,000/2,000 = $250 per unit

Inventory has fallen by 300 units in the period.

Absorption costing profit will be 300 × $250 = $75,000 lower than marginal costing profit as some fixed overhead from previous periods will be brought forward to be matched against sales in the period using absorption costing. In marginal costing only the fixed overhead incurred in the period will be included in the profit statement.

36

	A $	B $	C $
Selling price	200	150	150
Direct materials	41	20	30
Throughput	159	130	120
Machine P – minutes per unit	12	10	7
Return per factory minute	159/12	130/10	120/7
	13.25	13	17.14
Return per factory hour × 60 minutes	**$795**	**$780**	**$1,028**

Note: Product C return per factory hour = $1,029 with no rounding

37

	Assembly	Finishing	Stores	Maintenance	Total
Budgeted overhead	100,000	150,000	50,000	40,000	340,000
Reapportion maintenance	16,000	18,000	6,000	(40,000)	–
			56,000		
Reapportion stores	33,600	22,400	(56,000)		–
Total overhead	149,600	190,400			340,000

OAR for assembly department = $149,600/100,000 = $1.496 per unit

	$
Overhead absorbed 120,000 × 1.496	179,520
Overhead incurred	180,000
Under-absorption	480

STANDARD COSTING

38 **C**

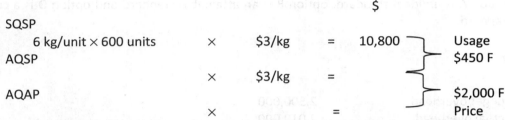

This is a 'backwards' question. Given some information including the variances, we then have to work backwards to find some missing numbers – here, the number of kg purchased.

SQSP
     6 kg/unit × 600 units   × $3/kg   =   10,800

AQSP
     3,450 kg$^{Bal\ 2}$ × $3/kg   =   10,350$^{Bal\ 1}$

AQAP
          ×   =

Usage $450 F · $2,000 F Price

The question can also be answered as follows:

	Kg	
600 units should use (× 6 kg)	3,600	
Usage variance in kg ($450(F)/3)	150	(F)
Therefore 600 units did use	3,450	

Given no change in stock levels, usage quantity = purchase quantity.

39 **D**

Direct labour variance

40   A

Variable overhead variance

$

SHSR
    2 hrs/unit × 11,000 units   × $6/hr   =   132,000 ⎤ Efficiency
AHSR   ⎬ $12,000 A
                24,000 hrs   × $6/hr   =   144,000 ⎦

41   C

Option A is an ideal standard, option B is an attainable standard and option D is a current standard.

42   D

	$
Budget overhead	2,500,000
Actual overhead	2,010,000
Expenditure variance	490,000 F

43   C

OAR = $2,500,000/500,000 = $5 per unit

Budgeted volume	500,000 units
Actual volume	440,000 units
	60,000 units
× OAR per unit	× $5
Volume variance	$300,000 A

44   A

	$
Expected cost = ($800 + $0.0002 × 4,100^2) × 1.03	4,287
Actual cost	5,000
	713A

45   C

This is the CIMA definition.

46 **B**

Absorption rate = $\dfrac{\$170,000}{42,500}$ = $4/unit

	Units
Budgeted output	42,500
Actual output	40,000
Volume variance in units	2,500 (A)
Standard fixed overhead cost/unit	× $4
Fixed overhead volume variance in $	$10,000 (A)

47 **C**

Labour variances

$

SHSR
    10 hrs/unit × 6,200 units   × $9.50/hr = 589,000 ⎤ Efficiency
AHSR $8,455 A
    62,890 hrs   × $9.50/hr = 597,455
AHAR $1,043 F
                                         = 596,412 ⎦ Rate

The variances could also be calculated as follows:

Rate variance:

	$
62,890 hours should cost (× $9.50)	597,455
They did cost	596,412
Labour rate variance	1,043 (F)

Efficiency variance:

	Hours
6,200 units should take (× 10)	62,000
They did take	62,890
Efficiency variance in hours	890 (A)

Efficiency variance in $ = 890 hours (A) × $9.50 per hour = $8,455 Adverse.

48   B

Inventories are valued at standard prices, so the material price variance must be calculated by reference to the quantity purchased.

Price variance

	Kgs
Actual quantity used	13,050
Reduction in stock	500
Quantity purchased	12,550 kgs

Material variances

$

SQSP

    6 kg/unit × 2,192 units   × $6.75/kg =   88,776

AQSP   Usage

    13,050 kg   × $6.75/kg =   88,087.50 $688.50 F

For a usage variance the quantity must be the quantity used.

$

AQSP

    12,550 kg   × $6.75/kg =   84,712.50

AQAP $11,812.50 A

                                  =   72,900   Price

As the price variance is calculated at the time of *purchase* then the quantity must be the quantity *purchased* and we had to use the more complicated format than the usual 3-line format.

	$
12,550 kgs should cost ($6.75/kg)	84,712.50
They did cost	72,900.00
Price variance	$11,812.50 (F)

	kgs
Usage variance	
2,192 finished units should use (× 6)	13,152
They did use	13,050
Usage variance in kgs	102 kgs (F)

Usage variance in $ = 102 kgs (F) × $6.75/kg (standard price) = $688.50 (F)

49   B

Labour variance

$

SHSR

0.75 hrs/unit × 11,000 units × $20/hr   =   165,000 ⎤ Efficiency

AHSR   ⎬ $5,000 F

8,000 hrs   × $20/hr   =   160,000 ⎦

The variances could be calculated as follows:

Hours

11,000 units should take (× 0.75 hr)   8,250

did take   8,000

Efficiency variance in hours   250   Favourable

Standard rate per hour   × $20

Efficiency variance in $ $5,000   Favourable

50   C

Variable overhead variance

$

AHSR

8,000 hrs   × $15/hr   =   120,000 ⎤

AHAR   ⎬ $12,000 A

=   132,000 ⎦ Expenditure

The variance could also be calculated as follows:

$

8,000 hours should cost (×$15)   120,000

did cost   132,000

Expenditure variance   12,000   Adverse

51   A

The operational labour efficiency variance uses the revised standard time of 12 minutes.

SHSR

$

$\frac{12}{60}$ × 370 × $10/hr =   740 ⎤

AHSR   ⎬ Efficiency $60 A

80 hrs × $10/hr = 800 ⎦

52   A

The fixed overhead volume variance is the difference between budgeted and actual production volume multiplied by the standard absorption rate per unit. This is the same as the difference between budgeted value of fixed overheads (budgeted volume × standard absorption rate per unit) and standard fixed overheads absorbed by actual production (actual volume × standard absorption rate per unit).

53 C

OAR = $1,500,000/300,000 = $5 per unit

Fixed production overhead variance is the level of over/under absorption. An adverse variance means that overhead is under absorbed.

	$
Overhead absorbed	
Actual output × $5	?
Actual overhead	1,950,000
Under absorbed	150,000

Working backwards, Overhead absorbed = 1,950,000 − 150,000 = 1,800,000 and actual output = 1,800,000/5 = 360,000 units

54 D

Sales price variance

	$	
Std selling price	500	
Actual selling price	465	
Sales price variance	35	(A)
× Actual no of units sold	× 642	
	22,470	

55 C

Sales volume contribution variance

	Units	
Budgeted quantity sold	600	
Actual quantity sold	642	
Sales volume variance in units	42	(F)
× Std contribution per unit (25% × $500)	× $125	
	$5,250	(F)

56

	Actual mix Litres	Standard mix Litres	Difference Litres		Price $	Variance $	
X	984	885.6	98.4	(A)	2.50	246.0	(A)
Y	1,230	1,328.4	98.4	(F)	3.00	295.2	(F)
Totals	2,214	2,214.0	nil			49.2	(F)

57

Expected output $= \dfrac{2,214}{30} = 73.8$ units

Actual output $= 72.0$ units

Shortfall $= 1.8$ units

1.8 units × $84/unit $= \$151.2$ (A)

An alternative would be only 73 complete units of output were expected, thus the shortfall would be 1 unit. The variance would be 1.0 × $84 per unit = $84 adverse.

58 Weighted average standard price per litre = $26/10 = $2.60

	Actual usage Litres		Standard mix Litres	Mix variance Litres		Rate $	Mix variance $	
Material C	200	(6/10)	180	20	(A)	(3 − 2.60)	8	(A)
Material D	75	(3/10)	90	15		(1 − 2.60)	24	
					(F)			(A)
Material E	25	(1/10)	30	5	(F)	(5 − 2.60)	12	(F)
	300		300	Nil			20	(A)

The variance for material C is adverse because actual usage was greater than standard, for a material costing more than the weighted average cost.

The variance for material D is adverse because actual usage was less than standard, for a material costing less than the weighted average cost.

The variance for material E is favourable because actual usage was less than standard, for a material costing more than the weighted average cost.

59

	Litres	
Standard usage for actual output of X2	280	
Actual usage	300	
Yield variance in litres	20	(A)
× weighted average standard price per litre	× $2.60	
Yield variance in $	$52	(A)

60 There are two methods of calculating mix and yield variances – one is the individual unit price method and the other is the weighted average price method. The two methods give different mix variances for individual materials, but give the same total mix variance. We are only asked for the total mix variance and so either method can be used. We have shown both methods. Most people would prefer the first.

(a) **Individual material price method**

Mix variance	Material D Litres	Material E Litres	Material F Litres	Total Litres
Actual input	4,300	3,600	2,100	10,000
Actual input in std proportions				⇓
4:3.5:2.5	4,000	3,500	2,500	⇐10,000
Difference in quantity	300 A	100 A	400 F	
× Std price	× $9	× $5	× $2	
Mix variance	$2,700 A	$500 A	$800 F	$2,400 A

Weighted average price method

Weighted average standard price per litre = $\dfrac{\$58.50}{4.0+3.5+2.5\,\text{litres}}$ = $5.85 per litre

Mix variance	Material D Litres	Material E Litres	Material F Litres	Total Litres
Actual input	4,300	3,600	2,100	10,000
Actual input in std proportions				⇓
4:3.5:2.5	4,000	3,500	2,500	⇐ 10,000
Difference in quantity	300	100	− 400	
× Difference in price (weighted av.std price − Ind. Material std price)				
× (5.85 − 9)	× − 3.15			
× 5.85 − 5)		× 0.85		
× (5.85 − 2)			3.85	
Mix variance	$945 A	$85 F	$1,540 A	$2,400 A

(b) **Yield variance**

This is calculated in exactly the same way under both methods.

$$\text{Std cost per litre of output} = \frac{\$58.50}{9\,\text{litres}} = \$6.50/\text{litre}$$

	Litres
Std yield	
10,000 × 90%	9,000
Actual yield	9,100
	100 F
× Std cost per litre of output	× 6.50
Yield variance	$650 F

61   C

Event (i) is more likely to result in a favourable usage variance therefore it is not correct. Event (ii) could cause an adverse usage variance since a lower quality material might lead to higher wastage and a higher level of quality control rejects. Event (iii) could cause an adverse usage variance because lower skilled employees might waste material and quality control rejects might again be higher. Event (iv) would not necessarily cause an adverse usage variance. The usage variance is based on the expected usage for the actual output, not on the budgeted usage for the budgeted output.

62   B

Less experienced employees are likely to take longer than standard to produce a given level of output. The result would be an adverse variable overhead efficiency variance. Option A is more likely to result in a favourable variable overhead efficiency variance because employees are likely to work faster than standard. Option C might also result in a favourable efficiency variance because higher quality material is likely to be easier to process, thus saving time against standard. Option D would result in an adverse variable overhead expenditure variance but would not directly affect the variable overhead efficiency variance.

63

Sales price variance		
Budgeted selling price	$10.00	
Actual selling price	$9.50	
	$0.50	adverse
Actual sales volume (units)	110,000	
	$55,000	adverse
Sales volume profit variance		
Budgeted sales volume (units)	100,000	
Actual sales volume (units)	110,000	
	10,000	favourable
Standard profit per unit ($10 − $8)	$2	
	$20,000	Favourable

64   Unfortunately there are different ways of calculating planning and operational variances and with the way that this question is written the correct answer could be B or D.

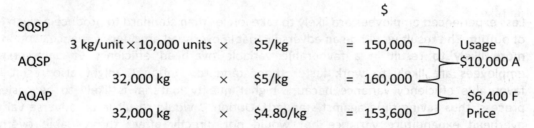

	Planning	**Operational**
Original Standard	Revised Standard	Actual
3 kg	3 kg	32,000 kg
$4	$5	$4.80
11,000 units	11,000 units	10,000 units

One way is to calculate planning variances as the difference between the original standard and revised standard.

Planning price variance = ($4 – $5) × 3 kg × 11,000 units = $33,000 A

The correct answer is D using the first method.

Alternatively the variance could be calculated on the actual number of units:

Planning price variance = ($4 – $5) × 3 kg × 10,000 units = $30,000 A

The correct answer is B using the second method.

65   **D (SEE NEXT ANSWER)**

66   **B**

Material variance

				$	
SQSP					
	3 kg/unit × 10,000 units ×	$5/kg	=	150,000	Usage
AQSP					$10,000 A
	32,000 kg ×	$5/kg	=	160,000	
AQAP					$6,400 F
	32,000 kg ×	$4.80/kg	=	153,600	Price

The standards here are the revised standards.

67   **B**

Mix variance

Liquid	Standard mix	Actual mix	Mix variance	Standard price	Mix variance
	ltr			$	$
X	2,250	2,200	50 F	16	800 F
Y	2,700	2,750	50 A	25	1,250 A
	4,950 l	4,950 l			450 A

68   Mix variance = $500 Favourable

	Actual mix (kg)	Actual quantity/ Standard mix (kg)	Difference (kg)	Standard price (£)	Mix variance (£)
P	1,030	1,000	30A	75	2,250 A
Q	560	600	40F	100	4,000 F
R	410	400	10A	125	1,250 A
	2,000	2,000			500 F

69   Yield variance = $11,306 Favourable

2,000 kgs should produce 2,000/100 × 90	1,800 kg of output
did produce	1,910 kg of output

Difference	110 F
Value at standard cost per kg ($9,250/90)	$11,306 F

70   Idle hours = 61,500 − 56,000 = 5,500

Standard rate per hour = $540,000/60,000 = $9

Idle time variance = 5,500 × $9 = $49,500 Adverse

71

14,650 units should take	60,000/15,000 = 4 hours per unit	58,600 hours
Did take		56,000 hours

Difference	2,600 hours F
Value at standard rate per hour ($9)	$23,400 F

72   **B**

8,200 × ($31 − $26) = $41,000 F

73   **A**

OAR = $34,800/8,700 = $4 per unit

Standard profit per unit = $26 − $10 − $4 = $12

Volume variance = (8,700 − 8,200) × $12 = $6,000 A

74   **A**

(8,700 − 8,200) × $4 = $2,000 A

75   **C**

Production volume ratio = standard hours produced/budgeted capacity = 95 %

So budgeted hours > standard hours

76 (a) Material price planning variance

Original standard price	$4.10
Revised standard price	$4.50

.40 A × 11,200 units = $4,480 A

(b) Operational material usage variance

1,600 units should use (× 7)	11,200 kg
did use	12,000 kg
	800 kg A

Valued at revised standard price ($4.50) $3,600 A

77

11,500 units should use 5 hours each	57,500 hours
Did use	?
Variance in hours	
Value at $12 per hour	
Labour efficiency variance	$30,000 A

Working backwards:

The variance in hours = $30,000/12 = 2,500 A

The actual hours used are 57,500 + 2,500 = 60,000

60,000 hours should cost (× $12)	720,000
Did cost	?
Labour rate variance	45,000 A

Working backwards:

The actual labour cost = $765,000

so the actual rate paid per hour = $765,000/60,000 = $12.75.

BUDGETING

78 C

The budget communicates to individual managers what is expected of them in the forthcoming budget period and how much expenditure they can incur in meeting their targets. Thus communication (i) is a purpose of budgeting. An agreed budget provides authorisation for individual managers to incur expenditure in undertaking the activities in their own budget centre. Therefore authorisation (ii) is a purpose of budgeting. Although an organisation might have an objective of maximising sales and might set a budget to enable them to achieve this objective, the maximisation of sales is not in itself a purpose of budgeting. Therefore (iii) is not correct. Individual budget targets are set within the framework of the plan for the organisation as a whole and in this way a budget provides a means of coordinating the efforts of everyone within the organisation. Therefore (iv) is correct.

79 D

80

	E	F	G	Total
Budgeted number of batches to be produced:	75,000/200	120,000/60	60,000/30	
	= 375	= 2,000	= 2,000	
Machine set-ups per batch:	5	3	9	
Total machine set-ups	1,875	6,000	18,000	25,875

So budgeted cost per set-up: $180,000/25,875 = $6.96 per set-up

Therefore the budgeted machine set-up cost per unit of F produced is:

($6.96 × 3)/60 = $0.35 per unit or $6.96 × 6,000/120,000 = $0.35 per unit

81 D

See workings in next answer.

82 D

In the year ended October 20X3 total variable costs were $850,000 × 60% = $510,000. These can be analysed as follows:

	People	Packages (kg)	Total
Variable costs 50:50	$255,000	$255,000	$510,000
Units in year	4,420	30,500	–
Cost per unit	$57.69	$8.36	–
Adjusted cost (× 1.02)	$58.84	$8.53	–
Activity for period to 31 January 20X4	1,150	8,100	–
Total related costs	$67,666	$69,093	$136,759

83 D

Production overhead:

	Units		$
High	800	(× 1.75)	1,400
Low	500	(× 2.50)	1,250
	300		150

Variable cost = $150/300 = $0.50

Fixed cost = $1,400 − (800 × $0.50) = $1,000

Other overhead:

	Units		$
High	800	(× 0.625)	500
Low	500	(× 1.00)	500

This is a wholly fixed cost.

Variable cost per unit:

	$
Direct material	2.00
Direct labour	1.50
Variable production overhead	0.50
	4.00

Period fixed cost:

	$
Fixed production overhead	1,000
Other overhead	500
	1,500

84   C

Note that the material usage figure is not required.

	Units
Sales	30,000
Add closing inventory (3,500 × 1.35)	4,725
Less opening inventory	(3,500)
Production	31,225

85   C

At output of 6,000 units, overhead = 6,000 × $3.20 = $19,200

At output of 10,000 units, overhead = 10,000 × $3.00 = $30,000

$\therefore$ Variable overhead / unit = $\dfrac{\$30,000 - \$19,200}{10,000 - 6,000}$ = $2.70

Fixed overhead = $19,200 − (6,000 × $2.70) = $3,000

At activity of 7,350 units, budgeted production overhead = $3,000 + (7,350 × $2.70) = $22,845

86   B

A zero based budgeting system begins each budget from scratch every time. All expenditure on the activity must be justified from zero and the method of carrying out each activity must be re-evaluated as if it were being carried out for the first time.

87   Orders = [100,000 + (30 × 240)] × 1.08 = 115,776

Overhead cost = $10,000 + (£0.25 × 115,776) = $38,944

Answer is $39,000

88 **D**

Quarter	Value of x		Trend units			Forecast sales units
1	25	y = (26×25) + 8,850	9,500	×85%	=	8,075.0
2	26	y = (26×26) + 8,850	9,526	×95%	=	9,049.7
3	27	y = (26×27) + 8,850	9,552	×105%	=	10,029.6
4	28	y = (26×28) + 8,850	9,578	×115%	=	11,014.7
						———
						38,169.0
						———

Difference between Q1 and Q4 budgeted sales = 11,014.7 − 8,075.0 = 2,939.7 units

89 **D**

Since no inventories are held, budgeted production will be equal to budgeted sales.

Budgeted production each quarter = 38,169/4 = 9,542.25 units

90 **D**

Trend	=	9.72 + (5.816 × 23)
	=	143.488
Seasonal factor	+	6.5
		———
Forecast		149.988
		———

To the nearest whole unit, the forecast number of units to be sold is 150.

91 **C**

Probability of rainy summer	=	1.0 − 0.4 = 0.6
Expected value of sales volume	=	(80,000 × 0.4) + (120,000 × 0.6)
	=	104,000 units

92 **D**

It is known that there is a stepped fixed cost of $10,000 above 35,000 units. Removing the stepped fixed cost at 40,000 units leaves $184,000.

(i)   Variable cost per unit = $\dfrac{\$184,000 - \$143,500}{40,000 - 25,000}$ = $2.70

(ii)   At 25,000 units

Total cost	143,500
Total variable cost $2.70 × 25,000	67,500
	———
Fixed cost	76,000
	———

Therefore fixed cost at 36,000 units = $76,000 + $10,000 = $86,000

93 **C**

Budgetary slack is also called budget bias. Budget holders may sometimes try to obtain a budget that is easier to achieve. They may do this either by bidding for expenditure in excess of what they actually need or, in the case of sales budgets, by deliberately setting easy revenue targets.

94 **C**

	Machine hours	$
High	12,212	39,477
Low	8,480	31,080
Change	3,732	8,397

Variable cost per machine hour = $8,397/3,732
= $2.25

Fixed cost = $39,477 − (12,212 × $2.25) = $12,000

Budget cost allowance for 9,340 machine hours:

		$
Fixed cost		12,000
Variable cost (9,340 × $2.25)	=	21,015
		33,015

95 We have been given the trend equation. We need to plug in the value for x so that we can find y.

X is the time period reference number and for the first quarter of year 1 is 1. The time period reference number for the third quarter of year 7 is 27. (Just keep adding 1 to the time period reference number for each new quarter, thus quarter 2, year 1, x = 2; quarter 3, year 1, x = 3; quarter 4, year 1, x = 4; quarter 1, year 2, x = 5, etc.)

$$y = 25,000 + 6,500 \times 27 = 200,500 \text{ units}$$

This is the trend we now need to multiply by the seasonal variation for quarter 3:

Forecast = 200,500 × 150/100 = 300,750 units.

96

	January units	February units	March units
Production budget			
Sales	4,000	5,000	6,000
Add closing inventory	1,500	1,800	
	5,500	6,800	
Less opening inventory	1,200	1,500	
Production	4,300	5,300	

Materials budget

Production (units)	4,300	5,300
× No. of units of material per unit of product	× 1 unit	× 1 unit
Usage quantity (units)	4,300	5,300
Add closing inventory	1,325	
	5,625	
Less op inventory	1,075	
Purchase quantity (units)	4,550	
× purchase price	× $8	
Purchase cost (£)	36,400	

The purchase cost of materials in January is $36,400. This will be paid in February.

97

$$\text{OAR} = \frac{\text{Budgeted overheads}}{\text{Budgeted level of activity}}$$

$$= \frac{\$22,000 + \$34,000 + \$32,000}{8,000 \text{ hours}} \quad = \$11 \text{ per direct labour hour}$$

$$\text{Labour rate} = \frac{\$128,000}{8,000 \text{ hours}} \quad = \$16 \text{ per direct labour hour}$$

	$
Direct materials	21.50
Direct labour	4.80
Overheads	3.30
	29.60

98

	$
Direct material	21.50
Direct labour	4.80
Overheads	
Set-up costs	16.67
Quality testing costs	11.33
Other overhead costs	1.20
	55.50

$$\text{Set-up costs} = \frac{\$22,000}{88 \text{ set-ups}} = \$250 \text{ per set-up}$$

Charge to Product Z = $250 per set-up × 2 set-ups per batch ÷ 30 units per batch = $16.67

$$\text{Quality testing costs} = \frac{\$34,000}{40\,\text{tests}} = \$850 \text{ per test}$$

Tests are performed every 75 units, therefore charge per unit = \$850/75 = \$11.33

$$\text{Other overhead costs} = \frac{\$32,000}{8,000\,\text{hours}} = \$4 \text{ per direct labour hour}$$

Charge to product Z = \$4 × 0.3 hours = \$1.20

99   C

The P/V line will move down as profit will be lower at all units of sales. The gradient represents the C/S ratio and this will be unchanged.

100   C

High Low Method

	Activity	$
	6,500	33,000
	4,500	29,000
Difference	2,000	4,000
So the variable cost	= \$4,000/2,000	= \$2 per unit
Substitute into either activity	6,500	33,000	Total cost
	6,500 × \$2	13,000	Variable cost
	Difference	\$20,000	Fixed cost

The estimated production cost for 5,750 units = 5,750 × \$2 + \$20,000 = \$31,500

101   D

The index values should add to 400 as there are four seasons.

80 + 80 + 110 + ? = 400

so ? = 130

102

Forecast sales volume for June, July and August is:

Month		Cumulative sales (units)		Monthly sales (units)
June		1,500		1,500
July	$1,500 \times 2^{0.6}$	2,274	2,274 – 1,500	774
August	$1,500 \times 3^{0.6}$	2,900	2,900 – 2,274	626

103

	Sales	
		$
Month 4	$108,000 × 20%	21,600
Month 3	$120,000 × 80% × 40% × 0.985	37,824
Month 2	$105,000 × 80% × 30%	25,200
Month 1	$90,000 x 80% x 28%	20,160
B/f		6,000
		$110,784

104 Purchases are sold at cost plus 25% so cost of sales is 100/125= 0.8 × Sales

Closing inventory = 0.5 × Following month's cost of sales

Closing inventory = Opening inventory of the following month

Month	Sales	Cost of sales	Opening inventory	Closing inventory	Purchase	Paid
July	100	80	40	36	76	
August	90	72	36	50	86	**76**
September	125	100	50	56	106	**86**
October	140	112	56			**106**

105 ($10M × 0.15) + ($20M × 0.1) + ?M = $5.5M + $2M

$3.5m + ?m = $7.5m   so ? = $4m

Revenue needed to ensure a profit of $2m = 4/0.25 = $16m

106 D

This is the definition of a master budget.

107

				Total
Number of purchase requisitions	1,200	1,800	2,000	5,000
Number of set-ups	240	260	300	800
	W	X	Y	Total
	$	$	$	$
Receiving/inspecting quality assurance (W1)	336,000	504,000	560,000	1,400,000
Production scheduling/machine set-up (W2)	360,000	390,000	450,000	1,200,000
Total overhead cost	696,000	894,000	1,010,000	2,600,000
Units produced and sold	10,000	15,000	18,000	
Overhead cost per unit	69.60	59.60	56.11	

Selling price	200	183	175
Direct material	50	40	35
Direct labour	30	35	30
Overhead cost per unit	69.60	59.60	56.11
Profit per unit	50.40	48.40	53.89

Workings

(W1) 1,200/5,000 × 1,400,000 = 336,000

  1,800/5,000 × 1,400,000 = 504,000

  2,000/5,000 × 1,400,000 = 560,000

(W2) 240/800 × 1,200,000 = 360,000

  260/800 × 1,200,000 = 390,000

  300/800 × 1,200,000 = 450,000

108

Labour hours for production

36,000 units x 4 hours = 144,000 hours

Idle time = 10% of total available hours, therefore total available hours need to be:

144,000 hours / 0.9 = 160,000 hours

Labour cost budget ($)

160,000 hours x 20% = 32,000 hours x ($12 x 1.50) = $576,000

160,000 hours x 80% = 128,000 hours x $12 = $1,536,000

109

Budgeted sales	24,000	units	
Plus closing inventory	2,000	units	
Less opening inventory	(500)	units	
Budgeted production	25,500	units	
Raw material required	25,500 units x 2 kg		= 51,000 kg
Plus closing inventory	2,000 units x 2 kg		= 4,000 kg
Less opening inventory			(300) kg
Raw material purchases			54,700 kg
Raw material purchases budget	54,700 kg x $12		= $656,400

110

Quarter	Trend sales units	Actual sales units	Variation units
1	13,000	14,000	+1,000
2	16,000	18,000	+2,000
3	19,000	18,000	-1,000
4	22,000	20,000	-2,000

Year 2 Quarter 1 = 10,000 + (3,000 x 5) = 25,000 + 1,000 = 26,000 units

Year 2 Quarter 2 = 10,000 + (3,000 x 6) = 28,000 + 2,000 = 30,000 units

Year 2 Quarter 3 = 10,000 + (3,000 x 7) = 31,000 - 1,000 = 30,000 units

Year 2 Quarter 4 = 10,000 + (3,000 x 8) = 34,000 - 2,000 = 32,000 units

111 The answer is 40.9 Days

Trade payables outstanding at end of this year = $474,500 / 365 x 45 = $58,500

Purchases budget for next year = $474,500 x 1.1 = $521,950

Trade payable days at end of next year = $58,500 / $521,950 x 365 = 40.9 days

112 The answer is $4,933,500

Budgeted sales	144,000	units
Plus Closing inventory	12,000	units
Less Opening Inventory	(6,500)	units
Budgeted Production	149,500	units

149,500 x 2 hours per unit = 299,000 hours

80% x 299,000 = 239,200 hours x $15 = $3,588,000

20% x 299,000 = 59,800 hours x $(15 x1.5) = 1,345,500

Total labour cost budget = $4,933,500

FINANCIAL INFORMATION FOR LONG-TERM DECISION MAKING

113 A

Annual contribution	= annual cash profit + annual cash fixed costs	
	= $450,000 + $190,000	= $640,000
Contribution / unit	= $220 − $55	= $165
∴ Units sold pa	= $640,000 ÷ $165	= 3,879 units.

The NPV of the project can fall by $127,600 before it becomes zero.

The NPV of total annual revenue is expected to be 3,879 × $220 × 4.623 = $3,945,175.

For this to fall by $127,600, it must suffer a decrease of:

$$\frac{127,600}{3,945,175} \times 100\% = 3.2\%$$

114 C

	$	Tax saved at 25%	Yr 1	Yr 2	Yr 3
Cost of asset	80,000				
Year 1 writing down allowance (20%)	16,000	4,000	2,000	2,000	
Balance	64,000				
Year 2 writing down allowance (20%)	12,800	3,200		1,600	1,600
				3,600	

Cash flows in the second year

	$
Tax relief on asset	3,600
Cash inflow	25,000
Tax due – year 1 cash flow $25,000 × 25% × 0.5	(3,125)
Tax due – year 2 cash flow $25,000 × 25% × 0.5	(3,125)
	22,350
Discount factor, year 2 at 5%	0.907
Present value of cash flows in Year 2	$20,271

115 A

Annual cost of capital: 10%. Inflation rate: 4%

Real rate: (1.10/1.04) − 1 = 0.0577

Year 1 discount rate:	$1/1.0577$	0.945
Year 2 discount rate:	$1/(1.0577^2)$	0.894
Year 3 discount rate:	$1/(1.0577^3)$	0.845
Year 4 discount rate:	$1/(1.0577^4)$	0.799
		———
		3.483
		———

Annual inflow years 1–4: 6,000 × $12 = $72,000

			Discount rate	$
Year 0	Investment	$250,000	0	250,000
Year 1–4	Inflow	$72,000	3.483	250,776
				———
	NPV			$776 i.e. $800
				———

Alternatively, you can reach the same solution (with some differences possibly for rounding error) by inflating all the cash flows at 4% to their 'out-turn' amount, and discounting these inflated cash flows at the money cost of capital, 10%. The cash flows would be ($72,000 × 1.04) $74,880 in year 1, $77,875 in year 2, $80,990 in year 3 and $84,230 in year 4.

116 C

The annual cash inflows over four years of $72,000 per annum will pay back the $250,000 investment in $250,000/$72,000 = 3.5 years. By looking at the cumulative present value table we can see that, over a four-year period, the rate that gives a discount factor of 3.5 over four years is between 5% (when the rate is 3.546) and 6% (when the rate is 3.465). To get to an approximate rate:

Rate at 5%	3.546
Rate at 6%	3.465
	———
	0.081
	———

This means that each 0.1% between 5% and 6% is worth 0.081/10 = 0.0081 discount rate.

Rate at 5%	3.546
Rate at x%	3.500
	———
	0.046
	———

The number of 0.1 percentage points to add to 5% is 0.046/0.0081 = 5.7

Therefore the discount rate x that gives a nil NPV after three years is 5.57.

Formula for discount rate where there is inflation: $[(1+r)/(1+I)] - 1 =$ discount rate

$$[(1 + r)/(1.06)] - 1 = 0.0557$$

$$r = (1.0557 \times 1.06) - 1$$

Real cost of capital $= 0.119$, i.e. 11.9%.

The answer is C, allowing for rounding errors in the calculations.

117 B

Year	Cash inflow/(outflow)	Discount factor @ 8%	Present value $
0	(60,000)	1.000	(60,000)
1	23,350	0.926	21,622
2	29,100	0.857	24,939
3	27,800	0.794	22,073
Net present value			8,634

Workings

Cash flows

Flow $	Probability	$
Year 1		
35,000	0.25	8,750
20,000	0.55	11,000
18,000	0.20	3,600
Expected value		23,350
Year 2		
40,000	0.25	10,000
26,000	0.55	14,300
24,000	0.20	4,800
Expected value		29,100
Year 3		
32,000	0.25	8,000
28,000	0.55	15,400
22,000	0.20	4,400
Expected value		27,800

118 **A**

Annual cost of capital: 8%

Inflation rate: 3%

Real rate: (1.08/1.03) − 1 = 0.0485

Year 1 discount rate:	1/1.0485	0.954
Year 2 discount rate:	$1/(1.0485^2)$	0.910
Year 3 discount rate:	$1/(1.0485^3)$	0.868
		2.732

Annual inflow years 1–3: 4,000 × $5 = $20,000

			Discount rate	$
Year 0	Investment	$50,000	0	50,000
Year 1–3	Inflow	$20,000	2.732	54,640
	NPV			4,640 i.e. $4,500

Alternatively, you can reach the same solution (with some differences possibly for rounding error) by inflating all the cash flows at 3% to their 'out-turn' amount, and discounting these inflated cash flows at the money cost of capital, 8%. The cash flows would be (20,000 × 1.03) $20,600 in year 1, $21,218 in year 2 and $21,855 in year 3.

119 **C**

The annual cash inflows over three years of $20,000 per annum will pay back the $50,000 investment in $50,000/$20,000 = 2.5 years. By looking at the cumulative present value table we can see that, over a three-year period, the rate that gives a discount factor of 2.5 over three years is between 9% (when the rate is 2.531) and 10% (when the rate is 2.487). To get to an approximate rate:

Rate at 9%	2.531
Rate at 10%	2.487
	0.044

This means that each 0.1% between 9% and 10% is worth 0.044/10 = 0.0044 discount rate.

Rate at 9%	2.531
Rate at x%	2.500
	0.031

The number of 0.1 percentage points to add to 9% is 0.031/0.0044 = 7

Therefore, the discount rate x that gives a nil NPV after three years is 9.7%.

Formula for discount rate where there is inflation: [1 + r)/(1 + I)] − 1 = discount rate

(1 + r)/(1.04) − 1 = 0.097

r = (1.097 × 1.04) − 1

Real cost of capital = 0.141 i.e. 14%

120 A

The present value of expected sales revenue is as follows:

Year	Item	Cash flow	Discount factor at 10%	PV
		$		$
1	Sales revenue	40,000	0.909	36,360
2	Sales revenue	40,000	0.826	33,040
3	Sales revenue	24,000	0.751	18,024
NPV				87,424

The NPV is $3,190, so the maximum reduction in sales price that can occur without the project ceasing to be viable is (3,190/87,424) = 0.036 = 3.6%.

121 B

The present value of the annual net cash flows, ignoring the machine cost and residual value, is: $(19,998 + 18,172 + 7,510) = $45,680.

If the machine costs $X, the net cost of the machine, in present value terms and allowing for the residual value at the end of year 3, is:

X – (0.751 × 20% of X)

= X – 0.1502X

= 0.8498X.

If 0.8498X exceeds $45,680, the project will not be viable. The maximum amount the machine can cost without the project ceasing to be viable is therefore $45,680/0.8498 = $53,754, say $54,000.

122 C

Sensitivity = NPV of project / PV of figures which vary = $320,000 / $630,000 = 51%

123

Year	Cash	15%	PV
	$		$
0	(75,000)		(75,000)
1 – 5	25,000	3.352	83,800
			8,800

Try 20%

Year	Cash	20%	PV
	$		$
0	(75,000)		(75,000)
1 – 5	25,000	2.991	74,775
			(225)

$$\text{IRR} = 15\% + \frac{8,800}{(8,800 + 225)} \times 5\%$$

$$\text{IRR} = 15\% + \frac{8,800}{9,025} \times 5\%$$

$$\text{IRR} = 19.88\%$$

124 PV of labour cost = $20,000 × 3.352

= $67,040

∴ Allowable change $= \frac{8,800}{67,040} \times 100$

= 13.13%

125 1.11/1.X6 = 1.0472

Real rate = 4.72%

126 Annuity factor $= \dfrac{1 - (1 + r)^{-n}}{r}$

$$= \frac{1 - (1.0472)^{-10}}{0.0472}$$

= 7.8278

NPV = 40,000 × 7.8278 − 300,000 = $13,112

127

Year	Discount factor	Increase in costs ($000)	Present value ($000)	Savings ($000)	Present value ($000)
1	0.833	16	13.328	150	124.95
2	0.694	20	13.880	160	111.04
3	0.579	24	13.896	170	98.43
4	0.482	30	14.460	180	86.76
			———		———
			55.564		421.18
			———		———

PV of costs increase by $55,564.

NPV falls to $22,900 − $55,564 = − $32,664

∴ PV of savings must rise by $32,664

or $\dfrac{32,664}{421,180} \times 100 = 7.8\%$

128

Year	Cash ($000)	17% discount factor	Present value ($000)
0	(400)	1.000	(400.00)
1	210	0.855	179.55
2	240	0.731	175.44
3	320	0.624	199.68
			———
			154.67

Maximum PV of advertising expenditure = $154,670.

Annualise by dividing by annuity factor for years 0 to 2 = 1 + 0.855 + 0.731 = 2.586.

Therefore, maximum cash = $154,670 ÷ 2.586 = $59,811, or $60,000 (rounded to the nearest $000).

129 NPV = $0

Let $x be annual rent.

Annuity factor for year 5 at 17% is 3.199.

∴ $x × 3.199 = 27,200

∴ $x = 8,502

130 Contribution per annum $\quad = \quad$ \$320,000 + \$160,000

$\qquad\qquad\qquad\qquad\qquad\quad = \quad$ \$480,000

Contribution per unit $\qquad = \quad$ \$180 − \$60

$\qquad\qquad\qquad\qquad\qquad\quad = \quad$ \$120 per unit

∴ Level of activity $\qquad\quad = \quad \dfrac{\$480,000}{\$120} = $ 4,000 units

NPV can fall by \$244,170.

Converted to annual cash equivalent:

$$= \quad \frac{\$244,170}{3.791} = \$64,408 \text{ per annum}$$

∴ Unit selling price can fall by up to:

$$\frac{\$64,408}{4,000\,\text{units}} \quad = \quad \$16.10 \text{ per unit}$$

As a percentage: $\dfrac{\$16.10}{\$180} \times 100 \quad = \quad 8.9\%$

131 (1 + real rate) $\quad = \quad \dfrac{(1+\text{money rate})}{(1+\text{inflation rate})}$

$$= \quad \frac{1.07}{1.04}$$

$$= \quad 1.0288$$

∴ Real rate = 2.88% per annum.

Discounting money cash flow at the money rate.

Money cash flow		Discount factor at 7%	Present value
Yr 0	(500,000)	1	(500,000)
Yr 1	$130,000 \times 1.04 = 135,200$	0.935	126,412
Yr 2	$130,000 \times 1.04^2 = 140,608$	0.873	122,751
Yr 3	$130,000 \times 1.04^3 = 146,232$	0.816	119,325
Yr 4	$130,000 \times 1.04^4 = 152,082$	0.763	116,039
	Net present value		(15,473)

Alternatively, discounting real cash flow at the real rate

		Discount factor at 7%	Present value
Yr 0	(500,000)	1	(500,000)
Yr 1–4	130,000	3.7278 (W1)	484,612
	Net present value		(15,387)

Annuity factor for a discount rate of 2.88% for four years is calculated using the formula $(1- (1+0.0288)^4)/0.0288$

132 Capital allowance in Year 2:

Year	Written down value	Capital allowance	Tax saving	Cash timing
1	$75,000	$25,000	$7,500	$3,750
2	$56,250	$18,750	$5,625	$3,750 + $2,812.50
				$2,812.50

Year	Capital allowance benefit	Annual cash inflow	Corporation tax	Net cash	Discount factor	Present value
2	$6,562.50	$20,000	$(6,000)	$20,562.50	0.857	$17,622

133 C

Profitability index = NPV per $ invested = $140,500 / $500,000 = 0.28

134 1.11/1.X6   =   1.0472

Real rate   =   4.72%

$$\frac{1-(1+r)^{-n}}{r}$$

Annuity factor   = $\dfrac{1-(1.0472)^{-10}}{0.0472}$

=   7.8278

NPV = 40,000 × 7.8278 − 300,000   = $13,112

135 The internal rate of return of the project is:

$$10\% + \frac{\$12,304}{(\$12,304 + \$3,216)} \times (15-10)\% = 14\%$$

136 B

$50,000 × 3.605 = $180,250

This would need to fall by $160,000 to make the project non-viable, a fall of

160,000/180,250 = 88.8%

137 34%

ARR	= Average annual profit / Average investment value

Cash flows received over project lifetime = $(80,000 + 90,000 + 100,000 + 60,000 + 40,000)

$$= \$370,000$$

No residual value, so depreciation over lifetime of project = full investment cost = $200,000

Lifetime profit	= $370,000 – $200,000 = $170,000
Average annual profit	= $170,000 / 5 = $34,000
Average capital invested	= $200,000 / 2
ARR = 34,000 / 100,000	= 34%

138 26%

NPV at 10% = $87,980. Discounting the cash flows using a higher discount rate, say 20% gives:

Year	Cash flow $	DF	PV $
0	(200,000)	1.000	(200,000)
1	80,000	0.833	66,640
2	90,000	0.694	62,460
3	100,000	0.579	57,900
4	60,000	0.482	28,920
5	40,000	0.402	16,080
			32,000

Using the formula:

$$IRR = A + (B - A)\frac{N_A}{N_A - N_B}$$

Where	A	=	lower discount rate	(10%)
	B	=	higher discount rate	(20%)
	N_A	=	NPV at rate A (87,980)	
	N_B	=	NPV at rate B (32,000)	

IRR (%) = 20 + (10 × 87,980/55,980) = 26%

139

Year	$000	$000
0	(400)	(400)
1	100	(300)
2	120	(180)
3	140	(40)
4	120	80

Payback period = 3 years + 40/120ths of year 4 = **3.33 years or 3 years 4 months**

140 Discounted cash flows are:

Year	$000	Present value $000	Cumulative present value $000
0	(450 × 1)	(450)	(450)
1	130 × 0.909	118.17	(331.83)
2	130 × 0.826	107.38	(224.45)
3	130 × 0.751	97.63	(126.82)
4	130 × 0.683	88.79	(38.03)
5	130 × 0.621	80.73	42.70

Discounted payback occurs in year 5 and can be estimated as:

4 years plus 38.03 / 80.73 of year five = 4.47 years

141 NPV at 10% is given as $48,000 in the question. Since the NPV is positive the IRR must be higher.

Try discounting at 20%

Year	Cash flow $000	Discount factor	Present value $000
0	(350)	1.000	(350)
1	50	0.833	42
2	110	0.694	76
3	130	0.579	75
4	150	0.482	72
5	100	0.402	40
NPV			(45)

IRR = 10% + [48/(48 + 45) × (20 − 10)%] = **15% (approx)**

142 C

Investment	J $000	K $000	L $000	M $000	N $000
Initial investment	400	350	450	500	600
Net present value (NPV)	125	105	140	160	190
Profitability index (NPV per $ invested)	0.3125	0.30	0.3111	0.32	0.3166
Ranking	3	4		1	2

J would be chosen before L and, as they are mutually exclusive, L can be disregarded.

The optimum investment plan is $500,000 in M and the remaining $500,000 in N.

143 Depreciation is not a cash flow so needs to be added back to profit to calculate cash flows.

Depreciation on straight line basis = ($400,000 − $50,000)/5 = $70,000 per year

Year	Profit ($)	Cash flow ($)	Cumulative cash flow ($)
0		(400,000)	(400,000)
1	175,000	245,000	(155,000)
2	225,000	295,000	140,000

Payback period = 1 + 145 / 295 years = 1.5 years to nearest 0.1 years

144 The present value of a $1 perpetuity is 1/r.

The present value of the rental income is $80,000/0.08 = $1,000,000

The NPV of the investment is $1,000,000 − $850,000 = $150,000

THE TREATMENT OF UNCERTAINTY IN DECISION MAKING

145 B

Project	EV $000	Workings
L	500	(500 × 0.2) + (470 × 0.5) + (550 × 0.3)
M	526	(400 × 0.2) + (550 × 0.5) + (570 × 0.3)
N	432.5	(450 × 0.2) + (400 × 0.5) + (475 × 0.3)
O	398	etc
P	497.5	

∴ Project M will maximise expected cash.

146 D

If market condition is forecast as Poor, then Project P should be chosen as this project yields the highest cash flow under a poor market.

However, if the market condition is forecast as Good or Excellent, then Project M should be chosen as M will yield the highest cash.

In summary:

Market condition	Selected project	Cash (x) $000	Probability (p)	px
Poor	P	600	0.20	120
Good	M	550	0.50	275
Excellent	M	570	0.30	171
			1.00	566

Expected return with perfect information	$566,000
Expected return without (answer to 1.2)	$526,000
∴ Value of information	$40,000

147 A probability tree may be used:

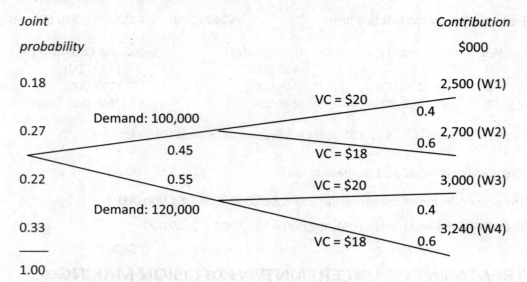

Joint   *Contribution*

probability $000

0.18   2,500 (W1)

                                                  VC = $20
                                                                  0.4
              Demand: 100,000

0.27   2,700 (W2)

                           0.45   0.6
                                                  VC = $18

0.22   0.55   VC = $20   3,000 (W3)

              Demand: 120,000   0.4

0.33   3,240 (W4)

                                                  VC = $18   0.6
_____

1.00

Existing contribution:

($50 − $21) × 90,000 units = 2,610 ($000)

Contribution is greater than this in (W2), (W3) and (W4) above.

∴ The probability of the profit being higher is:

0.27 + 0.22 + 0.33 = 0.82

Workings

(W1)   ($45 − $20) × 100,000 units

(W2)   ($45 − $18) × 100,000 units

(W3)   ($45 − $20) × 120,000 units

(W4)   ($45 − $18) × 120,000 units

148 Expected demand:

(100,000 × 0.45) + (120,000 × 0.55)   111,000 units

Expected variable cost:

($20 × 0.40) + ($18 × 0.60) $18.80

Contribution per unit:

$45 − $18.50 $26.20

Expected contribution:

111,000 × $26.20 $2,908,200

Less fixed costs   ($1,200,000)

                                             _____

Expected profit $1,708,200

                                             _____

149 Produce a payoff table:

Demand	Probability	Supply		
		100	200	300
100 units	0.25	$400	$0 (W1)	($400) (W2)
200 units	0.40	$400	$800	$400 (W3)
300 units	0.35	$400	$800	$1,200

Workings

(W1) $100 \times \$8 - 200 \times \$4$	=		$0
(W2) $100 \times \$8 - 300 \times \$4$	=		($400)
(W3) $200 \times \$8 - 300 \times \$4$	=		$400

Expected profits:

If supply 100 units, EVs = $400

If supply 200 units, EV = $0 × 0.25 + $800 × 0.4 + $800 × 0.35 = $600

If supply 300 units, EV = ($400) × 0.25 + $400 × 0.4 + $1,200 × 0.35 = $480

∴ Profit is maximised by supplying 200 units.

150 To generate a contribution greater than $20,000 it is necessary to earn a unit contribution greater than $20. Consider each of the feasible combinations:

Selling price $	Variable cost $	Contribution per unit $	Probability
50	20	30	0.45 × 0.55 = 0.2475
60	20	40	0.25 × 0.55 = 0.1375
60	30	30	0.25 × 0.25 = 0.0625
		Answer =	**0.4475**

Answer = 44.75%

151 D

Expected selling price		Expected cost	
	$		$
$20 × 0.25	5	$8 × 0.2	1.6
$25 × 0.4	10	$10 × 0.5	5
330 × 0.35	10.5	$12 × 0.3	3.6
	25.5		10.2

Expected unit contribution = $25.50 − $10.20 = $15.30 × 1,000 = $15,300

152 C

Monthly contribution will exceed $13,500 if unit contribution exceeds $13.50. This will be the case for the following combinations:

Sales price	Variable cost	Probability	Joint probability
$25	$8	0.4×0.2	0.08
$25	$10	0.4×0.2	0.20
$30	($8)		
$30	($10)	0.35×1	0.35
$30	($12)		
Total			0.63

153 Contribution table

		Daily demand		
		10	*11*	*12*
	10 (W1)	500	500	500
Batches baked	11 (W2)	480	550	550
	12 (W3)	460	530	600

Workings

(W1) If 10 batches are baked they will all be sold earning a contribution of $500

(W2) If 11 batches are baked and 10 are sold this earns a contribution of $10 \times 50 - 20 = 480$

(W3) If 12 batches are baked and 10 are sold contribution = $10 \times 50 - 40 = 460$

A regret table can now be produced which shows the shortfall from the maximum contribution that could be earned at each demand level. So, if demand is 12 batches, the maximum contribution is $600. If only 10 batches are baked, the contribution earned is $500, a regret of $100.

Regret table		Daily demand			
		10	*11*	*12*	*Max. Regret*
	10	0	50	100	100
Batches baked	11	20	0	50	50
	12	40	20	0	40

So to minimise the maximum regret bake 12 batches.

The following combinations of selling price and variable cost per unit yield a contribution of more than $20 per unit:

Selling price	Variable cost	Contribution	Probability
$50	$20	$30	$0.45 \times 0.55 = 0.2475$
$60	$30	$30	$0.25 \times 0.25 + 0.0625$
$60	$20	$40	$0.25 \times 0.55 + 0.1375$
			0.4475

Answer = 44.75%

MANAGING SHORT-TERM FINANCE

154 C

Businesses that regularly fail to pay their suppliers on time may find it difficult to obtain future credit.

155 D

A conservative working capital policy is one which only uses short-term financing for part of the fluctuating current assets..

156 The answer is $755,760.

		Cash received
		$
April sales	20% × $780,000	156,000
March sales	80% × 0.98 × $770,000 × 60%	362,208
February sales	80% × 0.98 × $760,000 × 30%	178,752
January sales	80% × 0.98 × $750,000 × 10%	58,800
		755,760

157 B

The current ratio is all current assets including inventory divided by current liabilities, while the acid test is the current asset figure *less inventory* divided by current liabilities. These can only be equal if a firm carries no inventory.

158 The answer is $4,800.

	Current assets	Current liabilities
	$	$
Credit purchase:		
Inventory	+ 18,000	
Trade payables		+ 18,000
Credit sale:		
Trade receivables	+ 24,000	
Inventory (24,000 × 100/125)	− 19,200	

Working capital will increase by $4,800, as a result of the credit sale.

159 The answer is $252,000.

	$
Budgeted sales	240,000
Expected decrease in receivables	12,000
	252,000

The reduction in receivables means that the company will expect to receive more cash next month than the total of its credit sales for the month. Changes in inventory levels have no effect on expected cash receipts.

160 The answer is 44.24 days.

Receivables

	$		$
B/f	68,000	Returns	2,500
Sales	250,000	Cash	252,100
		Irrecoverable debts	
		$(68,000 \times 0.05)$	3,400
		C/f	60,000
	318,000		318,000

Receivable days = $60/495 \times 365$ = 44.24 days

(**Note:** The estimated sales cover a period of only six months, so the annual sales figure is $495,000 ($2 \times 250,000 - 2,500$.)

161 B

Turnover cycle		Days
Inventory	$(8/30) \times 365$	97.3
Trade receivables	$(4/40) \times 365$	36.5
Trade payables	$(3/15) \times 365$	(73.0)
Cash conversion cycle		60.8

Note: The annual cost of purchases would be useful for measuring the inventory turnover period for raw materials. Since the question does not state whether inventory is mainly raw materials, work-in-progress or finished goods, it is probably appropriate to use the annual cost of sales to measure the average inventory turnover time. However, it is reasonable to assume that most trade payables relate to purchases of raw materials, and the annual purchases figure has been used to calculate the payment cycle for trade payables.

162 C

Average receivables = ($10 million + $12 million)/2 = $11 million

Average trade-related receivables = 90% × $11 million = $9.9 million

Annual sales on credit = $95 million

Average collection period = (9.9 million/95 million) × 365 days = 38 days

163 B

	$
Balance b/fwd	22,000
Credit sales	290,510
	312,510
Less: Balance c/fwd ($290,510 × 49/365)	(39,000)
Receipts	273,510

164 B

	$
Purchases on credit	360,000
Increase in trade payables	15,000
Therefore payments to suppliers	345,000

165 C

($82,000 − 12,250) × 97% = $67,657

166 The answer is $345,589.

	$
Owed to credit suppliers at 1 November 2006	42,000
Cost of goods sold	350,000
Less: Opening inventory reflected in cost of goods sold	(56,000)
Add: Closing inventory deducted from cost of goods sold	
60/365 × 350,000	57,534
Less: Amounts owed to credit suppliers at 31 October 2007	
50/365 × 350,000	(47,945)
Amount paid to credit suppliers during the year to 31 October 2007	345,589

167 The answer is 88.4 days.

Trade receivable days = 290/2,400 × 365 = 44.1 days

Inventory days (assuming that inventories are finished goods)

= 360/1,400 × 365 = 93.9 days

Trade payable days = 190/1,400 × 365 = 49.6 days

Working capital cycle = Inventory days + Receivable days − Payable days

= 93.9 + 44.1 − 49.6 = 88.4 days

168 The answer is $19,800.

Sales in	Total sales	Cash sales	Credit sales	Received in May	
	$	$	$		$
April	20,000	8,000	12,000	(97% × 12,000)	11,640
May	20,400	8,160	12,240		8,160
					19,800

169 B

Overtrading is associated with fast-growing companies that have insufficient long-term capital, and rely on short-term liabilities to finance their growth. The finance is largely provided by suppliers (trade payables) and a bank overdraft. As a result, there is an increasing bank overdraft (higher borrowing) and very low or even negative working capital. A typical overtrading enterprise is experiencing rapid growth and rising sales. Although it should be profitable, its problem will be a shortage of cash and liquidity. Cash balances will be not be rising, since the overdraft is increasing.

170 D

An aged analysis for trade payables is an analysis of unpaid invoices from suppliers according to the length of time since the issue of the invoice. It is not a list (therefore answer A and answer B are incorrect), but a table. A spreadsheet might be used to construct the analysis. The analysis can be used to decide which suppliers should be paid, and how much.

An aged analysis for trade receivables is similar, except that it relates to unpaid invoices sent to credit customers. This analysis is used to decide which customers to 'chase' for payment.

171 C

The equivalent annual return offered by supplier P is:

$(100/99)^{12} - 1 = 12.82\%$

This is below the minimum required rate of return of 12.85% and should not be accepted.

The equivalent annual return offered by supplier Q is:

$(100/98)^{12/2} - 1 = 12.89\%$

This is just above the minimum required rate of return of 12.85% and therefore should be accepted.

172 The answer is 27.86%.

Annual rate of interest $= (100/98)^{(365/30 - 0)} - 1$

$= 0.2786$ or 27.86%

173 The three main services provided by a without recourse factor are:

- sales ledger administration/debt collection
- credit insurance (which is the without recourse element of the service)
- factor finance (providing short-term finance against the security of the unpaid invoices).

174 C

Invoice discounting is a method of obtaining short-term funds. Specific invoices are 'sold' to a finance organisation, typically a factor, which provides finance up to a proportion (about 70%) of the value of the invoice. The invoice discounter is repaid with interest out of the money from the invoice payment, when it is eventually paid.

175 D

If $1 million is invested for one year at 7%, the value of the investment will be $1,000,000 × 1.07 = $1,070,000 after one year.

If $1 million is invested for three months at 6.5% per year and then for nine months at 7.5% per year, this means that the interest for the first three months will be 6.5% × 3/12 = 1.625%, and the interest for the next nine months will be 7.5% × 9/12 = 5.625%. The value of the investment after one year will therefore be:

$1,000,000 × 1.01625 × 1.05625 = $1,073,414.

This is $3,414 more than the income that would be obtained by investing at 7% for the full year. However, there is a risk that interest rates will not rise during the first three months, and XYZ will not be able to invest at 7.5% for the nine months, but only at a lower rate.

176 A

The customer cannot be asked for immediate payment once a bill of exchange has been accepted.

177 C

The instrument is a bill of exchange drawn on the bank. This is often called a bank bill (as distinct from a commercial bill, which is a bill drawn on a non-bank company). A bill drawn on a bank under a short-term financing arrangement is also known as an acceptance credit.

178 A

Forfaiting is a method of obtaining medium-term export finance, involving the issue of promissory notes by the importer/buyer, which the exporter is able to sell to a forfaiting bank at a discount to obtain finance. Promissory notes are promises to pay a specified amount of money at a specified future date. The importer's promissory notes have settlement dates spread over a number of years, often the expected useful economic life of the imported items. The importer is therefore able to pay for the imported goods over a period of several years, whilst the exporter can obtain immediate payment by selling the promissory notes.

179 Forms of short-term finance generally available to small entities include:

- trade credit
- bank overdraft
- term loan
- factoring
- hire purchase or leasing.

180 The answer is 40.4%.

AL offers 1.5% interest for 16 days

(100/98.5) (365/16) – 1 =

(1.015) 22.813 – 1 = 40.4%

181 A

Working capital financing involves deciding the mix of long-term and short-term debt. An aggressive policy involves using short-term finance to fund all the fluctuating current assets, as well as some of the permanent part of the current assets. So answer A is correct. A conservative policy is where all of the permanent assets (i.e. non-current assets and the permanent part of current assets) are financed by long-term funding. Short-term financing is only used for part of the fluctuating current assets. So answer B is incorrect. A moderate policy matches short-term finance to the fluctuating current assets and long-term finance to the permanent part of current assets plus non-current assets. So answer D is also incorrect.

182 The answer is 14.8%.

Annual cost = $(100/98.5)^{(365/(60-20))} - 1$

= $(100/98.5)^{9.125} - 1$

= 14.8%

183

	$
June debts: 345 + 520 + 150 – 200 – 520	295
July debts: 233 – 233	0
Augusts debts: 197 + 231 – 197	231
September debts: 319	319
	845

184 B

(70,000 + 10,000) : (88,000 + 7,000)

80,000 : 95,000

0.84 : 1

185   The answer is 500 units.

Optimal order quantity = $\sqrt{\dfrac{2 \times 200 \times 10,000}{[4 + (3\% \times 400)]}}$

= 500 units

186   B

With JIT purchasing, the objective is to receive deliveries exactly at the time required, so that the ideal inventory level is always 0. Therefore inventory holding costs should be lower. There will be an increased dependence on suppliers to deliver exactly on time, but there will be a risk (probably an increased risk) of inventory shortages due to failure by suppliers to deliver on time. However, since purchases will be made to meet demand requirements, there are likely to be much more frequent deliveries.

187   A

The simple EOQ model formula is:

EOQ $= \sqrt{\dfrac{2cd}{h}}$

where   d   =   annual demand
           h   =   cost of holding one unit for one year
           c   =   cost of placing order

188   C

EOQ $= \sqrt{\dfrac{2C_oD}{C_h}} = \sqrt{\dfrac{2 \times \$185 \times 2,500}{\$25}}$

     $= \sqrt{37,000}$

     = 192 units

Each week $\dfrac{2,500}{52}$ = 48 units are required.

Therefore each order of 192 units will last $\dfrac{192}{48}$ = 4 weeks.

189   The answer is $895.

$\sqrt{\dfrac{2 \times \$15 \times 32,000}{\$1.2}} = \sqrt{800,000} = 894.43\,\text{units}$

190   A

The cost of placing an order under the EOQ formula includes administrative costs, postage and quality control costs.

191   The answer is 98

$$Q = \sqrt{\frac{2C_oD}{C_h}}$$

$$\sqrt{\frac{2 \times 15 \times 95,000}{3}} = 974.68$$

$95,000/975 = 97.4$.

192   The answer is 10.5%.

The yield to maturity must be more than the coupon rate of 7% as the purchase price of the bond is less than maturity value. Using the maths tables to compute the present values of the sums receivable under the bond, the maturity value can be calculated as follows:

$t = 8$; $r = 10$

$(7 \times 5.335) + (100 \times 0.467) = 37.345 + 46.7 = \$84.045$

$t = 8$; $r = 11$

$(7 \times 5.146) + (100 \times 0.434) = 36.022 + 43.4 + \$79.422$

By interpolation:

$10\% + ((84.045 - 82.0)/(84.045 - 79.422)) = 10\% + (2.045/4.623) = 10.44\%$

193   The answer is $8,863.7.

$\$700 \times$ (Annuity factor for $t = 5$; $r = 10$) $+ 10,000 \times$ (Discount factor $t = 5$; $r = 10$) $=$
$(\$700 \times 3.791) + (10,000 \times 0.621) = 2,653.7 + 6,210 = \$8,863.7$

194   The answer is 7.2%

Using $t = 7$ and $r = 6$ and 8, from tables

(4×5.582) and $(100 \times 0.665) = 22.328 + 66.5 = 88.828$

(4×5.206) and $(100 \times 0.583) = 20.824 + 58.3 = 79.124$

$$6 + \left\{ \frac{88.828 - 83.00}{88.828 - 79.124} \right\} \times 2 = 6 + \left\{ \frac{5.828}{9.704} \times 2 \right\}$$

$6 + 1.20 = 7.20\%$

195   The answer is 7.77%.

Interest = 0.06 × 100 = 6 pa for 10 years

Gain on redemption = 100 − 88 = 12

The yield to maturity is effectively the internal rate of return of the bond, which is found by trial and error. Let us assume a discount rate of 8% for the first calculation:

Time	Cash flow	Discount factor @ 8%	Discounted cash flow
	$		$
T_0	(88)	1	(88)
$T_1 - T_{10}$	6	6.710	40.26
T_{10}	100	0.463	46.3
			(1.44)

As this gives an NPV close to zero, use 7% for our next calculation:

Time	Cash flow	Discount factor @ 7%	Discounted cash flow
	$		$
T_0	(88)	1	(88)
$T_1 - T_{10}$	6	7.024	42.14
T_{10}	100	0.508	50.8
			4.94

Change in NPV between 7% and 8% is 6.38 (4.94 + 1.44) so, to get an NPV of zero, rate needs to be:

8% − 1.44/6.38 = 8 − 0.23 = 7.77%

MARCH 12 EXAM ANSWERS

196   C

197   A

Net Present Value of the project = $180,000

Present value of the annual cash outflow = $100,000 x 3.312 = $331,200

Sensitivity = $180,000/$331,200 = 54.3%

198   C

Staffing mix	Fee level			
	Deluxe	High	Standard	Low
X	$5,000	0	$2,500	$20,000
Y	$15,000	$5,000	0	$5,000
Z	$35,000	$20,000	$7,500	0
Maximum regret	$35,000	$20,000	$7,500	$20,000

From the regret matrix, the Standard fee strategy minimises the maximum regret.

199 A

Co = (cost per order) = $160

D = (annual demand) = 26,000 units

Ch = (cost of holding one unit for one year) = $1.40

$$\text{EOQ} = \sqrt{\frac{2 \times 160 \times 26{,}000}{1.46}}$$

200 D

Number of orders = 26,000 / 2,600 = 10 per year

Ordering costs = 10 x $160 = $1,600

Holding costs = 2,600 x 0.5 x $1.40 = $1,820

Total ordering and holding costs = $3,420

201

The holders of an accepted bill of exchange can do one of the following:

(i)   Hold the bill until the due date and collect the money

(ii)   Discount the bill with the bank for immediate payment

(iii) Transfer the bill to a third party in settlement of an amount due.

202

Time	Cash flow $	Discount factor 12%	Present value $
0	(50,000)	1.000	(50,000)
1 - ∞	5,670	1 / 0.09 = 11.111	63,000
Net present value			13,000

The net present value of the project is $13,000

1.8The fixed costs will remain the same therefore the contribution has to exceed $2,880,000.

203

The possible outcomes and the probability of them occurring are given below:

100,000 x ($48 - $21) = $2,700,000 Joint probability is 0.40 x 0.25 = 0.10
100,000 x ($48 - $19) = $2,900,000 Joint probability is 0.40 x 0.75 = 0.30
120,000 x ($48 - $21) = $3,240,000 Joint probability is 0.60 x 0.25 = 0.15
120,000 x ($48 - $19) = $3,480,000 Joint probability is 0.60 x 0.75 = 0.45
                                                                      1.00

The probability therefore that the contribution will exceed $2,880,000 is 90%.

MAY 12 EXAM ANSWERS

204 D

205 A

206 A

Variable costs per unit	=($290,000 − $200,000) / (100,000 − 64,000)
	= $2.50
Fixed costs	=$290,000 − (100,000 x $2.50)
	= $40,000

At an activity level of 85,000 units, distribution costs will therefore be:

(85,000 x $2.50) + $40,000 = $252,500

207 B

Accounts receivable days	(10/48) x 365	76.0
Inventory days	(8/(48 x 0.6)) x 365	101.4
Accounts payable days	(5/(48 x 0.6)) x 365	(63.4)
		114.0

The cash operating cycle is 114 days.

208 C

Annual interest = ($250,000 x 80%) x 10% = $20,000

209

Payment will be made 38 days early.

Number of compounding periods = 365/38 = 9.60526

1+ r = (1.00/0.97) 9.60526

1+ r = 1.3399

The effective annual interest rate of the early settlement discount is 34.0%

210

The abandonment decision should be based on future cash flows:

Year	Cash flow $	Discount factor	Present value $
1	(90,000)	0.893	(80,370)
2	60,000	0.797	47,820
3	40,000	0.712	28,480
			(4,070)

As the net present value of the future cash flows is negative the project should be abandoned.

211

    (i)   The production budget for Product R for next year will be:

		units
Closing inventory	6,000 x 0.90	5,400
Plus: sales		80,000
		85,400
Less opening inventory		(6,000)
Production required		79,400

    (ii)   The purchases budget for Material T for next year will be

		kg
Closing inventory		75,000
Plus: production	79,400 units x 6 kg	476,400
		551,400
Less opening inventory		(60,000)
Purchases required		491,400

SEPTEMBER 12 EXAM ANSWERS

212 C

August credit sales	= 200,000 x 60% x 97%	= $116,400
September cash sales	= 204,000 x 40%	= $81,600
Total cash received	= $116,400 + $81,600	= $198,000

213 D

Selling price – material costs = $28.50 - $9.25 = $19.25

Return per hour = ($19.25 / 7.8) x 60 = $148.08

214 B

20% of October sales	= $ 56,000
65% of November sales	= $162,500
15% of December sales x 0.95	= $ 42,750
Total cash paid	= $261,250

215 A

216 D

217

(i) Costs that varied with number of parcels = $194,400 x 70% x 60% = $81,648

Cost per parcel last year = $81,648 /15,120 = $5.40

Parcel related cost for next year = $5.40 x 1.03 x 18,360 = $102,118

(ii) Costs that vary with kilometres travelled = $194,400 x 70% x 40% = $54,432

Cost per km = $54,432 / 120,960 = $0.45

Distance related costs for next year = $0.45 x 1.03 x 128,800 = $59,699

218

The net present value of the project is $98,200.

If the present value of the contribution was to decrease by more than $98,200 then the project would cease to be viable. As a percentage this is:

$98,200 / $389,340 = 25.2%

Which represents a decrease in the annual contribution of $108,000 x 0.252 = $27,216

219

(i) The labour rate planning variance for August

(22,000 units x 0.5) x ($17.50 - $14) = $38,500 A

(ii) The labour rate operational variance for August

11,400 hrs x ($17.50 - $15.50) = $22,800 F

(iii) The labour efficiency operational variance for August

((22,000 x 0.5 hour) - 11,400 hrs) x $17.50= $7,000 A

Section 5

ANSWERS TO SECTION B-TYPE QUESTIONS

COST ACCOUNTING SYSTEMS

220 MARGINAL COST PROFIT AND CASH FLOW

Marginal costing systems differ from absorption costing systems in the way that they treat fixed production overheads. In a marginal costing system the fixed production overheads are charged against the sales revenue in the period that they are incurred.

In contrast an absorption costing system will attribute some of the fixed production overheads to any units held in inventory and thus some fixed production overheads will be carried forward in inventory to future periods. These overheads will not be charged in calculating the profit in the month they are incurred, but in the month when the inventory is sold i.e. the charging of the fixed overheads against profit does not reflect the actual cash flow.

Thus marginal costing profits will provide a better indication of cash flow than will absorption costing profits, since more of the costs actually incurred will be charged against the sales revenue for the period. However there will still be a discrepancy between marginal costing profits and cash flow because of factors such as credit sales and purchases and the treatment of capital expenditure in profit calculations.

221 BACKFLUSH ACCOUNTING (SEPT 10)

In a traditional accounting system, inventory is a key item. Therefore detailed inventory records are kept and costs (for items such as labour, materials and overheads) are tracked at each stage of production and charged to inventory. This is done so that the cost of using inventory is accurately recorded in the income statement and that closing inventory is properly valued on the balance sheet.

Just-In-Time (JIT) control systems hold negligible levels of inventory and therefore the traditional costing system is less important. Companies who employ JIT are more likely to use backflush accounting. Instead of charging costs to inventory at each stage of production, backflush accounting values closing inventory (if there is any) at standard cost and the balance of costs are deemed to be production costs that get charged to the income statement.

This is a much simpler and quicker method, though it is less accurate than the traditional system. However, because inventory levels are very low, accuracy becomes much less important.

222 ACTIVITY BASED COSTING (MAR 12)

Cost driver rates

Set up costs	$200,000 / 800 = $250 per set up
Inspection/quality costs	$120,000 / 400 = $300 per test
Stores receiving	$252,000 / 1,800 = $140 per requisition

Product W cost per unit

Direct materials	$2.50
Direct labour	$0.54

Set up costs: 15,000/150 units = 100 batches x $250 = $25,000 / 15,000 units = $1.67

Inspection/ quality cost: quality tests 100/2 = 50 x $300 = $15,000 / 15,000 units = $1.00

Stores receiving costs: 80 x $140 = $11,200 / 15,000 units = $0.75

Total production costs = $2.50 + $0.54 + $1.67 + $1.00 + $0.75 = $6.46

Examiner's comments

This question was reasonably well answered. Most candidates calculated the cost driver rates correctly but some had difficulty in applying these rates to calculate a cost per unit. Some candidates assumed that the cost driver rate was the cost per unit of W.

Common errors

* Inability to calculate the cost per unit.

* Using the cost driver rate as the cost per unit.

* Failing to calculate a cost per unit.

* Omitting the labour and material costs.

---

223 ABSORPTION COSTING (MAR 12)

(i) **Gross profit**

	January $000	February $000
Gross profit	568.40	705.60
Over/(under) absorption of fixed overheads	(30.00)	28.00
Gross profit	538.40	733.60

Workings:

January:

Gross profit = 9,800 units x ($135 -$45 - $32) = $568,400

Under absorption of fixed overhead = (10,000 units x $32) − $350,000 = $30,000

February:

Gross profit = 11,200 units x ($140 - $45 - $32) = $705,600

Over absorption of fixed overhead = (11,500 units x $32) - $340,000 = $28,000

(ii)   **Reconciliation of profits**

Profit using absorption costing	$538.40k
Profit using marginal costing	$532.00k
Difference	$ 6.40k

Increase in inventory in January = 200 units

Absorbed fixed overheads included in inventory under absorption costing:

200 units x $32 = $6,400

Examiner's comments

This question was answered very poorly, clearly showing a knowledge gap. Although candidates could explain in part (ii) that under marginal costing the fixed overheads are period costs and that under absorption costing the fixed overheads are absorbed into inventory, they were unable to calculate the figures required for part (i).

Common errors

- Calculating absorbed overheads using normal capacity rather than actual production.

- Inability to calculate opening and closing inventory valuations.

In part (ii), not using calculations to explain the difference in profit figures.

---

224   IMPROVING THE THROUGHPUT ACCOUNTING RATIO

$$\text{TA ratio} = \frac{\text{throughput per hour of bottleneck resource}}{\text{operating expenses per hour of bottleneck resource}}$$

Three actions that could be considered to improve the TA ratio are as follows:

(i)   Increase the selling price of the product. This would improve the throughput per hour in the packing process, i.e. the numerator in the calculation and the TA ratio would increase.

(ii)   Reduce the operating expenses in the packing process. This would reduce the denominator in the ratio calculation.

(iii)   Improve the productivity of the employees engaged in the packing process, thus reducing the time taken to pack each unit of product C. Throughput per packing hour would increase, but the operating expenses per packing hour would remain unchanged. Therefore the TA ratio would increase.

225   ABC AND PROFITABILITY

Activity based costing (ABC) could provide more meaningful information about product costs and profitability in the following circumstances.

(i)   Where indirect costs are high relative to direct costs. The cost of direct materials, for example, can usually be attributed to cost units relatively easily. The attribution of overhead costs tends to be more problematic. Traditionally, overhead costs have been attributed to cost units by fairly arbitrary methods such as absorption costing on the basis of direct labour hours. The introduction of new technology has typically resulted in a reduction in labour cost and an increase in overhead cost and labour hours may no longer be an appropriate absorption basis. An ABC approach should lead to more accurate costings of products and departments by considering the processes that actually cause overhead costs to be incurred.

(ii)   Where products or services are complex. By identifying the activities that consume resources and the cost drivers for each activity, the costs incurred can be traced more accurately to products and services according to the number of cost drivers that they generate.

(iii)   Where some products or services are produced in large numbers but others are produced in small numbers. Products and services incur overhead costs because of the activities that go into producing them. These activities are not necessarily related to the volumes that are produced. An ABC system recognises that direct labour hours and machine hours are not the drivers of cost in many modern business environments.

(iv)   Where products or services are tailored to customer specifications. An ABC system is more likely to trace accurately the costs incurred on each specific customer order. The result will be more accurate cost determination which will help in decisions such as pricing.

226   MANUFACTURING RESOURCE PLANNING SYSTEM (MAY 07)

A manufacturing resource planning system contains details of all of the inputs into production, including raw materials, components, labour and machine capacity, and coordinates these to provide an optimal production and purchasing plan.

In order to ensure that a manufacturing resource planning system operates effectively it is essential to have:

- A master production schedule, which specifies both the timing and quantity demanded of each product.

- A bill of materials file for each sub-assembly, component and part, containing details of the number of items on hand, scheduled receipts and items allocated to released orders but not yet drawn from inventories.

- A master parts file containing planned lead times of all items to be purchased and sub-assemblies and components to be produced internally.

- A master labour and machine capacity file which specifies both the timing and quantity demanded to achieve planned production levels.

- Details of inputs can then be used in a standard costing system to set parameters for materials, labour and overhead capacity. These will then be used to measure performance through variance analysis.

227   JUST-IN-TIME (MAY 07)

Just-in-time (JIT) is a system whose objective is to produce or procure products or components as they are required by a customer or for use, rather than for inventory. It is a philosophy which aims to eliminate all waste and non value adding activities in an organisation. The main differences between JIT and a traditional manufacturing environment are:

- JIT is a 'pull system' which responds to demand, in contrast to a 'push system' in a traditional manufacturing environment, in which inventories act as buffers between the different elements of the system, such as purchasing, production and sales.

- The main focus in a traditional manufacturing environment is on maximising output and minimising costs. In a JIT environment it may be more cost effective to allow resources to stand idle than to produce goods for inventory.

- In a traditional manufacturing environment labour are organised into specialist roles and performance is measured against pre determined standards. In a JIT environment labour are multi skilled and carry out routine maintenance tasks as well as working on products. They are empowered to find methods of cost reduction.

- Companies using JIT are likely to have long term contracts with few, carefully chosen suppliers, whereas traditional producers will seek the cheapest quote from several suppliers for raw materials.

228 THROUGHPUT ACCOUNTING (SEPT 11)

(i) **Return per machine hour**

	Product A	Product B
	$	$
Selling price	46	62
Material cost	(18)	(16)
Throughput contribution	28	46
Machine hours per unit	0.5 hours	0.8 hours
Return per machine hour	56	57.50

(ii) **Profit for the period**

	Product A	Product B	Total
Return per machine hour	$56	$57.50	
Ranking	2	1	
Units produced	3,200	8,000	
Machine hours	1,600	6,400	8,000
Contribution per machine hour	$56	$57.5	
Total contribution	$89,600	$368,000	$457,600
Factory costs			$248,000
Total profit			$209,600

229 MRP AND ABB (MAY 10)

(a) **Manufacturing Resource Planning (MRP)**

MRP is a computerised planning system for materials. It determines the quantity and timing of the finished goods demanded and uses this to determine the requirements for raw materials etc. at each prior stage of production. It would therefore replace the existing EOQ system for ordering materials which relies on constant and predictable demand. The MRP system can cope with varying demand and take account of the changes in the company's environment.

An MRP system is very flexible and can account for sudden changes in demand. It can also cope better with bespoke/customised products and create a production and ordering system for each 'job'.

It should also reduce inventory levels as it would not order items that were not needed. However, in this particular instance it would appear that the biggest benefit would be in improved inventory levels – the purchasing department would know exactly what type and quantity of materials would be required and when it would be required. This should remove the difficulties that currently being experienced.

(b) **Activity Based Budgeting (ABB)**

ABB is defined as 'a method of budgeting based on an activity framework and utilising cost driver data in the budget-setting and variance feedback processes' (CIMA Official Terminology). This means that cost drivers would be identified for each activity and a cost per unit of activity in each cost pool would be used as a charge to products.

The company in question are likely to experiencing a rise in overheads due to a change in their production methods (for example, there might be more machine running costs or greater supervision etc.). ABB would give better detail on the make-up and causes of these overheads which would allow better cost control and planning.

The existing incremental system is likely to simply build on past deficiencies and not consider the changes in the company's environment and its production methods. It will also potentially have a poor identification of the nature and cause of overheads. ABB should eradicate both of these problems.

230 TOTAL QUALITY MANAGEMENT (MAY 08)

Three elements that are present in any business that is successfully focused on a TQM programme are:

- **Customer focus**. Quality is examined from a customer perspective and the system is aimed at meeting customer needs and expectations.
- **Continuous improvement**. The 'kaizen' system aims to make lots of small improvements over time that add up to overall large improvements.
- **Getting things right first time**. TQM aims for zero defects and zero waste. It recognises that it costs less to prevent problems than it does to rectify mistakes afterwards.

231 ENVIRONMENTAL COSTING (NOV 11)

Increased awareness of the impact of environment related activities on their financial statements

Organisations that alter their management accounting practices to incorporate environmental concerns will have greater awareness of the impact of environment related activities on their financial statements. This is because conventional management accounting systems tend to attribute many environmental costs to general overhead accounts with the result that they are "hidden" from management.

Cost reduction

Organisations which adopt environmental cost management principles are more likely to identify and take advantage of cost reduction and other improvement opportunities.

Improved decision making

A concern with environmental costs will also reduce the chances of employing incorrect pricing of products and services and taking the wrong options in terms of mix and development decisions. This in turn may lead to enhanced customer value while reducing the risk profile attaching to investments and other decisions which have long term consequences.

Avoidance of costs of failure

A lack of concern for the environment can result in significant costs, for example the associated costs of clean-up and financial penalties associated with environmental disasters.

Avoidance of damage to the company's reputation

A concern with environmental costs will also reduce the risk of damage to the company's reputation. The well publicised Brent Spar incident that cost the oil company Shell millions of pounds in terms of lost revenues via the resultant consumer boycott is an example of the powerful influence that environmental concern has in today's business environment. Shell learned the lesson, albeit somewhat belatedly and as a result completely re-engineered their environmental management system.

Tutorial note

The answer provides five examples. Only three of these are needed in the exam and students should not attempt to include more than three methods.

Examiner's comments

This was reasonably well answered, particularly since it has not previously been examined. Candidates obviously knew the area well although many strayed from discussions of environmental costing into general narrative about the benefits of being an environmentally friendly company, giving several examples of how a company could achieve that status. This was all very interesting but not worthy of any marks unless the discussion was linked to environmental costing. There was also evidence of very poor exam technique with far too much being written in answer to a question worth five marks.

Common errors

- Failure to specifically relate the answer to environmental costing
- Poor exam technique

---

232 ENVIRONMENTAL COSTS (MAR 12)

Environmental internal failure costs

These are costs that are incurred after hazardous materials, waste and/or other contaminants have been produced. The costs are incurred in order to comply with both externally and internally imposed standards. Examples include treating and disposing of toxic materials and recycling costs.

Environmental external failure costs

These are incurred when there are failures of internal control and hazardous materials, waste or contaminants have been introduced into the environment. Examples of costs that an organisation has to pay include decontaminating land or cleaning a river after leakages. Organisations may also be subject to penalties imposed by the government for these external failures. These costs can give rise to adverse publicity. Some external failure costs may be caused by the organisation but 'paid' by society.

233 MARGINAL COSTING AND THROUGHPUT ACCOUNTING (MAY 06)

The underlying methodology is the same except that throughput accounting (TA) assumes that direct materials are the only 'variable' cost and that labour is a fixed cost.

TA is based on the ideas of the 'Theory of Constraints' and seeks to maximise profits by maximising throughput by identifying and, where possible, removing bottlenecks.

Maximising throughput on a bottleneck is similar to the marginal costing (MC) idea of maximising contribution per unit of scarce resource.

TA controls production costs through a series of ratios that focus on throughput per bottleneck resource.

MC is used in many aspects of decision making such as pricing and breakeven analysis.

STANDARD COSTING

234 FIXED OVERHEAD VOLUME VARIANCE

The fixed production overhead volume variance is reported in a standard absorption costing system. It arises due to the use of a predetermined overhead absorption rate based on budgeted costs and activity levels.

The standard absorption rate is designed so that, if the actual costs and activity levels are exactly the same as budgeted, then there will be no fixed production overhead variances. In practice of course this is rarely the case and any difference between the actual and budgeted production volume results in a fixed production overhead volume variance.

The fixed production overhead volume variance is the difference in output volume multiplied by the absorption rate per unit of output. It represents the under- or over-absorbed fixed production overhead due to a change in production volume from the budgeted level. If the volume of output is higher than budgeted, the variance is favourable (over-absorbed overhead). If the volume of output is lower than budgeted, the variance is adverse (under-absorbed overhead).

If the variance is adverse, then it is necessary to investigate why output was lower than budgeted. This is not necessarily a bad thing, if output were deliberately reduced because sales volume was lower than expected. In this case the cause of the sales shortfall would need to be investigated, rather than questioning the shortfall in production. If production had proceeded as budgeted, then this would have reduced the volume variance but this would not necessarily be the correct action for the organisation as a whole, if as a result the units remained unsold in inventory.

Similarly, if the variance is favourable this is not necessarily a good thing. If the output were sold, then the increase in production was worthwhile. However, simply increasing output in order to produce a favourable overhead volume variance would not be the correct action, if the extra units cannot be sold.

In conclusion it is not the fixed production overhead volume variance itself which provides useful information for management but the reason why the production volume differed from that budgeted and the consequential effects of that volume difference.

235 DIAGNOSTIC RELATED GROUPS

Diagnostic related groups (DRGs) are a means of classifying patients according to certain characteristics such as their age, diagnosis and required treatment. Once a patient is classified into a certain group it is possible to determine a standard cost for their treatment and care. The standard cost will be based upon estimates of the standard consumption of hospital resources required and the expected length of stay.

This standard then provides a control measure against which the actual cost of the patient's treatment and care can be monitored. Therefore control by comparison can be achieved in the same way that product standard costs are used for control purposes.

The system was originally developed in the USA where the DRG classification provides a basis for determining the maximum payment that will be received by the hospital from a medical insurance company. This provides a direct incentive for hospital management to keep costs below the maximum payment that will be received from the insurance company.

236 MIX AND YIELD VARIANCES

When two or more materials are mixed together it may be possible to analyse further any recorded materials usage variance. The further analysis would subdivide the total usage variance into its component parts of materials mix variance and materials yield variance.

The materials mix variance is the change in standard cost caused by mixing the materials in a different proportion to standard. For example, if proportionately more of a cheaper material is used in the mix then a favourable mix variance will result.

The materials yield variance is the change in standard cost caused by using a different amount of material in total than the standard expected for the output achieved.

There are a number of limitations in the usefulness of material mix and yield variances.

(i)   Mix and yield variances can only provide useful control information where the mix of materials is within the control of management, and where the information about total yield is more useful than usage variances for the individual materials calculated separately.

(ii)   It is often found that the mix and yield variances are interdependent, and that one variance cannot be assessed without also considering the other. For example an adverse yield variance might be explained by the fact that the mix had a larger than expected proportion of cheaper material (favourable mix variance).

(iii) If management is able to achieve a cheaper mix of materials without affecting the yield then the standard becomes obsolete. The cheaper mix should become the new standard mix.

(iv)   Control measures to achieve a favourable mix variance are likely to affect the quality of the output. Analysing mix and yield variances for control purposes does not take account of quality issues.

237 LABOUR RATE VARIANCE

Possible causes of an adverse labour rate variance include the following:

(i)   The standard labour rate per hour may have been set too low.

(ii)   Employees may have been of a higher grade than standard, with a consequent increase in the hourly rate paid.

(iii)   There may have been an unexpected increase in the prevailing market rate of pay for employees with appropriate skills.

(iv)   Where bonuses are included as a part of direct labour costs, increased bonus payments may have been made, above the standard level expected.

(v)   There may have been a change in the composition of the work force, which resulted in an increase in the average rate of pay.

238   LABOUR VARIANCES (NOV 05)

Labour variance – senior consultant

$

SHSR

40 hours	×	$100/hr	=	4,000	Efficiency
AHSR					$1,000 A
50 hours	×	$100/hr	=	5,000	

Labour variance – junior consultant

$

SHSR

60 hours	×	$60/hr	=	3,600	Efficiency
AHSR					$900 F
45 hours	×	$60/hr	=	2,700	

The efficiency variance looks at whether people **work** fast or slow and looks at hours **worked.**

The total efficiency variance was thus $1,000 A + $900 F = $100 A.

Idle time variance

The idle time variance is the difference between the actual hours worked and the actual hours paid for, then multiplied by the standard labour rate per hour.

Idle time variance = 10 hours × $60 per hour = $600 A

Mix variance

	Senior consultant hrs	Junior consultant hrs	Total hrs
Actual hours	50	45	95
Actual hours in std proportions			⇓
4:6	38	57	⇐ 95
Difference in hours	12 A	12 F	
× Std rate	× 100	× 60	
Mix variance	$1,200 A	$720 F	$480 A

The mix and yield variances are sub-divisions of the efficiency variance and thus focus on hours worked. (**Note:** The mix variance was calculated using the individual unit prices; the weighted average method could also have been used.)

239   PLANNING AND OPERATING VARIANCES (MAY 07)

(i)   Budgeted wage rate = $30 per hour

Revised wage rate = $31.20 per hour

Standard hours for actual output = 680 × 900/600 = 1,020

Planning labour rate variance = standard hours for actual output × difference in wage rate = 1,020 × $1.20 = $1,224 Adverse

Operational labour efficiency variance

680 units should take	1,020 hours
did take	1,070 hours
	─────
	50 A
Value at revised rate per hour	$31.20
Operational labour efficiency variance	**$1,560 Adverse**

Tutorial note

Planning variance

The original labour rate variance is:

1,070 hours	*should cost $30 per hour*	*$32,100*
	did cost $32 per hour	*$34,240*
		─────
	$2,140 A	

It may be tempting to split this variance into a planning variance (1,070 × $1.20 = $1,284 A) and an operational variance (1,070 × $0.80 = $856 A). This approach ignores part of the effect of the revision to the wage rate; the part that impacts on the calculation of the efficiency variance. The original labour efficiency variance is 50 hours Adverse × $30 = $1,500 A. By revising the wage rate the operational efficiency variance increases to $1,560 A. There is a 'planning effect' of $60 F to reconcile back to the original variance. The net planning effect is $1,284 A − $60 F = $1,224 A. This is all caused by the revision to the wage rate and is therefore a planning labour rate variance.

(ii)   The major benefit of analysing the variances into planning and operational components is that the revised standard should provide a realistic standard against which to measure performance. Any variances should then be a result of operational management efficiencies and inefficiencies and not faulty planning.

240 INVESTIGATION OF VARIANCES (MAY 07)

Three factors that should be considered before deciding to investigate a variance are:

- *The benefit should exceed the cost.* This may depend on the importance (materiality) of the variance in the business and whether the cost can be controlled

- *Trend.* Actual costs will be expected to fluctuate around the standard from period due to it being a long run average. If there appears to be a trend of a variance steadily worsening this maybe an indication that the cost is out of control.

- *Interrelationships.* Some variances may be caused by the same factor. For example, purchasing cheaper material may lead to a favourable material price variance, an adverse material usage variance and an adverse labour efficiency variance. The net impact may be considered before deciding whether action is necessary.

241 FG (MAY 12)

(i) **Material mix variance**

	Actual input @standard mix (000 litres)	Actual input @ actual mix (000 litres)	Variance (000 litres)	Standard cost $	Variance $000
Chemical A	1,791	2,144	353 A	0.60	211.80 A
Chemical B	1,074	824	250 F	1.40	350.00 F
Chemical C	895	792	103 F	1.00	103.00 F
	3,760	3,760			241.20 F

Or alternatively:

Weighted average cost per litre of input

$0.97/1.05 litres = $0.9238

Material mix variance

	Actual input @standard mix (000 litres)	Actual input @ actual mix (000 litres)	Variance (000 litres)	Standard cost $	Variance $000
Chemical A	1,791	2,144	353 A	(0.60 – 0.9238)	114.30 F
Chemical B	1,074	824	250 F	(1.40 – 0.9238)	119.10 F
Chemical C	895	792	103 F	(1.00 – 0.9238)	7.80 F
	3,760	3,760			241.20 F

(ii) **Material yield variance**

Standard litres of input per litre of output = 1.05 litres

3,300k litres output x 1.05 litres = 3,465k litres input

Actual usage = 3,760k litres

Variance = 295k litres A

Standard cost per litre = $0.9238

Variance = 295k litres x $0.9238 = $272.5k A

Or alternatively:

3,760k litres should yield 3,760/1.05 = 3,580.95k litres

Actual yield = 3,300k litres

Yield variance = 280.95k litres A

Standard material cost = $0.97

Yield variance = 280.95k litres x $0.97 = $272.5k A

Examiner's comments

This question was well done by the majority of candidates with most scoring at least 3 marks. Candidates were generally better however at calculating the mix variance than the yield variance.

Common errors

- Using 3,465 litres or 3,948 litres to calculate the standard mix
- Multiplying the mix variance in litres by the actual cost rather than the standard cost
- Comparing 3,760 litres to 3,300 litres

---

242 HOSPITAL CARE (MAY 06)

	$	$
Standard cost for 2-day procedure		1,165
Length of stay variances		
Nursing costs: 1 day × 0.75 × $320 per day	240 A	
Space and food costs: 1 day × $175 per day	175 A	
Hospital overheads	110 A	525 A
Standard cost for 3-day stay		1,690
Drug and specific cost variances		205 A
Nursing staffing variance: 3 days × $320 × (0.9 − 0.75)		144 A
Actual cost		2,039

243 MODERN BUSINESS ENVIRONMENT (MAY 07)

Standard costing may not be appropriate in a modern business environment because:

- it is most appropriate for large volumes of similar products. In the modern environment products tend to be customised and produced in smaller batches;
- it is normally based on attainable working conditions. The modern environment emphasises continuous improvement and zero defects;
- it focuses on maximising the utilisation of capacity and minimising cost. In the modern environment breaks in production may be preferred to match production to demand and higher quality higher price inputs may be preferred such as highly skilled staff.

244 BENCHMARKING

Benchmarking is the practice of identifying an external organisation whose performance can be used as a comparator or benchmark for the organisation's own performance. The principle is that, by a close analysis of and comparison with other practices and processes, changes and adjustments can be made to those processes that will improve overall performance.

Four main types of benchmarking can be identified.

- *Internal benchmarking* involves comparisons with another department or division within the same company.
- *Competitive benchmarking* involves comparisons with the most successful competitors in the same field.
- *Functional benchmarking* is carried out by comparing the performance of a business function, for example the finance department, with the performance of the finance function in an organisation of similar size but which is not a direct competitor.
- *Strategic benchmarking* is a form of competitive benchmarking aimed at reaching decisions for strategic action and organisational change.

Benchmarking might help to improve overall performance by:

- providing managers with a warning about the need for change;
- enabling learning from others in order to improve performance;
- gaining a competitive edge (in the private sector);
- improving services (in the public sector).

BUDGETING

245 XY (SEPT 10)

ZBB starts each budget with the assumption that the function does not exist and that cost is zero. It ignores any past performance or budgets. It has the following advantages:

- All costs must be justified. Therefore if an activity cannot be justified it will not be performed. In this way it will force the charity to examine whether their activities are worthwhile.
- It should lead to improved resource utilisation by, for example, determining the best use of charity staff. This should assist managers in determining where discretionary expenditure gets allocated.

But the system also has some disadvantages:

- It is a complicated system. For a charity who's managers might lack financial expertise this may prove too difficult to implement.
- The charity's activities are unlikely to change drastically from year to year and therefore simpler systems such as incremental budgeting may be more appropriate.
- Donators may not be happy that too much time is spent on budgeting rather than on charitable activities.

246 PRODUCTION COST BUDGET (MAY 10)

Production cost budget		*Quarter 3*
Production (units)		23,000
		$
Direct materials	(W1)	262,200
Production labour	(W2)	219,000
Production overheads	(W3)	278,000
Total budgeted production cost		759,200

(W1) Materials

Cost per unit = ($180,000 / 15,000) = $12/unit.

Budgeted cost = 23,000 x $12 = $276,000.

This would qualify for the 5% discount so the actual cost would be $276,000 x 95% = $262,200.

(W2) Labour

Increase in cost in first two quarters = $195,000 - $155,000 = $40,000.

Increase in production in first two quarters = 5,000 units.

Variable cost per unit = $40,000 / 5,000 units = $8 per unit.

Fixed costs = $195,000 – ($8 x 20,000) = $35,000.

Budgeted cost for 23,000 units = $35,000 + (23,000 x $8) = $219,000.

(W3) Production overheads

Increase in cost in first two quarters = $240,000 - $210,000 = $30,000.

Increase in production in first two quarters = 5,000 units.

Variable cost per unit = $30,000 / 5,000 units = $6 per unit.

Fixed costs = $240,000 – ($6 x 20,000) = $120,000.

Budgeted cost for 23,000 units = $120,000 + (23,000 x $6) + $20,000 = $278,000.

247 BUDGET SETTING PROCESS (NOV 10)

There are three main stages in the budget setting process in a zero based budgeting system:

Description of activities in decision packages

The activities that are being proposed are described in a decision package. There will often be more than one decision package proposed e.g. one based on providing services at a minimum level and others at incremental levels above the minimum.

Some of these packages will be mutually exclusive and will require management to select the best solution to the issue involved. For example options for debt collection could be in-house or outsourced solutions and a decision package will be needed for each.

Evaluation and ranking

Each decision package is evaluated. Its costs are compared to its benefits and net present values or other measures calculated. The non-financial aspects are also considered as some packages might have legal obligations attached e.g. updating accounting systems.

Management will rank each package based on the benefits to the organisation. They may decide to reject packages even though the activity was undertaken last year. In this way the organisation is said to be starting from a zero base with each package given due consideration.

Allocation of resources

Once management decide which packages to accept a budget can be prepared for the resources required. This should include costs, revenues and other resource allocations necessary.

Examiner's comments

This question was badly done by the majority of students with most scoring only one mark. Students failed to answer the question; many discussed instead the advantages and disadvantages of zero based budgeting. Those that did refer to a budget setting process did so in a very general way rather than specifically discussing zero based budgeting. In terms of the zero based budgeting process, few students got further than to state that the budget started from scratch and that all expenditure had to be justified.

Common errors

- Failure to answer the question
- Discussion of the budget setting process in general terms without referring specifically to zero based budgeting.
- Discussion of the advantages and disadvantages of zero based budgeting.

---

248   ZBB (MAY 09)

(a)   **Zero Based Budgeting**

Incremental budgeting is a method of budgeting that starts with the current year's budget and adjusts this for known changes. The main problems associated with it are that:

- it can lead to inaccurate allocation of resources;
- managers may build in slack to make achieving targets easier.

Zero-Based Budgeting is a method of budgeting that requires all costs to be specifically justified by the benefits expected. Costs are built up from a zero base and ranked against other activities competing for limited resources. This should eliminate slack and lead to an optimal allocation of resources.

(b)   **Labour variances**

(i)   **Idle time variance**

The idle time variance is the difference between the actual hours worked and the actual hours paid for, then multiplied by the standard labour rate per hour.

Idle time variance = 10 hours × $80 per hour = $800 A

Mix variance

	Senior consultant hrs	Junior consultant hrs	Total hrs
Actual hours *worked*	60	80	140
Actual hours in std proportions			⇓
50:90	50	90	⇐ 140
Difference in hours	10 A	10 F	
× Std rate	× 120	× 80	
Mix variance	$1,200 A	$800 F	$400 A

The mix variance was calculated using the individual unit prices; the weighted average method could also have been used.

(ii) **Benefits of the labour mix variance**

One of the key factors that can determine the performance of a professional practice is the manner in which the work of senior staff is integrated with that of their juniors. In this scenario it will be important to discover that the senior consultants worked for ten extra hours than expected which cost the company $400. This could also explain the ten hours of idle time experienced by the junior staff – which gave a further cost of $800.

(c) **Variable costs**

Variable costs are defined as 'a cost which varies with a measure of activity'.

Under traditional costing methods a short-term view of variable costs is taken. This means that any cost that varies directly with changes in this year's production would be included as a variable cost and removed from overheads. However, for planning and control purposes, any costs that fall outside this definition are treated as a fixed cost and these are often apportioned between products on an arbitrary basis. This makes it more difficult to price products, gauge their profitability and to control costs due to a lack of understanding of their underlying cause.

However, in the longer term, all costs are variable. By identifying activities that use up resources that give rise to costs, ABC can provide useful information about product profitability, for controlling overhead costs over the longer term. Since costs are allocated to products on the basis of resource-consuming activities, ABC provides useful information about the economic cost of products, and which products are more profitable than others.

Traditional costing does not do this because there is no relationship between the overhead costs allocated to products and the consumption of overhead resources.

(d) **Variances**

(i) **Material usage planning variance**

		£
Original planned cost	400 units x 6 kgs x £12/kg	28,800
Revised planned cost	400 units x 6.75kgs x £12/kg	32,400
Planning Variance		3,600 A

(ii) **Operational materials price variance**

		£
Actually spent on materials cost		29,000
2500kgs should have cost	x £12/kg	30,000
Price Variance		1,000 F

(iii) **Operational materials usage variance**

380units should use	x 6.75 kgs	2,565 kgs
Actually used		2,500 kgs
Favourable Usage Variance		65 kgs
Standard price		£12 /kg
Material usage variance		£780 Fav

249   INCREMENTAL BUDGETING (SEPT 12)

An incremental approach to budgeting has a number of limitations as follows:

- It is based on what has happened in the past therefore the allocation of resources to specific activities is not justified. It is assumed that the activities will continue merely because they were undertaken in the previous year. This is inappropriate in a rapidly changing environment.

- Excessive costs included in the previous budget will be carried forward into the next budget. An incremental system does not look at reducing waste and overspending. Past inefficiencies will be continued as different approaches to achieving the objectives will not be examined.

- The performance targets in the budget tend not to be challenging. The approach does not encourage managers to look for ways to improve the business.

- It encourages managers to spend up to the budget as they know that if they fail to spend the budget it is likely to be cut in the next period.

250   MCDONALDIZATION AND BUDGETS (NOV 05)

The concept of McDonaldization comes from the successes of the fast food company. The term was defined by George Ritzer (1996) as 'the process by which the principles of the fast-food restaurant are coming to dominate more and more sectors of American society, as well as the rest of the world'. Ritzer identified four dimensions to McDonaldization which are critical to the success of the model:

(1) Efficiency

(2) Calculability

(3) Control

(4) Predictability.

Management should be able to set accurate budgets for what it takes, in terms of materials and time, to provide standard items to customers and it should be very cheap to provide that information. Owing to the supposed lack of variation the actual costs should be very close to the budgeted costs and thus any variances will be an indication of good or bad operational performance.

For UV Limited the provision of standard meals for large events does conform to the characteristics of McDonaldization and it should be very possible to flex the budgeted costs in accordance with the number of meals provided in order to predict costs accurately and then set prices which will guarantee a profit. These prices could then be used for a published price list.

UV Limited also provides meals to meet the exact requirements of a customer and prices are negotiated individually with each customer. This type of service does not have the characteristics of McDonaldization and the budgeting for this type of service will have to be different.

251 QR (SEPT 10)

Production cost budget

	Product Q	Product R
Number of batches produced	16	30
Number of machine set ups / batch	4	2
Total number of set ups	64	60

$$\text{Overhead recovery rate} = \frac{\text{Total overheads}}{\text{Total number of set ups}}$$

$$\text{Overhead recovery rate} = \frac{\$74,400}{124}$$

$$\text{Overhead recovery rate} = \$600 \text{ / set up}$$

Total charge to Product Q = $600 x 64 set ups = $38,400

Cost per unit of Product Q = $38,400 / 80,000 units = $0.48

Activity based budgeting can have the following advantages:

- It draws attention to overheads (which may be a large proportion of total costs) and should therefore improve cost control.

- The allocation of overheads between products can be improved which should, for example, improve product pricing.

252 DECISION PACKAGES (MAR 11)

The activities that are being proposed in a budget are described in decision packages. There will often be more than one decision package proposed for an activity e.g. one based on providing services at a minimum level and others at incremental levels above the minimum.

Some of these packages will be mutually exclusive and will require management to select the best solution to the issue involved. For example options for refuse collection could be in-house or outsourced solutions and a decision package will be needed for each.

Each decision package is evaluated. Its costs are compared to its benefits and net present values or other measures calculated. The non-financial aspects are also considered as some packages might have legal obligations attached e.g. updating accounting systems.

Management will rank each package based on the benefits to the organisation. They may decide to reject packages even though the activity was done last year. In this way the organisation is said to be starting from a zero base with each package given due consideration.

The process of ranking decision packages is inherently difficult as value judgements are necessary. In a public sector body, for example, decision packages will relate to very disparate activities. It is extremely difficult to formulate criteria that would allow unambiguous ranking where decision packages, for example, related to education services are measured against those relating to health services. It can also be difficult to place a monetary value on the output of some of the services provided.

> **Examiner's comments**
>
> This question was badly done by the majority of candidates with most scoring only one or two marks. Many candidates did little more than state that zero based budgets start from scratch and are justified, while others merely restated the statement in the question. Few explained how the decision packages are formed or ranked/evaluated. Most candidates thought that charities would not use zero based budgeting because of lack of knowledge and due to the time and expense involved. Most candidates did mention that as the organisations were non profit making, a more subjective method of ranking may have to be used which would be difficult to measure. However candidates' explanations were not sufficiently developed to achieve a good mark for this section.
>
> *Common errors*
>
> - Failure to answer the question.
>
> - Failure to explain the statement as required by the question.
>
> - Lack of explanation of the points made.

253 BUDGET CONFLICTS (MAY 11)

One of the main purposes of budgeting is planning. It will help to ensure that managers think ahead, planning and reviewing their activities and that this is done in a co-ordinated way. It also acts as a control mechanism, with actual results being compared against budget. In order for the budget to fulfil these purposes it need to be based on realistically achievable estimates.

Another purpose of a budget is to set targets to motivate managers and optimise their performance. Evidence suggests that the existence of a defined goal or target is likely to motivate managers and result in higher levels of performance than when no target is established. The manager has to accept the target set for it to be effective, but the problem is in determining the optimum degree of difficulty for the target. As the degree of difficulty increases it has been shown that the managers' aspiration level and performance increases up to a point where the target is seen as impossible to achieve. Thereafter, the aspiration level and performance of the manager declines dramatically.

This suggests that challenging targets should be established to motivate managers. However it is unlikely that these will be suitable for planning purposes since they have a high probability of not being achieved. There is therefore a need for two separate budgets to be produced; however this is unlikely to be realistic in practice.

> **Examiner's comments**
>
> This question was particularly badly done with few candidates scoring highly. Answers included activity based budgeting, zero based budgeting and a lot of discussion of planning and operational variances. Every budgeting question that has been set under the new syllabus has been badly answered with disappointingly few candidates being able to apply their knowledge to address the question that was set and many answering the question that was set the time before. Poor exam technique was used in answering this question. The question asks for an explanation of the statement therefore marks were available for candidates explaining the two purposes of budgeting and then explaining why they conflict.

Common errors

- Failure to answer the question
- Failure to explain the statement as required by the question
- Discussion of a wide variety of budgeting techniques which were irrelevant to the question

254 BUDGET PARTICIPATION (SEPT 11)

One of the main purposes of budgeting is to act as a control mechanism, with actual results being compared against budget. Another purpose of a budget is to set targets to motivate managers and optimise their performance. The participation of managers in the budget setting process has several advantages. Managers are more likely to be motivated to achieve the target if they have participated in setting the target. Participation can reduce the information asymmetry gap that can arise when targets are imposed by senior management. Imposed targets are likely to make managers feel demotivated and alienated and result in poor performance. Participation however can cause problems; in particular, managers may attempt to negotiate budgets that they feel are easy to achieve which gives rise to 'budget padding' or budgetary slack. They may also be tempted to 'empire build' because they believe that the size of their budget reflects their importance within the organisation. This can result in budgets that are unsuitable for control purposes.

255 X PLC (NOV 06)

(a)

Tutorial note

The budget for the next four quarters is required. However, closing stock values are determined by the following quarter's sales demand and material usage, so the budget for Q5 will also be prepared.

	Q1	Q2	Q3	Q4	Q5
Sales demand	2,250	2,050	1,650	2,050	1,250
Add closing inventory (W1)	615	495	615	375	616
Less opening inventory (W2)	(675)	(615)	(495)	(615)	(375)
Production budget	2,190	1,930	1,770	1,810	1,490
Raw material usage (× 3kg)	6,570	5,790	5,310	5,430	4,470
Closing inventory (W3)	2,605.5	2,389.5	2,443.5	2,011.5	
Opening inventory (W4)	(2,956.5)	(2,605.5)	(2,389.5)	(2,443.5)	
Purchases budget for B in kgs	6,219	5,574	5,364	4,998	
Purchases budget for B in $	43,533	39,018	37,548	34,986	

Total purchases budget for material B for Quarters 1–4 = $155,085

Workings

(W1) Q1 0.3 × 2,050

(W2) The opening inventory for any quarter is the same as the closing inventory of the previous quarter. The opening inventory for Q1 is 0.3 × 2,250 = 675

(W3) Q1 0.45 × 5,790

(W4) The opening inventory for any quarter is the same as the closing inventory of the previous quarter. The opening inventory for Q1 is 0.45 × 6,570 = 2,956.5

(b) If Material A is in short supply then this becomes the principal budget factor. This will affect budget preparation because the first step in the budgetary process will be to determine the optimum mix of products according to their contribution per kg of Material A. The optimum production plan can then be determined and the sales budget can be derived from the production plan. It may be necessary to revise the policy for holding inventory whilst Material A is in short supply.

Once the production plan has been determined then Material B, labour and overhead budgets can be derived. The limit on the level of production may mean that there is spare capacity in the factory and the fixed overhead absorption rate will increase. This will increase the cost per unit of products and lower profitability. In addition lower production levels may mean that there are spare labour resources. This could mean that output of products which do not use Material A could be increased.

In the long term, if the supply of Material A continues to be limited, X plc may wish to seek alternative sources of supply, change product design or produce alternative products.

(c) Incremental budgeting is a method of budgeting that starts with the current year's budget and adjusts this for known changes. The main problems associated with it are that:

- it can lead to inaccurate allocation of resources;
- managers may build in slack to make achieving targets easier.

Zero-Based Budgeting is a method of budgeting that requires all costs to be specifically justified by the benefits expected. Costs are built up from a zero base and ranked against other activities competing for limited resources. This should eliminate slack and lead to an optimal allocation of resources.

(d) Linear regression analysis can be used to forecast sales when it can be assumed that there is a linear relationship between sales and time. Sales data can be plotted on a scattergraph and a line of best fit fitted by eye for forecasting purposes. Regression analysis is a statistical technique that calculates the line of best fit using formulae given for a and b in the straight line equation:

$y = a + bx$

where y = sales and x = time

Once the formula has been established, this can be used to forecast sales at any future time.

It can be seen that sales of Product W do not appear to have a linear trend over time. Linear regression analysis will therefore not be a suitable method for X plc to use for forecasting.

256 TIME SERIES IN FORECASTING

The strengths of time series analysis as a basis for forecasting are that:

- forecasts are based on clearly understood assumptions;
- trend lines can be reviewed after each successive time period to assess the reliability of the forecasts;
- forecasting accuracy can be improved with experience.

The limitations of the technique stem from the following assumptions that are made in its application. These assumptions may not be valid:

- that past events are a reliable guide to what will happen in the future;
- that there is a straight line trend;
- that seasonal variations are constant, either in absolute values if the additive model is used, or as a proportion of the trend line value in a multiplicative model.

257 BUDGETARY CONTROL (NOV 11)

Planning

Budgeting forces an organisation's management to look ahead and set performance targets. This ensures that management anticipates any future problems and gives the organisation direction. It also ensures that managers are aware of their own targets and responsibilities and how they relate to those of other managers within the organisation.

Control/Evaluation

The budget acts as a control mechanism, with actual results being compared with budget. Appropriate actions can then be taken to correct any deviations from plan. The budget also provides an internal benchmark against which performance can be evaluated. The performance measured may be that of a department or division or of an individual manager.

Co-ordination

The budget ensures actions of different parts of the organisation are co-ordinated and reconciled otherwise managers take actions for the benefit of their own part of organisation that may not benefit the organisation as a whole. The budget compels managers to examine the relationship between their own operation and other departments.

Communication

Every part of the organisation needs to be informed of plans, policies and constraints. In that way, everyone should have a clear understanding of the part they need to play in achieving the budget. It is through the budget that top management communicates it expectations to lower level managers and in return lower level managers can communicate what they consider to be achievable targets.

Motivation

Another benefit of budgeting is to set targets to motivate managers and optimise their performance. The budget is a useful device for influencing managers' behaviour and motivating managers to perform in line with the organisation's objectives. It provides a standard which managers may be motivated to achieve. It can also encourage inefficiency and conflict between managers particularly if the budget is imposed from above, whereby it may act as a threat rather than as a challenge.

Tutorial note

The answer provides five examples. Only three of these are needed in the exam and students should not attempt to include more than three methods.

Examiner's comments

This question was reasonably well answered although as the question was fairly straightforward it was surprising how many candidates did not make a good attempt at it. To obtain full marks candidates need to discuss three distinct benefits. In many cases there was duplication of points which earned no marks. Candidates need to take a more structured approach to these questions, clearly identifying the benefit and explaining why it is of benefit. Candidates score much better with this type of approach rather than producing two pages of general, non-specific material in the vain hope of picking up some marks.

Common errors

- Not considering three distinct benefits

- Duplication of points made

- Not addressing the question set but instead discussing various aspects of budgeting e.g. rolling budgets and flexible budgets

258 CENTRALISED PURCHASING (MAY 12)

The advantages of a centralised purchasing system are as follows:

- A centralised buyer is able to order in larger quantities and may be able to negotiate bulk buying discounts.
- A centralised buyer may have a wider network of suppliers than a local buyer and should be able to ensure that the best available prices are identified.
- With centralised purchasing it is easier to enforce common quality standards for purchased materials.
- Centralised purchasing should result in more efficient management of inventory. The buyer should have access to information about the current inventory levels at all locations in the organisation and where appropriate can arrange for inventory to be transferred from one location to another to avoid purchasing additional quantities.
- In an organisation where the operating units are all within a small geographical area it should also be possible to operate a single centralised stores location. It should be easier to control inventory levels within a centralised store rather than with several localised stores.
- The company should benefit from economies of scale and the reduction in administration costs. As larger orders are being placed with suppliers it will also reduce inventory ordering and handling costs.
- Centralised purchasing should enable closer relationships with suppliers and allow the use of JIT inventory management techniques.

> **Examiner's comments**
>
> This question was usually very well answered with many candidates giving significantly more detail than was required for a five mark question. While it is pleasing to see a question being so well answered, candidates should be aware of the need to more effectively manage their time. Candidates generally discussed the effect of large volume purchases giving bulk discounts as well as overhead cost reductions from going from multiple locations to just one department. They also discussed the benefits in terms of control/monitoring, transferring stock between locations, information in one place so easier to get reports / budget etc.
>
> *Common error*
>
> - Assuming that stock would be centrally managed and giving a detailed discussion on the benefits of this rather than addressing the question that was asked.

259 PROBLEMS IN CENTRALISED PURCHASING (SEPT 12)

The disadvantages of a centralised purchasing system are as follows:

- It may result in increased transport costs with a consequential impact on the environment.
- A centralised purchasing system is likely to be more bureaucratic and unable to respond to inventory shortages as quickly as a local buyer.
- A local buyer may be more flexible and able to respond to temporary reductions in local prices that a central purchasing manager may be unaware of.
- Local buyers may be able to develop stronger relationships with local suppliers thus possibly ensuring greater reliability of supply and the opportunity for JIT purchasing and reduced inventories.
- Local suppliers may offer varied products thus enabling differentiation of finished products.
- The opportunity to delegate responsibility for aspects of the management of the business and the benefits in terms of management development will not be available.
- A centralised purchasing system is not appropriate where managers have been given responsibility for the financial management of their particular operating unit. Where this is the case the responsibility for purchasing and inventory management decisions should also be given to the managers.

260 TOP DOWN BUDGETING (MAY 12)

The participation of managers in the budget setting process has several advantages. Managers are more likely to be motivated to achieve the budget if they have participated in the budget setting process. Participation can also reduce the information asymmetry gap that can arise when targets are imposed by senior management and should result in more realistic budgets. Imposed budgets are likely to make managers feel demotivated and alienated and result in poor performance.

Participation however can cause problems; in particular, managers may attempt to negotiate budgets that they feel are easy to achieve which gives rise to 'budget padding' or budgetary slack. They may also be tempted to 'empire build' because they believe that the size of their budget reflects their importance within the organisation. This can result in budgets that are unsuitable for control purposes. Manager participation is only effective if it is true participation. Pseudo participation can be worse for motivation than no involvement at all. The involvement of managers in the budget setting process is time consuming and the benefits of participation would need to weighed against the cost of the resources used.

Examiner's comments

This question was also well answered with most candidates achieving at least 4 marks. Most candidates discussed motivation, superior knowledge of own business area and realistic budgets as arguments for participation and budget slack as an argument against participation.

Common errors

- Failure to answer the question set.

- Discussing top-down budgeting rather than participative budgeting.

- Assuming senior management was no longer involved in the budget process.

THE TREATMENT OF UNCERTAINTY IN DECISION MAKING

261 GT (NOV 11)

(i) **Decision tree: Build a new restaurant or not**

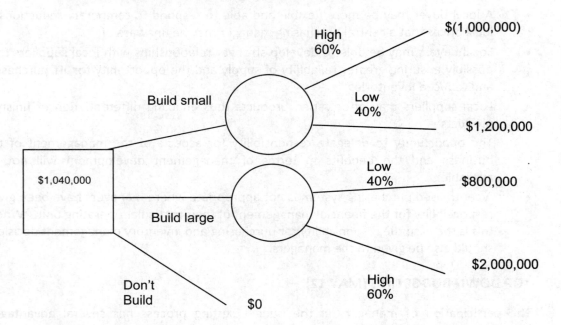

(ii) **Value of survey**

Expected value with the survey

= (0.4 x $800,000) + (0.6 x $2,000,000)

= $320,000 + $1,200,000

= $1,520,000

Expected value without the survey

= $1,040,000 (see diagram)

Therefore maximum value of the survey = $1,520,000 - $1,040,000 = $480,000

262   DECISION TREE (SEPT 11)

Decision tree: Develop an overseas market or not

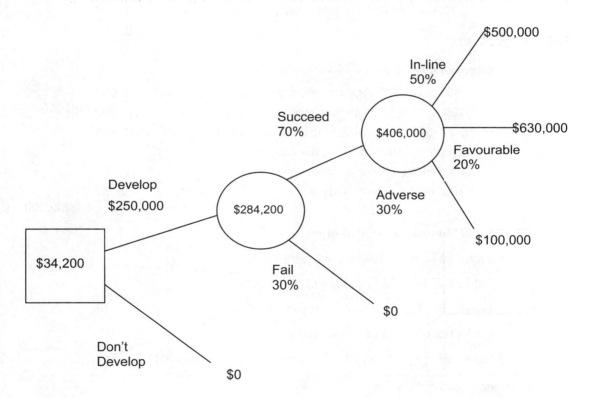

Therefore the overseas market should be developed

Tutorial note

The figures in the circles are calculated using expected values. You should started with the circle furthest to the right. This calculates the expected value of the different exchange rates as follows:

= (50% x $500,000) + (20% x $630,000) + (30% x $100,000) = $406,000

> *Moving to the left, the expected value figure in the next circle is calculated as:*
>
> *= (70% x $406,000) + (30% x $0) = $284,200*
>
> *Finally, to get the overall value of the developing (for the final circle on the left) we deduct the development cost:*
>
> *= $284,200 - $250,000 = £34,200*

263 NEW PRODUCT (NOV 11)

(i) **Calculation of probability**

$ 80 - $40 = $40 Joint probability is 0.25 x 0.20 =	0.0500
$100 - $40 = $60 Joint probability is 0.30 x 0.20 =	0.0600
$100 - $60 = $40 Joint probability is 0.30 x 0.55 =	0.1650
$120 - $40 = $80 Joint probability is 0.45 x 0.20 =	0.0900
$120 - $60 = $60 Joint probability is 0.45 x 0.55 =	0.2475
$120 - $80 = $40 Joint probability is 0.45 x 0.25 =	0.1125
	0.7250

Alternatively:

$ 80 - $40 = $40 Joint probability is 0.25 x 0.20 =	0.050
$100 - $40 = $60 Joint probability is 0.30 x 0.20 =	0.060
$100 - $60 = $40 Joint probability is 0.30 x 0.55 =	0.165
At a selling price of $120, the contribution per unit under all three alternatives is greater than $40 therefore probability is	0.450
	0.725

(ii) **Expected value of contribution**

Expected value of selling price per unit

($80 x 0.25) + ($100 x 0.30) + ($120 x 0.45) = $104

Expected value of variable cost per unit

($40 x 0.20) + ($60 x 0.55) + ($80 x 0.25) =$61

Expected value of contribution per unit = $104 - $61 = $43

Examiner's comments

Part (i) of the question caused difficulties for some candidates but overall the question was well answered.

Some candidates answered part (ii) as part (i) and many candidates made careless errors in the calculations, particularly in part (i).

Common errors

- Failure to sum the probabilities in part (i)

- Arithmetic errors

264 RISK ATTITUDES (MAR 11)

(i)   **A risk neutral** decision maker will tend to ignore risk and choose the course of action that gives the best expected value. The probability distribution results in an expected value of $13 which is more than the current delivery cost of $12.50 therefore the risk neutral decision maker will want to remain with the third party delivery service.

(ii)   **A risk averse** decision maker is one that focuses on the poor results and seeks to avoid a high degree of risk. A risk averse decision maker will focus on the 51% chance that delivery costs per unit will be higher than the current cost of $12.50. They will ignore the fact that there is also a 35% probability that the delivery cost per unit will be lower than the current unit cost of $12.50. A risk averse decision maker will want to remain with the third party delivery service.

(iii)   **A risk-seeker** is a decision maker that is interested in the best possible outcomes no matter how unlikely they are to occur. They are not put off by the low probability of an outcome but choose to focus on potential large returns instead. A risk-seeker will focus on the 23% probability that the delivery cost per unit will be $11 or lower and will want to establish the in-house delivery service. A risk-seeker will ignore the fact that there is a 35% chance that delivery costs per unit will be $14.20 or higher.

Examiner's comments

This question was reasonably well done with some candidates achieving full marks. The most disappointing error was that many candidates believed that the decision maker could select a cost and did not appreciate that the data provided was only the probabilities of incurring those costs. It would help candidates if they read through their answers to check that what they have written makes sense. Other candidates chose not to use the table of costs and probabilities at all despite the fact that the question asked for an explanation of the decision that each manager would take based on the probability distribution. Candidates who chose to define the three attitudes to risk struggled to explain a risk neutral decision maker.

Common errors

*   Stating the decision that would be made without explaining why this would be the case.

*   Selecting a cost that the decision maker would choose.

*   Not explaining the different attitudes to risk.

*   Inability to explain the term 'risk neutral'.

*   Failure to refer to the probability distribution.

---

265 PERFECT INFORMATION (MAR 11)

Competitor reaction	Probability	Product A expected value $000s	Product B Expected value $000s	Product C expected value $000s
Strong	0.3	200 x 0.3 = 60	400 x 0.3 = 120	600 x 0.3 = 180
Normal	0.2	300 x 0.2 = 60	600 x 0.2 = 120	400 x 0. 2 = 80
Weak	0.5	500 x 0.5 = 250	800 x 0.5 = 400	500 x 0.5 = 250
Expected Value		370	640	510

Product B is the best choice (without the benefit of perfect information) as it has the highest expected value (EV) of $640k.

With perfect information:

If research suggests strong competitor reaction: select C and earn $600k – probability 0.3

If research suggests normal competitor reaction: select B and earn $600k – probability 0.2

If research suggests weak competitor reaction: select B and earn $800k – probability 0.5

EV (with perfect information) = ($600k x 0.3) + ($600k x 0.2) + ($800k x 0.5) = $700k

Value of perfect information is $700k – $640k = $60k

Examiner's comments

Many candidates scored full marks for this question but others could only earn 1 ½ marks for calculating the expected value of the products. The weakest candidates calculated the expected values of strong, normal and weak reactions rather than the expected value of products A, B and C.

Common errors

- Calculating the expected value of the competitor reaction rather than the expected value of the products.

- Comparing the total of the expected values of the products to the total of the three best outcomes.

- Lack of understanding of how to calculate the expected value with perfect information.

---

266 CONSUMER DEMAND (MAY 11)

Consumer demand	Probability	Project A expected value $000s	Project B expected value $000s	Project C expected value $000s
Above average	0.20	400 x 0.2 = 80	300 x 0.2 = 60	800 x 0.2 = 160
Average	0.45	500 x 0.45 = 225	400 x 0.45 = 180	600 x 0.45 = 270
Below average	0.35	700 x 0.35 = 245	600 x 0.35 = 210	300 x 0.35 = 105
Expected value		550	450	535

Product A is the best choice (without the benefit of perfect information) as it has the highest expected value (EV) of $550k.

With perfect information:

If research suggests above average consumer demand: select C and earn $800k

If research suggests average consumer demand: select C and earn $600k

If research suggests below average consumer demand: select A and earn $700k

EV (with perfect information) = ($800k x 0.2) + ($600k x 0.45) + ($700k x 0.35) = $675k

Value of perfect information is $675k – $550k = $125k

267 CLOTHING RETAILER (MAY 12)

Expected values ($000)

Package A ($700 x 0.25) + ($600 x 0.4) + ($400 x 0.35) = $555

Package B ($900 x 0.25) + ($500 x 0.4) + ($300 x 0.35) = $530

Package C ($800 x 0.25) + ($400 x 0.4) + ($500 x 0.35) = $535

Expected value of perfect information ($000)

If good select Package B = ($900 x 0.25) = $225

If moderate select Package A = ($600 x 0.4) = $240

If poor select Package C = ($500 x 0.35) = $175

Expected value of perfect information is $225 + $240 + $175 = $640

Value of information

The maximum amount that should be paid is ($640k – $555k) = $85k

268   ELECTRONIC GOODS (SEPT 12)

(i)   **Regret matrix**

Customer reaction	Agreement A $	Agreement B $	Agreement C $
Strong	12,100	19,900	0
Moderate	0	7,500	2,100
Weak	0	3,700	5,100

The maximum regret if Agreement A is chosen is $12,100

The maximum regret if Agreement B is chosen is $19,900

The maximum regret if Agreement C is chosen is $5,100

To minimise the maximum regret the manager will choose Agreement C.

(ii)   **Risk averse**

A risk averse decision maker is one that focuses on the possibility of poor results and seeks to avoid a high degree of risk. A risk averse decision maker faced with a choice between two alternatives with identical expected values will choose the less risky alternative. These decision makers are often viewed as pessimists.

269   MAXIMIN AND MAXIMAX (NOV 10)

(i)   **The order level**

(a)   If AP applied the maximin decision criterion it would order at the medium level. The worst result is a profit of $300 and this is the best "worst result".

(b)   If AP applied the maximax decision criterion it would order at the high level, since the maximum return of $600 is to be gained at this level.

(ii)   **Minimax regret**

Minimax Regret Table			
Demand level	Level of order		
	High	Medium	Low
Good	0	$300	$500
Average	$200	0	$300
Poor	$400	0	$100

The maximum regret if AP orders at the high level is $400

The maximum regret if AP orders at the medium level is $300

The maximum regret if AP orders at the low level is $500

Therefore if AP wants to minimise the maximum regret it will order at the medium level.

Examiner's comments

This question was reasonably well done with many candidates achieving full marks. Weaker candidates struggled to produce an accurate regret table. A number of candidates added the figures in the regret table therefore losing marks as it was difficult to determine the basis on which the selection had been made.

Common errors

- Selecting a demand level rather than an order level

- Stating an amount rather than an order level

- Totalling the columns in the regret table

FINANCIAL INFORMATION FOR LONG TERM DECISION MAKING

270 TS (MAY 11)

Replace after year:		1		2		3	
Year	Discount factor	Cash flows	Present value	Cash flows	Present value	Cash flows	Present value
0	1.000	(25,000)	(25,000)	(25,000)	(25,000)	(25,000)	(25,000)
1	0.943	13,000	12,259	(5,000)	(4,715)	(5,000)	(4,715)
2	0.890			7,000	6,230	(8,000)	(7,120)
3	0.840					(6,000)	(5,040)
Present value			(12,741)		(23,485)		(41,875)
Cumulative discount factor			0.943		1.833		2.673
Annualised equivalent			13,511		12,812		15,666

The lowest annualised equivalent cost occurs if the vehicles are kept for 2 years. Therefore the optimum replacement cycle is to replace the vehicles every 2 years.

Examiner's comments

This question was not particularly well done. Few candidates knew the correct approach to take. Although most recognised the need to calculate the net present value for each of the alternatives they did not know what to do once they had calculated the NPV. Many went no further and selected the replacement cycle based on the NPV. Some decided on a basic approach and divided by 1, 2 and 3 years. Surprisingly few knew that the cumulative discount factor needed to be used to find the annualised equivalent cost. The more ambitious candidates tried to do rolling cycles but most who did this went for a three year approach rather than a more sensible six year cycle so the results were not comparable.

Common errors

- Including the cost of the vehicle in year 1 rather than in year 0

- Allocating the cost to the wrong years

- Failure to calculate an annualised equivalent cost

271 TWO ASSETS (SEPT 12)

Asset 1

Present value of purchase cost = $120,000

Present value of lease cost = $18,000 + ($18,000 x 5.759) = $121,662

Asset 1 should be purchased as the present value of the purchase cost is lower.

Asset 2

Present value of purchase cost = $51,000 - ($20,000 x 0.621) = $38,580

Present value of lease cost = $10,000 x 3.791 = $37,910

Decision

Asset 2 should be leased as the present value of the lease payments is lower.

272 SENSITIVITY ANALYSIS (MAY 12)

(i) **Calculation**

If the present value of the fixed costs were to increase by more than $8,675 then the project would cease to be viable. As a percentage increase this is:

$8,675 / $90,125 = 9.6%

(ii) **Benefits**

Tutorial note

The answer provides four examples. Only two of these are needed in the exam and students should not attempt to include more than two methods.

- Sensitivity analysis enables a company to determine the effect of changes to variables on the planned outcome.
- Sensitivity analysis enables a company to assess the risk associated with a project.
- Sensitivity analysis enables identification of variables that are of special significance.
- Sensitivity analysis enables risk management strategies to be put in place to focus on those variables of special significance.

Examiner's comments

This question was usually well answered with many candidates getting full marks. There were some candidates who didn't understand sensitivity analysis and merely calculated the net present value of the project. Candidates were generally good at the second part of the question usually citing risk analysis and the change in the variable that would lead to a negative NPV as potential benefits.

Common errors

- Using 100,000 as the denominator
- Expressing the NPV as a percentage of the annual fixed costs i.e. $25,000.

273 ST (SEPT 11)

Year	Discount Factor	Van A Cash Flows	Van A Present Value	Van B Cash Flows	Van B Present value
	@ 8%	$	$	$	$
0	1.000	(25,000)	(25,000)	(30,000)	(30,000)
1	0.926	(2,000)	(1,852)	(3,000)	(2,778)
2	0.857	(2,000)	(1,714)	(3,000)	(2,571)
3	0.794	(3,000)	(2,382)	(3,000)	(2,382)
4	0.735	5,000	3,675	(4,000)	(2,940)
5	0.681			6,000	4,086
Present Value			(27,273)		(36,585)
Cumulative discount factor			3.312		3.993
Annualised equivalent			8,234		9,162

The lowest annualised equivalent cost is for Van A therefore the company should replace its fleet of delivery vans with Van A.

274 SENSITIVITY AND UNCERTAINTY (MAR 12)

Project appraisal involves the estimation of cash flows over several years. As the cash flows can only be estimated with varying degrees of certainty it is useful to see the impact of changes in assumptions on project viability. Sensitivity analysis enables a company to determine the effect of changes to variables on the planned outcome. Particular attention can then be paid to those variables that are identified as being of special significance. In project appraisal, an analysis can be made of all the key variables to ascertain by how much each variable would need to change before the net present value (NPV) reaches zero i.e. the indifference point. Alternatively, specific changes can be tested to determine the effect on NPV.

MANAGING SHORT-TERM FINANCE

275 WCC (NOV 10)

The number of days for each component of the working capital cycle is as follows:

Component	Calculation	Days
Raw material inventory days	85/915 x 365	33.9
Finished goods inventory days	90/1215 x 365	27.0
Receivable days	185/(0.80 x 1,400) x 365	60.3
Payables days	125/(0.95 x 915) x 365	-52.5
Working capital cycle		68.7

The working capital cycle is therefore 68.7 days.

Examiner's comments

It was disappointing to see how many students were unable to calculate basic working capital ratios. Most students were able to calculate the working capital cycle.

Common errors

- Calculating raw material inventory days using cost of sales rather than purchases as the denominator.

- Failing to adjust sales and purchases to credit sales and credit purchases.

- Adding payable days and deducting receivable days when calculating the working capital cycle.

---

276 JE (NOV 09)

	20X8	*20X9*
Inventory days	$= \dfrac{160}{1,910} \times 365$	$= \dfrac{200}{2,800} \times 365$
	$= 31$ days	$= 26$ days
Receivables days	$= \dfrac{250}{2,250} \times 365$	$= \dfrac{390}{3,150} \times 365$
	$= 41$ days	$= 45$ days
Payables days	$= \dfrac{300}{1,910} \times 365$	$= \dfrac{500}{2,800} \times 365$
	$= 57$ days	$= 65$ days
Current ratio	$= \dfrac{250+160+90}{300}$	$= \dfrac{390+200+10}{500+100}$
	$= 1.67$	$= 1.00$
Quick ratio	$= \dfrac{250+90}{300}$	$= \dfrac{390+10}{500+100}$
	$= 1.3$	$= 0.67$

277 HL (MAY 09)

(i) Overtrading means a company it growing too quickly without the long term finance to support its growth. This will result in rapid increase in turnover, high levels of inventory, receivables, payables, little increase in share capital and long term loans and problems with liquidity when short term funding is used to support the growth.

(ii) The actions HL could take to correct the problem could be:

- Inject more long term capital into the business by issuing more share capital or raising long term loans;

- Cut back on trading and be more selective of who they sell to;

- Reduce the working capital cycle to improve liquidity, i.e. chase receivables to collect cash faster, reduce inventory levels and delay payables within reasonable

---

278 DISCOUNTS (MAR 12)

(i) Cost of the discount

The percentage =

$$= [(100/(100 - d))]^{365/t} - 1$$

$$= [100/98]^{365/35} - 1$$

$$= 1.02041^{10.43} - 1$$

$$= 1.2346 - 1$$

$$= 23.5\%$$

(ii) Cost of the discount

> ***Tutorial note***
>
> *The answer provides three examples. Only two of these are needed in the exam and students should not attempt to include more than two methods.*

Bank references - These may be provided by the prospective customer's bank to indicate the customer's financial standing.

Financial statements - The most recent financial statements of the prospective customer can be obtained either direct from the customer, or for limited companies, from Companies House.

Personal contact - A representative of TJ might visit the business premises of the prospective customer.

Examiner's comments

Part (i) was fairly well done although there were occasionally some errors in applying the formula. Part (ii) was also well done although some candidates failed to read the question properly and stated trade references as a potential method.

Common errors

- Incorrect application of the formula e.g. forgetting to deduct 1 or not multiplying the answer by 100.

- Incorrect calculation of the compounding periods e.g. using 35/365 or 365/20.

- Stating trade references as a potential method.

---

279 CREDIT LIMITS (NOV 11)

Bank references

These may be provided by the customer's bank to indicate the customer's financial standing. However, the law and practice of banking secrecy determines the way in which banks respond to credit enquiries, which can render such references uninformative, particularly if the company is experiencing financial difficulties.

Trade references

Companies already trading with the customer may be willing to provide a reference. This can be extremely useful, providing that the companies approached are a representative sample of all of the customer's suppliers. Such references can be misleading, as they are usually based on direct credit experience and contain no knowledge of the underlying financial position of the customer.

Financial statements

The most recent financial statements of the customer can be obtained either direct from the customer or for limited companies from Companies House. While subject to certain limitations, past accounts can be useful in assessing the creditworthiness of the customer. In circumstances where the credit risk appears high or substantial levels of credit are required, the supplier may ask to see evidence of the customer's ability to pay in accordance with proposed payment terms. This would require access to internal future budget data.

Personal contact

A representative of the supplier might visit the business premises of the customer. Through visiting the premises and interviewing the senior management, the representative of the supplier should gain an impression of the efficiency and financial resources of the customer and the integrity of its management. The management will however be keen to give the best impression of the company and the standard of the premises and other resources will reflect past rather than present financial standing.

Past experience

If the credit limit is being determined for an existing customer, the supplier will have access to their past payment record. However, if it is a key supplier to the customer, the supplier should be aware that many failing companies preserve solid payment records with key suppliers in order to maintain supplies, but only do so at the expense of other creditors. Indeed, many companies go into liquidation with excellent payment records with key suppliers.

Tutorial note

The answer provides five examples. Only two of these are needed in the exam and students should not attempt to include more than two methods.

Examiner's comments

This question was generally well answered although most candidates did not appreciate the significance of the use of the verb 'discuss' in the question. To achieve full marks candidates were expected to give both advantages and disadvantages of the suggested sources of information. It was also not clear in many cases what exactly was the source of information. Some candidates discussed using ratio analysis but did not explain where these figures were going to come from. Candidates need to take a more methodical approach to answering questions. No further credit was given to those candidates who chose to give three or four sources of information.

> Common errors
>
> - Giving more than TWO sources of information
> - Not explaining the disadvantages of the suggested sources
> - Not describing the sources of information
> - Confusing credit terms/period with credit limit

280 WITHOUT RECOURSE FACTORING (MAR 11)

(i) Annual sales revenue = $1,095,000

Factoring fee	$1,095,000 x 2.5%	= $27,375
Annual interest	(90% x $180,000) x 12%	= $19,440
		$46,815
Savings in credit control costs		$20,000
Net cost of factoring		$26,815

(ii) The company requires to borrow – $180,000 x 90% =$162,000

The cost of borrowing is therefore – $162,000 x 15% = $24,300

There is therefore no financial benefit in factoring as the cost of borrowing is less than the cost of factoring.

> **Examiner's comments**
>
> Very few candidates achieved full marks in this question. Many candidates showed a lack of understanding of the factoring process by calculating the interest on the total sales revenue of $1,095k. Candidates were rarely able to gain more than two or three marks with various extraneous items included in the answer and incorrect calculations of the relevant items.
>
> *Common errors*
> - Calculating the interest cost based on the total sales revenue rather than on 90% of the outstanding trade receivables.
> - Deducting $20,000 in both part (i) and part (ii).
> - Failure to recognise that the factor advanced only 90% of the outstanding invoice value.

281 FACTORING (MAY 11)

Advantages

Factoring has the advantage that 80 – 85% of the cash is received immediately with the remainder received when the client settles the debt. Factoring can also be provided on a non-recourse basis, i.e. the factor guarantees settlement even if they are not paid by the customers. The factor will also administer the client's sales ledger including the assessment of credit worthiness of the customer, invoicing and collection. The factor has considerable expertise in all of these areas that a small business in particular may not have available. Factoring also provides flexibility since as sales increase with the corresponding demand for finance, so finance from this source increases. It may be a cost effective source of finance for a company that has no assets, other than its receivables, to offer as security.

Disadvantages

Factoring has in the past been associated with financial difficulties and many companies are reluctant to use factors for this reason. It may also be difficult, if using factoring, to raise more traditional forms of finance except at high interest rates. The services provided by a factor are expensive and may not be cost effective. The company will also lose the benefits of being in personal communication with the customer. Once established with a factor, it may be difficult for a company to withdraw from the arrangement and re-establish a sales ledger function.

Examiner's comments

This question was very well answered with candidates showing a good knowledge of both the advantages and disadvantages of factoring. The majority of candidates scored full marks for this question.

---

282 AGED RECEIVABLES ANALYSIS (MAY 10)

(i) **Aged debtor analysis**

Outstanding invoices only

	Jan	Feb	Mar	Apr	Total
Invoice no: 234	118				
Invoice no: 365			135		
Invoice no: 379			232		
Invoice no: 391			71		
Invoice no: 438				145	
Totals	118		438	145	701

(ii) **Benefits of an aged debtor analysis**

- This can help determine tactics for trying to collect overdue payments
- It can help collection staff prioritise debtors to prioritise
- It may highlight customers who should no longer be supplied
- It may indicate when cash is likely to come into the business and how much

(choose any two of the above)

283 CREDIT TERMS (SEPT 12)

(a) (i) **Effective annual interest rate**

Payment will be received 80 days early.

Number of compounding periods = 365/80 = 4.5625

$1 + r = (1.00/0.97)^{4.5625}$

$1 + r = 1.14909$

The effective annual interest rate of the early settlement discount is 14.9%

(ii) **Bank loans**

Tutorial note

The answer provides four examples. Only two of these are needed in the exam and students should not attempt to include more than two methods.

- The bank will normally include additional conditions such as security in the form of fixed/floating charges and other debt covenants. These are likely to result in reduced financial flexibility for GH.
- Bank loans will increase the company's gearing ratio.
- Interest charges on bank loans are normally based on the bank's base rate. This makes it harder to forecast the interest payable and exposes the business to future increases in interest rates
- A bank loan is generally inflexible in terms of amount and time period whereas working capital requirements are likely to fluctuate.

(b) **Debt Factoring**

Advantages

Factoring has the advantage that GH will received 80 – 85% of the cash immediately with the remainder being received when the customer settles the debt thus reducing the need for working capital financing. Factoring can also be provided on a non-recourse basis, i.e. the factor guarantees settlement even if they are not paid by the customers. The factor will also administer GH's sales ledger including the assessment of credit worthiness of customer, invoicing and collection which will result in reduced administration costs. The factor has considerable expertise in all of these areas that a small business in particular may not have available. Factoring also provides flexibility since as sales increase with the corresponding demand for finance, so finance from this source increases. It may be a cost effective lender to GH, if it has no assets, apart from its receivables, to offer as security.

Disadvantages

Factoring is sometimes associated with financial difficulties and many companies are reluctant to use factors for this reason. GH will also lose personal communication with its customers. The services provided by a factor are expensive and may not be cost effective. It may be difficult for GH in the future to withdraw from the arrangement and re-establish a sales ledger function. It may also be difficult to raise more traditional forms of finance except at high interest rates. Debt factoring would involve factoring GH's total sales ledger. It may be more appropriate to use invoice discounting where only the invoices relating to this contract would be discounted.

284   EOQ (SEPT 10)

(i)   **Total annual costs**

$$EOQ = \sqrt{\frac{2C_oD}{C_h}} \quad = \quad \sqrt{\frac{2 \times \$360 \times 150,000}{\$3.00}}$$

$$= \quad \sqrt{36,000,000}$$

$$= \quad 6,000 \text{ units}$$

Cost of holding	=	Holding cost per unit x average stock levels (i.e. EOQ/2)
	=	$3.00 x (6,000 / 2)
	=	$9,000
Cost of ordering	=	Cost per order x no. of orders (i.e. demand / EOQ)
	=	$360 x (150,000 / 6,000)
	=	$9,000

(Note that at the EOQ, the cost of holding and ordering are equal. So there is technically no need to do a full calculation for the cost of ordering.)

(ii)   **Bulk discount**

Existing total costs:

		$
Purchase cost	150,000 x $2	300,000
Holding cost		9,000
Order cost		9,000
		–––––––
Total cost		318,000

New total costs

		$
Purchase cost	150,000 x $2 x 99%	297,000
Holding cost	$3 x (10,000/2)	15,000
Order cost	$360 x (150k/10k)	5,400
		–––––––
Total cost		317,400

Benefit of the bulk discount =   318,000 – 317,400   = $600

285   INVENTORY LEVELS (MAY 10)

(i)   **Total annual costs**

$$EOQ = \sqrt{\frac{2C_oD}{C_h}} = \sqrt{\frac{2 \times \$150 \times 64,000}{\$1.20}}$$

$$= \quad \sqrt{16,000,000}$$

$$= \quad 4,000 \text{ units}$$

Cost of holding	=	Holding cost per unit x average stock levels (i.e. EOQ/2)
	=	$1.20 x (4,000 / 2)
	=	$2,400

Cost of ordering	=	Cost per order x no. of orders (i.e. demand / EOQ)	
	=	$150 x (64,000 / 4,000)	
	=	2,400	

(Note that at the EOQ, the cost of holding and ordering are equal. So there is technically no need to do a full calculation for the cost of ordering.)

(ii) **Reorder level**

Average demand per week = 64,000 / 52 = 1,231 units.

Maximum lead time = 3 weeks

Minimum inventory level at which to place an order = 1,231 x 3 = 3,693 units.

286 CH (NOV 11)

	January $000	February $000	March $000
Cash sales	75	80	90
Receipts from credit sales (W1)	245	253	254
Total receipts	320	333	344
Payment for purchases (W2)	(180)	(195)	(200)
Expenses paid	(122)	(123)	(123)
Forklift trucks		(100)	
Total payments	(302)	(418)	(323)
Net cash	18	(85)	21
Opening balance	15	33	(52)
Closing balance	33	(52)	(31)

Workings

(W1) Credit sales – receipts

	Total sales $000	January $000	February $000	March $000
October	250	20		
November	250	25	20	
December	250	200	25	20
January	260		208	26
February	260			208
Total		245	253	254

(W2) Credit purchases – payments

	Total purchases $000	January $000	February $000	March $000
November	180	45		
December	180	135	45	
January	200		150	50
February	200			150
Total		180	195	200

287   JL (MAR 12)

	Quarter 1 $	Quarter 2 $	Quarter 3 $
Receipts			
b/f trade receivables	125,000		
20% cash sales	100,000	90,000	96,000
56% in same quarter	280,000	252,000	268,800
24% in quarter following sales		120,000	108,000
Total receipts	505,000	462,000	472,800
Payments			
b/f trade payables	60,000		
Materials 50% in same Quarter	69,000	75,600	57,800
Materials 50% in next Quarter		69,000	75,600
Labour and overheads	284,000	284,000	284,000
Loan repayment			100,000
Total payments	413,000	428,600	517,400
Opening balance	49,400	141,400	174,800
Net cash flow	92,000	33,400	-44,600
Closing balance	141,400	174,800	130,200

288   BILLS OF EXCHANGE (MAY 09)

Three ways to use a bill of exchange are:
- Hold the bill of exchange until maturity and collect the money;
- Transfer the bill of exchange to a bank to gain immediate cash. The bank will discount the bill as this is effectively a loan until the maturity date;
- Transfer the bill of exchange to a supplier as payment of a debt. This again will be at a discount.

When the due date of maturity arises whoever has the bill of exchange will receive payment.

The maximum price that HG should be willing to pay should be:

7% = a year, therefore for 91 days = 91/365 x 7% = 0.017452

The price is calculated by deducting this from 1 = 1 − 0.017452 = 0.982548 x $1,000 (face value) = $982.55

289 TREASURY BILLS (MAR 11)

The returns given are over different time periods. It is necessary to calculate a rate per annum to enable the investments to be compared:

The annual return on the treasury bills is ($5/$995) x 365/91 = 2.02%

The annual return on the bank deposit account is 2.5%.

Treasury bills are generally considered risk free as they are guaranteed by the government of the country of issue. However during the present economic recession it has become evident that investment with countries that have previously been considered financially secure are not risk free. It should be borne in mind that the treasury bills are fixed dated and although they are negotiable this would incur costs and expose the company to price movement which will reflect the change in market interest rates. Although the return is fixed, if the company holds the bills for 91 days, market interest rates may rise with the result that the return on the treasury bills may be below market rates.

The deposit account has a variable interest rate which will introduce variability in the return, although this is likely to reflect market rates. Investments in banks are generally considered very low risk however after the world banking crisis in 2008/2009 it is now conceivable for a bank to fail. This introduces another albeit small element of risk in that there is liquidation risk of the bank itself. The deposit account lacks flexibility as it requires the company to give 30 days' notice of withdrawal or accept penalty interest charges.

The choice of investment will depend on the company's attitude to risk and whether they prefer to have a fixed return. The bank deposit account currently offers a higher return but may not continue to do so in the future.

Examiner's comments

Candidates generally scored reasonably well, often making the expected points regarding risk in relation to capital and income. Many nevertheless were unable to make a valid interest rate comparison between the two investments and invariably thought that it would not be possible to recover the capital in the treasury bills before the end of the 91-day period. This led many to conclude that the 30 day notice account was the most liquid of the two investments.

Common errors

- Failure to clearly explain the points made.
- Inability to correctly calculate the return on the Treasury bills.
- Failure to recognise that the Treasury bills were negotiable.

---

290 COUPON RATE (MAR 11)

When a bond is issued it carries a 'coupon' rate. This is the rate that is payable on the face, or nominal, value of the bond. Unlike shares which are rarely issued at their nominal value, debt is frequently issued at par, usually $100 payable for $100 nominal value of the bond. At the time of issue, the interest rate will be fixed according to interest rates available in the market for bonds of similar maturity i.e. the coupon rate and the yield to maturity of the bond will be the same. As market interest rates change during the life of the bond, so the market value of the bonds will change and the yield to maturity, from interest and capital gain on the bond, will then differ from the coupon rate of the bond. If market interest rates increase the market value of the bond will fall to a level where the yield to maturity to an investor, at that point, reflects market interest rates.

> **Examiner's comments**
>
> This question was answered very poorly. Candidates did not understand the difference between the coupon rate and the yield to maturity, but assumed that it was to do with discount factors, NPVs and IRRs. Many consequently tried to provide calculations which were not requested in the question. Candidates would have done better if they had started by defining the coupon rate and the yield to maturity.
>
> *Common errors*
>
> - Failure to explain the coupon rate and the yield to maturity.
>
> - Making irrelevant calculations.
>
> - General lack of knowledge of the topic area.

291 RISK AND YIELD (NOV 06)

Notes on risk and effective yield of potential investments:

Treasury bills

Treasury bills reflect the credit rating of the country, so are generally low risk. However, as the risk is low, the investment is relatively attractive, such that the rate of interest is generally relatively low. In this case a yield of $10 would be earned over three months, which is an effective interest rate of only 1% per quarter.

Yield is achieved through a combination of interest payments and a growth in the value of the bill over time.

Equities

The value of equities can go down as well as up. In this case, the equity index has increased for the last 14 months. However, this cannot be taken as a guarantee of future continued good performance.

The risk associated with a particular share depends upon the risk associated with the market in general and the risk associated with the particular company. In this case, the proposed companies are multinationals, which can result in a lower risk due to diversification.

Due to the higher risk associated with equities, the yield is generally relatively high.

Bank deposit

A bank deposit is an investment in the business of the bank. However, banks are generally very secure, such that it is normally assumed that the investment will be recovered in full.

As with treasury bills, the yield is low to reflect the low risk, so carries a low rate of interest. However, in this case, the company would be required to give 30 days' notice of any withdrawals. This gives the bank more certainty and is reflected in an increased return on the deposit, in the form of an increased interest rate.

292 YIELD TO MATURITY (MAY 11)

Year(s)	Description	Cash flow	Discount factor (3%)	Present value $	Discount factor (6%)	Present value $
0	Purchase	103	1.000	(103.00)	1.000	(103.00)
1-4	Interest	6	3.717	22.30	3.465	20.79
4	Redemption	100	0.888	88.80	0.792	79.20
NPV				8.10		(3.01)

By interpolation

3% + (($8.10 /($8.10 + $3.01)) x 3) = 5.19%

The bond's yield to maturity is 5.19%

Examiner's comments

This question was answered very poorly. Candidates did not understand the difference between the coupon rate and the yield to maturity, but assumed that it was to do with discount factors, NPVs and IRRs. Many consequently tried to provide calculations which were not requested in the question. Candidates would have done better if they had started by defining the coupon rate and the yield to maturity.

Common errors

- Failure to explain the coupon rate and the yield to maturity.

- Making irrelevant calculations.

- General lack of knowledge of the topic area.

---

293 EXPORT FINANCING (MAY 11)

(i)   Bills of exchange

The bill of exchange requires the customer to pay the amount due at some fixed future date. The supplier signs the bill and sends it to the customer, who also signs it to signify that they agree to pay. The supplier can either, hold the bill until the due date and collect the money, discount the bill with the bank for immediate payment or transfer the bill to their own supplier in settlement of an amount due.

(ii)   Forfaiting

The forfaiting bank buys at a discount to face value a series of promissory notes (or bills of exchange). The promissory notes may be in any of the world's major currencies. For promissory notes to be eligible for forfaiting (and to provide the forfaiting bank security), the notes must be guaranteed by a highly rated international bank, usually in the importers country.

(iii)   Documentary credits

A documentary credit is an undertaking that payment to the exporter will be guaranteed provided that the exporter complies with certain specific requirements. The foreign buyer would advise its bank (the issuing bank) to provide credit in favour of the exporter. The issuing bank would then ask the exporters bank to advise or confirm credit to the exporter. The issuing bank is effectively guaranteeing payment for the goods. The exporter's bank will provide payment to the exporter on receipt of satisfactory documentation for the goods. The documents are sent to the issuing bank who if satisfied will reimburse the exporter's bank and release the documents to the foreign buyer after payment has been received. The foreign buyer can then take delivery of the goods.

Examiner's comments

This question demonstrated a lack of knowledge in some areas of the syllabus. Candidates showed some knowledge of bills of exchange but few candidates had any knowledge whatsoever of forfaiting and documentary credits. This question examines an important learning outcome and yet has obviously been considered a peripheral part of the syllabus and not studied by candidates.

Common errors

- Inability to answer the question due to lack of knowledge
- Making general statements for all three methods in a vain hope of gaining some marks

---

294 OVERDRAFT (SEPT 11)

Advantages

Flexibility: The bank will agree an overdraft limit or facility. The borrower may not require the full facility immediately but may draw funds up to the limit as and when required. If the funds are no longer required they can be repaid without suffering any penalty.

Minimal documentation: Legal documentation is fairly minimal when arranging an overdraft. The documents will state the maximum overdraft limit, the interest payable and the security required.

An overdraft is seen as a relatively cheap source of finance. Banks usually charge between 2 and 5% above base rate depending on the creditworthiness and security offered by the borrower. Savings come from the fact that interest is only paid on the daily outstanding balance therefore a large cash inflow can offset the balance outstanding and temporarily lower the interest payable, whilst still retaining the ability to borrow up to the overdraft limit when required.

Disadvantages

An overdraft is strictly speaking repayable on demand.

The interest rate payable will vary depending on the perceived credit risk of the borrower.

Banks will normally expect security either in the form of a fixed charge or a floating charge.

295 INVESTMENT RISKS (SEPT 11)

Default risk

This refers to potential doubt about the payment of interest or the eventual repayment of the capital invested. Investments in government securities are generally considered to have very low default risk however the recent financial crisis has shown that even investment in government securities is not risk free. Investment in equities is generally considered high risk and is not a suitable form of short-term investment.

Interest rate risk

This refers to the risk that market interest rates will change and the investor will be worse off. Interest rates cannot be predicted with any degree of accuracy. Variable rate bank deposits will leave the company vulnerable to a fall in interest rates. If the investment is in a fixed rate term deposit, whilst the investor will receive a guaranteed return, there will be an opportunity cost if market interest rates increase above the fixed rate.

296 INVESTING CASH SURPLUSES (MAY 12)

Three factors that would need to be considered when deciding how to invest short term cash surpluses are:

Maturity

A short term investment will involve investing the money for a specified period of time and receiving interest and the payment of the capital at a specified future date. The maturity date of the investment should be no longer than the duration of the cash surplus. If the cash is required before the maturity of the investment and the investment is 'cashed in' early, there will be the risk of loss of interest or capital value.

Risk v Return

Risk refers to the possibility that the investment might fall in value or that there may be some doubt about the eventual payment of interest or repayment of capital. Generally a higher risk investment will offer a higher return.

Investing in equities is high risk since the value of the equities depends on the profitability and future prospects of the company and stock market movements. Share prices can fall by a large amount in a short period of time therefore equities are generally regarded as an unsuitable form of short-term investment.

Liquidity

Liquidity refers to the ease with which an investment can be 'cashed in' without any significant loss of value or interest. All short-term investments are less liquid than cash in a bank current account but some are more liquid than others. For example, many savings accounts or deposit accounts are reasonably liquid and a depositor can withdraw cash immediately without penalty or for the loss of only several days' interest.

Examiner's comments

This question was not well answered. Candidates considered return as a separate factor and stated that the company should invest in the option that gave the highest return. They did not appear to appreciate that the return offered on an investment would depend on the other three factors. Candidates occasionally talked about liquidity but rarely maturity. Some candidates just listed three different investment options and discussed the merits or otherwise of the three options which scored few marks. Some candidates misread the question and considered other opportunities for the use of the funds such as paying off an overdraft or keeping the cash just in case. This was not relevant as the question asked 'how' to invest not 'whether' to invest.

Common errors

- Failure to answer the question requirements set.
- Assuming return was not dependent on other factors.
- Lack of consideration of liquidity and maturity.

Section 6

ANSWERS TO SECTION C-TYPE QUESTIONS

COST ACCOUNTING SYSTEMS

297 RETAIL COMPANY (NOV 09) *Walk in the footsteps of a top tutor*

Key answer tips

Part (a) of this question is in an unusual format that many students may not have seen before. The key to success will be to read the requirement carefully. Notice that each of the three changes must be dealt with *independently* (for example, the results from part (i) should be ignored when attempting part (ii)). Also, rather than simply stating the effect a number, the revised number must be stated. The final element to be careful with is that the changes take place at the *start* of the accounting year. There will be easy marks for filling in figures that do not change – so make sure you put a figure in every box.

In part (b) of the question, it will be important that you know the break even formulae (a commonly examined area). In this scenario you have to work with the contribution margin (contribution as a % of selling price) rather than the contribution per unit. Part (iii) is the easier part and should be dealt with first (even if you cannot do the calculations).

Part (c) covers an uncommonly examined area and only very well prepared students would score well in this section. This highlights the need for comprehensive syllabus coverage in order to maximise the chance of success in this paper. There are two element – Beyond Budgeting and TQM. There will be marks available for defining each element, so that even if Beyond Budgeting is unfamiliar to you, you should still pick up some marks on TQM (which is regularly examined). Having defined each element, to get full marks you need to link the two elements together and explain why this might be a better relationship than traditional budgeting techniques.

Overall, this is a tricky question where it will be important that you pick out the easy marks available first. There are easy marks for explaining TQM, assessing the proposal, putting figures in the table that don't change etc. Good technique should gain you enough marks to gain a pass. But this needs to be backed up with good syllabus knowledge if you want to gain all the marks.

(a) **Sensitivity analysis**

	(i)	*(ii)*	*(iii)*
Operating profit	440,000	440,000	245,000
Inventory	200,000	182,280	182,280
Receivables	501,000	641,100	475,950
Cash	271,580	149,200	119,350
Payables	428,980	428,980	428,980

Workings

(i) **Increase inventory to £200,000**

Assumptions: he change is arrived at from a revaluation of opening *and* closing inventory.

This means that there will be reduction in cash (£17,720) and an increase in closing inventory. All other figures (such as operating profit) will remain unaffected.

(ii) **Increase receivable days to 60**

Revised receivables can be calculated as follows:

$$= \frac{60}{365} \times \text{Sales revenue}$$

$$= \frac{60}{365} \times 3,900,000$$

$$= £641,100$$

This represents an increase in receivables of £140,100. There would be no impact on sales or operating profit, but cash would reduce by this amount as customers pay later.

(iii) **Reduce selling prices by 5%**

This would have the effect of reducing both sales revenue and receivables by 5%. It would also mean that the cash received from collected sales would also reduce by 5%.

Reduction in sales revenue (and operating profit)	=	5% x 3,900,000	=	£195,000
Reduction in receivables	=	5% x 501,000	=	£25,050
Reduction in cash recovered	=	195,000 – 25,050	=	£169,950

(b) **Break even analysis**

(i) **Break even point**

$$\text{Break even point} = \frac{\text{Fixed costs (W1)}}{\text{Contribution margin (W2)}}$$

$$= \frac{516,000}{24.5\%}$$

$$= £2,106,122$$

Workings

(W1) **Fixed Costs**

	=	60% of selling and administration costs
	=	60% x 860,000
	=	516,000

(W2) **Contribution margin**

Gross profit		=	1,300,000
Variable selling and administration costs	= 40% x 860,000	=	344,000
Contribution		=	£956,000
As a % of sales revenue		=	24.5%

(ii) **Break even point**

Break even point $= \dfrac{\text{Fixed costs (W1)}}{\text{Contribution margin (W2)}}$

$= \dfrac{1,116,000}{37.8\%}$

$= £2,952,380$

Workings

(W1) **Fixed Costs**

	=	old fixed costs + annual fee
	=	516,000 + 600,000
	=	1,116,000

(W2) **Contribution margin**

Revised gross profit = 1,300,000 + (20% x 2,600,000)	=	1,820,000
Variable selling and administration costs	=	344,000
Contribution	=	£1,476,000
As a % of sales revenue	=	37.8%

(iii) **Assessment of the proposal**

Advantages

- Dealing with only one supplier will reduce administration and inbound logistics costs. So there may further cost advantages that have not been accounted for.

- The reduction in cost of sales may allow a reduction in selling prices. This might stimulate more sales volume and allow the retailer to become more competitive.

Disadvantages

- The costs outweigh the benefits. The reduction in cost of sales will be £520,000 based on existing (optimistic) forecasts, against an annual fee of £600,000.

- The retailers risk will increase. Because a greater proportion of costs will be fixed the breakeven point rises by £800,000. This might be more difficult to achieve in the current economic climate.

(c) **Beyond Budgeting**

It has been argued that the budgeting process is limiting and unsuitable for businesses, and better budgeting (for example, by using, say, zero based budgeting) is not an answer to the problem. Instead, budgets should be abandoned.

The argument for abolishing budgets, referred to as **'beyond budgeting'**, is that the modern business environment is constantly changing. Managers need to be flexible and facilitate change. The budgeting system is too rigid. It acts as a barrier to change because managers are expected to conform to budget. The emphasis in budgeting is on minimising costs, not maximising value. Therefore, managers are held back by the budgeting system from achieving the organisation's goals.

Total Quality Management (TQM) has been defined as: 'an integrated and comprehensive system of planning and controlling all business functions so that products or services are produced which meet or exceed customer expectations. TQM is a philosophy of business behaviour, embracing principles such as employee involvement, continuous improvement at all levels and customer focus, as well as being a collection of related techniques aimed at improving quality such as full documentation of activities, clear goal setting and performance measurement from the customer perspective.' (CIMA *Official Terminology*)

Traditional budgets restrict flexibility because individuals feel they are expected to achieve the budget targets. This is a deterrent to continual improvement (and so is inconsistent with TQM). A shift to a 'beyond budgeting' approach would facilitate the flexibility and change needed to support TQM and make it successful. Beyond Budgeting is likely to empower individuals to make the changes needed in a TQM environment and to find more efficient ways to perform tasks. Everyone will be involved in the process – not just the budget setters and budget owners. This will support the 'total' element of TQM.

298   HIP, KNEE AND SHOULDER (NOV 10)

Key answer tips

This is a typical ABC question. There are lots of 'easier' marks available for discussing the benefits of ABC (part (c)) and for performing traditional costing techniques (part (a)). So those students with good technique should have attempted these parts first and got themselves well on the way to a pass in the question. Some students may have been thrown by the scenario as it was not a traditional production company and instead involved a company performing healthcare operations. There was also a lot of information to take in. But it was well laid out in tabular form (for example, even cost drivers were clearly flagged and students would not have had to work these out for themselves) and any reasonable progress towards a standard cost card should have been enough to ensure a pass overall.

(a) **Profit per procedure using the current basis**

	Hip	Knee	Shoulder
	$	$	$
Fee charged to patient	8,000	10,000	6,000
Surgeon's fee	(1,200)	(1,800)	(1,500)
Fee for follow-up consultations	(24)	(15)	(30)
Medical supplies	(400)	(200)	(300)
Overhead cost	(5,200)	(6,500)	(3,900)
Profit per procedure	1,176	1,485	270

Follow-up consultations working:

Hip - $300 per consultation x 8% = $24

Knee - $300 per consultation x 5% = $15

Shoulder - $300 per consultation x 10% = $30

Overhead cost workings:

	Hip	Knee	Shoulder	Total
	$	$	$	$
Sales revenue	$8,000 x 600 = $4,800,000	$10,000 x 800 = $8,000,000	$6,000 x 400 = $2,400,000	$15,200,000
Overheads				$9,880,000
Overheads / sales revenue				65%
Cost per procedure	$8,000 x 65% $5,200	$10,000 x 65% $6,500	$6,000 x 65% $3,900	

(b) **Profit per procedure using ABC**

Activity	Cost Driver	Overheads $000	No. of cost drivers	Cost per driver $
Theatre preparation for each session	Number of theatre preparations	864	(600/2 + 800/1 + 400/4) = 1,200	$720 per theatre preparation
Operating theatre usage	Procedure time	1,449	(600 x 2hrs) + (800 x 1.2hrs) + (400 x 1.5hrs) = 2,760	$525 per hour
Nursing and ancillary services	In-patient days	5,428	(600 x 3) + (800 x 2) +(400 x 1) = 3,800	$1,428 per day

Activity	Cost Driver	Overheads $000	No. of cost drivers	Cost per driver $
Administration	Sales revenue	1,216	15,200,000	$0.08 per $ sales revenue
Other overheads	Number of procedures	923	(600 + 800 + 400) = 1,800	$513 per procedure

Overhead cost per procedure	Hip	Knee	Shoulder
Theatre preparation for each session	$720/2 = $360	$720/1 = $720	$720/4 = $180
Operating theatre usage	($525 x 2) = $1,050	($525 x 1.2) =$630	($525 x 1.5) = $788
Nursing and ancillary services	($1,428 x 3) =$4,284	($1,428 x 2) =$2,856	($1,428 x 1) =$1,428
Administration	(8,000 x $0.08) = $640	(10,000 x $0.08) = $800	(6,000 x$ 0.08) = $480
Other overheads	$513	$513	$513
Total overhead cost per procedure	$6,847	$5,519	$3,389

	Hip	Knee	Shoulder
	$	$	$
Profit per procedure per (a) above	1,176	1,485	270
Add back overhead cost per (a) above	5,200	6,500	3,900
Less overhead cost using ABC	(6,847)	(5,519)	(3,389)
Profit per procedure using ABC	(471)	2,466	781

(c) **Usefulness of the information**

Under an activity based costing (ABC) system the various support activities that are involved in the process of making products or providing services are identified. The cost drivers that cause a change to the cost of these activities are also identified and used as the basis to attach activity costs to a particular product or service. Through the tracing of costs to product in this way ABC establishes more accurate costs for the product or service.

The identification of cost drivers provides information to management to enable them to take actions to improve the overall profitability of the company. Cost driver analysis will provide information to management on how costs can be controlled and managed. Variance analysis will be more useful as it is based on more accurate costs.

The establishment of more accurate procedure costs should also help hospital managers to assess procedure profitability and make better decisions concerning pricing and procedure mix decisions.

In the above example, the use of an ABC system has resulted in different levels of profit for each of the procedures. It is apparent that the knee replacement procedure and the shoulder replacement procedure are more profitable than was thought under the absorption costing system. The shoulder replacement procedure however is making a significantly lower margin that the knee replacement procedure. The hip replacement procedure is now shown to be loss making. This additional information will enable management to make important decisions regarding pricing of the procedures. The price of the knee replacement procedure could potentially be reduced to make it more competitive and increase volumes. The price of both the hip replacement and shoulder replacement procedures could be increased to make these procedures more profitable. Before making any decision regarding pricing however they would need to review market prices and consider the effect any adjustment would have on the company's market position. If market conditions would not allow an increase in price of both hip and shoulder replacement procedures they could look at ways to reduce the costs of these procedures. ABC gives more detailed information about how costs are incurred and the potential for cost reduction by reducing activity levels. Alternatively they may want to consider whether to discontinue the hip replacement procedures altogether and replace them with a more profitable use of resources. This decision may not be appropriate however if part of the marketing strategy is for the company to provide a range of complementary procedures.

An activity based costing system can be extended beyond product and service costing to a range of cost management applications known as activity based management. These include the identification of value added and non value added activities and performance management in terms of measuring efficiency through cost driver rates.

Examiner's comments

This question was generally very well done although some calculations caused difficulty, in particular the calculation of follow up fees in part (a) and theatre preparation costs in part (b). Students lost marks and time because they did not read the question properly. In part (a) some students apportioned the overhead by activity which wasted a lot of valuable time and gained no marks. Some students failed to show workings in part (b) which potentially lost them marks. Too many students are still not laying out workings in a clear, structured way, potentially resulting in the loss of marks. Part (c) was well answered by the majority of students.

Common errors

- Failure to calculate follow-up fees correctly, using instead a flat rate of $300.

- Allocating overhead costs based on units sold rather than on sales revenue.

- Calculating the number of cost drivers for theatre preparations as 3,600 rather than 1,200.

- Multiplying the cost driver rate for theatre preparation by 2, 1 and 4 respectively rather than dividing by 2, 1 and 4.

299 RJ (MAY 07)

> **Key answer tips**
>
> In part (a) you will need to calculate the total machine hours in order to determine the overhead recovery rate for absorption costing.

(a)   **Budgeted Operating Statement**

Fixed production overhead = $35,000,000

Budgeted machine hours = (1,100 × 200) + (1,600 × 300) = 700,000 machine hours

Fixed production overhead absorption rate = $35,000,000/700,000 = $50 per machine hour.

	Car X $ per car	Car Y $ per car
Total production cost per unit		
($44,000,000/1,100)	40,000	
($75,200,000/1,600)		47,000
Fixed overhead absorbed		
(200 × $50)	10,000	
(300 × $50)		15,000
Variable production cost per car	30,000	32,000

Marginal costing operating statement – year ending 30 June 2008

	Car X $000	Car Y $000	Total $000
Sales	52,500	105,000	157,500
Variable production costs			
(1,000 × $30,000)	30,000		
(1,750 × $32,000)		56,000	86,000
Variable administration costs	6,300	12,600	18,900
Contribution	16,200	36,400	52,600
Specific fixed costs			
Marketing	2,000	4,000	6,000
Contribution to general fixed costs	14,200	32,400	46,600
General fixed costs			
Production			35,000
Administration ($16,000 – $6,000)			10,000
Profit			**1,600**

(b) **Reconciliation of Profits**

The difference in the profit figures will be caused by the fixed production overheads that are absorbed into closing inventories. If inventory levels increase, the absorption costing profit will be higher than the profit calculated using marginal costing since a proportion of fixed overhead will be carried forward to be charged against future revenue.

	Car X	Car Y
Change in inventory (units)	+100	−150
Fixed production overhead per car	$10,000	$15,000
Total difference in profits	$1,000,000	$2,250,000

Reconciliation

	$000
Absorption costing profit	350
Car X: inventory impact	(1,000)
Car Y: inventory impact	2,250
Marginal costing profit	1,600

(c) **Budgeted Production Cost**

Activity	Cost Driver		Drivers
Machining costs	Machine hours	From part a)	700,000
Set up costs	No. of production runs	(1,100/10) + (1,600/40)	150
Quality inspections	No. of inspections	(110 × 20) + (40 × 80)	5,400
Stores receiving	No. of deliveries	492 + 900	1,392
Stores issues	No. of issues	4,000 + 7,000	11,000

Activity	$000	Driver	Cost per driver
Machining costs	7,000	700,000	$10 per machine hour
Set up costs	12,000	150	$80,000 per set up
Quality inspections	7,020	5,400	$1,300 per inspection
Stores receiving	3,480	1,392	$2,500 per delivery
Stores issues	5,500	11,000	$500 per issue

	Car X		Car Y		
	Driver	$000	Driver	$000	
Machining costs	220,000	2,200	480,000	4,800	
Set up costs	110	8,800	40	3,200	
Quality inspections	2,200	2,860	3,200	4,160	
Stores receiving	492	1,230	900	2,250	
Stores issues	4,000	2,000	7,000	3,500	
Total overhead		17,090		17,910	
Direct costs		33,000		51,200	
Total production costs		50,090		69,110	
Cars produced		1,100		1,600	
Cost per car		**$45,536**		**$43,194**	

(d)   **Report**

To: Production Director

From: Management Accountant

Date: 22 May 2007

Subject: Activity Based Budgeting – Performance Evaluation

Introduction

This report presents the potential benefits of adopting an activity based budgeting approach for performance evaluation.

Benefits of activity based budgeting

(1)   **Better understanding of activities which cause costs**

Activity based budgeting provides a clear framework for understanding the link between costs and the level of activity. This would allow us to evaluate performance based on the activity that drives the cost.

The modern business environment has a high proportion of costs that are indirect and the only meaningful way of attributing these costs to individual products is to find the root cause of such costs, that is, what activity is driving these costs. The traditional absorption costing approach collects overhead costs using functional headings which may make many overhead costs appear to be fixed as they are not linked to the volume of output but they may be related to other activities which are variable for a batch or product line.

(2)   **Clearer responsibility for costs**

With an activity based costing approach responsibility for activities and therefore costs can be broken down and assigned accordingly. Individual managers can provide input into the budgeting process and subsequently be held responsible for the variances arising.

(3)   **More detailed analysis of overhead costs**

There is greater transparency with an ABB system due to the level of detail behind the costs. The traditional absorption costing approach combines all of the overheads together using a machine hour basis to calculate an overhead absorption rate and uses this rate to attribute overheads to products. ABB will drill down in much more detail examining the cost and the driver of such costs and calculate a cost driver rate which will be used to assign overheads to products. Therefore ABB has greater transparency than absorption costing and allows for much more detailed information on overhead consumption and so on. This then lends itself to better performance evaluation.

Conclusion

The traditional absorption costing approach to product costing does not enable us to provide a satisfactory explanation for the behaviour of costs. In contrast ABB will provide such details which will allow us to have better cost control, improved performance evaluation and greater manager accountability. If you require any further information please do not hesitate to contact me.

300 PHOTOCOPYING COMPANY (MAR 11)

Key answer tips

In part (a) students should identify the direct costs for each procedure and then calculate the overhead absorption rate. This rate can then be applied to each procedure and the profit calculated. In part (b) students need to calculate a cost driver rate for each of the activities and then apply this cost driver rate to calculate the overhead cost for each activity per procedure. The profit per procedure can then be recalculated using the activity-based overhead costs per procedure. In part (c) students need to clearly explain the potential benefits to the company of using activity-based costing in the areas of planning, decision making and control.

(a)   **Profit per machine**

	Small	Medium	Large
	$	$	$
Copy charge per machine	(60,000 x $0.03) = 1,800	(120,000 x 0.04) = 4,800	(180,000 x $0.05) = 9,000
Cost of parts per machine	($100 x 5) = (500)	($300 x 7) = (2,100)	($400 x 14) = (5,600)
Labour cost per machine	($60 x 5) = (300)	($80 x 7) = (560)	($100 x 14) = (1,400)
Overhead cost (W1)	(324)	(864)	(1,620)
Profit per machine	676	1,276	380

(W1) **Overhead cost workings**

	Small	Medium	Large	Total
	$	$	$	$
Sales revenue	$1,800 x 300 = $540,000	$4,800 x 800 = $3,840,000	$9,000 x 500 = $4,500,000	$8,880,000
Overheads				$1,596,000
Overheads / sales revenue				18%
Cost per machine	$1,800 x 18% = $324	$4,800 x 18% = $864	$9,000 x 18% = $1,620	

(b)   **Cost driver rates**

Activity	Cost Driver	Overheads $000	No. of cost drivers	Cost per driver $
Customer account handling	Number of customers	126	(300 / 2) + (800 / 2) + (500 / 2) = 800	$157.50 per customer
Planned maintenance scheduling	Number of planned maintenance visits	480	(300 x 4) + (800 x 6) + (500 x 12) = 12,000	$40 per planned maintenance visit
Unplanned maintenance scheduling	Number of unplanned maintenance visits	147	(300 x 1) + (800 x 1) + (500 x 2) = 2,100	$70 per unplanned maintenance visit
Spare part procurement	Number of purchase orders	243	(500 + 1,200+ 1,000) = 2,700	$90 per purchase order
Other overheads	Number of machines	600	(300 + 800 + 500) = 1,600	$375 per machine

Overhead cost per machine

	Small	Medium	Large
Customer account handling	($157.50 / 2) = $79	($157.50 / 2) = $79	($157.50 / 2) = $79
Planned maintenance scheduling	($40 x 4) = $160	($40 x 6) = $240	$40 x 12 = $480
Unplanned maintenance scheduling	($70 x 1) = $70	($70 x 1) = $70	($70 x 2) = $140
Spare part procurement	($90 x 500/300) = $150	($90 x 1,200/800) = $135	($90 x 1,000/500) = $180
Other overheads	$375	$375	$375
Total overhead cost per machine	$834	$899	$1,254

Profit per machine

	Small $	Medium $	Large $
Copy charge per machine	1,800	4,800	9,000
Parts and labour per machine	(800)	(2,660)	(7,000)
Overhead cost per machine	(834)	(899)	(1,254)
Profit per machine using ABC	166	1,241	746

(c)   **Benefits of ABC**

The potential benefit for the company will be in the areas of planning, control and decision making.

Planning

The implementation of an activity based costing system will allow the company to use activity based budgeting. The activities necessary to allow a particular output level of services can be determined and the quantity of activity cost driver can be established for each activity. The resources required to perform that quantity of cost drivers can then be estimated.

Control

Under an activity based costing (ABC) system the various support activities that are involved in the process of providing services are identified. The cost drivers that cause a change to the cost of these activities are also identified and used as the basis to attach activity costs to the service. The identification of cost drivers provides information to management to enable them to take actions to improve overall profitability of the company. Cost driver analysis will provide information to management on how costs can be controlled and managed. Variance analysis will be more useful as it is based on more accurate costs. ABC gives more detailed information about how costs are incurred and the potential for cost reduction by reducing activity levels.

Decision Making

The establishment of more accurate service costs should also help managers assess machine profitability and make better decisions concerning pricing and product mix decisions. In the above example, the use of an ABC system has resulted in different levels of profit for each machine type. It is apparent that the large machines are more profitable than under the absorption costing system. The small machines however are making a lower margin than was originally thought. This additional information will enable management to make important decisions regarding pricing. The copy charge for the large machine could potentially be reduced to make it more competitive and increase volumes. The copy charge for the small machines could be increased to make these machines more profitable. Before making any decision regarding pricing however they would need to review market prices and consider the effect any adjustment would have on the company's market position. If market conditions would not allow an increase in the copy charge they could look at ways to reduce the costs of these machines. Alternatively they may want to consider whether to drop the small machines altogether and replace them with a more profitable use of resources. This decision may not be appropriate however if part of the marketing strategy is for the company to provide a range of complementary products.

Examiner's comments

This question was generally very well done although some calculations caused difficulty, in particular the customer account handling costs in part (b). Candidates lost marks and time because they did not read the question properly. In part (a) some candidates apportioned the overhead by activity which wasted a lot of valuable time and gained no marks. Some candidates failed to show workings in part (b) which potentially lost them marks. Too many candidates are still not laying out workings in a clear, structured way, potentially resulting in the loss of marks. Part (c) was reasonably well answered by most candidates although many tended to focus on one particular area rather than considering planning, control and decision making.

Common errors

- Failure to include either the overhead cost or parts and labour costs in part (a).

- Allocating overhead costs based on number of machines or number of copies rather than based on sales revenue in part (a).

- Incorrect calculation or incorrect application of cost driver rates.

- Confusion between total $000 and $ per single machine.

- Lack of reference to the calculations in part (a) and (b) in the answer to part (c).

STANDARD COSTING

301   HB (MAY 12)

Key answer tips

Overall this should be a straightforward question for students, but, as is usual, it will be important to approach it in the correct manner. Students should attempt the discursive part (c) first. For students who start with part (a), there may be a temptation to spend too long on the calculations and not leave enough time for the easier marks that are available in part (c). In part (c) only the advantages of absorption costing are required, but this is an area that students at this level should be very comfortable with.

In part (a), students should start by setting up a reconciliation statement and then pick off the calculations that they find easiest. Tougher variances, such as the variable overhead ones, should be left until last. In part (b), students need to know that when using the absorption costing method then the two variances that are affected are the sales volume variance and the fixed overhead volume variance.

(a)   **Operating statement**

	$	$	
Budgeted profit (W1)		466,000	
Add back fixed production overheads		170,000	
Budgeted contribution		636,000	
Sales volume contribution variance		63,600	A
(9,000 units - 10,000 units) x $63.60			
Standard contribution on actual sales volume		572,400	
Other variances:			
Selling price variance		36,000	F
9,000 units x ($184 - $180)			
Cost variances:			
Direct material price variance	29,600 A		
74,000 kg x ($10.80 – $11.20)			
Direct material usage variance	21,600 A		
((9,000 x 8 kg) – 74,000 kg) x $10.80			
Direct labour rate variance	10,800 A		

10,800 x ($18.00 - $19.00)

Direct labour efficiency variance	8,100 F	
((9,000 x 1.25) – 10,800) x $18.00		
Variable overhead expenditure variance	5,200 A	
(10,800 hours x $6) - $70,000		
Variable overhead efficiency variance	2,700 F	56,400 A
((9,000 x 1.25) – 10,800) x $6.00		
Actual contribution		552,000
Budgeted fixed overheads	170,000	
Fixed overhead expenditure variance	2,000 F	
$170,000 - $168,000		
Actual fixed overheads		(168,000)
Actual profit (W2)		384,000

Workings:

(W1) Budgeted profit for the period

			$
Sales	10,000 units x $180		1,800,000
Direct materials	10,000 units x $86.40	864,000	
Direct labour	10,000 units x $22.50	225,000	
Variable production overheads	10,000 units x $7.50	75,000	(1,164,000)
Contribution	10,000 units x $63.60		636,000
Fixed production overheads			(170,000)
Budgeted profit			466,000

(W2) Actual profit for the period

			$
Sales	9,000 units x $184		1,656,000
Direct materials	74,000 kg @ $11.20	828,800	
Direct labour	10,800 hours @ $19	205,200	
Variable production overheads		70,000	(1,104,000)
Contribution			552,000
Fixed production overheads			(168,000)
Actual profit			384,000

(b) (i) **Marginal vs Absorption Costing**

In a standard marginal costing variance statement the sales volume contribution variance is calculated using the standard contribution per unit. In a standard absorption costing variance statement, standard contribution is replaced by the standard profit per unit which includes a fixed overhead absorption rate. The difference in the variance is represented in the absorption costing variance statement by the fixed production overhead volume variance which is calculated as the difference in actual and budgeted volume x the fixed overhead absorption rate. The fixed production overhead volume variance represents a part of the under absorbed fixed overhead as a result of producing a lower volume than budgeted.

(ii) **Absorption costing variances**

Sales volume profit variance

(9,000 units - 10,000 units) x $46.60 = $46,600 A

It would also be necessary to include a fixed production overhead volume variance as follows:

Fixed production overhead volume variance

(9,000 units – 10,000 units) x $17 = $17,000 A

(c) **Benefits of absorption costing**

The arguments used in favour of using absorption costing for profit reporting and inventory valuation are as follows:

- Fixed production overheads can be a large proportion of total production costs. It is therefore important that these costs are included in the measurement of product costs as they have to be recovered to make a profit.

- Absorption costing follows the matching concept by carrying forward a proportion of the fixed production overhead costs in the inventory valuation to be matched against the sales revenue generated when the items are sold.

- It is necessary to include fixed production overheads in inventory valuations for financial statements.

- It has been argued that in the longer term all costs are variable and it is appropriate to try to identify overhead costs with the products or services that cause them.

Examiner's comments

Part (a) was reasonably well done. Most candidates produced a reconciliation statement. The majority of candidates were able to calculate the variances for materials and labour, fixed overhead expenditure and selling price. However calculation of the variable overhead variances and the sales volume contribution variance caused difficulty for some candidates. Parts (b) and (c) were not well answered. In part (b) few candidates went further than stating that fixed overheads were treated differently under the two costing methods. Some candidates discussed over/under absorption but it was quite rare for candidates to mention the sales volume variance using contribution/profit. The calculations in part (b)(ii) were also poorly done which to some extent is not surprising since candidates clearly showed in part (i) that they didn't understand the difference between variances under the two costing systems. A number of candidates managed to calculate the fixed overhead volume variance but few candidates even attempted to calculate the sales volume profit variance. Part (c) was very poorly answered with few candidates scoring more than one or two marks.

Many candidates went off on a tangent discussing the effect on profits of a company holding stocks valued either at marginal or absorption cost. Candidates also failed to read the question properly by including disadvantages of using absorption costing or advantages of marginal costing which were not asked for.

Common errors

- Calculating the sales volume contribution variance using the selling price rather than the contribution per unit.

- Failure to calculate separate variances for variable overhead expenditure and variable overhead efficiency.

- Calculating a total variable overhead variance as (10,000 x ($6 x 1.25)) - $70,000 = $5,000A

- Lack of knowledge of difference between variance calculations under an absorption and marginal costing system.

- Failure to calculate the sales volume profit variance.

- Calculating the total fixed overhead variance rather than the fixed overhead volume variance.

- Lack of knowledge of the benefits of absorption costing.

- Failure to answer the question asked.

- Discussing the effect of the two systems on reported profits.

302 PRODUCT MANAGER (NOV 09) *Walk in the footsteps of a top tutor*

Key answer tips

For students who are comfortable with variances it might be best to skip the unusual part (a) of the question and get straight into the calculations in parts (b) and (c). This is a common scenario type for this paper – the examiner has started with a tricky/unusual part (a), which might knock the confidence of some students (and some might give up completely at that stage). But if (a) has proven to be tough you could leave it out completely and still get full marks in the remaining question parts. This highlights the importance of continuing to tackle each part of a question even when one part proves too difficult.

Part (a) of this question is in an unusual format that many students may not have seen before. It will be important that you don't simply explain the type of cost, but focus instead on how it is behaving in the scenario. This will mean that you will have to refer to the particular levels of outputs and may have to perform some calculations in order to define the exact relationship between the variables. To score full marks you will also have to discuss the possible causes of these relationships.

Part (b) is a much more straightforward variance question. In order to succeed in this requirement you have to begin by calculating the standard cost of materials, labour and overheads for one unit of production using the budgeted information. From that point onwards you then have to work through 6 variances in your usual approach.

Part (c) is an operational variance question for 4 marks. The marks available should provide a hint that there is nothing too complicated expected here. The key to success will be to remember to use the revised standard materials price to calculate the operational variances.

(a) **Cost behaviour**

Average variable cost per unit

This cost appears to exhibiting features of both economies and diseconomies of scale. As the production increases there is a fall in the average cost which reflects economies of scale that could come from bulk discounts, learning curve effects etc. But when production reached 25,000 units, the average cost rises again and exhibits diseconomies of scale. These can be caused by factors such as the duplication of effort or inertia in the business.

Fixed costs

These costs appear to be stepped in nature. They are fixed at certain levels of production, but they appear to rise by $300,000 after each 10,000 units of production. This could be caused by the need for more space or more supervisors as production increases beyond certain levels.

Head office costs

This cost appears to be related directly at 6% of production. Therefore, as production increases this cost increases in a direct, variable nature.

(b) **Operating statement**

					$
Budgeted production cost (3,200,000 x 76,000/80,000)					3,040,000

Variances:	Workings	Fav $	Adv $		
Materials price	(W1)	52,000			
Materials usage	(W1)		64,500		
Labour rate	(W2)		48,000		
Labour efficiency	(W2)		58,800		
Overhead expenditure	(W3)	50,000			
Overhead volume	(W3)		32,000		
		102,000	203,300	101,300	A

Actual production cost		3,141,300

(W1) **Material variances**

$

SQSP

6 kg/unit × 76,000 units × $2/kg = 912,000 — Usage

AQSP — $52,000 F

430,000 kg × $2/kg = 860,000

$64,500 A

AQAP = 924,500 Price

(W2) **Labour variances – surgical team fees**

$

SHSR

    2.5 hrs/unit × 76,000 units ×$8/hr =1,520,000   Efficiency

AHSR $48,000 A

    196,000 hrs   × $8/hr   =1,568,000

AHAR   =1,626,800 $58,800 A

                                        Rate

(W3) **Fixed overhead expenditure variance**

	$
Budgeted Cost	640,000
Actual Cost	590,000
	50,000 F

Fixed overhead volume variance

	Units
Budgeted output	80,000
Actual output	76,000
	4,000 A
× Std fixed overhead cost per unit	× $8
	$32,000 A

The variances can also be calculated in a more traditional manner as follows:

(W1) Material:

    Rate variance   =   ($2/kg x 430,000hrs) – 924,500

                      = $64,500 (A)

    Usage variance   =   (6 kgs × 76,000 × $2) – ($2 x 430,000kgs)

                      = $52,000 (F)

(W2) Labour:

    Rate variance   =   ($8/hr x 196,000hrs) – 1,626,800

                      = $58,800 (A)

    Efficiency variance   =   (2.5 hrs × 76,000 × $8) – ($8 x 196,000hrs)

                      = $48,000 (A)

(W3) Fixed overhead:

    Expenditure variance = $640,000 – 590,000

                      = $50,000 (F)

    Volume variance   =   (80,000 – 76,000) × ($640,000 / 80,000)

                      = $32,000 (A)

(c) **Planning variance**

Materials price planning variance:	$	
Original planned price	2.00	
Revised price	2.10	
Variance	0.10	A
Actual quantity	430,000	kgs
Direct materials planning variance	$43,000	A

Operational variances

SQSP $

     6 kg/unit × 76,000 units × $2.10/kg   = 957,600   ⎫ Usage

AQSP   ⎬ $54,600 F

     430,000 kg × $2.10/kg   = 903,000   ⎫

AQAP   ⎬ $21,500 A

                                             = 924,500   ⎭ Price

303 WESTERN EUROPE (MAY 10)

Key answer tips

The key to obtaining a good mark in this question is to attempt part (b) first. A well prepared student should be aware of the limitations of standard costing in modern environments and be able to get at least 4 out of 6 in part (b). If you start with part (a) there is a risk that you will run out of time before getting these easier marks which are available in part (b). By attempting part (b) first, a good student can avoid the temptation to spend too long on numbers that he or she may find difficult.

In part (a), the mix and yield variances will be the hardest element. It will therefore be important to set up a proforma operating statement and do the other variances first. With a good part (b) and a solid attempt at the other variances, a good student should be able to pick up enough marks to pass the question even if they get no marks at all in the mix and yield calculations.

(a) **Operating statement**

April - Product CP1			$	
Budgeted profit	(W1)		432,000	
Sales volume variance	(W2)		6,000	Adv
Sales price variance	(W3)		21,300	Fav
Profit before cost variances			447,300	
Cost variances		*Fav*	*Adv*	
		$	$	
Materials price				
ETH1	(W4)		2,210	
RXY2	(W4)	9,580		

Materials mix

ETH1	(W5)		19,800		
RXY2	(W5)	6,600			
Materials yield	(W6)	18,000			
Fixed overhead expenditure	(W7)	2,000			
Fixed overhead volume	(W8)		4,000		
		36,180	26,010	10,170	Fav

Actual profit   (W9)   457,470

Workings

(W1) **Budgeted profit**

		$
Budgeted sales	(72,000 x $20)	1,440,000
Budgeted production costs	(70,000 x $14)	(980,000)
Opening stock		(28,000)
Budgeted profit		432,000

(W2) **Sales volume variance**

Actual sales volume	71,000	
Budgeted sales volume	(72,000)	
Variance (kgs)	1,000	Adv
Standard profit per unit ($20 - $14)	$6	
Variance ($)	$6,000	Adv

(W3) **Sales price variance**

Actual selling price	20.30	
Budgeted selling price	(20.00)	
Variance (per kg)	0.30	Fav
Actual sales volume	71,000 kgs	
Variance ($)	$21,300	Fav

(W4) **Materials price variance**

		ETH1 $	RXY2 $
Standard cost of actual purchases	(22,100 x $18.00) (47,900 x $6.00)	397,800	287,400
Actual cost of actual purchases	(22,100 x $18.10) (47,900 x $5.80)	400,010	277,820
Variance		2,210 A	9,580 F

(W5) Materials mix variance

	Standard mix	Actual material usage (Kg)	Actual usage at standard mix (Kg)	Mix variance (Kg)	Standard price per kg	Mix variance
ETH1	30%	22,100	21,000	1,100 A	18	19,800 A
RXY2	70%	47,900	49,000	1,100 F	6	6,600 F
Total		70,000	70,000			11,400 A

(W6) Materials yield variance

Standard input (69,000 kgs / 96%)	71,875	
Actual input	(70,000)	
Variance (per kg)	1,875	Fav
Standard price per kg of input	$9.60	
Variance ($)	$18,000	Fav

(W7) Fixed overhead expenditure variance

Budgeted overheads – actual overheads = $280,000 – $278,000 = $2,000 Fav

(W8) Fixed overhead volume variance

Actual sales volume	71,000	
Budgeted sales volume	(72,000)	
Variance (kgs)	1,000	Adv
Standard fixed overheads per kg	$4	
Variance ($)	$4,000	Adv

(W9) Actual profit

	$	$
Sales		1,441,300
Cost of sales:		
Opening stock	28,000	
Material – ETH1	400,010	
Material – RXY2	277,820	
Fixed overheads	278,000	
Closing stock	–	983,830
Actual profit		457,470

(b)   **Standard costing**

Standard costing might be inappropriate in an advanced manufacturing environment for the following reasons:

- In advanced manufacturing environments, products are often personalised/ bespoke for customer needs and therefore there is no longer one 'standard' set of production inputs. In such systems, cost for resources would still be useful (if standard resources are used, which in itself might not be true), but the usage is likely to become less relevant.

- An advanced manufacturing environment is constantly evolving and changing and therefore standards can quickly become out of date. The standards will therefore be of little use in planning and control – for example, variances would become more common and larger and any investigation is likely to highlight planning errors rather than operational ones.

- Production is highly automated in modern manufacturing environments. This means that overhead costs will increase and labour costs will decrease. Overhead variances will become more important and labour variances will become less important. Normal standard costing overhead variances lack detail and are often poorly related to the actual cause of the variance (as it often assumes that overhead costs are linked to the efficiency of the workforce).

304   PQ (SEPT 12)

Key answer tips

It may be best to attempt the discursive elements of this question first. Part (c) should provide an easier three marks than other elements of the question and doing this part first should ensure that if a student runs out of time then they are not missing out on these easy marks. Even part (b) can be attempted to some degree before the calculations (although ideally your answer needs to make some reference to the output from part (a)). Two different methods are illustrated for part (a), but only one is needed in the exam and students should pick the method that they are most comfortable with. If elements of part (a) prove too tricky students should avoid them and leave them until last. There should be enough easier marks available (for example, in attempting the cost variances) to give students an overall pass in what is a difficult syllabus area.

(a)   **Operating statement for August**

	$	$		$	
Budgeted profit (W1)				206,750	
Sales mix profit margin variance (W3)					
Product B		26,250	F		
Product C		28,219	A	1969	A
Sales quantity profit variance (W4)					
Product B		13,750	F		
Product C		12,094	F	25,844	F
Standard profit on actual sales				230,625	F
Selling price variance (W2)					
Product B: 3,000 units x ($110 - $100)		30,000	F		
Product C: 1,500 units x ($105 - $107.50)		3,750	A	26,250	F

Cost variances	Fav	Adv	
Direct material price variance	3,200		
((25,600 kg x $5) – $124,800)			
Direct material usage variance		500	
((3,000 x 5 kg) + (1,500 x 7 kg)) – 25,600 kg) x $5			
Direct labour rate variance		4,000	
(9,140 x $7) - $67,980			
Direct labour efficiency variance		6,230	
((3,000 x 2hrs) + (1,500 x 1.5 hrs)) – 9,140) x $7			
Variable overhead expenditure variance		590	
(9,140 hours x $1.50) - $14,300			
Variable overhead efficiency variance		1,335	
((3,000 x 2hr) + (1,500 x 1.5hr)) – 9,140) x $1.50			
Fixed overhead expenditure variance	1,400		
((2,200 x $8) + (1,800 x $6)) - $27,000			
Fixed overhead volume variance	6,400	1,800	
Product B: (3,000 – 2,200) x $8			
Product C: (1,500 – 1,800) x $6			
Actual profit (W5)	11,000	14,455	3,455 A
			253,420

Workings:

(W1) **Budgeted profit for the period**

	Product B	Product C	Total
Sales (units)	2,200	1,800	
Budgeted profit per unit	$50	$53.75	
Total budgeted profit	$110,000	$96,750	$206,750

(W2) **Standard selling price per unit**

Product B: $50 x 2 = $100

Product C: $53.75 x 2 = $107.50

(W3) **Sales mix profit margin variance**

	Actual sales @standard mix (units)	Actual sales @ actual mix (units)	Variance (units)	Standard profit $	Variance $
Product B	2,475	3,000	525 F	50.00	26,250 F
Product C	2,025	1,500	525 A	53.75	28,219 A
	4,500	4,500			1,969 A

Or alternatively:

Weighted average profit per unit

$206,750 / 4,000 = $51.6875

	Actual sales @standard mix (units)	Actual sales @ actual mix (units)	Variance (units)	Standard profit difference $	Variance $
Product B	2,475	3,000	525 F	(50.00 – 51.6875)	886 A
Product C	2,025	1,500	525 A	(53.75 – 51.6875)	1083 A
	4,500	4,500			1,969 A

(W4) **Sales quantity profit variance**

	Actual sales @standard mix (units)	Budget sales @ standard mix (units)	Variance (units)	Standard profit $	Variance $
Product B	2,475	2,200	275 F	50.00	13,750 F
Product C	2,025	1,800	225 F	53.75	12,094 F
	4,500	4,000			25,844 F

Or alternatively:

	Actual sales @standard mix (units)	Budget sales @ standard mix (units)	Variance (units)	Standard profit $	Variance $
Product B	2,475	2,200	275 F	51.6875	14,214 F
Product C	2,025	1,800	225 F	51.6875	11,630 F
	4,500	4,000			25,844 F

(W5) **Actual profit for the period**

	$	$
Sales (3,000 x $110) + (1,500 x $105)		487,500
Direct materials	124,800	
Direct labour	67,980	
Variable production overheads	14,300	
Fixed production overheads	27,000	
Total production cost		234,080
Actual profit		253,420

(b) **Benefits of splitting the sales volume variance**

By separating the sales volume profit variance into the quantity and mix variance, we can explain how the sales volume is affected by a change in the total physical volume of sales and a change in the relative mix of products. The sales quantity profit variance indicates that if the original planned sales mix had been maintained for the actual sales volume of 4,500 units, profits would have increased by $25,844. However because the actual sales mix was not in accordance with the budgeted sales mix, an adverse mix variance of $1,969 occurred. The adverse mix variance arose because there was an increase in the percentage of units sold of Product B which has the lowest profit margin and a decrease in the percentage sold of Product C which has the highest profit margin.

The separation of the sales volume variance into the quantity and mix components demonstrates that increasing or maximising sales volume may not be as beneficial as promoting the sales of the most profitable mix of products.

(c) **Standard costing in modern manufacturing environments**

Tutorial note

The answer provides five examples. Only two of these are needed in the exam and students should not attempt to include more than two methods.

In a JIT environment measuring standard costing variances may encourage dysfunctional behaviour. A JIT production environment relies on producing small batch sizes economically by reducing set up times. Performance measures that benefit from large batch sizes or producing for inventory should therefore be avoided.

In an AMT environment the major costs are those related to the production facility rather than production volume related costs such as materials and labour which standard costing is essentially designed to plan and control. Fixed overhead variances do not necessarily reflect under or overspending but may simply reflect differences in production volume. An activity based cost management system may be more appropriate, focusing on the activities that drive the cost.

In a total quality environment, standard costing variance measurement places an emphasis on cost control to the detriment of quality. Cost control may be achieved at the expense of quality and competitive advantage.

A continuous improvement environment requires a continual effort to do things better rather than achieve an arbitrary standard based on prescribed or assumed conditions. In today's competitive environment cost is market driven and is subject to considerable downward pressure. Cost management must consist of both cost maintenance and continuous cost improvement.

In a JIT/AMT/TQM environment the workforce is usually organised into empowered, multi-skilled teams controlling operations autonomously. The feedback they require is real time. Periodic financial reports are neither meaningful nor sufficiently timely to facilitate appropriate control action.

305 PRE-PREPARED MEALS (MAY 11) *Walk in the footsteps of a top tutor*

Top Tutor Tips

With all exam questions you should start with the requirements to understand all that is being asked of you and to determine whether there are any 'easier' elements that can be attempted first. A read of the requirements in this question throws up some tough areas such as flexing budgets and sales mix and quantity variances.

You should always attempt the discursive elements of a section C question first. Your ability to score well in these areas is no different to your ability to score well if the same question was asked in section B, and it is often not influenced by your calculations in other parts of the question. The two discursive elements on this question (on the benefits of flexible budgeting and the sales mix and quantity variances) does expect some reference to be made to your calculation answers. But you should still attempt them first and leave space for a final couple of sentences which will make reference to these calculations. This should allow you to gain around seven or eight marks of the 12 available and set you well on your way to gaining a pass.

Now let's look at the calculations. Part (a) is on overheads. We are told very clearly in the scenario that the company uses the high-low method to estimate overheads and it will therefore be important that you use this method. The important element of this technique is that you choose the highest and lowest output. This means that we should work on the observations for 680,000 and 840,000 units and ignore the other observation. If you manage to do this then these three marks should be easily achievable by most students.

The key to part (b) is to prepare a flexed budget. A flexed budget takes the original budget and adjusts it to the actual level of activity. In this scenario, the actual quantity sold is 396,000 units compared to an original budgeted sales of 360,000. Therefore actual sales are 10% greater than budget sales (396,000/360,000 − 1). To prepare a flexed budget we therefore need to increase the original sales and variable costs by 10%. Note that there will be no adjustment to fixed costs, as, due to their fixed nature, they do not change as activity levels change. Variances are then calculated as the difference between the actual results and the (revised or) flexed budget.

To get to this point should be the target for most students. If you have managed to achieve everything to this point then you should have around 15 out of the 19 marks available. Even if you have made errors in flexing the budget, you should still have enough marks to gain a pass is in what is a tough exam question.

We are left with part (d) on the sales mix and quantity variances. The question states that the variances are needed in terms of contribution and you should gain a mark or two by first calculating the contribution per unit of each product. These variances can be tricky, but you need to have a proforma layout and fill in as many elements as you can. Also be careful with the direction of the variances – remember that because this is sales, any increase in volume will give a favourable variance.

Overall, there are some challenging elements in this question. But if you approach it in the right manner you should be able to achieve a marginal pass at least.

(a) **Cost estimation**

High-Low Method applied to total overhead costs.

Variable costs = ($1,096,000 - $992,000) / (840,000 - 680,000) = $0.65 per tray

Total budgeted variable costs = 800,000 x $0.65 = $520,000

Fixed costs = $1,096,000 - (840,000 x $0.65) = $550,000

(b) **Budget control statement for Premium product**

	Original budget	Flexed budget	Actual	Variance
Sales (units)	360,000	396,000	396,000	
	$	$	$	$
Sales revenue	1,152,000	1,267,200	1,271,160	3,960 F
Direct materials	576,000	633,600	594,000	39,600 F
Direct labour	180,000	198,000	213,840	15,840 A
Variable overheads	234,000	257,400	261,360	3,960 A
Contribution	162,000	178,200	201,960	23,760 F

Workings

	Standard contribution per unit	Flexed budget (396,000 Trays)
		$
Sales revenue	$3.20	1,267,200
Direct material	$1.60	633,600
Direct labour	$0.50	198,000
Variable overhead	$0.65	257,400
Contribution	$0.45	178,200

(c) Benefits of flexible budgeting

A fixed budget will not provide meaningful control information when actual activity differs from budget and variable costs are significant. If, for example, actual sales revenue is compared to a fixed budget it is not possible to tell whether a favourable sales variance is due to an increase in units sold or an increase in sales price. The flexed budget statement highlights that there is a favourable sales price variance of $3,960. Similarly, if sales volumes were well above budget, adverse variable cost variances will probably be reported, against the fixed budget, since more variable costs have to be incurred to support the higher level of activity. In the question, if the original budget had been used for direct materials an adverse variance of $18,000 ($576,000 - $594,000)) would have been reported compared to the favourable variance of $39,600 shown above. Reporting against a fixed budget tells management nothing about the efficiency of operations. However, if a flexible budget is prepared then the budget variances calculated will provide a better indication of performance since actual results will be compared against an appropriate benchmark.

It should be noted that actual results will always be compared against the original approved budget in the first instance. The flexed budget however provides more insight into actual performance.

(d) (i) Sales quantity contribution variance

Contribution per unit

	Economy per unit	Premium per unit	Deluxe per unit
Selling price	$2.80	$3.20	$4.49
Direct labour	$0.50	$0.50	$0.50
Direct material	$1.00	$1.60	$2.20
Variable overheads	$0.65	$0.65	$0.65
Contribution	$0.65	$0.45	$1.14

Sales Quantity Contribution Variance

	Budget sales quantity	Actual sales at budget mix	Difference	Contribution	Variance
Economy	180,000	193,500	13,500 F	$0.65	$8,775 F
Premium	360,000	387,000	27,000 F	$0.45	$12,150 F
Deluxe	260,000	279,500	19,500 F	$1.14	$22,230 F
	800,000	860,000	60,000		$43,155 F

Or alternatively:

	Budget sales quantity	Contribution	Total contribution
Economy	180,000	$0.65	$117,000
Premium	360,000	$0.45	$162,000
Deluxe	260,000	$1.14	$296,400
	800,000		$575,400

Weighted average contribution: $575,400 / 800,000 = $0.71925

Sales quantity contribution variance = (860,000 − 800,000) x $0.71925 = $43,155F

(ii)   **Sales Mix Contribution Variance**

	Actual sales quantity	Actual sales at budget mix	Difference	Variance from weighted average contribution per unit	Variance
Standard	186,000	193,500	7,500 F	($0.65 - $0.71925)	$519.37 F
Premium	396,000	387,000	9,000 A	($0.45 - $0.71925)	$2,423.25 A
Deluxe	278,000	279,500	1,500 A	($1.14 - $0.71925)	$631.12 A
					$2,535.00 A

Or alternatively:

	Actual sales quantity	Actual sales at budget mix	Difference	Contribution	Variance
Standard	186,000	193,500	7,500 A	$0.65	$4,875 A
Premium	396,000	387,000	9,000 F	$0.45	$4,050 F
Deluxe	278,000	279,500	1,500 A	$1.14	$1,710 A
					$2,535 A

N.B. The analysis of the variances by product shown in the method above is not meaningful.

(e)   **Benefits of quantity and mix variances**

By analysing the sales volume variance into sales quantity and mix variances we can explain how the sales volume variance has been affected by a change in the total quantity of sales and a change in the relative mix of products sold. From the figures calculated in part (d) we can say that the contribution would have been $43,155 higher if the increase in quantity sold had been in the budgeted sales mix. The change in the sales mix however has resulted in a reduction in profit of $2,535. The change in the sales mix has resulted in a relatively higher proportion of sales of the Premium product which is the product that earns the lowest contribution. This is important information for future planning and pricing purposes. An overall increase in quantity of products sold may not result in an increase in profits if the increased sales are from a lower margin product at the expense of products with a higher profit margin.

Examiner's comments

This question was generally poorly done. Disappointingly few candidates scored highly on this question despite the fact that part (a) and part (b) are at Certificate level standard. Flexible budgeting is a fundamental concept but it was obvious from the answers to part (c) that some candidates had never heard the term despite the fact that the technique is used in variance analysis.

In part (a) many candidates decided not to use the high-low method but instead to perform a medium-high or medium-low calculation of their own invention. Candidates did usually manage to follow through with their own incorrect variable cost per unit to derive at least one of the fixed or variable overheads.

In part (b) most candidates did not produce a flexible budget statement despite being asked for one. However, most did attempt to reconcile what ended up to be the flexible figures against the actuals. The weaker candidates gave the variances for the flexible budget against the original budget and some, despite using the heading flexible budget, gave the actual figures and calculated the variances just between the actual and the original budget. Candidates obviously expected a variance analysis question that required them to reconcile the original budgeted profit with the actual profit and, despite the fact that this was not what was asked, decided to do this anyway. The result was lot of unnecessary work for only 5 marks.

Candidates who did not produce a flexible budget statement in part (b) struggled in part (c) to explain the benefits of flexible budgeting. Many candidates discussed changing budgets for movements in prices and other external factors but few discussed the flexing in terms of activity level.

In part (d) most candidates were unable to calculate the sales quantity contribution variance with the majority clearly not knowing what it was. Many candidates calculated a volume variance but even this was badly done since the variance was calculated using sales price rather than contribution. The sales mix contribution variance was tackled much better with candidates usually deriving correctly the actual sales at budget mix. Quite a few then got the signs of the variances the wrong way round and many used incorrect contribution figures (or sales prices).

In part (e) candidates were able to discuss the mix variances and how the change in the mix had affected the contribution. A number of candidates however decided to explain why a material mix variance was calculated.

Common errors

- Inability to apply the high-low method to cost estimation
- Failure to produce a budget control statement
- Comparison of original budget with actual figures to calculate variances
- Comparison of flexed budget with the original budget to calculate variances
- Lack of knowledge of the purposes of flexible budgeting
- Assuming the budget was changed for a number of different variables rather than just volume
- Calculation of sales volume contribution variance rather than sales quantity contribution variance
- Using sales price to evaluate sales volume and sales mix variances
- Using actual contribution rather than standard contribution to evaluate variances
- Lack of knowledge of reasons to calculate a sales mix and sales quantity contribution variance
- Discussion of material mix variances rather than sales mix variances

306   TP (NOV 11)

Key answer tips

As with most section C questions, it is probably best to start with the written elements of the questions first. These can be done without the calculations and a reasonable mark here means that there is less pressure to do well on the calculation areas. It should also allow students to manage their time better – weaker students have a tendency to spend too long on the calculations and not leave enough time to even attempt the discursive areas.

Part (c) is likely to be easier than part (a) and therefore this part should be attempted next. This leaves a very tricky part (a). The key here is to notice that we are only asked to reconcile the material variances, so there is no need to do any other variances. The question covers both planning and mix variances and students should focus on whichever of these areas that they are strongest on. If the other parts of the question have gained reasonable marks(say, 8 out of 13), then students could probably still pass the question overall with a poor effort on this difficult part (a) (they may only need 5 out of 12 marks here).

(a)   **Reconciliation Statement**

			$	
Flexed budget material cost (original standard)	9,000 units x $189		1,701,000	
Material price planning variances:				
Ingredient A	36,000kg x ($25 - $23)		72,000	F
Ingredient B	27,000kg x ($22 - $20)		54,000	F
Flexed budget material cost (revised standard)			1,575,000	
Material price operational variances:				
Ingredient A	(35,000kg x $23) - $910,000		105,000	A
Ingredient B	(28,000kg x $20) - $630,000		70,000	A
Ingredient C	(27,000kg x $11.50) - $296,000		14,500	F
Material mix variance	See workings below		74,500	F
Material yield variance	See working below		175,000	A
Actual material cost			1,836,000	

Material mix variance

	Actual input @ standard mix kg	Actual input @ actual mix kg	Variance kg	Standard price $	Variance $
Ingredient A	40,000	35,000	5,000 F	23.00	115,000 F
Ingredient B	30,000	28,000	2,000 F	20.00	40,000 F
Ingredient C	20,000	27,000	7,000 A	11.50	80,500 A
	90,000	90,000			74,500 F

Or alternatively:

Material mix variance

	Actual input @standard mix	Actual input @ actual mix kg	Variance Kg	Standard price difference $	Variance $
Ingredient A	40,000	35,000	5,000	(23 – 19.444)	17,778 F
Ingredient B	30,000	28,000	2,000	(20 – 19.444)	1,111 F
Ingredient C	20,000	27,000	(7,000)	(11.50 – 19.444)	55,611 F
	90,000	90,000			74,500 F

Material yield variance

Standard kg per cake = 9kg

9,000 cakes x 9kg = 81,000kg

Actual usage = 90,000kg

Variance = 9,000kg A

Standard price per kg = $19.4444

Variance = 9,000 kg x $19.4444 = $175,000 A

Or alternatively:

90,000 kg should produce 10,000 cakes

Did produce 9,000 cakes

Yield variance = 1,000 A

Standard material cost = $175

Yield variance = 1,000 x $175 = $175,000 A

(b) **Usefulness of planning variances**

The calculation of planning and operational variances will be useful to TP for the following reasons:

- The use of planning and operational variances will enable TP's management to draw a distinction between variances caused by factors extraneous to the business and planning errors (planning variances) and variances caused by factors that are within the control of management (operational variances). In this case they can separate the materials price variance caused by general price rises (planning variance) and the price variance as a result of efficient or inefficient procurement.

- The purchasing managers' performance can be compared with the adjusted standards that reflect the conditions the manager actually operated under during the reporting period. If planning and operational variances are not distinguished, there is potential for dysfunctional behaviour especially where the manager has been operating efficiently and effectively and performance is being judged by factors outside the manager's control. In the case of TP it became evident during the period that the prevailing market prices for materials were significantly less than those set during the budget process. It can be seen from the reconciliation statement that the operational performance of the material buyers was poor with large adverse operational price variances on both of the ingredients A and B which was slightly offset by a favourable variance on ingredient C.

- The use of planning variances will also allow TP's management to assess how effective the company's planning process has been. Where a revision of standards is required due to environmental changes that were not foreseeable at the time the budget was prepared, the planning variances are uncontrollable. However standards that failed to anticipate known market trends when they were set will reflect faulty standard setting. It could be argued that some of the planning variances due to poor standard setting are in fact controllable at the planning stage.

(c) **Sales price and volume variances**

Total sales price variance

(9,000 units x $400) - $3,456,000 = $144,000A

Total sales volume contribution variance

(9,000 units − 10,000 units) x $151 = $151,000 A

(d) **Just In Time (JIT)**

JIT purchasing involves having an arrangement with a small number of key suppliers where the supplier is able to provide raw materials or components on demand or with a very short lead time. This means that the company can hold zero or very little inventory thus reducing the costs involved with holding inventory including storage costs, insurance costs and obsolescence costs. The costs involved with ordering inventory may however increase. The use of a small number of suppliers should also reduce administrative costs for the company and result in greater quantity discounts. The successful operation of a JIT purchasing system involves the company working together with their suppliers to ensure that they can rely on receiving supplies at the right time and at the required quality level. This should result in a reduction in quality control costs for the company. Quality standards should improve resulting in lower wastage in the production process.

Examiner's comments

In part (a) very few candidates produced a reconciliation statement despite the fact that this was clearly required by the question. A large number of candidates calculated labour and overhead variances when the question asked for a reconciliation of material costs. It was apparent that most candidates were unsure which material variances to calculate and there was duplication of variances i.e. calculation of material usage variances as well as material mix and yield variances. There was an apparent lack of knowledge of how to deal with planning and operational variances. A number of candidates managed to calculate a material price planning variance for ingredient C despite the fact that its standard price has not changed. Too many candidates did not appreciate that the operational variances should be calculated based on the revised standard.

Part (b) was consequently not well answered because candidates did not know how to calculate planning and operational variances and therefore were unlikely to be able to discuss the usefulness of the calculation. Some candidates defined planning and operational variances but did not go on to explain why they would be useful to management. A significant number of candidates described the generic benefits of variance analysis and commented on all the variances that had been calculated in part (a) explaining what they measured, even to the extent of discussing the labour and overhead variances that they had calculated.

Part (c) was well answered. Most candidates could calculate the sales price variance but many had more difficulty with the sales volume contribution variance. The sales volume revenue variance was often calculated rather than the sales volume contribution variance.

Part (d) was generally well answered although many candidates, as well as discussing just in time purchasing, also discussed just in time production which was given no credit. Some of the answers were too narrowly focused, merely considering the low inventory holding costs.

Common errors

- Calculation of labour and overhead variances in part (a)
- Failure to produce a reconciliation statement
- Duplication of material usage variances and material mix and yield variances
- Duplication of material price variances and material price planning and operational variances
- Calculation of material price planning variances using actual or budgeted quantities rather than standard quantities
- Lack of understanding of the benefits of planning and operational variances
- Failure to answer the question asked
- Valuing the sales volume variance at selling price per unit.
- Discussion of JIT production
- Too narrow a focus in part (d)

307   FA AND FB (NOV 08) *Walk in the footsteps of a top tutor*

Top Tutor Tips

The question starts with a tough part (a) which may have put some students off (it required the calculation of a usage variance in a process that contained losses).But it was only worth 6 marks and the question got easier from that point.

To some extent it may have been easier to do this question backwards as it gets easier as it goes along and no part relates to previous parts. So start with the discursive elements at the end of the question, then try the (simple) purchases budget, then the discussion on planning variances and you've already attempted 17 of the 30 marks and hopefully built up some marks in case you find the other sections tougher. It may be more difficult to pick up full marks on the other, trickier calculations but if you show a reasonable level of knowledge you should get enough marks overall to pass.

For the variance calculations in part (b) you could start with the usage variances and gain most of the marks. It will be important to use the revised price for materials, but even if the original price is used you will still pick up the majority of the marks and score a high mark in the question overall.

> *Part (a) is made very tough by the treatment loss percentage and the weaker students who start with part (a) are likely to become disheartened and struggle with the question overall.*

(a) **Chemical C1**

    (i) **Materials usage variance**

63,000 units (combined) of products FA and FB were actually produced. Each product is expected to use 0.2 kg of chemical C1. Therefore the standard quantity should have been 0 .2 kgs for each unit = 12,600 kgs for the finished product.

However, this is after an expected 30% loss in C1 due to the treatment process. So the total C1 used should have been:

$$= \frac{12,600\,\text{kgs}}{70\%} = 18,000 \text{ kgs}$$

The actual quantity used was 17,740 kgs of C1. This allows us to calculate the total usage variance:

Output of 53,000 units should have used	18,000 kgs	
Actual Quantity used	17,740 kgs	
	_____	
Variance	260 kgs	Favourable
Standard Price	$8/ kg	
	_____	
Total usage variance	$2080	Favourable
	_____	

    (ii) **Treatment loss percentage**

Actual quantity used was 17,740 kgs. There were 12,600 kgs of C1 in the finished product. Therefore 5,140 kgs were lost in the treatment of C1. This is 29% of the materials actually used. Alternatively:

Actual quantity used	17,740 kgs
Output of 53,000 units × 0.2kgs per unit	12,600 kgs
	_____
Loss	5,140 kgs
$\% = \dfrac{5,140\,\text{kgs}}{17,740\,\text{kgs}} \times 100\%$	29%

(b) (i) **Planning, operational and usage variances**

        Planning variance

		$
Original planned expenditure	(25,000 units × 0.25kgs × $12/unit)	75,000
Revised planned expenditure	(25,000 units × 0.25kgs × $14.50/unit)	90,625
		_____
		15,625 A
		_____

Operating variances

Price variance

		$	
Revised budgeted price		14.50	
Actual price	($94,000 / 6,450kgs)	14.57	
Price variance		0.07	Adv
Materials purchased		6,450	kg
Materials price variance		$475	Fav

Usage variance

25,000 units of production should use	(× 0.25 kg)	6,250	kg
They did use		6,450	kg
Usage variance (in kg)		200	Adv
Revised standard price		$14.50	/kg
Materials usage variance		$2,900	Adv

(ii) **Problems with reporting planning variances**

- There is a possibility that planning variances are not investigated so that future plans and the planning function overall are not improved.
- Operational managers may argue that a change in circumstances is outside their control and should therefore be deemed to be a planning variance rather than an operational one.

(c) **Purchases budget**

Production Units		40,000units
C2 per unit		0 .15kg / unit
Materials Usage		6,000 kgs
Opening Stock	Note 1	(3,000 kgs)
		3,000 kgs
Closing Stock	Note 2	3,300 kgs
Purchases (kgs)		6,300 kgs
Cost / kg		$15 / kg
C2 Purchases Budget		$94,500

Notes:

1 Opening stock = 50% × 40,000 units × 0.15 kg / unit = 3,000 kgs

2 Closing stock = 50% × 44,000 units × 0.15 kg / unit = 3,300 kgs

(d)   **Usefulness of variance analysis**

A number of criticisms have been suggested concerning the applicability of standard costing in a modern manufacturing environment. Arguments to support the statement that variance analysis is of little use in modern manufacturing environments are:

1   In modern manufacturing there is an increasing trend away from mass production towards customised and non-standard products. This leads to a greater variability in operating conditions, where constant standards are less useful and measurement against them gives meaningless results.

2   The constant changes that happen in a modern environment (for example, due to shorter product life cycles) would also make it too costly to constantly update and review the standards. It also means that any standard that is used to assess performance will quickly become out of date and its usefulness diminished.

3   The move towards strictly monitored input systems, such as JIT, decreases the variability in input costs, thus rendering variance analysis unnecessary anyway.

4   In modern manufacturing environments direct labour and direct material play a smaller role in the total product cost so that lots of the variances calculated in variance analysis become less useful. Whereas important factors such as quality, customer satisfaction etc. might be ignored.

5   It may now be too late to do anything about the problem. By the cause is discovered for any variance that has been calculated the environment may have moved on so that new problems become more relevant and solving old problems only results in the business falling further behind its rivals.

However, whilst it is true that variance calculation and analysis takes place after the actual events have taken place, variance analysis can still play some role in planning and control – even in a modern manufacturing environment. Examples of this might be:

1   Cost and mix changes from plan will still be relevant in many processing situations. A change in material mix, for example, may continue to warrant investigation to determine whether quality standards and technical specification is being met.

2   If the product mix is relatively stable, performance management may be enhanced by the use of planning and operating variances.

3   Variance trends can be monitored to assess whether a situation is in control or out of control.

4   Even in a TQM environment, budgets will need to be quantified. For example, the level of staff training needs to be planned. Variance analysis can then be focused more on overheads and adapted to techniques such as activity based costing by extending variances to cost drivers.

5   Although variances are calculated after the event has taken place they still provide vital information to managers: they can indicate when a process might need investigation, they can continue to indicate when a process is out of control, and they can be used in feed forward control to improve standard setting and budgeting in the future.

Overall, whilst variance analysis needs to be adapted to modern business environments, it can still play an important role in the planning and control of processes – even after the events have taken place.

308   HR (MAR 12)

Key answer tips

The best approach to this question is to try to pick up the easy marks which are available for the discursive elements on variance investigation and the benefits of planning variances. There are 9 marks available for these areas and if you can achieve, say, 6 of these marks then they only need to get 7 out of 16 on the more difficult calculation areas in order to pass the question. For the calculations it will be best to focus on the areas you are comfortable with rather than getting bogged down in areas that you find difficult. So if you can't do materials yield variances well then skip this element and move on to the labour variances. The great thing in this question is that very few of the marks follow on so that the elements can effectively be attempted in any order – just ensure you leave space in your exam paper to come back and try the bits that you skip if you have time to do so later.

(a)   **Reconciliation statement for February**

			$	
Standard material cost		78 x $210	16,380	
Material price variance	Material A	2,800 litres x ($1.40 - $1.50)	280	A
	Material B	2,700 litres x ($1.20 - $1.30)	270	A
	Material C	1,000 litres x ($3.65 - $4.00)	350	A
	Material D	1,900 litres x ($2.60 - $2.50)	190	F
Material mix variance	Material A	(W1)	784	A
	Material B	(W1)	648	A
	Material C	(W1)	1,314	A
	Material D	(W1)	3,796	F
Material yield variance		(W2)	420	A
Actual material cost			16,460	

Workings:

(W1) **Material mix variance**

Raw material	Actual input @ standard mix litres	Actual input @ actual mix litres	Variance Litres	Standard cost $	Variance $
A	2,240	2,800	560 A	1.40	784A
B	2,160	2,700	540 A	1.20	648A
C	640	1,000	360 A	3.65	1,314A
D	3,360	1,900	1,460 F	2.60	3,796F
	8,400	8,400			1,050F

Or alternatively:

Raw material	Actual input @ standard mix litres	Actual input @ actual mix litres	Variance Litres	Standard cost differences $	Variance $
A	2,240	2,800	560 A	(1.40 – 2.00)	336F
B	2,160	2,700	540 A	(1.20 – 2.00)	432F
C	640	1,000	360 A	(3.65 – 2.00)	594A
D	3,360	1,900	1,460 F	(2.60 – 2.00)	876F
	8,400	8,400			1,050 F

NB: *either method of calculating the individual mix variances would be acceptable*

(W2) **Material yield variance**

Standard input per 100 litres = 105 litres

7,800 litres x 1.05 = 8,190 litres

Actual usage = 8,400 litres

Variance = 210 litres A

Standard input cost per litre = $2.00

Variance = 210 A x $2.00 = $ 420 A

Or alternatively:

8,400 litres input should produce 8,000 litres output

Did produce 7,800 litres

Yield variance = 200 litres A

Standard output material cost per litre = $2.10

Yield variance = 200 A x $2.10 = $420 A

(b) **Variance investigation**

(i) The size of the variance

(ii) The likelihood of the variance being controllable

(iii) The likely cost versus the potential benefits of the investigation

(iv) The interrelationship between variances

(v) The type of standard that was set

Tutorial note

The answer provides five examples. Only three of these are needed in the exam and students should not attempt to include more than three methods.

(c)   **Direct labour rate planning variance**

(7,800 x 0.08 hours) x ($24 - $26) = $1,248 A

Direct labour rate operational variance

(640 x $26) - $16,500 = $140 F

Direct labour efficiency operational variance

[(7,800 x 0.08) – 640] x $26 = $416 A

(d)   **Importance of planning variances**

The calculation of planning and operational variances is important for the following reasons:

- The use of planning and operational variances will enable management to draw a distinction between variances caused by factors extraneous to the business and planning errors (planning variances) and variances caused by factors that are within the control of management (operational variances).

- The manager's performance can be compared with the adjusted standards that reflect the conditions the manager actually operated under during the reporting period. If planning and operational variances are not distinguished, there is potential for dysfunctional behaviour especially where the manager has been operating efficiently and effectively and performance is being affected by factors that the manager cannot control. In part c) the labour rate variance was $1,108A however it can be clearly seen that $1,248A was a result of a planning error and was not within the control of the operational managers.

- The use of planning variances will also allow management to assess how effective the company's planning process has been. Where a revision of standards is required due to environmental changes that were not foreseeable at the time the budget was prepared, the planning variances are uncontrollable. However standards that failed to anticipate known market trends when they were set will reflect faulty standard setting. It could be argued that some of the planning variances due to poor standard setting are in fact controllable at the planning stage.

Examiner's comments

This question was fairly well done with a higher average mark than normally seen on this type of question. Part (a) was well done with most candidates demonstrating ability to calculate the material price and mix variance although the yield variance caused more difficulty. Part (b) was well answered although a number of candidates seemed to think that only adverse variances should be calculated and that cost in itself was a reason not to investigate. Part (c) was not so well done with few candidates able to correctly calculate the planning variance. Part (d) required explanation of the benefits of distinguishing between planning and operational variances. This part was badly answered by most candidates despite this topic having been examined in the previous diet. Many candidates chose to define a planning and an operational variance and say nothing about the importance of separating the variances. If candidates did discuss separating the variances, very general statements were given but the points were not expanded to explain why this was useful.

Common errors

- Calculating material price variances as the differences between standard and actual price without multiplying by the number of litres.

- Calculating the mix variance using the actual cost per litre instead of the standard cost per litre.

- Calculating the yield variance using either $210 or $8.85 as the standard cost per litre.

- Failing to calculate the actual material cost.

- Failing to produce a reconciliation statement.

- Assuming only adverse variances should be investigated.

- Assuming part (b) referred to the specific variances calculated in part (a)

- Calculating the planning variance using actual hours rather than standard hours.

- Failing to address the question asked in part (d)

- Discussing why the variances in part (c) might have arisen as an answer to part (d).

- Lack of understanding of benefits of planning and operational variances.

BUDGETING

309   Q (MAY 08)

Key answer tips

In part (a) I4 marks available for a 3 month cash budget. There were some easier parts to this:

- fixed overheads (the trick will be to ignore depreciation)

- variable overheads (with some payment deferred to second month)

- labour cost (very straight forward)

These therefore should have been attempted first. If you also put in the initial capital investment you should now be close to a pass. You are left with sales and materials but should now only need 2/3 marks to pass so anything that makes sense should get you over the pass mark.

Part (b) would rely on students having a fair attempt at materials in part (a). The key was then to calculate the materials savings/increase rather than re-doing the entire budget. But this was the trickiest part of the question. The key trick was to notice that each Trackit used one and half components so to get the cost per Trackit you had to multiply the cost per component given by 1.5.

For part (c) you should have spotted that this new product makes a positive contribution which would have given you a few marks to discuss. Extra calculations such as first year profit and breakeven point would also have been useful.

(a) **Cash budget**

Cash Budget

For the first three months

	Month 1 £	Month 2 £	Month 3 £	Total £
Receipts				
Sales (W1)	20,160	65,240	148,820	234,220
Capital Investment	250,000			250,000
Total	270,160	65,240	148,820	484,220
Payments				
Materials (W2)		106,800	104,640	211,240
Wages (W3)	14,500	16,500	21,200	52,200
Var. Overheads (W4)	18,850	31,600	39,110	89,560
Fixed O/Hs (W5)	42,000	52,500	52,500	147,000
Total	75,350	207,400	217,450	500,200
Net inflow/(outflow)	194,810	(142,160)	(68,630)	(15,980)
Balance b/f	0	194,810	52,650	0
Balance C/f	194,810	52,650	(15,980)	(15,980)

Workings

(W1) **Sales receipts**

		Month 1	Month 2	Month 3
Units		1,000	1,500	2,000
Revenue	(@ $140)	140,000	210,000	280,000
Receipts				
– 0 months	15% × 96%	20,160	30,240	40,320
– 1 month	25%		35,000	52,500
– 2 months	40%			56,000
– 3 months	15%			
Total		20,160	65,240	148,820

(W2) Materials cost

	Month 1	Month 2	Month 3	Month 4
Production units	1,450	1,650	2,120	2,460
+ Closing inventory	330	424	492	
	1,780	2,074	2,612	
– Opening inventory	0	(330)	(424)	(492)
Units purchased	1,780	1,744	2,188	
Purchases (@ $60)	106,800	104,640	131,280	
Payments	0	106,800	104,640	131,280

(W3) Labour cost

	Month 1	Month 2	Month 3	Month 4
Production units	1,450	1,650	2,120	2,460
Wages (@ $10)	14,500	16,500	21,200	

(W4) Variable overhead cost

		Month 1	Month 2	Month 3	Month 4
Production units		1,450	1,650	2,120	2,460
Cost (@ $20)		29,000	33,000	42,400	
Paid					
– 0 months	65%	18,850	21,450	27,560	
– 1 month	35%		10,150	11,550	
Payments		18,850	31,600	39,110	

(W5) Fixed overhead cost

		Month 1	Month 2	Month 3	Month 4
Cost	(excl dep'n)	52,500	52,500	52,500	
Paid					
– 0 months		42,000	42,000	42,000	
– 1 month			10,500	10,500	
Payments		42,000	52,500	52,500	

(b)   **Revised component cost**

(i)   Cost = $32 per Trackit (or 32 × 1.5 = $48 per unit)

Units purchased		1,780	1,744	2,188
Saved cost	(@ $12)	21,360	20,928	26,256
Savings		0	21,360	20,928

	$
Original net cash flow	(15,980)
Total savings (21,360 + 20,928)	42,288
Revised cash flow	12,212

(ii)   Cost = $50 per Trackit (or 50 × 1.5 = $75 per unit)

Units purchased		1,780	1,744	2,188
Extra cost	(@ $15)	26,700	26,160	32,820
Extra payments		0	26,700	26,160

	$
Original net cash flow	(15,980)
Extra costs (26,700 + 26,160)	(52,860)
Revised cash flow	(68,840)

(c)   **REPORT**

To: The shareholders of Q

From: Management Accountant

Date:

Subject: Company Profitability

This report discusses the company's overall profitability and issues raised by the business plan.

Overall profitability

Overall the Trackit is a profitable product. It will make a contribution of $50 per unit. First year's profits will therefore be:

		$
Contribution	($50 × 27,700 units)	1,385,000
Fixed costs		(840,000)
Bad debts	(5% × 27,700 × $140)	(193,900)
		$351,100

Based on monthly fixed overheads of $70,000 it has a breakeven point of only ($70,000/ $50 contribution per unit) 1,400 units per month. This is achieved as quickly as month two.

Even if the component price rose to $50 so that contribution fell to $40, the breakeven point would be ($70,000/ $40 contribution per unit) 1,750 units which would be achieved by month three.

Cash position

The problem facing Q is that profitability and cash flow are not the same thing. The company's cash flow forecast shows that the owners' initial $250,000 investment will be completely wiped out within three months of operations. In fact, Q will be overdrawn and may need either further short-term investment or other sources of finance.

The main cause of this problem is in the management of working capital. Materials are paid for within one month of purchase, whereas it takes three months to receive all monies from sales.

This problem will create bigger negative outflows as the company grows – but by month five growth will stop and the cash flow problems will start to ease up. So this is a short term problem and not a long term one.

Impact of changing component prices

It can be seen that the component price could have a significant impact on Q's cash position. If the cost is at the lower end of the scale then the overdrawn position disappears.

Q plans to purchase and pay for 3,524 units in the first three months so that each $1 reduction/increase in the component price will save/cost it 3,524 × 1.5 = $5,286. Therefore to wipe out the original planned overdraft of $15,980 the price would have to fall by:

$$\frac{\$15,980}{\$5,286} = \$3.03 \text{ per component}$$

Q should look for ways to achieve this reduction from the component manufacturer.

Conclusion

It can be seen that the company has short-term cash flow problems. But if it can solve this by either injecting some extra short-term finance or reducing the component cost, long-term profitability is good.

310   RF LTD (MAY 07)   *Walk in the footsteps of a top tutor*

Top Tutor Tips

As with all cash budget questions it is best to have a standardised approach rather than attempting to work through the question on a line-by-line basis. So you should start by setting up a proforma cash budget then put in the easier figures – these are typically the opening balance (in this case it is actually a capital injection in the first month of the business) and the fixed overheads (in this question we actually have to do a working for these but it should still be straightforward).At this stage you will have gained 2/3 marks without having to do anything too challenging.

Next you need to attempt the sales working. The key is to be careful and methodical. Remember that bad debts are not a cash flow and should be ignored. The trick in this calculation is to deal with the discount given in the first month. Lots of students will get this wrong and it is only worth one mark – therefore, if you find it tricky you should leave it out rather than spend lots of time trying to get it right for only one mark (i.e. if you can't deal with it in less than two minutes then it is not worth attempting and it is better for you to move on).

At this stage you should have racked up 7 or 8 marks put of 15. It is not yet enough to pass because if, as is likely, you will find part (b) tough, then you may still have to pick up another 5 or 6 marks to pass the question overall (subject to a reasonable attempt at part (c)). So next we have to deal with the production plan. The key here is to be aware that production = sales –opening stock + closing stock.

If you manage to get the production plan correct then the remaining costs are straightforward. Even if you get it wrong (for example by adding opening stock and deducting closing stock), as long as your technique is fine, you should still get full marks for your workings on materials, labour and variable overhead costs if you base them on your incorrect production but apply the correct technique.

Adding the cash budget up at the end will be worth only around one mark – so keep an eye on the clock. If you have run out of time by now (which is likely) then this is a mark that is not worth spending 5 minutes to acquire.

-Part (b) is a much tougher part of the question and it would be advisable to skip it for now and attempt part (c) first. This is mainly 'bookwork' and you should be able to get a good strong mark in order to pass the question overall.

If you have time, return to part (b). This will rely on the production budget in part (a) – but again, you will not be punished if your answer in part (a) was incorrect. Examine how the answer lays out the approach to the question. If you did not get it right this time then you should learn from this for future, similar questions. If you managed to have a go at part (b) then the final marks in the question will be awarded for discussing the results of part (b) in your report in part (c).

(a)   **Cash Budget**

	Month 1 $	Month 2 $	Month 3 $	Total $
Sales receipts (W1)	2,940	10,180	15,545	28,665
Capital	16,250			16,250
Total receipts	19,190	10,180	15,545	44,915
Outflow				
Material purchases (W2)	0	3,515	3,420	6,935
Labour (W3)	6,105	5,940	6,666	18,711
Variable overhead (W4)	1,332	2,184	2,318	5,834
Fixed overhead (W5)	3,750	5,625	5,625	15,000
Total payments	11,187	17,264	18,029	46,480
Net cash flow	8,003	(7,084)	(2,484)	(1,565)
Bal b/fwd	0	8,003	919	0
Bal c/fwd	8,003	919	(1,565)	(1,565)

Workings

(W1) **Sales receipts**

	1	2	3
Sales units	1,500	1,750	2,000
Sales (Units x $10)	15,000	17,500	20,000
Paid in month – 20% x 0.98	2,940	3,430	3,920
45% in the following month		6,750	7,875
25% in 3rd month			3,750
Receipts	2,940	10,180	15,545

(W2) **Production**

	1 units	2 units	3 units	4 units
Required by sales	1,500	1,750	2,000	2,100
Opening inventory		(350)	(400)	
	1,500	1,400	1,600	
Closing inventory (20% × following month's sales)	350	400	420	
Production	1,850	1,800	2,020	
Material price	$1.90	$1.90	$1.90	
Material cost	$3,515	$3,420	$3,838	
Payment		£3,515	$3,420	

(W3) Labour

Production units	1,850	1,800	2,020
Rate per unit	$3.30	$3.30	$3.30
Payment	$6,105	$5,940	$6,666

(W4) Variable Overhead

Production units	1,850	1,800	2,020
Rate per unit	$1.20	$1.20	$1.20
Variable overhead cost	$2,220	$2,160	$2,424
60% in month	1,332	1,296	1,454
40% in following month		888	864
Payment	1,332	2,184	2,318

(W5) Fixed overhead

	6,250	6,250	6,250
60% in month	3,750	3,750	3,750
30% in following month		1,875	1,875
Payment	3,750	5,625	5,625

(b) (i)

	Month 1	Month 2	Month 3
Production	1,850	1,800	2,020
Material price saving ($1.90 – $1.50)	$0.40	$0.40	$0.40
Total saving ($)	740	720	808
Received		740	720
Total cash benefit	$1,460		
Current cash flow at $1.90	$(1,565)		
Revised cash flow at $1.50	**$(105)**		

(ii)

	Month 1	Month 2	Month 3
Production units	1,850	1,800	2,020
Additional cost ($2.20 – $1.90)	$0.30	$0.30	$0.30
Total additional cost ($)	555	540	606
Payment ($)		555	540
Total additional payment	$1,095		
Current cash flow at $1.90	$(1,565)		
Revised cash flow at $2.20	$(2,660)		

(c)   **'What if' analysis and cash budgets**

Benefits of 'what-if' analysis

(1)   It provides an assessment of how responsive the cash flows are to changes in variables.

For example, in preparing the cash budgets it has been identified that there is a degree of uncertainty concerning the direct material cost. The following results have been calculated:

Direct material cost per component	Increase/(decrease) in cash flow	Budgeted cash flow
$2.20	($1,095)	($2,660)
$1.50	$1,460	($105)
$1.90		($1,565)

A 16% increase in material cost to $2.20, results in a negative cash flow of -$2,660. This is a 70% increase in the closing cash negative balance. A 21% decrease in direct material cost to $1.50, results in a revised cash flow of -$105. This is a 93% reduction in the closing cash negative balance. It can be seen that the closing cash balance is sensitive to changes in the price of materials because a small change in price results in a large change in the total cash balance.

(2)   *Directs attention to critical variables*

The sensitivity of each variable can be calculated and the most sensitive variables identified. These can be closely monitored and action taken quickly if they vary from forecast.

(3)   *Assess the risk to the closing cash balance*

'What-if' analysis can be used to assess how likely the expected cash balance is to occur. Managers may decide to take an alternative course of action if the outcome is very risky. For example they may negotiate an overdraft limit if there is a possibility of a cash deficit.

Limitations of 'what-if' analysis

(1)   *Only one variable changes at a time*

'What-if' analysis assesses the impact on the outcome of one variable changing at a time and assumes that each variable is independent. In reality variables are likely to be interdependent.

(2)   *Probabilities of changes unknown*

There is no indication of the likelihood of a key variable changing and therefore the use of 'what if' analysis is limited.

Conclusion

Despite the limitations of 'what-if' analysis it can provide an insight into key variables which can impact on an outcome and give managers a better understanding of the risks involved in a cash budget.

311 THIRTEEN WEEKS (MAY 09)

Key answer tips

There are some tricks in almost every part of this question so it is important to be careful in your approach and to ensure you understand all the data that has been provided. However, a lot of marks will be awarded for technique – so if you make a mistake you will not be punished for it more than once.

In part (a) the trick is to account for the bad debts and the loan interest. Recognise that the former is a variable cost and should be included in the calculation of contribution, and the latter is a fixed cost that should be included with other fixed costs. Also, the question asks for the answers in units so there is no need to calculate the margin of safety percentage.

In part (b), the trick is to identify the axis for the diagram. These are given in the question: "budgeted profit to.....the price of raw materials". Draw the relationship as a straight line. We already have one point (the current profit position, so you need to calculate profit from another material cost in order to plot the line required.

For part (c) the trickiest element will be in dealing with a 13 week period and the unusual sums that gives as a result. But the format and style should be familiar to students. The stock adjustment is the hardest part of the requirement, but it should not make the difference between a pass and a fail.

Part (d) is more straightforward – though you should attempt to relate it to part (c) where possible.

(a)   **Breakeven point**

Contribution per unit:		£
Selling price		30.00
Bad debts (2% x 30.00)		(0.60)
Variable selling costs		(1.60)
Raw materials		(9.50)
Production wages		(8.20)
Variable expenses		(1.10)
		_____
Contribution		9.00
		_____

Fixed costs:		£
Depreciation	(2.70 x 860,000)	2,322,000
Fixed expenses	(3.20 x 860,000)	2,752,000
Loan interest	(9% x 10,000,000)	900,000
		_____
		5,974,000
		_____

Breakeven point:

$$= \frac{\text{Fixed costs}}{\text{Contrib'n/unit}}$$

$$= \frac{5,794,000}{9.00}$$

$= 663,777.8$

$= $ **663,778 units**

Margin of safety

$= $ Budgeted sales – breakeven point

$= $ 810,000 – 663,778

$= $ **146,222 units**

(b) **Sensitivity analysis**

Current profit (with materials price @ £9.50 per unit) $= $ £1,611,000

Change in profit for every £2 change in materials $= $ £2 x 810,000 units

$= $ £1,620,000

If price is reduced by £2 per unit the revised profit will be:

$= $ 1,611,000 + 1,620,000

$= $ £3,231,000

If price is reduced by £2 per unit the revised profit will be:

$= $ 1,611,000 – 1,620,000

$= $ £(9,000)

Diagram:

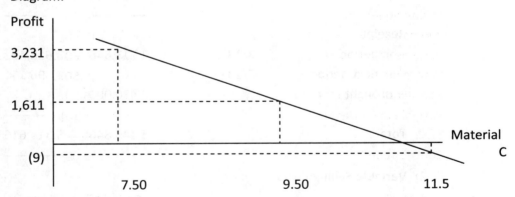

(c) **Cash Budget**

	Period 1	Period 2
	£	£
Receipts		
Sales (W1)	5,143,846	5,314,616

Payments

Variable selling costs (W2)		240,000	320,000
Materials (W3)		2,139,071	2,201,509
Wages (W4)		1,719,538	1,722,000
Variable expenses (W5)		231,000	231,000
Fixed expenses (W6)		1,376,000	
Loan interest (W7)			450,000
		_____	_____
Total payments		5,705,609	4,924,509
		_____	_____
Net inflow/(outflow)		(561,763)	390,107
Balance b/f		76,000	(485,763)
		_____	_____
Balance C/f		(485,763)	(95,656)
		_____	_____

Workings

(W1) **Sales Receipts**

		Period 1	Period 2
Units		150,000	200,000
Revenue	(@ £30)	4,500,000	6,000,000
Bad debts (@ 2%)		(90,000)	(120,000)
		_____	_____
Net sales		4,410,000	5,880,000
		_____	_____
Receipts			
– in period	8/13	2,713,846	3,618,462
– in next period	5/13		1,696,154
– brought forward		2,430,000	
		_____	_____
Total		5,143,846	5,314,616
		_____	_____

(W2) **Variable Selling Costs**

	Period 1	Period 2
Sales units	150,000	200,000
Cost per unit	£1.60	£1.60
Total cost	£240,000	£320,000

(W3) **Materials Cost**

	Period 1	Period 2	Period 3
Production Units	210,000	210,000	220,000
	£	£	£
Total cost (@ £9.50 / unit)	1,995,000	1,995,000	2,090,000
+ Closing Inventory			
(Period 1 = 6/13 x £1995k)	920,769		
(Period 2 = 7/13 x £2090k)		1,125,385	
	2,915,769	3,120,385	
− Opening Inventory	(710,000)	(920,769)	
Purchases	2,205,769	2,199,616	
Payments			
brought forward	612,000		
9/13ths in period	1,527,071	1,522,811	
4/13ths in next period		678,698	
Total payments	2,139,071	2,201,509	

(W4) **Labour cost**

	Period 1	Period 2
Production Units	210,000	210,000
	£	£
Wages (@ £8.20)	1,722,000	1,722,000
Payments		
brought forward	130,000	
12/13ths in period	1,589,538	1,589,538
1/13th in next period		132,462
Total payments	1,719,538	1,722,000

(W5) **Variable expenses**

	Period 1	Period 2
Production Units	210,000	210,000
	£	£
Expenses (@ £1.10)	231,000	231,000

(W6) **Fixed expenses**

Depreciation is ignored as it is not a cash flow.

Total fixed expenses = £3.20 x 860,000 = £2,752,000

Half are paid at the beginning of period 1 = £1,376,000

(W7) **Loan interest**

Total interest = £10m x 9% = £900,000

Half are paid at the end of period 2 = £450,000

(d) **Possible problems**

Three areas that may cause concerns for management are:

- The company is overdrawn in the first two quarters of the year. Management may need to consider arranging an overdraft or organising a capital injection into the company

- These figures could be made worse if some cash flows have not been included. For example, tax payments have not been considered nor have dividends from previous years.

- The change in stock policy requires over £200,000 of extra investment – perhaps this could be delayed until cash flows are more stable/positive.

THE TREATMENT OF UNCERTAINTY IN DECISION MAKING

312   A BANK (MAY 08)

Key answer tips

A long and complex question on relevant cash flows, but the examiner helps by splitting requirements into sizeable chunks. In part (a), calculating bank balances for all types of customers should have been feasible by most students, however the calculation of investment revenue foregone would only have been incorporated by the best prepared. Nevertheless, 2 marks would have been given for the calculation of transaction charges under each option, with one mark for interest revenue and a couple for opportunity costs – the savings income at 3%. (2 marks for the calculation of net balances under the existing option.)

In part (b), even if filled up incorrectly, the two-way data table should have been setup by most and grabbed a mark. Correct calculations could have marked as much as a mark each, and the correct working would also have got the students well over the 4 marks required to pass this question. There would also be marks on the marking scheme for mentioning the need to obtain probabilities for the forecasts of demand and level of loan balance, and how this would enable the decision maker to calculate the probability that the advertising campaign will generate a profit that is higher than the existing profit.

In part (c) a couple of marks were available for general comments on other factors. Follow-through marks from the options in the two-way data table could have been as many as 3. This should remind students that easy marks are available in each requirement and that even a poor performance in the previous requirements should not discourage candidates to attempt all parts of questions.

(a) (i) **Continuing with existing bank account**

	Workings	Profit £
Business Customers	1 million × (1–20%) = 800,000	
Routine Transactions per year	800m	
Transaction charges	800m × 0.60	480,000,000
Customers with positive bank balances	45% × 800,000 = 360,000	
Interest paid to 'positive' customers	£2,000 average balance × 0.1% × 360,000	(720,000)
Customers with negative bank balances	55% × 800,000 = 440,000	
Interest charged to overdrawn customers	£4,000 average balance × 20% × 440,000	352,000,000
Current profit		**£831,280,000**

Note: Current business customers net balances:

(360,000 × £2000 average balance) − (440,000 × £4000 average overdraft) = £(1,040,000,000)

Account Option One

	Workings	Profit £
Business Customers	1 million × 1.05 = 1,050,000	
Charges	£10 × 12 months × 1,050,000 customers	126,000,000
Customers with positive bank balances	45% × 1,050,000 = 472,500	
Interest paid to 'positive' customers	£2,000 average balance × 0.5% × 472,500	(4,725,000)
Customers with negative bank balances	55% × 1,050,000 = 577,500	
Interest charged to overdrawn customers	£4,000 average balance × 20% × 577,500	462,000,000
Business Customers net balances	(472,500 × £2000 average balance) − (577,500 × £4000 average overdraft) = £(1,365,000,000)	
Opportunity cost	(£1,365,000,000 − £1,040,000,000) × 3%	(£9,750,000)

Option 1 annual profit   **£573,525,000**

Account Option Two

	Workings	*Profit £*
Business Customers	1 million × 1.10 = 1,100,000	
Customers with positive bank balances	45% × 1,100,000 = 495,000	
Interest paid to 'positive' customers	NIL	
Customers with negative bank balances	55% × 1,100,000 = 605,500	
Interest charged to overdrawn customers	£4,000 average balance × 20% × 605,500	484,000,000
Business Customers net balances	(495,000 × £2000 average balance) – (605,000 × £4000 average overdraft) = £(1,430,000,000)	
Opportunity cost	(£1,430,000,000 – £1,040,000,000) × 3%	(11,700,000)

Option 2 annual profit   **£472,300,000**

Conclusion

On the basis of the above calculations, the bank should keep its existing charging structure.

(b)   (i)   **Profit matrix**

Average Balance	Number of loans	250,000	280,000	300,000
£7,500		£106,750,000 (see working)	£133,000,000	£150,500,000
£14,000		£188,000,000	£224,000,000	£248,000,000
£15,000		£200,500,000	£238,000,000	£263,000,000

Example working

250,000 loans × arrangement fee £500	£125,000,000
Add:	
Interest income 5% × £7500 × 250,000 loans	£93,750,000
Less: Advertising campaign cost	(£112,000,000)
Profit	£106,750,000

(ii)   The bank needs to calculate whether going ahead with the advertising campaign makes financial sense, i.e. whether there are incremental profits to be gained compared to its existing profits.

Existing profits =

Arrangement fees £500 × 200,000 loans	=	£100,000,000

Add: Revenue from Interest charges

£5000 × 5% × 200,000 loans	=	£50,000,000
Total	=	**£150,000,000**

The two-way table shows that two of the three options at the £7500 increase level do not result in incremental profit for the bank, and that the third only increases this value by £500,000.

However, as there are seven options out of nine that do give a positive incremental profit, the bank should be advised to proceed with the campaign.

For decision making, we need to obtain probabilities for the forecasts of Demand and level of loan balance. Having obtained this information it will be possible to calculate the probability that the advertising campaign will generate a profit that is higher than the existing profit, in other words, the probability that we will benefit from the campaign. This information will help the management understand some of risks involved in the decision.

Other considerations include:

- Extra staff level and / or training to support the increase in business due to the higher number of loans;
- The bank's attitude to risk in view of the conclusions in i), particularly with an analysis of the probability of each outcome occurring.

313 H PRINTING (MAY 07)

Key answer tips

Although part (b) does not specifically ask you to give examples from the scenario in part (a), as there are 10 marks allocated to part (b) it is not sufficient just to make general points. Also, using specific examples may make it easier to put across the points than just using general arguments.

(a)

	$	
Relevant costs		
Material A	15,000	10,000 sheets @ $1.50/sheet. Material is in regular use so must be costed at market price
Material B	2,000	250l @ $8 per litre. Cost of entire order as surplus is unlikely to be used.
Direct labour	500	50 hours @ $10/hr. Overtime only as 100 hours idle time already paid for un guaranteed minimum wage.

Machine A	240	20 hrs @ $12/hr.
		Opportunity cost of lost income.
Machine B	100	25 hrs @ $4/hr.
		Cost of overtime as machine fully utilised in normal hours.
Despatch	400	Additional cost which will be incurred due to this contract
Total relevant costs	18,240	
Not relevant		
Technical report	0	This is a sunk cost.
Supervisor	0	This cost will be incurred irrespective of decision on project.
Overhead	0	This cost is not specific to the project and will be incurred irrespective of decision.
Profit mark-up	0	Profit mark-up is not a relevant cost of the project.

(b) Relevant costs are those costs that are appropriate to a specific management decision.

It is appropriate to use relevant costs when considering the best use of resources at a particular point in time, and to base prices on relevant costs on a one-off basis to win a contract to utilise spare capacity if fixed costs are unchanged by the decision and there is no other profitable work. However, in the long run it is important to ensure that prices are set at a level which covers the underlying fixed costs of the organisation.

When routinely reporting profit within an absorption costing system, the costs will be attributed to the work based on the time taken, overhead absorption rates and inventory levels. These costs will be different from those used in the relevant cost calculation.

For example, in the case of the direct labour costs in this scenario, under absorption costing the labour cost would be reported as 150 hours at a rate of $8 per hour, that is $1,200 rather than the relevant cost of $500. In addition, fixed overheads of $20 per hour of direct labour will be allocated to the work even though the actual level of fixed costs will not be changed by undertaking the contract. In both cases the costs reported for the contract will be greater than the additional costs incurred, thus decreasing the reported profit on the contract.

In the case of machine A, the cost allocated to the contract will be 20 hours at the running cost of $5 per hour. This is lower than the relevant cost which took account of the impact on the overall profitability of the company of not selling spare machine hours. This means that reported profit on the contract is higher, but the income reported elsewhere in the company will be lower.

If the total costs allocated to the contract under the absorption costing system are greater than the relevant costing on which the price is based, it is possible that a contract which was worthwhile from a decision-making perspective may appear to make a loss. This could present a problem to a manager whose performance is measured based on the results from the absorption costing system.

314 HEALTH CLINIC (MAY 06) *Walk in the footsteps of a top tutor*

Top Tutor Tips

With all exam questions you should start with the requirements to understand all that is being asked of you and to determine whether there are any 'easier' elements that can be attempted first. A read of the requirements in this question will indicate that the easiest marks are likely to lie in part (c) on the non-financial factors.

Read the question and it is clear that we are focusing mainly on financial factors. For non-financial factors you should think about the impact on other stakeholders such as customers, staff and the wider community. It should be straight forward to think of at least three other factors that the clinic should consider. It is important to do part (c) as it is common in the exam for students to run out of time in section C questions. Doing this part first means that you can get these three or four marks first and if you run out of time you are only missing out on marks which are harder to pick up on anyway.

This question does not want you to include the numerical values which should help simplify things for you. Many students will possibly miss the 'No investment' option but should still manage to pick up four of the six marks available.

For part (b) there is a lot of information to take in, but the decision tree created in part (a) should help you understand what information is needed and where. Remember that no further discounting is needed, so although the NPV method is mentioned we won't actually need to perform any calculations other than expected values.

Year 0 and Year 1 costs for each of the three options should be the easier parts, and getting this much correct should easily get you enough marks to pass the question overall if you have picked up 3 marks in part (c) and 4 marks in part (a). So although the remainder of the question is tougher, this should be your target in the exam room. After this you need to keep your eye on the time available so that you do not overrun. You've passed the question, which is the aim of the exam. You need to ensure that you do not spend too much time on this question at the expense of gaining marks in another question.

In the remaining time available you need to deal with years two and three for each option. Firstly you need to be aware that what happens in year 1 affects the outcomes of years 2 and 3. You will therefore need to determine joint probabilities. These are calculated as the probability in year 1 multiplied by the associated probability in year 2. The table at the start of the answer to part (b) explains this well, and again your decision tree should help you.

The other trick to deal with is the extra investment needed if demand exceeds the level of investment. This will be relevant for the 'don't invest' and 'option A' investments. These require careful reading, but, as highlighted above, if you have managed to get this far then you are likely to have already passed the question anyway. So any marks picked up at this stage should be an advantage which distinguishes the very top students in the exam.

Overall, there is a lot of information to deal with in this question and at times it is not well structured. A good decision tree should help you bring all the information together.

(a)   See decision tree overleaf.

Health clinic

Requirement (a)

Years 2 & 3 Demand

Year 1 Demand

Low
Medium
Low
Medium
High
Medium
High
Low
Medium
Low
Medium
High
Medium
High
Low
Medium
Low
Medium
High
Medium
High

Low
Medium
High

Low
Medium
High

Low
Medium
High

Investment B

Investment A

No Investment

Tutorial note

Part (a) you need to draw a decision tree. Some key tips are:

- Turn your page on its side to make it easier to fit everything in
- Each branch should represent the possible options
- Do not forget to include an option of no investment
- Use clear labels for each branch
- Remember that chance points should be shown as circles and decision points as squares. If you are unsure then you should include a key alongside your diagram.

(b)   Three options are available. With no investment, facilities will have to be bought in to satisfy medium and high demand in all three years.

The probabilities of low, medium or high demand in years 2 and 3 are dependent on the level of demand in year 1, so a good place to start may be to calculate joint probabilities.

Year 1 demand	Year 2 and 3 demand	Probability		
Low	Low	0.3 × 0.4	0.12	
Medium	Low	0.5 × 0.3	0.15	
High	Low	0.2 × 0.0	0.00	**Total 0.27**
Low	Medium	0.3 × 0.6	0.18	
Medium	Medium	0.5 × 0.4	0.20	
High	Medium	0.2 × 0.3	0.06	**Total 0.44**
Low	High	0.3 × 0.0	0.00	
Medium	High	0.5 × 0.3	0.15	
High	High	0.2 × 0.7	0.14	**Total 0.29**

No further investment

Year 1	Annual cost ($)	Additional facilities ($)	Total cost ($)	Probability	Expected cost
Low	300,000	0	300,000	30%	$90,000
Medium	300,000	100,000	400,000	50%	$200,000
High	300,000	250,000	550,000	20%	$110,000
					————
					$400,000
					————

Years 2 & 3	Annual cost ($)	Additional facilities ($)	Total cost ($)		
Low	300,000	0	300,000	27%	$81,000
Medium	300,000	100,000	400,000	44%	$176,000
High	300,000	250,000	550,000	29%	$159,500
					$416,500
					× 2 years =
					$833,000

Total present value of cost					$1,233,000

Investment in facility A requires additional facilities to be bought in for high demand. Don't forget to include the fixed and variable cost for high demand. The additional facility cost only represents the cost of the *additional* facilities.

Investment in facility A	Annual fixed cost ($)	Annual variable cost ($)	Additional facility cost ($)	Total cost ($)	Probability	Expected cost ($)
Year 0 cost						500,000
Year 1						
Low	100,000	150,000		250,000	30%	75,000
Medium	100,000	250,000		350,000	50%	175,000
High	100,000	250,000	150,000	500,000	20%	100,000
						350,000
Years 2 & 3 expected cost per year:						
Low	100,000	150,000		250,000	27%	67,500
Medium	100,000	250,000		350,000	44%	154,000
High	100,000	250,000	150,000	500,000	29%	145,000
						$366,500
						× 2 years =
						$733,000

Total present value of cost $1,583,000

Investment in facility B provides sufficient capacity to cover all levels of demand so there are no additional facility costs.

Investment in facility B	Fixed cost ($)	Variable cost ($)	Total cost ($)	Probability	Expected cost ($)
Year 0 cost					800,000

Year 1 expected cost:

Low	200,000	100,000	300,000	30%	90,000
Medium	200,000	150,000	350,000	50%	175,000
High	200,000	200,000	400,000	20%	80,000
					345,000

Years 2 & 3 expected
cost per year:

Low	200,000	100,000	300,000	27%	81,000
Medium	200,000	150,000	350,000	44%	154,000
High	200,000	200,000	400,000	29%	116,000
					$351,000
					× 2 years
					= $702,000

Total present value of cost   **$1,847,000**

The expected cost of the three options are:

- No investment $1,233,000
- Facility A $1,583,000
- Facility B $1,847,000

So on financial grounds the decision would be not to invest and to use existing facilities.

(c)   Non-financial factors may be important and include:

- The health clinic will have to use additional facilities to satisfy demand which are not under its direct control. This may lead to quality and reliability issues.

- Demand has only been estimated for the forthcoming three years. A longer time period may need to be considered. By not carrying out investment now it may be more difficult to expand facilities in three years' time if required.

- Reliance on outside contractors may mean that the health clinic is vulnerable to price rises which would be out of its control.

- Employees may become demotivated if there is a perception that the health clinic is unwilling to invest in new facilities.

Users of the health clinic may prefer to be treated in a known environment.

FINANCIAL INFORMATION FOR LONG-TERM DECISION MAKING

315 REGIONAL AIRPORT (MAY 10) *Walk in the footsteps of a top tutor*

Top Tutor Tips

You should begin questions by reading the requirement first (in the exam hall this can be done during the reading time at the start of the). From reading the requirement to this question you can determine that in part (a) you need to calculate the NPV of a project (which can be a time consuming requirement), and that part (b), the discursive element of the question, does not relate in any way to part (a). So this would allow you to attempt part (b). This means that you can pick up a few marks here that you may otherwise miss if you spend too long on part (a).

Part (b) refers to standard deviation – a topic that many students would have struggled with and is likely to be the area that distinguishes the outstanding students from the average students. So don't worry if you are not familiar with this concept. There are still plenty of easy marks available for explaining expected values, NPV, IRR etc. Remember to make points that are relevant to the scenario rather than simply answer in very general terms. But even a mark of only 3 or 4 out of 9 in this section might be enough to distinguish between those students who pass the question and those who fail due to spending too long on part (a).

It will be important to have a methodical approach to part (b). Start by determining whether the question includes tax and/or inflation, the length of the project and the cost of capital. These will influence which proforma is used to answer the question. As is normal in section C questions we discover that it is a short project (4/5 years) and includes both tax and inflation so that we need the columnar NPV proforma. You should therefore set up this proforma and insert the discount factors (which should score an easy mark to get you going).

Now try to deal with the remainder of the information in a logical order. Begin with the initial investment and disposal (putting these in the proforma will gain another easy mark or two). The writing down allowances should come next. These appear very regularly in these types of exam question and you should have practiced lots of them before you enter the exam hall. They are typically worth 4 or 5 marks and you really should aim to achieve as many of these marks as possible by practicing the technique a number of times. It should mean that by this stage you will have around 7 marks for part (a), and if you've already picked up 4 marks for part (b) you've almost got enough marks to pass the question overall.

You are now left with revenue (the toughest part of the calculation), variable costs and overheads. Salaries and overheads are probably the easiest of these elements to deal with so do these first which should be enough to push you up over the pass mark overall. Any reasonable attempt at the remaining, trickier areas should then boost your marks to well over the required target to pass.

(a)

Year	0	1	2	3	4	5
	$000	$000	$000	$000	$000	$000
Sales (W2)		1,620,000	1,782,000	1,960,200	2,156,220	
Variable costs (W3)		(900,000)	(990,000)	(1,089,000)	(1,197,900)	
Lost revenue (W4)		(432,000)	(475,200)	(522,720)	(574,992)	
Salaries		(80,000)	(80,000)	(100,000)	(100,000)	
Increased overheads		(70,000)	(70,000)	(70,000)	(70,000)	
Net operating CF		138,000	166,800	178,480	213,328	
Taxation						
Current Year		(20,700)	(25,020)	(26,772)	(31,999)	
Previous Year			(20,700)	(25,020)	(26,772)	(31,999)
Initial investment	(350,000)				30,000	
Tax depreciat'n (W1)		13,125	22,969	17,227	25,031	17,648
Net CF Post Tax	(350,000)	130,425	144,049	143,915	209,588	(14,351)
DF @8%	1.000	0.926	0.857	0.794	0.735	0.681
Present Value	(350,000)	120,774	123,450	114,269	154,047	(9,773)

NPV   **$152,767**

As the NPV is positive, the project is worthwhile and should be accepted.

Workings

(W1) **Tax depreciation allowances**

Year	Written-down value	Tax saving at 30%	Saving in year	Saving in following year	Cash flow
0	350,000				
1	(87,500)	26,250	13,125		13,125
	262,500				
2	(65,625)	19,688	9,844	13,125	22,969
	196,875				
3	(49,219)	14,766	7,383	9,844	17,227
	147,656				
4	(30,000)				
BA	117,656	35,297	17,648	7,383	25,031
5				17,648	17,648

(W2) Revenue

Year	1	2	3	4
Passenger numbers	180,000	198,000	217,800	239,580
Revenue per customer	$9	$9	$9	$9
Total revenue ($)	1,620,000	1,782,000	1,960,200	2,156,220

(W3) Variable costs

Year	1	2	3	4
Passenger numbers	180,000	198,000	217,800	239,580
Revenue per customer	$5	$5	$5	$5
Total revenue ($)	900,000	990,000	1,089,000	1,197,900

(W4) Lost revenue from cold food

Year	1	2	3	4
Lost passengers (1,200 x 40% x 360)	172,800	190,080	209,088	229,997
Lost contribution	$2.5	$2.5	$2.5	$2.5
Total revenue ($)	432,000	475,200	522,720	574,992

(b) Interpretation of project information

Expected NPV

Net Present Value (NPV) represents the increase in shareholders wealth that should arise if the project is accepted. The project with the biggest NPV, in this case Projects B and C have equal value, will be the most beneficial for shareholders and should be accepted. Because B and C are of equal weighting they are equally preferable.

The 'expected' part of the data provided highlights that the project includes a number of chance points and that probabilities have been allocated to these different potential outcomes to allow a weighted average to be calculated for each set of possibilities. These calculations will ignore any attitudes to risk that the managing director might have – and therefore different risk attitudes might result in different calculations and different decisions by the managing director.

Standard Deviation of Expected NPV

This set of figures aims to give an indication of the risk of each project. It shows how much variation there is from the average. So, the higher the standard deviation, the higher the perceived risk. It can be seen from the data that Project B has the highest standard deviation – this indicates that the expected NPV could typically be up to $50,000 different (either higher or, more importantly, lower). This indicates that Project B is more risky than the other projects (and, likewise, that Project A is the least risky). When coupled with the expected NPV data, a risk averse investor is likely to prefer Project C to B as it has a lower standard deviation.

IRR

The internal rate of return (IRR) gives another indicator of risk. It tells us how high the company's cost of capital (i.e. the cost at which it obtains finance) would have to rise before the expected NPV would fall to zero. Generally, the lower this figure is then the more risky the project becomes. Using this data, Project C now becomes the most risky and least attractive investment.

Deciding factors

The managing director needs to make a decision between the projects. What we know is that B and C are best for investors, A is the least risky, and that Project C would be much less attractive if the cost of capital was to rise. Therefore in order to make his decision, the managing director must determine a number of issues:

- An attitude to risk – a risk seeker might take on project B but an investor who is risk averse might prefer project A.

- The likelihood of a change in the cost of capital – if the cost of capital as been arranged and fixed in advance, then the risk to project C is reduced.

- The validity of the data used – all of this data will be based on predictions about the future and the managing director may want to investigate some of the underlying assumptions that have been made.

316 GYMNASIUM (SEPT 10)

Key answer tips

In this question it may be easiest to start with part (c) if you are comfortable with the two techniques for dealing with inflation. Part (b) requires an IRR calculation (this may catch out a lot of students) and cannot be completed until after part (a). In part (a) it is best to use a methodical approach whereby you perform the calculations in the easiest order, for example, putting in the discount factors first, the investment and proceeds next, then doing the tax depreciation, before moving on to the salaries and overheads, before attempting the difficult revenue calculations last.

(a) **Net Present Value**

Year	0	1	2	3	4	5
	$000	$000	$000	$000	$000	$000
New revenue (W2)		3,099,600	3,223,584	3,352,527	3,486,628	
Old revenue (W3)		(2,880,000)	(2,995,200)	(3,115,008)	(3,239,608)	
Salaries		(120,000)	(124,800)	(129,792)	(134,984)	
Increased overheads		(42,000)	(43,680)	(45,427)	(47,244)	
Net operating CF		57,600	59,904	62,300	64,792	
Taxation – Current		(8,640)	(8,986)	(9,345)	(9,719)	
– Previous			(8,640)	(8,985)	(9,345)	(9,719)
Installation + equip	(150,000)				15,000	
Tax depreciat'n (W1)		5,625	9,844	7,383	10,406	7,242
Net CF Post Tax	(150,000)	54,585	52,122	51,353	71,134	2,477
DF @12%	1.000	0.893	0.797	0.712	0.636	0.567
Present Value	(150,000)	48,744	41,541	36,563	45,241	(1,404)
NPV		**$20,685**				

As the NPV is positive, the project is worthwhile and should be accepted.

Workings

(W1) **Tax depreciation allowances**

Year	Written-down value	Tax saving at 30%	Saving in year	Saving in following year	Cash flow
0	150,000				
1	(37,500)	11,250	5,625		5,625
	112,500				
2	(28,125)	8,438	4,219	5,625	9,844
	84,375				
3	(21,094)	6,328	3,164	4,219	7,383
	63,281				
4	(15,000)				
BA	48,281	14,484	7,242	3,164	10,406
5				7,242	7,242

(W2) **Revenue**

Year	1	2	3	4
Occupancy @ 82%	11,808	11,808	11,808	11,808
Average room rate ($)	262.50	273.00	283.92	295.277
Total revenue ($)	3,099,600	3,223,584	3,352,527	3,486,628

Note: Total capacity = 40 rooms x 360 nights = 14,400 room rentals per annum.

(W3) **Old revenue**

Year	1	2	3	4
Occupancy @ 80%	11,520	11,520	11,520	11,520
Average room rate ($)	250.00	260.00	270.40	281.22
Total revenue ($)	2,880,000	2,995,200	3,115,008	3,239,608

(b) **Point of indifference**

The cost of capital at which the hotel will be indifferent to the project will the internal rate of return (IRR) of the project.

This can be calculated as follows:

If we calculate the present values of the cashflows at, say 15%, we get the following:

Net CF Post Tax	(150,000)	54,585	52,122	51,353	71,134	(2,477)
DF @15%	1.000	0.870	0.756	0.658	0.572	0.497
Present Value	(150,000)	47,489	39,404	33,790	40,689	(1,231)

NPV =$10,141

We can then use this along with the earlier NPV to calculate the IRR:

$$\text{IRR} = 12\% + \frac{20{,}685}{20{,}685 - 10{,}141} \ (15\% - 12\%)$$

$$\text{IRR} = 12\% + \frac{20{,}685}{10{,}544} \ (3\%)$$

$$\text{IRR} = 12\% + \ 1.96 \ (3\%)$$

$$\text{IRR} = 17.9\%$$

This is the post-tax money cost of capital at which the hotel will be indifferent to accepting/rejecting the project.

(c)   **Treatment of inflation**

An alternative approach to dealing with inflation would be to leave the cash flows in present day terms (i.e. do not inflate them), and instead adjust the cost of capital to an effective cost of capital.

This would be calculated as follows:

$$\text{Effective cost of capital} = \frac{1 + \text{money cost of capital}}{1 + \text{inflation rate}} - 1$$

$$\text{Effective cost of capital} = \frac{1.12}{1.04} - 1$$

$$\text{Effective cost of capital} = 7.7\%$$

However, a major problem with this method is in dealing with taxation. The tax charges calculated above will be in 'money' terms – that is, they will include an element of inflation. This is particularly true of the tax depreciation charges. Therefore this inflation needs to be 'stripped out' of the money flows to find their equivalent flow in 'real terms'. This matter is further complicated by the fact that the tax is paid over two years.

Overall, this effective method would make the calculation much more difficult. Therefore it would be normal to use the 'money method' illustrated in part (a) to keep the calculation more straightforward.

317   SQ (NOV 07) *Walk in the footsteps of a top tutor*

Top Tutor Tips

Initially it is not clear from the question whether the new facility is a replacement for or in addition to the existing one – however if there is to be a saving in maintenance costs then the new investment must be a replacement.

What follows is a step by step approach to the question:

1   Read the requirement – we discover that we are only interested in incremental contribution.

2   Read and annotate the question trying to pick up the key pieces of information – is there tax? Inflation? How long will the project last?

3   *Because it mentions savings in maintenance costs this is what tells us that the new machine will be a replacement for the existing machine.*

4   *Set up workings for corporation tax and WDA's.*

5   *Set up the NPV proforma – you are likely to find it easiest if you set this up in landscape form with the years going across the top of your page. But the answer provides a tabular layout if you find that more comfortable.*

6   *Deal with the section headed 'Proposed new production facility' as this is likely to be a big mark scorer and reasonably easy to deal with. You should be able to put in:*

- *the initial investment*

- *the scrap proceeds*

- *now attempt the capital allowances working. This is a common area in NPV questions and you should practice a lot of these until you can consistently get them right.*

- *produce a working for the increase in production capacity (W1)*

- *produce a working for the increased contribution per unit (W2)*

- *produce a working for the overall net benefit for the investment (W3)*

- *transfer the values from this working to the face of the NPV calc.*

7   *Next deal with the maintenance costs – putting them straight onto the face of the NPV calc.*

8   *Add together additional contribution and the maintenance cost savings and multiply this by 30% to calculate the tax we will pay on this saving. These savings will have a one year time lag – though this is something that only the very top students are likely to spot and deal with properly. You will need an extra column for your NPV calc now. This shows that when setting up proformas in NPV calculations you should always leave a spare column for just this kind of scenario.*

9   *Now all that's left is to apply the discount factors and add up the NPV – but leave this final step out if you are short of time.*

(a)   (i)   Relevant cash flows are:

- Investment and residual value
- Increase in contribution due to investment
- Increased sales
- Change in variable costs
- Change in tax payment
- Change in contribution
- Depreciation/ capital allowances
- Saving in maintenance costs

Fixed overheads are not relevant with the exception of the change in maintenance costs

Year 0 is 2007

Yr	Investment ($)	Contribution + cost saving ($) (W1, W2, W3)	Corporation tax ($) (W3)	Change in tax due to depreciation adjustment ($) (W4)	Net cash flow ($)	DF 12%	Present value ($)
0	(4,000,000)				(4,000,000)	1.000	(4,000,000)
1		1,850,000	(277,500)	150,000	1,722,500	0.893	1,538,193
2		2,320,000	(625,500)	262,500	1,957,000	0.797	1,559,729
3		2,642,000	(744,300)	196,875	2,094,575	0.712	1,491,337
4		2,994,000	(845,400)	147,657	2,296,257	0.636	1,460,419
5	400,000	3,106,000	(915,000)	193,125	2,784,125	0.567	1,578,599
6			(465,900)	129,843	(336,057)	0.507	(170,381)
						NPV	3,457,896

Workings

(W1) **Sales revenue**

New facility will increase capacity to 130% of previous level

New capacity = 130% × 120,000 = 156,000 units

Sales for next five years

Year	Sales	Increase on previous level	Comment
2008	130,000	10,000	Limited by demand
2009	140,000	20,000	Limited by demand
2010	147,000	27,000	Limited by demand
2011	154,000	34,000	Limited by demand
2012	156,000	36,000	Limited by capacity

(W2) **Change in contribution per unit**

	Existing equipment	New facility
Selling price	150	150
Direct material	(50)	(50)
Direct labour	(30)	(24)
Variable production overhead	(25)	(20)
Variable selling overhead	(10)	(10)
Contribution per unit	35	46

(W3) Additional contribution, maintenance cost saving, corporation tax on additional contribution

	Existing equipment	New facility					
		2008 Year 1	2009 Year 2	2010 Year 3	2011 Year 4	2012 Year 5	2013 Year 6
Sales (units)	120,000	130,000	140,000	147,000	154,000	156,000	–
Contribution per unit ($)	35	46	46	46	46	46	–
Total contribution ($000)	4,200	5,980	6,440	6,762	7,084	7,176	–
Additional contribut'n		1,780	2,240	2,562	2,884	2,976	–
Maintenance cost saving		70	80	80	110	130	
Contribution + cost saving		1,850	2,320	2,642	2,994	3,106	
Additional tax (30% of contribution + saving)		555	696	792.6	898.2	931.8	
Payment of tax ($000)							
50% in year		277.5	348	396.3	449.1	465.9	
b/f			277.5	348	396.3	449.1	465.9
Cash flow		277.5	625.5	744.3	845.4	915	465.9

(W4) Tax depreciation/capital allowances

It is assumed that the existing facility has no residual value

Year	Written-down value	Tax saving at 30%	Saving in year	Saving in following year	Cash flow
	4,000,000				
2008	(1,000,000)	300,000	150,000		150,000
	3,000,000				
2009	(750,000)	225,000	112,500	150,000	262,500
	2,250,000				
2010	(562,500)	168,750	84,375	112,500	196,875
	1,687,500				
2011	(421,875)	126,563	63,282	84,375	147,657
	1,265,625				
2012	(865,625)	259,688	129,844	63,281	193,125
scrap	400,000				
2013				129,843	129,843

(ii)

Tutorial note

You are only asked for two factors. More are included here for completeness.

Other factors which SQ should consider before making decision:

- SQ should consider the validity of the estimates – this calculation is based on forecasts of changes in revenue and costs over a five year period which may not materialise. The company should consider undertaking sensitivity analysis to test how sensitive the NPV is to changes in estimates.

- This analysis is based purely on financial considerations. There may be non-financial risks associated with the project which should also be considered. One possible way of accounting for an element of any risks would be by using a risk-adjusted discount rate.

- If access to capital funding is limited SQ may need to consider alternative used for the $4 million it plans to invest in this project. There may other opportunities which provide a better or less risky return than this proposal which should be considered alongside this.

- SQ should also marketing issues and possible changes in the market in which it operates, for example increased competition from companies producing similar products. This may have an impact on the future demand for the product and the price which can be charged.

- There will be excess capacity in the facility for the first four years if sales volume estimates are accurate. The company should consider whether there are other ways of utilising this additional capacity which could generate additional contribution and improve the returns from the project.

(b)   (i)   The IRR can be estimated using the formula:

$$IRR \approx A + (B - A)\frac{N_A}{N_A - N_B}$$

where   A   =   lower discount rate

             B   =   higher discount rate

             NA   =   NPV at rate A

             NB   =   NPV at rate B

Calculating an NPV at 20%

Annual net cash flow from project   = cash inflow – cash outflow

                                     = $(30,000 – $22,500)

                                     = $7,500

NPV = annual net cash flow × cumulative discount factor at 20% – investment

NPV = $7,500 × 2.106 – $15,000

NPV = $795

Substituting in formula:

A	= 10%
B	= 20%
NA	= $3,652.50
NB	= $795.00
IRR	≈ 10 + ((10 × 3,652.50) / (3,652.50 − 795.00))
IRR	≈ 10 + 12.78
IRR	≈ 22.78 %

(ii) The sensitivity to changes in annual cash inflows is the percentage change in the cash inflows which would change the investment decision, that is which would produce an NPV of $0.

Sensitivity of project   = NPV of project / PV of cash inflow × 100%

Cumulative discount factor for three years at 10%   = 2.487

PV of cash inflow   = $30,000 × 2.487   = $74,610

Sensitivity of project   = 3,652.50 / 74,610 × 100%   = 4.90%

318 HOTEL GROUP (NOV 09)

Key answer tips

This can be a difficult question at first glance. But if you use your exam technique well there should be enough marks available that any well prepared student should be able to gain a pass. There are 'easy' marks in part (a) for standard areas such as the discount factors, the investment, the tax depreciation (which with lots of practice you should be well prepared for in time for the real) etc. Part (b) on sensitivity analysis is a part of the syllabus that many students can find difficult. But, again, there will be easy marks for available for providing the formula and making any reasonable progress towards an answer – even if your answer to part (a) is incorrect you will not get punished again in part (b).

(a) **Net Present Value of the proposed hotel investment ($000)**

$000	1 Jan 20X0	Year 1 20X0	Year 2 20X1	Year 3 20X2	Year 4 20X3	Year 5 20X4	Year 6 20X5
Sales revenue (W3)		130	234	252	284	306	
Guest related costs (W4)		(20)	(37)	(40)	(45)	(48)	
Other fixed costs (W2)		(65)	(68)	(68)	(70)	(72)	
Net taxable flows		45	129	144	169	186	
Tax on profit							
Paid in year		(7)	(19)	(21)	(25)	(28)	
Paid in following year			(7)	(20)	(22)	(26)	(28)
Investment in building	(650)					650	

$000	1 Jan 20X0	Year 1 20X0	Year 2 20X1	Year 3 20X2	Year 4 20X3	Year 5 20X4	Year 6 20X5
Investment in equipment	(250)					100	
Tax relief on equipment (W1)		7	14	11	9	4	
	———	———	———	———	———	———	———
Net cash flow	(900)	45	117	114	131	886	(28)
Discount factor at 8%	1.000	0.926	0.857	0.794	0.735	0.681	0.630
Present value	(900)	42	100	91	96	603	(18)

Net present value = $14,000.

Since the investment has a positive NPV it is financially worthwhile.

Workings

(W1) **WDA's on equipment**

	$000	Tax relief	Year 1	Year 2	Year 3	Year 4	Year 5
Yr 0 Cost	250						
Yr 1 tax depreciation	(50)	15	7	8			
	———						
NBV	200						
Yr 2 tax depreciation	(40)	12		6	6		
	———						
NBV	160						
Yr 3 tax depreciation	(32)	10			5	5	
	———						
NBV	128						
Yr 4 tax depreciation	(26)	8				4	4
	———						
NBV	102						
Yr 4 sale	(100)						
	———						
Balancing allowance	2	0*					
Total tax relief			7	14	11	9	4

* the total tax relief on the balancing allowance will be $2,000 x 30% = £600, paid in two instalments of £300. But as figures are being rounded to the nearest £1,000 these have been ignored in the calculation of the NPV. It should not materially affect the decision to invest.

(W2) **Fixed costs**

Base cost = $40,000 (guest related costs) + $25,000 (other fixed costs)

Year	Base cost	Indexation	Money cost
	$		$
1	65,000	100	65,000
2	65,000	104	67,600
3	65,000	105	68,250
4	65,000	107	69,550
5	65,000	110	71,500

(W3) Sales revenue

Year	Base revenue	Increase in guest numbers (index)	Indexation	Money cost
	$			$
1	130,000	100	100	130,000
2	130,000	180	100	234,000
3	130,000	190	102	251,940
4	130,000	210	104	283,920
5	130,000	220	107	306,020

(W4) Guest related costs

Year	Base cost	Increase in guest numbers (index)	Indexation	Money cost
	$			$
1	20,000	100	100	20,000
2	20,000	180	104	37,440
3	20,000	190	105	39,900
4	20,000	210	107	44,940
5	20,000	220	110	48,400

(b) Sensitivity analysis

$$\text{Sensitivity analysis} = \frac{\text{NPV}}{\text{PV of fixed charges}} \times 100\%$$

$$= \frac{14,000}{73,470 \,(\text{W1})} \times 100\%$$

$$= 19\%$$

(W1) Present value of other fixed charges

Year	Base cost	Index-ation	Money cost	Tax relief (year)	Tax relief (next)	Net flows	DF @ 8%	PV
	$		$	$	$	$		$
1	25,000	100	25,000	(3,750)		21,250	0.926	19,677
2	25,000	104	26,000	(3,900)	(3,750)	18,350	0.857	15,726
3	25,000	105	26,250	(3,938)	(3,900)	18,412	0.794	14,619
4	25,000	107	26,750	(4,013)	(3,937)	18,800	0.735	13,818
5	25,000	110	27,500	(4,125)	(4,102)	19,273	0.681	13,125
6					(4,125)		0.630	(3495)
								73,470

319 CAR MANUFACTURER (NOV 10)

Key answer tips

This is a tricky question on NPV and IRR. Students will need a clear understanding of both techniques - including why they can give conflicting answers. Students have to assess 2 projects – though for one of the projects the NPV and IRR had already been calculated. For this first project students have to identify the relevant costs that had been used in the calculation. This is tricky as there was a lot of information to take in. But there should be 2 or 3 easy marks here for illustrating the sunk consultancy fee, the initial investment and the savings on materials. The question is also made a little easier as students are told to ignore taxation. So students should have reasonably been expected to pick up the necessary half marks on this part of the question.

The second project has less information to deal with but the students had to complete both the NPV and IRR calculations. There is a tricky bit in removing depreciation from fixed overheads, but even if a mistake is made here there should still be enough marks available for students to achieve a pass.

Overall, success or failure on this question will have come down to a student's familiarity with NPV and IRR. But as these are core syllabus areas and have appeared regularly in exams to date, this should not have been a shock to most students.

(a) **Project 1**

Internal Failure Cost Savings:

Current Expected Value = ($300k x 0.5) + ($500k x 0.3) + ($700k x 0.2)   = $440k

Expected Savings Year 1 = $440k x 80% x 1.04   = $366k

External Failure Cost Savings:

Current Expected Value = ($1,300k x 0.6) + ($1,900k x 0.3) + ($3,000k x 0.1) = $1,650k

Expected Savings Year 1 = $1,650k x 80% x 1.04   = $1,373k

Raw Material Cost:

Expected savings Year 1 = 50,000 x $62 x 1.04   =$3,224k

Net cash flows Year 1

$366,080 + $1,372,800 + $3,224,000   = $4,963k

(b) **Project 2**

(i) **NPV**

Component Costs:

Expected savings Year 1 = 50,000 x $110 x 1.04 =$5,720k

Depreciation per annum = $15,000,000 / 5 = $3,000k

Additional fixed costs (excl. dep'n) per annum = $5,000k - $3,000k = $2,000k

	Year 0 $000	Year 1 $000	Year 2 $000	Year 3 $000	Year 4 $000	Year 5 $000
Initial Investment	(15,000)					
Working capital	(1,000)					1,000
Cost savings		5,720	5,949	6,187	6,434	6,691
Fixed costs		(2,000)	(2,000)	(2,000)	(2,000)	(2,000)
Net cash flows	(16,000)	3,720	3,949	4,187	4,434	5,691
Discount Factor @ 8%	1.000	0.926	0.857	0.794	0.735	0.681
Present value	(16,000)	3,445	3,384	3,324	3,259	3,876

Net present value = $1,288k

(ii) **Internal Rate of Return**

	Year 0 $000	Year 1 $000	Year 2 $000	Year 3 $000	Year 4 $000	Year 5 $000
Net cash flows	(16,000)	3,720	3,949	4,187	4,434	5,691
DF @ 12%	1.000	0.893	0.797	0.712	0.636	0.567
PV	(16,000)	3,322	3,147	2,981	2,820	3,227

Net present value = - $503k

IRR

NPV at 8% = $1,288k

NPV at 12% = -$503k

By interpolation

8% + (1,288/(1,288 + 503)) x 4% =10.9%

(c) **Overall advice**

The general rule in discount cash flow analysis where projects are mutually exclusive is that the project with the highest net present value should be selected. In this case project 1 has a NPV of $1,338K and project 2 has a NPV of $1,288K. Therefore on the basis on NPV alone project 1 should be selected.

Project 2 requires an investment of $16m while project 1 requires an investment of $20m. While project 2 has a marginally lower NPV than alternative 1, if the additional $4m of funds can be invested in other projects with NPVs in excess of this difference, it would be worthwhile investing in project 2.

The company directors will also have to consider the risk of the two projects and other non-financial factors.

(d)   **NPV vs IRR**

The IRR measures the project return as a percentage whereas NPV measures the absolute amount. This can result in a problem if the IRR is used to select projects where the projects are mutually exclusive. Decisions based on IRR may result in the selection of a project with a lower investment and a higher return, when it may be preferable to invest a greater sum which generates a lower percentage return but produces a greater absolute amount. Where projects are mutually exclusive NPV should be used to select projects.

Even if mutually exclusive projects have the same initial investment, NPV and IRR can give conflicting results due to the assumption regarding the reinvestment of surplus cash flows generated by an investment. The assumption if the NPV method is adopted is that the cash flows generated by an investment will be reinvested at the cost of capital. The IRR method assumes that cash flows generated by the investment will be reinvested at the IRR of the original project. IRR may favour an investment with high early cash flows, reinvested at the IRR, while NPV may prefer a different project with later cash flows. The NPV ranking of the projects depends on the discount rates used. When the discount rate exceeds a certain level the choice of projects will change and the conflict will no longer exist.

Examiner's comments

Part (a) and (b) were reasonably well done although there were a lot of fairly basic errors. Many students wasted valuable time in part (a) as they did not read the question properly and gave cash flows for all five years. In some cases they even carried out a discounted cash flow analysis. In part (b) some students failed to appreciate that the benefits from an investment can be in terms of cost savings and decided to make up sales revenue to put into the analysis. Parts (c) and (d) were not well answered with few students scoring more than one or two marks. It was not clear whether students had run out of time or just had a general lack of knowledge, particularly in part (d).

Common errors

- Giving cash flows for five years instead of only Year 1.

- Including 20% of cost saving rather than 80%.

- Failing to increase the production volume by 4% in Year 1.

- Failing to include the working capital as a cash inflow in Year 5

- Increasing the fixed costs by $5,000k each year.

- Treating depreciation as a cash flow.

- Using a second discount rate higher than 8%, to calculate IRR even though the students' original calculation at 8% incorrectly gave a negative NPV. Using the NPV for project 1 to calculate the IRR for project 2.

- Failing to state the superiority of NPV when choosing between mutually exclusive projects

- Inability to explain the conflict that can arise between NPV and IRR.

---

320 RESTAURANT (NOV 08 EXAM)

Key answer tips

In (a) Calculating the NPV, an average student, who would have omitted price increases and not dealt with variable costs and fixed costs separately, should have been able to layout the proformas and fill in enough information to almost pass this section –6 or 7 marks is a realistic target.

In (b) any attempt at calculating an IRR, even based on incorrect values from a), would have got credit. The actual formula would have got one mark, and the result of around 15% would have enabled the candidate to score full marks here.

In (c), the sensitivity calculation would have been challenging without the right results in a) but any attempt would have got credit. The skill here is in identifying the right cash flows for the sensitivity calculation.

(a)   The approach taken will be to evaluate the NPV of the increases in the relevant cash flows.

Relevant cash Flows:

- Sales

   Incremental cash flows   = £330,000 × 30%   = £99,000

   Applying a 3% price increase year-on-year, the following cash flows will be relevant:

   20X9 : £99,000 × 1.03 = £101,970

   20Y0 : £99,000 × 1.03² = £105,029

   20Y1 : £99,000 × 1.03³ = £108,180

   20Y2 : £99,000 × 1.03⁴ = £111,425

- Costs

   Food and Drink costs incremental cash outflows = (£125,000 + £70,000) × 30%

                                                                                                = £58,500

   Staff costs incremental cash outflows   = £55,000 × 20%

                                                                                          = £11,000

   Variable costs   = 30% × £45,000 ×30%

                                                                                          = £4,050

   Fixed Costs increases   = £10,000

   Total Cost increase   = £83,550

Applying a 4% inflation rate year-on-year, the following cash flows will be relevant :

20X9 : £83,550 × 1.04 = £86,892   20Y0 : £83,550 × 1.04² = £90,368

20Y1 : £83,550 × 1.04³ = £93,982   20Y2: £83,550 × 1.04⁴ = £97,742

	t=0	20X9	20Y0	20Y1	20Y2	20Y3
		£	£	£	£	£
Investment	(40,000)					
Increase in Cash flows (W1)		15,078	14,661	14,198	13,683	
Tax Savings from Capital Allowances (W2)			6,400	320	256	1,024
additional CT to pay 20%			3,016	2,932	2,840	2,737
Net operating CF	(40,000)	15,078	18,045	11,586	11,099	(1,713)
DF at 8%	1	0.926	0.857	0.794	0.735	0.681
Discounted Cash flows	(40,000)	13,962	15,465	9,199	8,158	(1,167)
NPV	**5,617**					

As the proposed investment yields a positive NPV, it is worthwhile on financial grounds.

Workings

(W1) **Net increases in Cash Flows**

	20X9	20Y0	20Y1	20Y2
Total Revenue increases	101,970	105,029	108,180	111,425
Total Cost Increases	86,892	90,368	93,982	97,742
Increase in Cash flows	15,078	14,661	14,198	13,683

(W2) **Capital Allowances**

Year	Written-down value	Tax saving at 20%
	£30,000	
20X9	£(30,000)	£6,000
	————	
	£10,000	
20X9	£(2,000)	£400
	£8,000	
20Y0	£(1,600)	£320
	6,400	
20Y1	£(1,280)	£256
	£5,120	
20Y2 Bal. Allowance	£5,120	£1,024

(b) (i) The IRR can be estimated using the formula:

$$IRR \approx A + (B - A)\frac{N_A}{N_A - N_B}$$

where   A   =   lower discount rate

B   =   higher discount rate

NA   =   NPV at rate A

NB   =   NPV at rate B

Calculating an NPV at 15%:

Net CF	(40,000)	15,078	18,045	11,586	11,099	(1,713)
DF at 15%	1	0.870	0.756	0.658	0.572	0.497
PV	(40,000)	13,118	13,642	7,624	6,349	(851)
NPV				**(£118)**		

Substituting in formula:

A = 8%

B = 15%

NA = £5,617

NB = (£118)

IRR ≈ 8 + ((7 × 5,617) / (5,617+118))

IRR ≈ 8 + 6.86

IRR ≈ 14.86 %

Interpretation

The IRR can be thought of as the return generated by the project. As the return (around 15%) is greater than the company's cost of capital (8%), then the project should be accepted.

(ii) The sensitivity to changes in the percentage capacity utilisation is the percentage change in the cash inflows which would change the investment decision.

Sensitivity of project = NPV of project / PV of cash inflow × 100%

Here, the cash inflow under consideration is the total post-tax increase in contribution, as a variation in capacity utilisation will affect our contribution (i.e. revenues less variable costs.)

	20X9	20Y0	20Y1	20Y2	20Y3
Sales Revenue increases (from (a))	£101,970	£105,029	£108,180	£111,425	
Total Variable costs (from (a))	£65,052	£67,654	£70,360	£73,175	
Increased Contribution from investment	£36,918	£37,375	£37,820	£38,250	
Corporation tax 20%		£7,384	£7,475	£7,564	£7,650
Net Post-tax contribution	£36,918	£29,991	£30,345	£30,686	(£7,650)
Discount Factor 8%	0.926	0.857	0.794	0.735	0.681
Discounted Cash flows	£34,186	£ 25,702	£24,094	£22,554	(£5,210)
Total Discounted Cash Flows			**£ 101,326**		

321 DP (MAY 12)

Key answer tips

In (a), calculating the NPV, the key calculation will be in determining the expected value of the parking charges. After that, the key challenge will be in dealing with the amount of information provided in the scenario so it will be important to have a careful an methodical approach.

In (b), any attempt at calculating an IRR, even based on incorrect values from a), would have got credit. The actual formula would have got one mark, and the result of around 11% would have enabled the candidate to score full marks here.

In (c), it will be important to use the three terms using the examiner's terminology from the syllabus. Although students are familiar with using the time value of money principles, this question shows that they also need to be able to explain it.

(a)   **Net present value**

		Year 0	Year 1	Year 2	Year 3	Year 4	Year 5	Year 6
		$000	$000	$000	$000	$000	$000	$000
Land		(8,000)					10,000	
Net cash flows	(W1)		681	722	766	812	859	
Tax payment	(W5)		(102)	(108)	(115)	(122)	(129)	
Tax payment	(W5)		0	(102)	(109)	(115)	(122)	(129)
Net cash flow after tax		(8,000)	579	512	542	575	10,608	(129)
DF @ 8%		1.000	0.926	0.857	0.794	0.735	0.681	0.630
Present value		(8,000)	536	439	430	423	7,224	(81)

Net present value = $971k

The project has a positive net present value and therefore should be accepted

Workings

(W1) **Cash Flows**

		Year 1	Year 2	Year 3	Year 4	Year 5
		$000	$000	$000	$000	$000
Contribution	(W2)	1,199	1,259	1,322	1,388	1,457
Leasing costs		(50)	(50)	(50)	(50)	(50)
Staff costs	(W3)	(364)	(379)	(394)	(409)	(426)
Security system costs	(W4)	(104)	(108)	(112)	(117)	(122)
Net cash flows		681	722	766	812	859

(W2) **Contribution**

Year 1 car parking charges

($60 x 40%) + ($50 x 25%) + ($70 x 35%) = $61 x 1.05 = $64.05

Year 1 sales revenue = (600 x 0.75) x $64.05 x 52 weeks = $1,499k

Year 1 contribution = $1,499k x 0.8 = $1,199k

(W3) **Year 1 Staff costs**

= $350k x 1.04 = $364k

(W4) **Year 1 Security system cost**

= $100k x 1.04 = $104k

(W5) **Taxation**

		Year 1 $000	Year 2 $000	Year 3 $000	Year 4 $000	Year 5 $000
Net cash flows	(W1)	681	722	766	812	859
Taxation @ 30%		(204)	(217)	(230)	(244)	(258)

(b) **Internal rate of return**

Firstly, a new NPV needs to be calculated at a different cost of capital. Let's try 12%:

	Year 0	Year 1	Year 2	Year 3	Year 4	Year 5	Year 6
Net cash flow after tax	(8,000)	579	512	542	575	10,608	(129)
DF @ 12%	1.000	0.893	0.797	0.712	0.636	0.567	0.507
Present value	(8,000)	517	408	386	366	6,015	(65)

Net present value = -$373k

We now have two NPVs:

@8%   NPV = $971k

@12%   NPV = ($373)k

These can then be used in the calculation of the IRR.

IRR = 8% + (($971k/($971k + $373k)) x (12% - 8%))

= 8% + 2.9%

= 10.9%

(c) **Time value of money**

The time value of money relates to the return required by investors and has three main elements:

Delayed Consumption

There is an opportunity cost involved with the investment of funds. Generally the value of $1.00 now is greater than the value of $1.00 in one year's time since investors have to give up present consumption. An investor will give up present consumption for the potential of higher future consumption i.e. they need to be rewarded for giving up certain current consumption for certain future consumption.

Inflation

If there is inflation then investors also need to be compensated for the loss in purchasing power as well as for time.

Risk

The promise of money in the future carries with it an element of risk. The payout may not take place or the amount may be less than expected. An investor therefore needs to be compensated for time, inflation and also risk.

The objective of investment within a company is to create value for its owners. Investors have alternative uses for their funds and therefore have an opportunity cost if money is invested in a corporate project. Investments therefore must generate enough cash for all investors to receive their required returns. The use of net present value in investment appraisal recognises the time value of money and discounts cash flows at the investors' required rate of return.

Examiner's comments

Part (a) was well done with many candidates scoring high marks. Part (b) was also well answered although some candidates still have problems applying the interpolation formula. Candidates often didn't realise that their answers could not be correct since if they had a positive and a negative NPV they needed to get an IRR between the two interest rates used. This showed a lack of understanding of the calculations. Part (c) was poorly answered with few candidates able to get further than stating that a pound today is worth more than a pound in five years' time and that this needed to be taken into account when appraising investments. Some candidates discussed inflation or risk but in very general terms.

Common errors

Part (a)

- Not inflating the year 1 price from $61 to $64.05.

- Incorrectly applying the inflation rate or not inflating cash flows at all.

- Not calculating contribution or deducting variable costs twice.

- Not evaluating whether or not the project should go ahead.

Part (b)

- Inability to apply interpolation to calculate the IRR.

- Inability to assess whether the answer derived was realistic.

Part (c)

- Lack of knowledge of the elements of the time value of money.

---

322   BUS OPERATOR (MAR 11)

Key answer tips

In part (a)(i) students should identify the relevant cash flows for each year of the project and discount these at the rate of 8% to calculate the net present value (NPV) of the project. They should then select the project for investment based on the highest NPV. In part a(ii) students should explain relevant non-financial factors that should be considered before making a final decision. In part (b) students should calculate the present value of the contribution from passengers in Project 2 and use this to calculate the sensitivity of the decision to changes in this value. Students should recognise that the decision would change when the NPV of project 2 falls below the NPV of project 1. In part (c) students should calculate the profitability index for each project and rank the projects on the basis of this index. The funding should then be allocated based on this ranking.

(a)   (i)   **Choice of project**

Project 1

Current contribution   = (20,000 passengers x $1.50) x 365 days = $10,950k

Revised contribution = (20,000 x 1.20 x $1.30) x 365 = $11,388k

Incremental contribution in year 1 = $11,388k - $10,950k = $438k

Incremental costs = $100k

Year	Cash flows $000	Discount factor	Present value $000
0	1,000	1.000	(1,000.0)
1-5	338	3.993	1,349.6
NPV			349.6

Project 2

Expected passenger numbers Year 1

= (6,000 x 50%) + (9,000 x 30%) + (12,000 x 20%) = 8,100

Expected contribution Year 1 = 8,100 x $1.50 x 365 days =$4,435k

Depreciation per annum = $5,000,000 / 5 = $1,000k

Additional fixed costs (excluding depreciation) per annum = $3,500k - $1,000k = $2,500k

Net Present Value

	Year 0 $000	Year 1 $000	Year 2 $000	Year 3 $000	Year 4 $000	Year 5 $000
Initial Investment	(5,000)					
Working capital	(1,000)					1,000
Expected contribution		4,435	4,568	4,705	4,846	4,991
Fixed costs		(2,500)	(2,500)	(2,500)	(2,500)	(2,500)
Net cash flows	(6,000)	1,935	2,068	2,205	2,346	3,491
DF @ 8%	1.000	0.926	0.857	0.794	0.735	0.681
Present value	(6,000)	1,792	1,772	1,751	1,724	2,377

Net present value ($000) = 3,416

Project 2 has a significantly higher NPV than project 1 and if the decision was made on NPV alone then the company should go ahead with Project 2.

(ii)   **Other factors to consider**

- Project 2 requires a significantly higher level of investment than project 1 and the company needs to consider whether it can raise the capital required.

- There is more risk involved in Project 2. In particular the estimated passenger numbers on the new routes is critical to the success of the project.

- Project 2 is on a much larger scale and will cause many operational issues for the company. There may be a requirement for a new depot for the buses and there will be a substantial increase in staffing.

- The level of competition and potential competitor reaction on the new routes needs to be considered.

- Project 2 will increase the company's market share and may be important for future growth of the company.

(b)   **Sensitivity analysis**

Tutorial note

The sensitivity to changes in the passenger numbers is the percentage change in the cash inflows which would change the investment decision.

Sensitivity = Difference in the NPV's / PV of cash inflow × 100%

First we need to calculate the present value of the expected contribution:

	Year 1	Year 2	Year 3	Year 4	Year 5	Total
	$000	$000	$000	$000	$000	$000
Expected contribution	4,435	4,568	4,705	4,846	4,991	
Discount Factor @ 8%	0.926	0.857	0.794	0.735	0.681	
Present value	4,107	3,915	3,736	3,562	3,399	18,719

Tutorial note

The difference in the NPV's of the projects is 3,066 ($3,416 - $350). Therefore the sensitivity is:

$3,066/ $18,719 = 16.4%

Assuming that the 3% annual increase is maintained, if passenger numbers in year 1 reduce by more than 16.4% the NPV of Project 2 will be less than that of Project 1 and therefore the choice will be to accept Project 1. Passenger numbers in year 1 need to therefore be greater than 6,772 (8,100 x 83.6%) for the project to be worthwhile.

(c) **Capital rationing**

The projects should be ranked on the basis of the profitability index as follows:

Project	Investment $000	NPV at 12% $000	Profitability Index	Ranking
A	50	13.6	1.27	4
B	40	15.2	1.38	3
C	20	10.2	1.51	1
D	30	12.3	1.41	2

The company will select projects D, C and B which will use $90,000 of the available funding. The remaining $20,000 can be used for part of project A.

Examiner's comments

Part a(i) was reasonably well done although candidates are still making fundamental errors such as including depreciation and sunk costs in the cash flows. The quality of answers to part a(ii) was fairly mixed, with some candidates failing to expand on the points made while others gave very good, thoughtful answers about the environment, competitors and the public's attitude to the new services.

Part (b) was badly answered although candidates invariably knew the general formula required. The difference in NPV between Project 2 and Project 1 was very rarely calculated as the numerator. Candidates frequently simply used passenger numbers as the denominator, rather than the contribution.

In part (c), there were relatively few correct answers. Most candidates ranked on absolute NPV values, although it was not always made clear that absolute NPV had been used as the basis for the ranking. The better candidates who knew that the profitability index needed to be used earned all four marks but unfortunately these candidates were in the minority.

Common errors

- Failure to calculate the incremental contribution for Project 1.
- Including the sunk costs in Project 1.
- Including the depreciation in Project 1.
- Failure to multiply the contribution in Project 2 by 365 days.
- Failure to show the release of working capital as a cash flow in Year 5.
- Failure to adjust the fixed cost for depreciation in Project 2.
- Inability to apply sensitivity analysis to the scenario.
- Use of passenger numbers rather than contribution in part (b)
- Failure to use the profitability index to rank projects in part (c).

323 GR (NOV 11)

Key answer tips

There are a couple of key elements in part (a) – firstly, students need to be familiar with the annual equivalent cost technique which firstly calculates the NPV and then divides it by the annuity factor for the length of the useful economic life. Secondly, there is a trick with the maintenance costs as they are paid out in advance and therefore must be brought to their present value by multiplying by one plus a two year annuity factor. Otherwise, the calculations are relatively straightforward for students familiar with the equivalent cost technique.

Parts (b) and (d) are likely to be easier than part (c) so it may be best to leave part (c) until last.

(a)   **Annual equivalent cost**

   System 1

	Cash flows	Annuity factor/ discount factor	Present value
	$000	@12%	$000
Initial investment	(600)	1.000	(600)
Contribution	580	2.402	1,393
Operating costs (W1)	(180)	2.402	(432)
Maintenance costs	(20)	1+ 1.690	(54)
Residual value	60	0.712	43
Net present value			350
Expected life			3 years
Cumulative discount factor			2.402
Annualised equivalent cash flow			146

   System 2

	Cash flows	Annuity factor/ discount factor	Present Value
	$000	@12%	$000
Initial Investment	(800)	1.000	(800)
Contribution	600	3.605	2,163
Operating costs	(155)	3.605	(559)
Maintenance costs	(40)	1+3.037	(161)
Residual value	50	0.567	28
Net present value			671
Expected life			5 years
Cumulative discount factor			3.605
Annualised equivalent cash flow			186

System 2 has the highest annualised equivalent discounted cash flows and therefore should be purchased.

Workings

(W1) **Other operating costs**

System 1

Depreciation per annum ($600k - $60k) / 3 = $180k

Operating costs excluding depreciation = $360k - $180k = $180k

System 2

Depreciation per annum ($800k - $50k) / 5 = $150k

Operating costs excluding depreciation = $305k - $150k = $155k

(b) **Purpose of sensitivity analysis**

Sensitivity analysis recognises the fact that not all cash inflows and cash outflows for a project are known with certainty. Sensitivity analysis enables a company to determine the effect of changes to variables on the planned outcome. Particular attention can then be paid to those variables that are identified as being of special significance. In project appraisal, an analysis can be made of all the key variables to ascertain by how much each variable would need to change before the net present value (NPV) reaches zero i.e. the indifference point. Alternatively, specific changes can be made to the variables to determine the effect on NPV.

(c) **Calculation of sensitivity**

The annualised equivalent NPV for System 1 is $40k less (i.e. $186k - $146k) than for System 2 therefore it would need to increase by more than $40k before the decision would be to invest in System 1.

The present value of the contribution would need to increase by $40k x 2.402 = $96k. This is an increase of $96k/$1393k = 6.9%

Alternatively, the increase would need to be $40k/$580k = 6.9%.

(d) **Tax calculations**

Year	Reducing balance	Tax deprecation	Tax benefit @ 30%	Tax benefit	Tax benefit	Total tax benefit
	$000	$000	$000	$000	$000	$000
1	800	200	60	30	0	30
2	600	150	45	23	30	53
3	450	113	34	17	22	39
4	337	84	25	13	17	30
5	253	203	61	31	12	43
6				0	30	30

Examiner's comments

The performance in part (a) was varied. Most candidates were able to make a reasonable attempt at calculating the NPV. However many did not then go on to calculate an annualised equivalent despite the clear instruction in the question. A large number of candidates did not adjust the operating costs for depreciation and many of those that did failed to take account of the residual value for the systems. Most candidates did not appreciate the significance of the maintenance costs being payable in advance. For those candidates that did calculate the annualised equivalent figures some then treated them as costs and therefore made an incorrect decision about the system to purchase.

Part (b) was fairly well answered although few candidates actually discussed risk or taking measures to mitigate the risk of certain variables. Part (c) was not well answered with very few candidates getting the correct answer. Some candidates calculated the break even contribution for system 1 or system 2 rather than the change in contribution that would lead to a changed recommendation between the two systems.

Part (d) was generally well answered although many candidates calculated the tax cash flows for the whole system 2 project which was not required. This was given full credit but did involve extra work in calculating the figures.

Common errors

- Including sunk costs and depreciation as cash flows

- Incorrect calculation of depreciation

- Failure to treat the maintenance costs as payable in advance

- Treating the annualised equivalent figures as an annualised cost

- Failure to calculate annualised equivalent figures

- Dividing the net present value by 3 or 5 years

- Multiplying rather than dividing the net present value by the cumulative discount factor

- Failure to discuss risk in part (b)(i)

- Calculating the break even contribution for System 1 or 2

- Attempting to calculate an IRR for one of the systems

- Failure to calculate the correct balancing allowance for year 5

- Calculating the tax cash flows for system 1 rather than system 2

- Failure to extend the tax savings into Year 6

- Including the sunk costs as part of the initial investment

324 EF (SEPT 12)

Key answer tips

This question follows a similar pattern to many other past exam questions. Students should start with the discursive element to ensure that poor time management doesn't mean that they don't leave enough time to make any attempt at this section at all. In part (a), the key to success will be to cope with the expected value calculation. Students will then need a methodical approach to working through the remainder of the information. In part (b), any attempt at the calculations will score marks, even if the wrong numbers are carried forward from part (a).

(a)   **Net present value**

	Year 0	Year 1	Year 2	Year 3	Year 4	Year 5	Year 6
	$000	$000	$000	$000	$000	$000	$000
Structure cost	(120,000)					50,000	
Net cash flows (W1)	0	31,324	32,597	33,921	35,298	36,730	
Tax payment (W4)	0	(198)	(1,514)	(2,557)	(3,396)	(7,314)	
Tax payment		0	(199)	(1,515)	(2,557)	(3,397)	(7,314)
Net cash flow after tax	(120,000)	31,126	30,884	29,849	29,345	76,019	(7,314)
DF @ 12%	1.000	0.893	0.797	0.712	0.636	0.567	0.507
Present value	(120,000)	27,796	24,615	21,252	18,663	43,103	(3,708)

Net present value = $11,721

The project has a positive net present value and therefore should be accepted

Workings

(W1) **Cash Flows**

		Year 1	Year 2	Year 3	Year 4	Year 5
		$000	$000	$000	$000	$000
Contribution	(W2)	32,032	33,313	34,646	36,032	37,473
Lease costs		(500)	(500)	(500)	(500)	(500)
Maintenance costs	(W3)	(208)	(216)	(225)	(234)	(243)
Net cash flows		31,324	32,597	33,921	35,298	36,730

(W2) **Year 1 Contribution**

Visitor numbers

Year 1 = (1.2m x 30%) + (0.8m x 50%) + (0.6m x 20%) = 880k

Contribution per visitor

Year 0 = $60 - $25 = $35

Year 1 = $35 x 1.04 = $36.40

Year 1 total contribution = $36.40 x 880k = $32,032k

(W3) **Year 1 Maintenance costs**

= $200k x 1.04 = $208k

(W4) Taxation

		Year 1	Year 2	Year 3	Year 4	Year 5
		$000	$000	$000	$000	$000
Net cash flows	(W1)	31,324	32,597	33,921	35,298	36,730
Tax Depreciation		(30,000)	(22,500)	(16,875)	(12,656)	12,031
Taxable profit		1,324	10,097	17,046	22,642	48,761
Tax @ 30%		(397)	(3,029)	(5,114)	(6,793)	(14,628)

(b)   (i)   Internal Rate of Return (IRR)

Firstly, we need the NPV at a different discount rate. Let's use 20%:

	Year 0	Year 1	Year 2	Year 3	Year 4	Year 5	Year 6
	$000	$000	$000	$000	$000	$000	$000
Net cash flow after tax	(120,000)	31,126	30,884	29,849	29,345	76,019	(7,314)
DF @ 12%	1.000	0.833	0.694	0.579	0.482	0.402	0.335
Present value	(120,000)	25,928	21,433	17,283	14,144	30,560	(2,450)

Net present value = -$13,102

IRR

NPV at 12% = $11,721

NPV at 20% = $(13,102)

By interpolation

IRR = 12% + (($11,721 / ($11,721 +$13,102)) x (20% - 12%)

IRR = 12% + 3.78%

IRR = 15.78%

(b)   (ii)   Payback period

Year	Cash flow	Cumulative cash flow
0	(120,000)	(120,000)
1	31,126	(88,874)
2	30,884	(57,990)
3	29,849	(28,141)
4	29,345	1,204

Payback period   = 3 yrs + ((28,141/29,345) x 12)

= 3 yrs 11.5 months

(c) **Real cost of capital**

The real cost of capital is the rate of return that would be required in the absence of inflation. If prices rise then investors will demand compensation for general inflation. If the real cost of capital was 8% and the general rate of inflation was 4%, investors will require a return of

1.08 x 1.04 = 1.1232

Investors will be indifferent from a financial perspective as to whether they hold $1,000 now or receive $1,123.20 in one year's time. The money cash flow of $1,123.20 is equivalent to $1,000 now i.e. the money rate of return is 12.32%. The money rate of return includes a return to compensate for inflation.

325 5G MOBILE PHONE (MAY 11)

Key answer tips

In part (a) students should identify the relevant cash flows for each year of the project including the loss of contribution from the 4G model. They should then calculate the tax depreciation and tax payments. The net cash flows after tax should be discounted at the discount rate of 8% to calculate the NPV of the project.

In part (b) the same cash flows should then be discounted at a higher discount rate and the IRR calculated using interpolation. The discounted payback period should also be calculated using the discounted cash flows from part a).

In part (c) students should discuss the reasons why IRR and discounted payback may be used in investment appraisal despite the theoretical superiority of NPV.

In part (d) students should clearly explain the potential benefits to a company of carrying out a post-completion audit.

(a) **Net Present Value**

		Year 0 $m	Year 1 $m	Year 2 $m	Year 3 $m	Year 4 $m	Year 5 $m
Net cash flows	(W1)		225	700	103	(228)	
Manufacturing facility		(600)				100	
Tax payment	(W3)		(12)	(88)	(3)	57	
Taxable payment				(11)	(88)	(3)	57
Net cash flow after tax		(600)	213	601	12	(74)	57
DF @ 8%		1.000	0.926	0.857	0.794	0.735	0.681
Present value		(600)	197	515	10	(54)	39

Net present value = $107m

As this is positive, the project is worthwhile.

Workings

(W1) **Cash Flows**

	Year 1 $m	Year 2 $m	Year 3 $m	Year 4 $m
Contribution from 5G sales(W2)	875	1,150	503	72
Reduction in contribution from 4G sales	(200)			
Fixed manufacturing costs	(300)	(300)	(300)	(300)
Technical improvement and marketing	(150)	(150)	(100)	
Net cash flows	225	700	103	(228)

(W2) **Contribution**

Unit sales Year 1 = 25,000,000 x 20% = 5,000,000

Unit sales Year 2 = 25,000,000 x 40% = 10,000,000

Unit sales Year 3 = 25,000,000 x 30% = 7,500,000

Unit sales Year 4 = 25,000,000 x 10% = 2,500,000

Contribution per unit Year 1 = $300 - $125 = $175

Contribution per unit Year 2 = $240 - $125 = $115

Contribution per unit Year 3 = $192 - $125 = $67

Contribution per unit Year 4 = $153.60 - $125 = $28.60

Total contribution Year 1 = $175 x 5m = $875m

Total contribution Year 2 = $115 x 10m = $1150m

Total contribution Year 3 = $67 x 7.5m = $502.5m

Total contribution Year 4 = $28.60 x 2.5m = $71.5m

Loss of contribution from 4G model sales:-

Year 1 – $100 x 2m = $200m

(W3) **Taxation**

	Year 1 $m	Year 2 $m	Year 3 $m	Year 4 $m
Net cash flows	225	700	103	(228)
Tax depreciation	(150)	(113)	(84)	(153)
Taxable profit	75	587	19	(381)
Taxation @ 30%	(23)	(176)	(6)	114

(b)   (i)   **Internal rate of return (IRR)**

	Year 0	Year 1	Year 2	Year 3	Year 4	Year 5
	$m	$m	$m	$m	$m	$m
Net cash flows	(600)	213	601	12	(74)	57
DF @ 20%	1.000	0.833	0.694	0.579	0.482	0.402
Present value	(600)	177	417	7	(36)	23

Net present value = $(12)m

IRR

NPV at 8% = $107m

NPV at 20% = $(12)m

By interpolation

= 8% + (107/(107 + 12)) x 12

IRR =18.8%

(ii)   **Discounted payback period**

1 yr + ((600 − 197) / 515) x 12 = 1 yr 9 months

(c)   **Comparison of methods**

IRR is used in practice because users are familiar with interpreting percentage rates such as return on capital employed, return on investment, bank rates etc. Since the IRR is expressed as a percentage it is easy to understand. It also avoids the need to have to specify a discount rate in advance. The IRR is particularly useful for indicating the excess percentage above the cost of capital for projects that earn a positive net present value.

Discounted payback tends to be used in practice as a supplementary method of project appraisal. Projects which return their cash outlay quicker can be seen as less risky. It can be used at an early stage to eliminate projects that have unacceptable risk and return characteristics. It is also seen as useful when funds are in short supply since early payback of funds allows investment in other profitable opportunities. Discounted payback is also easy to use and is a simple way to communicate product acceptability to managers.

(d)   **Post completion audit**

Post completion audit has benefits in terms of the current project and future projects. In terms of the current project, it enables changes to be made to over or under performing projects at an early stage. This also makes it more likely that unsuccessful projects will be terminated.

In terms of future projects, it improves the quality of decision making as past experience is made available to future decision makers. It encourages greater realism in predicting future outcomes as past inaccuracies are made public. It highlights reasons for successful projects which may be important in achieving greater benefits from future projects and in future project selection.

Examiner's comments

Overall this question was well done. Most candidates scored well in part (a) although too many candidates are still showing the initial investment occurring in Year 1 of the project. The weakest area was in the tax calculations with many candidates being unable to deal with a taxable loss arising on the project.

Part (b) (i) was fairly well done but it is surprising how many candidates are unable to calculate an IRR. The weaker candidates performed two further calculations, with different discount rates, which was a poor use of time given that they had already calculated the net present value using one discount rate in part (a).

In part (b) (ii) most candidates knew what was required although many candidates used undiscounted cash flows and again the weaker candidates looked at the payback from just the revenue rather than from the present value of the cash flows. A significant percentage of candidates were unable to calculate the correct payback period despite having correctly calculated the cumulative cash flows.

In part (c) candidates stated that IRR was easy to understand and that payback was useful in explaining when the investment would be returned. Few candidates discussed risk. Many candidates relied on providing definitions of IRR and discounted payback and explaining why NPV was superior – unfortunately these details were not relevant to the question.

Part (d) on post completion audits was very well answered with many candidates scoring full marks.

Common errors

- $600m initial investment included in Year 1 rather than in Year 0
- Treating $100m residual value as working capital
- Inclusion of $35m sunk costs as a cash outflow
- Failure to treat the $200m lost contribution from 4G sales as a cash outflow
- Calculation of tax before all costs had been included
- Including $100m residual value in calculation of corporation tax payable
- Treating the tax on a taxable loss as zero rather than as a tax credit
- Calculating net present value at a different discount rate using already discounted cash flows
- Calculating discounted payback using undiscounted cash flows
- Counting year 0 as one year when calculating payback period
- Defining discounted payback and IRR rather than explaining why they are used in practice

326 OWN BRAND PRODUCTS (SEPT 11) *Walk in the footsteps of a top tutor*

Top Tutor Tips

You should begin questions by reading the requirement first (in the exam hall this can be done during the reading time at the start of the). From reading the requirement to this question you can determine that in part (a) you need to calculate the NPV of a project (which can be a time consuming requirement), and that parts (b) and (c) have a combination of a calculation and a discursive element (as is quite common in the).

It is these discursive elements that you should attempt first. Your ability to do well in these areas will not be influenced by how well you do in the other (calculation) areas. There are discussions on sensitivity analysis and the payback period, of which the second may be easier and more familiar to you. Overall you should have a target of getting at least five of the seven marks available here, which will mean that you only need to get eight out of eighteen on the calculation elements in order to garner an overall pass.

For the calculations it is best now to work through the question in order. Part (a) wants a NPV calculation and therefore you should quickly scan the question to determine the length of the project and the discount rate. We're normally told the length of the project near the start of the question (here the first paragraph tells us that it will consider sales over four years) and the discount rate near the end of the question (here the final sentence tells us that the cost of capital is 8%). This allows you to set up a proforma NPV layout. You will need 6 columns for the years (year 0 to 5, remembering to leave an extra column for tax paid in year 5). You can also include the discount factors from the present value tables.

Now we need to determine the relevant cash flows. The second paragraph looks complicated initially, and it would therefore be good exam technique to skip this for the moment and return to it later. So skipping to the third paragraph we get information on the level of investment and its residual value. Put these figures into the NPV proforma and perform a working for the tax depreciation. This is a very common exam area that you should be very familiar with and have practiced a lot. By this stage you should already have around four marks out of the twelve available.

Also include the working capital flow – this should be shown as an outflow at the start of the project (year 4) with an identical inflow at the end of the project (year 4). This is a tricky mark to pick up, so don't worry if you can't get it. Getting it wrong shouldn't make a difference between pass or fail and it is only likely to be worth one mark. When you find yourself in a situation where you don't know what to do with a figure it is best to just skip it and leave it out rather than to spend five minutes trying to work out what to do with a tough area that is only worth one mark.

In the next paragraph the marketing costs should be an easy mark to pick up. With the fixed costs it is important to remember that only cash flows are included and therefore depreciation should not be included. So you need to work out the annual depreciation charge and remove this from the total fixed costs to get the figure required for our NPV calculation. The contribution to sales ratio will be used later when we have determined the sales value.

Even if you have failed to get the working capital figure correct, if you have got everything else correct at this point you should have the six marks that you need to pass part (a) at this point. If you've also got five out of seven on the discursive elements it means that you now only need to get two more things correct to pass the question overall. This illustrates the power of good exam technique. Doing the easier parts first and avoiding the tougher areas is the best and quickest way to pass an exam question. Weaker students are likely to start with the tougher areas and run out of time before they can get to the easy marks.

Now we have to return and deal with the second paragraph. We are told that a consultancy firm was employed at a cost of $0.5m. As this is in the past tense (an historic cost) it should not be included in the NPV calculation.

For the sales you need to perform and expected value calculation for year 1. When you have that figure you then need to add $100m to it each year to get the sales over the entire life of the project. With a sales to contribution ratio of 60% you can either take these sales and multiply them by 60% to get the contribution, or you could have a line for 'variable costs' and this would be equal to 40% of the sales. Either approach will give the same answer and you should use the one that you are most comfortable with.

Now attempt the tax calculation and add up the overall NPV. If you have made an error at some prior point (for example if you have miscalculated the sales figure), you will not get punished again at this point. So as long as your approach is correct you will get all the marks even if your answer is ultimately incorrect.

Part (b) (i) of the question is a challenging syllabus area that students can often be uncomfortable with. But a good student would already have passed the question by this point. You need to know the sensitivity formula which will highlight the need to calculate the present value of the fixed costs (post tax). The calculation itself is not then too difficult as long as you remember to take account of tax and the fact that it is paid in two instalments. If your answer in part (a) has a different NPV than the correct one, you will not get punished again here for using your answer in the calculation.

For part (c) (i), the payback period is normally a quick calculation. But it relies on you having determined the figures in part (a) and good time management. Again, follow through errors will not be punished.

Overall, this is a typical exam question where good technique will be as important as good syllabus knowledge. Approaching and tackling questions in the correct manner will always be the key to success in this exam.

(a)   **NPV Calculation**

Year 1 expected sales revenue = ($450m x 50%) + ($300m x 30%) + ($600m x 20%) = $435m

Year 2 sales revenue = $435m +100m = $535m

Year 3 sales revenue = $535m + 100m = $635m

Year 4 sales revenue = $635m + 100 = $735m

Contribution Year 1 = $435m x 60% = $261m

Contribution Year 2 = $535m x 60% = $321m

Contribution Year 3 = $635m x 60% = $381m

Contribution Year 4 = $735m x 60% = $441m

Fixed Costs

Depreciation per annum ($600m - $400m) / 4 = $50m

Fixed costs excluding depreciation = $150m - $50m = $100m

Cash Flows

	Year 1 $m	Year 2 $m	Year 3 $m	Year 4 $m
Contribution	261	321	381	441
Fixed Costs	(100)	(100)	(100)	(100)
Marketing Costs	(50)	(50)	(50)	(50)
Net cash flows	111	171	231	291

Taxation

	Year 1 $m	Year 2 $m	Year 3 $m	Year 4 $m
Net cash flows	111	171	231	291
Tax Depreciation	(150)	(113)	(84)	147
Taxable profit	(39)	58	147	438
Taxation @ 30%	12	(17)	(44)	(131)

Net present value

	Year 0 $m	Year 1 $m	Year 2 $m	Year 3 $m	Year 4 $m	Year 5 $m
Development and fit out costs	(600)				400	
Working capital	(60)				60	
Net cash flows		111	171	231	291	
Tax payment		6	(9)	(22)	(66)	
Tax payment			6	(8)	(22)	(65)
Net cash flow after tax	(660)	117	168	201	663	(65)
Discount factors @ 8%	1.000	0.926	0.857	0.794	0.735	0.681
Present value	(660)	108	144	160	487	(44)

Net present value = $195m

The net present value is positive therefore on this basis the company should go ahead with the project.

(b) **Sensitivity analysis**

(i) **Calculation**

Tutorial note

The sensitivity to changes in the fixed costs is the percentage change in the cash inflows which would change the investment decision.

Sensitivity = Difference in the NPV's / PV of cash inflow × 100%

First we need to calculate the post-tax present value of the fixed costs:

	Year 1	Year 2	Year 3	Year 4	Year 5
	$m	$m	$m	$m	$m
Fixed costs	100	100	100	100	
Tax @ 30%	30	30	30	30	
Tax payment	(15)	(30)	(30)	(30)	(15)
Net cash flow	85	70	70	70	(15)
Discount Factor @ 8%	0.926	0.857	0.794	0.735	0.681
Present value	79	60	56	51	(10)

Total present value = $236m

Tutorial note

The NPV's of the project is $195m. Therefore the sensitivity is:

$195 / $236 = 82.6%

If fixed costs increase by more than 82.6% the NPV of the project will be negative and the decision will be to reject the project.

(ii) **Benefits of sensitivity analysis**

Sensitivity analysis recognises the fact that not all cash flows for a project are known with certainty. Sensitivity analysis enables a company to determine the effect of changes to variables on the planned outcome. Particular attention can then be paid to those variables that are identified as being of special significance. In project appraisal, an analysis can be made of all the key input factors to ascertain by how much each factor would need to change before the net present value (NPV) reaches zero i.e. the indifference point. Alternatively, specific changes can be calculated to determine the effect on NPV.

(c) **Payback period**

(i) **Calculation**

	Year 0	Year 1	Year 2	Year 3	Year 4	Year 5
	$m	$m	$m	$m	$m	$m
Net cash flows	(660)	117	168	201	663	(65)
Cumulative cash flows	(660)	(543)	(375)	(174)		

Payback period

3 yrs + (174 / 663) x 12 = 3 yr 3 months

(ii) **Benefits of the payback method**

Projects which return their cash outlay quicker can be seen as less risky. Payback is therefore used by companies at an early stage to eliminate projects that have unacceptable risk and return characteristics. In this case there is uncertainty surrounding the potential of the market and the management may be concerned to ensure that the payback period is relatively short in the event that it becomes necessary to withdraw from the market. Alternatively, a long payback period may persuade management not to enter the market in the first place.

Payback is also seen as useful when funds are in short supply since early payback of funds allows investment in other profitable opportunities. Payback is also easy to use and is a simple way to communicate project acceptability to managers.

Examiner's comments

Part (a)(i) of question 4 was generally well done with most candidates achieving a pass in this part of the question. Some candidates however are still making fundamental errors such as including depreciation and sunk costs in the cash flows. The calculation of the tax depreciation particularly in the final year is still causing problems for some candidates. Many candidates either ignored the residual value or if it was treated correctly the tax was included as a credit rather than a charge.

Part (b)(i) was badly answered although candidates invariably knew the general formula required. Few candidates thought to adjust the fixed costs for tax. Many candidates also did not discount the fixed costs and some just used one year's fixed costs. Part (b)(ii) was well answered with most candidates understanding the benefits of carrying out a sensitivity analysis.

In part (c)(i), there were relatively few correct answers. The payback period was often calculated using the discounted cash flows or even the cash flows before tax, using contribution only or using sales revenue only. Some candidates counted the investment in year 0 as the first year, so the payback period ended up being a year longer than it should have been. In part (c)(ii) the reasons for management's interest in payback were reasonably well explained.

Common errors

- Including sunk costs and depreciation as cash flows.

- Failure to release the working capital in Year 4.

- Including both sales revenue and contribution as positive cash flows.

- Demonstrating confusion between variable costs and contribution.

- Treating the balancing charge in Year 4 as a tax benefit.

- Including the working capital in the tax depreciation calculation.

- Failing to adjust the fixed costs for tax.

- Failing to discount the cash flows related to fixed costs.

- Using only one year's fixed costs.

- Using incorrect cash flows to calculate the payback period.

- Treating Year 0 as one year when calculating the payback period.

- Inability to correctly calculate a proportion of a year.

---

327 MGC (MAR 12)

(a) (i) **Net present value**

Expected value of increase in demand

(1,000 x 0.30) + (700 x 0.50) + (500 x 0.2) = 750 members

Contribution per member

$800 x 55% = $440

Additional contribution Year 1 = $440 x 750 = $330k

Cash Flows

	Year 1 $000	Year 2 $000	Year 3 $000	Year 4 $000	Year 5 $000
Contribution	330	343	357	371	386
Additional fixed costs	(120)	(125)	(130)	(135)	(140)
Net cash flows	210	218	227	236	246

Taxation

	Year 1 $000	Year 2 $000	Year 3 $000	Year 4 $000	Year 5 $000
Net cash flows	210	218	227	236	246
Tax depreciation	(150)	(113)	(84)	(63)	(160)
Taxable profit	60	105	143	173	86
Taxation @ 30%	18	32	43	52	26

Net present value

	Year 0	Year 1	Year 2	Year 3	Year 4	Year 5	Year 6

	$000	$000	$000	$000	$000	$000	$000
Net inflows		210	218	227	236	246	
Investment	(600)					30	
Tax payment		(9)	(16)	(21)	(26)	(13)	
Tax payment			(9)	(16)	(22)	(26)	(13)
Net cash flow	(600)	201	193	190	188	237	(13)
DF @ 12%	1.000	0.893	0.797	0.712	0.636	0.567	0.507
PV	(600)	179	154	135	120	134	(7)

Net present value = $115k

The net present value is positive therefore on this basis the company should go ahead with the project.

(ii) **Non-financial factors**

Two non-financials factors that could be considered are as follows:

- The risk of the project. The cash flows used in the project appraisal are estimates and will depend on a number of factors that are uncertain. The club will need to be aware of the risk involved in the project.

- The prospect of obtaining planning permission for the new facilities. The success of the project will depend on the club obtaining planning permission for the new facilities. The planning conditions may also have an effect on the cost involved in the project.

(b) **Internal rate of return**

Firstly, we need the NPV at a different discount rate. Let's use 20%:

	Year 0	Year 1	Year 2	Year 3	Year 4	Year 5	Year 6
	$000	$000	$000	$000	$000	$000	$000
Net cash flows	(600)	201	193	190	188	237	(13)
DF @ 20%	1.000	0.833	0.694	0.579	0.482	0.402	0.335
PV	(600)	167	134	110	91	95	(4)

Net present value = $(7)k

IRR

NPV at 12% = $115k

NPV at 20% = $(7)k

By interpolation

12% + (115/(115+7)) x 8% =19.5%

(c)   (i)   **Real cost of capital**

The company's real cost of capital

$$\left(\frac{1 + 0.12}{1 + 0.04}\right) - 1 = 7.7\%$$

(ii)   **Using the real cost of capital**

An alternative approach would be to express the cash flows in today's value terms and to discount the cash flows at the real cost of capital. There are problems however in taking this approach when there are tax implications. If there are tax implications the tax cash flows would need to be treated separately. Capital allowances are based on original cost rather than replacement cost and do not change in line with changing prices. Each tax depreciation figure would have to be reduced by expected inflation over the relevant period to obtain a current value. Similarly the residual value of the equipment is stated at year 5 values and would need to be adjusted to present day values. 50% of the tax payable for any year will be a money cash flow in the following year. This second stage payment in each year would have to be reduced by one year's inflation to determine its 'real' value in that year.

Examiner's comments

Part (a) of this question was reasonably well done although many candidates seemed unable to deal with the tax calculations. Candidates came up with some good suggestions in part (a)(ii) but sometimes failed to explain their ideas and consider the effect that these factors would have on the project. Part (b) was generally well done although many candidates were unable to perform what should be a basic calculation. In part (c)(i) many candidates did not know the formula to use and part (c) (ii) was either very poorly answered or ignored by most candidates.

Common errors

• Not adjusting the revenue by 55% to derive the contribution figures.

• Applying the inflation rate incorrectly or not inflating cash flows at all.

• Calculating the tax depreciation balancing charge in Year 5 incorrectly.

• Not applying the 30% tax rate to the tax depreciation figures

• Not evaluating whether or not the project should go ahead.

• Failing to explain the points made in part (a)(ii).

• Inability to apply interpolation to calculate the IRR.

• Lack of knowledge of the formula to be applied to calculate the real cost of capital.

• Lack of knowledge in part (c)(ii).

328   H (MAY 08 EXAM)

Key answer tips

In Part (a), calculating the NPV, an average student, who would have omitted indexation and not dealt with variable costs and fixed costs separately, should have been able to layout the proformas and fill in enough information to almost pass this section – 6 or 7 marks is a realistic target.

In (b) any attempt at calculating an IRR, even based on incorrect values from a), would have got credit. The actual formula would have got one mark, and the result of around 13% would have enabled the candidate to score full marks here.

In (c), the alternative calculation involving the real cost of capital is independent from numerical answers in a) and b); Students should have been able to grab 2/3 marks here from a theoretical point well covered in class.

(a)

	20X8 $000	20X9 $000	20Y0 $000	20Y1 $000	20Y2 $000	20Y3 $000	20Y4 $000
Sales (W1)		578.45	613.27	662.09	675.94	722.69	
Variable prod^n costs (W2)		(259.56)	(277.83)	(302.83)	(312.14)	(336.94)	
Fixed prod^n costs		(105.00)	(110.25)	(115.76)	(121.55)	(127.63)	
Non-production costs		(82.40)	(84.87)	(87.42)	(90.04)	(92.74)	
Net operating CF		131.49	140.32	156.09	152.21	165.38	
Taxation							
Current Year		(19.72)	(21.05)	(23.41)	(22.83)	(24.81)	
Previous Year			(19.72)	(21.05)	(23.41)	(22.83)	(24.81)
Investment in machinery	(500)					100.00	
Tax savings wrt CAs (W3)							
Current Year		15.00	12.00	9.60	7.68	15.72	
Previous Year			15.00	12.00	9.60	7.68	15.72
Net CF Post Tax	(500)	126.76	126.54	133.23	123.25	241.14	(9.09)
Discount Factor @14%	1.000	0.877	0.769	0.675	0.592	0.519	0.456
Present Value	(500)	111.17	97.31	89.92	72.96	125.15	(4.14)
NPV	**(7.62)**						

The NPV calculations show that the project should not be undertaken, as it shows a negative result of around $7,600.

Workings

(W1) **Sales revenue**

Growth in price **and** volume need to be incorporated:

		$000
20X9	$540 \times 103\% \times 1.04$	578.45
20Y0	$540 \times 105\% \times 1.04^2$	613.27
20Y1	$540 \times 109\% \times 1.04^3$	662.09
20Y2	$540 \times 107\% \times 1.04^4$	675.94
20Y3	$540 \times 110\% \times 1.04^5$	722.69

(W2) **Variable Production Cost**

		$000
20X9	$240 \times 103\% \times 1.05$	259.56
20Y0	$240 \times 105\% \times 1.05^2$	277.83
20Y1	$240 \times 109\% \times 1.05^3$	302.83
20Y2	$240 \times 107\% \times 1.05^4$	312.14
20Y3	$240 \times 110\% \times 1.05^5$	336.94

(W3) **Tax Savings and Capital Allowances**

Year		Written-down value	Tax saving at 30%	Saving in year	Saving in next year
		$	$	$	$
		500,000			
20X9	CA@20%	(100,000)	30,000	15,000	
		———			
		400,000			
20Y0	CA@20%	(80,000)	24,000	12,000	15,000
		———			
		320,000			
20Y1	CA@20%	(64,000)	19,200	9,600	12,000
		———			
		256,000			
20Y2	CA@20%	(51,200)	15,360	7,680	9,600
		———			
		204,800			
20Y3	BA	(104,800)	31,440	15,720	7,680
		———			
	Proceeds	100,000			
20Y4					15,720

(b) The post-tax money cost of capital at which H would be indifferent to accepting or rejecting the project is the Internal Rate of Return. With another discount factor of, say, 5%:

Net CF	(500)	126.76	126.54	133.23	123.25	241.14	(9.09)
DF @14%	1.000	0.952	0.907	0.864	0.829	0.784	0.746
PV	(500)	120.68	114.78	115.10	102.17	189.06	(6.78)
NPV	**135.01**						

NPV is now positive.

IRR = 14% − (7.62 / (7.62 + 135)) × 9% = 13.52%

(c) In (a) above, each of the annual sales revenues and cost cash flows have been inflated using their respective inflation rates and then, the money cost of capital has been used to discount the resulting cash flow.

An alternative method would have been the calculate the real cost of capital, using the following formula: (1+ money cost of capital)/(1+ inflation) = (1+ real cost of capital)

And then, discount each of the un-inflated cash flows by the real post-tax of capital.

MANAGING SHORT-TERM FINANCE

329 BF *Walk in the footsteps of a top tutor*

Key answer tips

Parts (a) and (b) are both standard textbook material. In part (a), for six marks you should discuss at least three factors. Don't forget the requirement is to "discuss" not "state" so you must give some commentary: 'the length of the working capital cycle' will not get the full marks available.

In part (b) the requirement is again to "discuss". Given the emphasis is on how both factoring and invoice discounting can assist in the management of accounts receivable, there should be more discussion on factoring than invoice discounting (the latter being a tool for managing cash flow rather than managing accounts receivable). Don't forget to define each of the terms to collect some easy marks.

The calculation in part (c) requires some "out of the box" thinking in order to see how the brief information provided can be used to work out the size of the overdraft. Not only does it involve re-arranging the usual working capital ratios we're used to seeing, it also requires a disaggregation of the operating cycle to reveal the inventory holding period.

In contrast, part (d) is a fairly straightforward application of the EOQ model which shouldn't pose many difficulties.

Throughout the discursive areas, the highlighted words are key phrases that markers are looking for.

(a)   There are a number of factors that determine the level of investment in current assets and their relative importance varies from company to company.

Length of working capital cycle

The working capital cycle or operating cycle is the period of time between when a company settles its accounts payable and when it receives cash from its accounts receivable. Operating activities during this period need to be financed and as the operating period lengthens, the amount of finance needed increases. Companies with comparatively longer operating cycles than others in the same industry sector, will therefore require comparatively higher levels of investment in current assets.

Terms of trade

These determine the period of credit extended to customers, any discounts offered for early settlement or bulk purchases, and any penalties for late payment. A company whose terms of trade are more generous than another company in the same industry sector will therefore need a comparatively higher investment in current assets. BF are likely to smaller than many of its rivals and this may explain why it must offer 12 weeks of credit to customers.

Policy on level of investment in current assets

Even within the same industry sector, companies will have different policies regarding the level of investment in current assets, depending on their attitude to risk. A company with a comparatively conservative approach to the level of investment in current assets would maintain higher levels of inventory, offer more generous credit terms and have higher levels of cash in reserve than a company with a comparatively aggressive approach. While the more aggressive approach would be more profitable because of the lower level of investment in current assets, it would also be more risky, for example in terms of running out of inventory in periods of fluctuating demand, of failing to have the particular goods required by a customer, of failing to retain customers who migrate to more generous credit terms elsewhere, and of being less able to meet unexpected demands for payment.

Industry in which organisation operates

Another factor that influences the level of investment in current assets is the industry within which an organisation operates.   Some industries, such as aircraft construction, will have long operating cycles due to the length of time needed to manufacture finished goods and so will have comparatively higher levels of investment in current assets than industries such as supermarket chains, where goods are bought in for resale with minimal additional processing and where many goods have short shelf-lives. BF should be experiencing a much shorter life cycle given the nature of the industry in which it competes.

(b)   Factoring involves a company turning over administration of its sales ledger to a factor, which is a financial institution with expertise in this area. The factor will assess the creditworthiness of new customers, record sales, send out statements and reminders, collect payment, identify late payers and chase them for settlement, and take appropriate legal action to recover debts where necessary.

The factor will also offer finance to a company based on invoices raised for goods sold or services provided. This is usually up to 80% of the face value of invoices raised. The finance is repaid from the settled invoices, with the balance being passed to the issuing company after deduction of a fee equivalent to an interest charge on cash advanced.

If factoring is without recourse, the factor rather than the company will carry the cost of any bad debts that arise on overdue accounts. Factoring without recourse therefore offers credit protection to the selling company, although the factor's fee (a percentage of credit sales) will be comparatively higher than with non-recourse factoring to reflect the cost of the insurance offered.

Invoice discounting is a way of raising finance against the security of invoices raised, rather than employing the credit management and administration services of a factor. A number of good quality invoices may be discounted, rather than all invoices, and the service is usually only offered to companies meeting a minimum turnover criterion.

(c) **Calculation of size of overdraft**

The operating cycle = Inventory period - payables period + receivables period. This can then be re-arranged as follows:

Inventory period = operating cycle + payables period − receivables period = 15 + 4 − 12 = 7 weeks

Inventory	= Cost of sales × 7/52
	= (80% x $72m) x 7/52
	= $57.6m x 7/52
	= $7.75 m
Accounts receivable	= $72m × 12/52 = $16.6m
Current assets	= $7.75m +$16.6m = $24.35m
Accounts payable	= $57.6m × 4/52 = $4.4m

Current liabilities = current assets/current ratio = $24.35/1.2 = $20.3m

Overdraft = $20.3m − $4.4m = $15.9m

Net working capital = current assets − current liabilities = $24.35m − $20.3m = $4m

Short-term financing cost = $15.9m × 0.11 = $1.75m

Long-term financing cost = $4m × 0.08 = $0.32m

Total cost of financing current assets = 1.75 + 0.32 = $2.1m

(d) (i) $$EOQ = \sqrt{\frac{2cd}{h}}$$

Where d = annual demand

h = cost of holding one unit for one year

c = cost of placing order

Therefore: $\sqrt{\dfrac{2 \times 25 \times 65{,}000}{3}} = 1{,}041$

Total cost using the EOQ of 1,041:

	$
Purchase cost (65,000 × $10)	650,000
Procurement cost (65,000/1,041 × $25)	1,561
Holding cost (1,041/2 × $3)	1,562
Total annual costs	653,123

(ii)   Total cost if order size increased to 2,000:

	$
Purchase cost (65,000 × $9.80)	637,000
Procurement cost (65,000/2,000 × $25)	813
Holding cost (2,000/2 × $3)	3,000
Total annual costs	640,813

It is therefore worth increasing the order size as it will reduce costs by $12,310 a year.

330   MISHA ARIF

Key answer tips

The scenario in this question is very long so it's important that you read the requirement first and think about the sort of information you will need. For example, for cash inflows you will be expecting sales data (the requirement tells us there will be some probabilities given) together with some details on credit terms with customers. Make notes in the margin as you read it to flag up what each piece of information can be used for. Ensure you also highlight easy marks; cash flows that can be immediately entered into your pro-forma. You should start writing your answer by putting in the easy numbers before doing any more complex workings.

(a)

	January $	February $	March $	April $	May $	June $
Receipts						
Capital	150,000					
Sales (W2)	–	69,000	229,100	462,200	610,200	777,800
	150,000	69,000	229,100	462,200	610,200	777,800
Payments						
Machinery		800,000				
Labour (W4)	36,225	51,450	72,450	79,800	111,825	111,825
Materials (W5)	–	108,675	154,350	217,350	239,400	335,475
Overheads (W6)	–	–	72,450	102,900	144,900	159,600
Fixed costs	98,000	98,000	98,000	98,000	98,000	98,000
Consultant		100,000				
	134,225	1,158,125	397,250	498,050	594,125	704,900
Net cash flow	15,775	(1,089,125)	(168,150)	(35,850)	15,875	72,900
Opening balance	–	15,775	(1,104,900)	(1,273,050)	(1,308,900)	(1,293,025)
Closing balance	15,775	(1,104,900)	(1,273,050)	(1,308,900)	(1,293,025)	(1,220,125)

Workings

(W1) Expected demand

	Low demand	Medium demand	High demand	Expected demand (units)
February	6,000 × 0.15	7,000 × 0.80	8,000 × 0.05	6,900
March	8,000 × 0.15	10,000 × 0.80	12,000 × 0.05	9,800
April	12,000 × 0.15	14,000 × 0.80	16,000 × 0.05	13,800
May	10,000 × 0.15	16,000 × 0.80	18,000 × 0.05	15,200
June	16,000 × 0.15	22,000 × 0.80	26,000 × 0.05	21,300

(W2) Cash from sales

	Jan	Feb	Mar	Apr	May	Jun
	$	$	$	$	$	$
Sales (@$50)		345,000	490,000	690,000	760,000	1,065,000
Cash sales (20%)		69,000	98,000	138,000	152,000	213,000
Credit sales:						
(80% × 0.5 × 95%)			131,100	186,200	262,200	288,800
(80% × 0.5)				138,000	196,000	276,000
Total	-	69,000	229,100	462,200	610,200	777,800

(W3) Production

	Jan	Feb	Mar	Apr	May	Jun
Production (net)	6,900	9,800	13,800	15,200	21,300	21,300
Defects (5%)	345	490	690	760	1,065	1,065
Production	7,245	10,290	14,490	15,960	22,365	22,365

(W4) Labour costs – based on the production from (W3)

	Jan	Feb	Mar	Apr	May	Jun
@ $5 per unit	36,225	51,450	72,450	79,800	111,825	111,825

(W5) Material costs – based on the production from (W3)

	Jan	Feb	Mar	Apr	May	Jun
@ $15 per unit	-	108,675	154,350	217,350	239,400	335,475

(W6) Variable overhead costs – based on the production from (W3)

	Jan	Feb	Mar	Apr	May	Jun
@ $10 per unit	-	-	72,450	102,900	144,900	159,600

Tutorial note

Materials paid one month in arrears and variable overheads two months in arrears.

(b)   The introduction of better working capital management is often a good way of solving short-term cash flow problems. Misha could consider some or all of the following:

    (i)   it could be considered whether better payment terms could be negotiated with creditors. Any delay in payments would mean that the business would be closer to matching them with incoming receipts. However, the business has already negotiated a 1 month credit period with material suppliers, and as a new venture, it is unlikely that labour or materials suppliers would be willing to accept greater delays in payments.

    (ii)   the business could consider ways to improve the receipts recovery from debtors. It could consider attempting to make more cash sales or perhaps offer a larger discount for early credit payments. However, moving towards more cash sales might mean a reduction in volume that can be provided by distributors, and any increase in settlement credits might outweigh any short-term benefits from quicker receipts.

    (iii)   better inventory management would also improve cash flow as it would delay the need for such high early payments for labour materials and overheads. For example, if material was held at only 50% of the following months sales then the first payment for materials etc. would be halved –saving almost $55,000 in February on materials alone.

The introduction of better inventory management would appear to be a workable solution, but the savings made from better working capital management are unlikely to be enough to remove the need to raise over $1.3m by the end of April.

(c)   The introduction of better working capital management is unlikely to sufficiently solve the cash demands of the new business. Misha should therefore consider the following alternatives:

    (i)   a bank overdraft. Bank overdrafts are a very flexible source of finance and Misha could attempt to gain an overdraft facility of at least $1.35m. However, although the business will only pay interest on the outstanding balance at the end of each month, this is an expensive source of finance and it may also be difficult to raise this amount as a new business with no credit history.

    (ii)   a bank loan. A bank loan may be more appropriate. It can be seen that from June the business can expect to begin making around $70k per month (subject to other business changes in the future). On that basis it would take around 19 months to repay a loan of $1.3m. Misha could aim to borrow around $1.5m to cover contingencies and perhaps consider a 2 or 3 year period. The bank could be offered the machine as security, but Misha may have to consider offering his home as further back-up.

Section 7

SPECIMEN PAPER QUESTIONS

We are grateful to CIMA for their kind permission to reproduce their specimen papers. They are © Chartered Institute of Management Accountants.

SECTION A – 20 MARKS

(*Note:* The indicative time for answering this section is 36 minutes.)

Answer ALL SEVEN sub-questions in this section

1.1 The original budgeted profit statement for a product is as follows:

	$
Revenue	200,000
Variable costs	100,000
Fixed costs	36,000
Profit	64,000

It has now been realised that sales volume will be 10% higher than budgeted volume with no change in selling price. The product has also been redesigned to lower variable costs by 20% per unit.

The percentage increase in the budgeted profit as a result of the two changes will be:

A   2.0%

B   30.0%

C   50.0%

D   62.5%   (2 marks)

1.2 A project has the following present values when discounted at the company's cost of capital of 8% per annum:

	$
Initial investment	250,000
Cash inflows	500,000
Cash outflows	200,000

The sensitivity of the project to changes in the cash inflows is:

A   8%

B   10%

C   20%

D   50%   (2 marks)

The following data is for questions 1.3 and 1.4

D provides a motorist rescue service to its members. It has been proposed to change the annual membership fee to $120 for the next year. The impact of this on the number of members is uncertain but the following estimates have been made:

Number of members	Probability
20,000	0.1
30,000	0.6
40,000	0.3

It is thought that the variable operating costs vary in relation to the number of members but the cost per member is uncertain. The following estimates have been made:

Variable cost per member	Probability
$70	0.3
$60	0.5
$40	0.2

D expects to incur annual fixed costs of $1,100,000.

1.3 Calculate, based on expected values, the profit for the next year **(2 marks)**

1.4 The Management Accountant of D has produced a two-way data table.

(i) Calculate the value that would be shown in that table in the cell for the profit from 40,000 members with a variable cost per member of $40. **(2 marks)**

(ii) Calculate the joint probability of having 20,000 members and a variable cost per member of $40. **(2 marks)**

1.5 GF wants to sell an unquoted bond. The bond has a coupon rate of 5% and will repay its face value of $1,000 at the end of four years.

GF estimates that the market requires a yield to maturity of 11% from this type of bond. GF has asked you to recommend a selling price for the bond.

Calculate the selling price for the bond. **(4 marks)**

1.6 A company has the following information:

	Actual 31 December 2009	Forecast 30 June 2010
Balances	$000	$000
Trade receivables	75	80
Trade payables	47	40
Inventory of raw materials	29	31

The production budget for the six month period to 30 June 2010 shows that the cost of raw materials to be used in that period will be $331,000.

Calculate the cash that will be paid to suppliers during the six month period to 30 June 2010. **(3 marks)**

1.7 **A company's trade payables days outstanding at 30 September 2009 were 45 days. Purchases for the year to 30 September 2009 were $324,444 occurring evenly throughout the year.**

The company's budgeted purchases for the year ending 30 September 2010 are $356,900 occurring evenly throughout the year.

Calculate the budgeted trade payables days outstanding at 30 September 2010.

(Assume that the trade payables outstanding balance at 30 September 2010 will be the same amount as at 30 September 2009.) **(3 marks)**

(Total: 20 marks)

SECTION B – 30 MARKS

(*Note:* The indicative time for answering this section is 54 minutes.)

Answer ALL SIX sub-questions in this section – 5 marks each

2 OFFICE EQUIPMENT MANUFACTURER

(a) A company manufactures office equipment in England but sells it in the UK and to overseas customers.

Current situation UK customers (£2.1m annual revenue)

The company offers a cash discount of 3% for payment within 10 days to UK customers. Approximately 40% of customers take advantage of the early payment discount whilst the remainder pay in 30 days.

Overseas customers (£0.9m annual revenue)

All sales are on credit but customers are required to pay a 20% deposit when they place their orders and the balance in 60 days.

Debt factoring

The company is thinking about debt factoring. Investigations have revealed that a non-recourse factor will accept 85% of the company's UK customers. It is assumed that the remaining 15% will not take advantage of the early settlement discount.

Required:

Calculate, based on a 365-day year, the total debtors' days if

(i) the current situation continues

(ii) debt factoring is introduced   **(5 marks)**

(b) Discuss the non-financial factors that a company would need to consider before making a decision to factor its debts.   **(5 marks)**

(c) The manager of a hotel is deciding if he should carry out repairs to the hotel immediately or postpone them for a year. He has made the following estimates for the coming year:

The cost of the repairs would be £90,000.

If the repairs are started immediately there is only a two-in-three chance of them being completed in time. If the repairs are completed in time the contribution for the hotel could be any one of the three levels below with equally probability. If the repairs are not completed on time some rooms will be unavailable and consequently demand could be either medium or low, with equal probability.

Contribution for the coming year if the repairs are undertaken could be:

    £200,000 if there is high demand

    £150,000 if there is medium demand

    £100,000 if demand is low

If the repairs are not undertaken the contribution for the coming year is estimated to be £37,500.

Required:

Demonstrate, using a decision tree, if the repairs should be started immediately or postponed for a year. **(5 marks)**

(d) A fast food outlet served the following number of burgers in the past 13 quarters:

	2007				2008				2009				2010
	Q1	Q2	Q3	Q4	Q1	Q2	Q3	Q4	Q1	Q2	Q3	Q4	Q1
Burgers (000)	75	80	110	175	92	96	122	210	111	116	164	259	135

Regression analysis was used to determine the following equation for the trend of sales:

S = 134.23 + 7.945Q where

S = quarterly sales ('000)

Q = quarter number. (The 13 quarters in the period Q1 2007 to Q1 2010 were coded from −6 through to +6).

Previous research has established that the sales follow a seasonal pattern:

Quarter	1	2	3	4
Seasonality	−25%	−25%	0	+50%

Required:

Calculate the number of burgers that are forecast to be sold in quarters 2, 3 and 4 of 2010. **(5 marks)**

(e) **Explain how a budget can cause conflict between "motivation" and "control".**
(5 marks)

(f) **Two classifications of environmental costs are "environmental internal failure costs" and "environmental external failure costs".**

Explain each one of the two classifications of environmental costs mentioned above. Your answer should include, for each classification, an example of an activity that would cause such costs. **(5 marks)**

(Total: 30 marks)

SECTION C – 50 MARKS

(*Note:* The indicative time for answering this section is 90 minutes.)

Answer BOTH questions in this section – 25 marks each

3 MUTUALLY EXCLUSIVE PROJECTS

The Board of Directors of a company are considering two mutually exclusive projects. Both projects necessitate buying new machinery and both projects are expected to have a life of five years.

Project One

This project has already been evaluated. Details of the project are:

Initial investment needed	£500,000
Net present value	£41,000
Accounting rate of return	31%

Project Two

Details of Project Two are:

Year	1	2	3	4	5
Revenue (£000)	370	500	510	515	475
Operating costs (£000)	300	350	380	390	400
Depreciation (£000)	90	90	90	90	90

The figures for revenue and operating costs in the table above are cash flow estimates, have been stated at current values and are assumed to occur at the year end. However differential inflation is expected: 8% per annum for revenue and 6% per annum for operating costs.

The machinery will cost £500,000 and will be sold for £50,000 cash at the end of year 5.

Additional information

The company pays tax at 30%. Tax is paid and / or received one year in arrears.

The machines qualify for tax depreciation at the rate of 25% per annum on a reducing balance basis.

The company's cost of capital is 12% per annum. The current rate of return on investments in the money market is 7%.

The project chosen will be funded by internal funds.

The target accounting rate of return is 30%. The company defines "Accounting rate of return" as the average profit before tax divided by the average investment.

Required:

(a) (i) **Calculate the Net Present Value and the Accounting Rate of Return of Project Two.** **(12 marks)**

   (ii) **Prepare a report for the Board of Directors which**

   - **recommends which of the projects, if any, they should invest in;**
   - **identifies two non-financial factors that are relevant to the decision;**
   - **explains the strengths and weaknesses of net present value and accounting rate of return.** **(8 marks)**

(b) A government organisation has a fixed interest ten-year loan. The interest rate on the loan is 8% per annum. The loan is being repaid in equal annual instalments at the end of each year. The amount borrowed was £250,000. The loan has just over 4 years to run.

   Ignore taxation.

Required:

Calculate the present value of the amount outstanding on the loan. **(5 marks)**

(Total: 25 marks)

4   HOSPITAL BUDGETS

A hospital specialises in the provision of a particular surgical procedure. The hospital seeks to provide a value-for-money service. In order to do this it hires teams of specialist staff on a sub-contract basis and pays them only for the hours that they have worked. The hospital uses a standard marginal costing system.

Overhead costs are attributed to the procedures based on direct labour cost.

Budget for November

Budgeted number of procedures to be performed: 20 procedures Standard marginal cost per procedure:

		$
Team fee	2 hours @ $1,500 per hour	3,000
Variable overheads	65% of team fee	1,950
		4,950

The budgeted fixed overheads for November were $48,000

Actual results for November

Procedures performed: 22 procedures

Costs incurred:

Team fees: the team worked 47 hours and were paid a total of $75,400.

Variable overheads: $48,000

Fixed overheads: $46,000

Required:

(a)   **Prepare a statement which reconciles the original budget cost for November and the actual costs incurred, in as much detail as possible.**   **(14 marks)**

(b)   **It has now been realised that the budgeted rate for the team should have been $1,625 per hour.**

      Calculate the planning variance and the operational rate and efficiency variances for the team fees for November.   **(6 marks)**

(c)   **Explain why budgetary control and standard costing are most effective when used together as a means of cost control in service-based organisations.**   **(5 marks)**

(Total: 25 marks)

Section 8

ANSWERS TO SPECIMEN PAPER QUESTIONS

We are grateful to CIMA for their kind permission to reproduce their specimen papers. They are © Chartered Institute of Management Accountants.

1.1   **C**

Contribution after reduction in variable cost = $120,000

Contribution following volume increase = $132,000

Increase in contribution = increase in profit = $32,000

Original profit was $64,000 therefore increase = 50%

1.2   **B**

Net present value = $50,000

Present value of cash inflows = $500,000

Sensitivity = 50,000/500,000 = 10%

1.3   **EV of variable cost = $(70*0.3) + (60*0.5) + (40*0.2) = $59**

Therefore the expected contribution is $61 per member

EV of number of members = (20,000*0.1) + (30,000*0.6) + (40,000*0.3) = 32,000

Expected total contribution = $61*32,000 = $1,952,000

Expected profit = $1,952,000 – 1,100,000 = **$852,000**

1.4

(i)   If VC = $40 then the contribution per member will be $80

Total contribution = 40,000*$80 = $3,200,000

Profit = $2,100,000

(ii)   Joint probability of 20,000 members and $40 variable cost = 0.1*0.2 = 0.02

1.5   **Selling price= ($50 × (annuity factor t = 4, r = 11) + ($1,000 × (disc factor t = 4, r = 11)**

From tables:

Selling price = $(50 × 3.102) + (1,000 × 0.659) = 155.1 + 659 = $814.10

GF should sell the bond for $814.10

1.6

	$000
Inventory used in production	331
Adjustment for increase in inventory	2
	333
Add reduction in trade payables	7
Forecast cash required	340

1.7   **The outstanding balance of trade payables in 2008 is $40,000. This is calculated as shown below:**

$$\frac{\chi}{324,444} \times 365 = 45$$

$$\chi = 45 \times \frac{324,444}{365}$$

$$\chi = 40,000$$

Days outstanding = 41 days

2   OFFICE EQUIPMENT MANUFACTURER

(a)   (i)

		£
UK non-discount	60%*£2.1m*30/365	103,561
UK discount	40%*£2.1m*10/365	23,014
Overseas	80%*£0.9m*60/365	118,356
Total debtors		**244,931**

Debtors days = £244,931 * 365/£3m = 29.8 days

(ii)

		£
UK non factored	15%*£2.1m*30/365	25,890
Overseas	80%*£0.9mm*60/365	118,356
Total debtors		**144,246**

Debtors days = £144,246 * 365/£3m = **17.5 days**

(b)   Flexibility – it offers a flexible source of finance, as sales increases with a corresponding demand for finance, so finance from this source increases.

Security – it allows the firm to pledge other assets as security for the finance.

Last resort – it may be the most cost effective lender to a firm that has no assets to offer as security.

Administration – it relieves management of the responsibility for the sales ledger and the factor can probably perform credit checking better than the firm.

Risk of future changes – Management must balance the disruption from cutting back its administrative function with the financial and other advantages of factoring. However, the financial advantage may change and it may be costly to re-establish a sales ledger function.

Reputation – factoring is associated in many people's mind with financial difficulties or at best with small businesses, which may have an impact on the image of the business in the eyes of its suppliers.

Customer relationship – The use of factoring may create a barrier between the firm and its customers.

(c)   EV with repairs = £51,670 Earnings without repairs = £37,500

Therefore do the repairs.

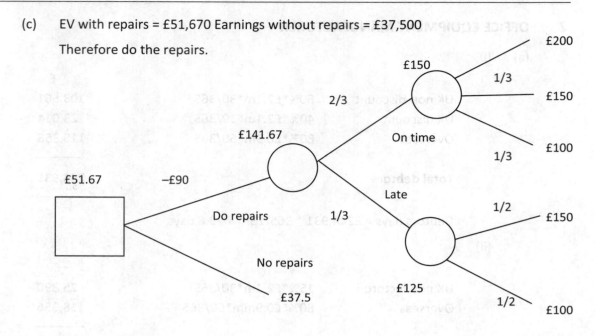

(d)

	Trend values	Seasonal adjustment	Forecast
2009 Q2	134.23 + (7.945 * 7)	0.75	142
2009 Q2	134.23 + (7.945 * 8)	1.00	198
2009 Q2	134.23 + (7.945 * 9)	1.50	309

(e)   When preparing the whole company's budget it is important to have a realistic forecast of what is likely to happen, particularly for cash, purchases, labour and capital budgets. However, for a budget to be effective for motivation, targets must be set that are challenging. It is also argued that for control purposes the budget must be a realistic benchmark against which actual performance can be compared, that is, it must be close to a forecast.

The difficulty is that both of these objectives are valid and beneficial. Thus the issue becomes whether one budget can do both tasks or whether companies need to choose which task the budget will be used for.

(f)   Environmental internal failure costs are costs that are incurred after hazardous materials, waste and / or contaminants have been produced. The costs are incurred in an attempt to comply with expected or enforced standards. Examples include treating and disposing of toxic materials and recycling scrap.

Environmental external failure costs are the most significant costs: they are incurred after the hazardous materials have been introduced into the environment. Examples of costs that an organisation has to pay include decontaminating land and clearing a river after leakage. These costs can give rise to adverse publicity. Some external failure costs may be caused by the organisation but 'paid' by society.

3   MUTUALLY EXCLUSIVE PROJECTS

(a)   ***Workings*** £000

Year	0	1	2	3	4	5	6
Money Sales		399.600	583.200	642.453	700.652	697.931	
Money costs		318.000	393.260	452.586	492.366	535.290	
Tax profit		81.600	189.940	189.867	208.286	162.641	
Tax		24.480	56.982	56.960	62.486	48.792	
tax offset			24.480	56.982	56.960	62.486	48.792
Capital value		500	375	281.25	210.9375	158.2031	
Allowance		125	93.75	70.3125	52.73438	108.2031	
C/f		375	281.25	210.9375	158.2031		
Tax		37.5	28.125	21.09375	15.82031	32.46094	
offset			37.5	28.125	21.09375	15.82031	32.46094

Cash flows

	0	1	2	3	4	5	6
Investment	−500					50	
Sales-costs		81.600	189.940	189.867	208.286	162.641	
Tax			−24.480	−56.982	−56.960	−62.486	−48.792
Tax allow			37.5	28.125	21.09375	15.82031	32.46094
net cash flow	−500	81.6	202.96	161.01	172.4194	165.9752	−16.3312
Discount factor	1.00	0.893	0.797	0.712	0.636	0.567	0.507
Present Value	−500	72.87	161.76	114.64	109.66	94.11	−8.28

Net present value = £44,760

Sales Revenue	399.600	583.200	642.453	700.652	697.931
Operating Costs	318.000	393.260	452.586	492.366	535.290
Depreciation	90.00	90.00	90.00	90.00	90.00
Profit	(8.40)	99.94	99.867	118.286	72.641

Total profit = £382,334.

Average profit = £382,334/5 = £76,467

Average investment = (500,000+50,000)/2 = £275,000

Accounting Rate of Return = £76,467 /£275,000 = 0.278

Accounting Rate of Return = 28%

To: Board of Directors

From: Management Accountant

Date: July 2009

Subject: Investment projects

From a financial perspective based on the information given and that the projects are mutually exclusive the company should invest in Project 2. Investment decisions should be based on Net Present Values as this methodology is consistent with maximising company wealth. However, the company will also need to consider non-financial factors that could affect the decision.

Examples include:

- Consistency with the company's strategy

- Impact on other areas of the business

- Technical compatibility and obsolescence

Accounting rate of return is a simple method of investment appraisal but has many disadvantages. In particular it is based on accounting profit rather than cash flow. Accounting profit is a subjective and dependant on the choice of accounting methods used. Accounting rate of return also ignores the time value of money.

The Net Present Value method is preferable as it ensures that shareholders wealth is maximised and recognises that cash received in the future is less valuable than cash received today. Net present value does suffer from a number of disadvantages as follows:

- The speed of the repayment of the original investment is not highlighted

- Non-financial managers may have difficulty in understanding the concept

- Determination of the correct discount rate can be difficult

(b) Annual repayments = £250,000/(10 year 8% annuity factor)

   = £250,000/6.71

   = £37,258

There are just over years remaining therefore the company will be about to make a payment and then will have four more annual payments to make. The value of these five payments is:

£37,258 + (37,258 * 3.312) = **£160,656**

4   HOSPITAL BUDGETS

(a) **Surgical procedure – November reconciliation**

Original budget (20 procedures)	$	$	$
Team			60,000
Variable overheads			39,000
Fixed overheads			48,000
Total cost			147,000
Flexed budget (22 procedures)			
Additional variable costs			9,900
Expected total cost of 22 procedures			**156,900**

Variances	F	A
Team fee rate (47 × 1,500) − 75,400		4,900
Team efficiency ((22 × 2) − 47) × 1,500		4,500
Variable overhead expenditure (47 × 975) − 48,000		2,175
Variable overhead efficiency ((22 × 2) − 47) × 975		2,925
Fixed overhead expenditure (48,000 − 46,000)	2,000	−
	2,000	14,500	12,500

Actual cost 169,400

(b) Revised standard cost = $1,625 per hour

Original standard cost = $1,500 per hour

Original total team cost for 22 procedures (22 * 2 * $1,500)	66,000
Actual cost	75,400
Total variance	**9,400** adverse

Planning variance (22 * 2 * (1,500 − 1,625))	5,500 adverse
Operational team rate variance (75,400 − (47*1,625))	975 favourable
Operational team efficiency variance (3 * 1,625)	4,875 adverse

9,400

(c) Budgets are projected cost (and/or revenue) aggregates which quantify expectations about future performance. They are used as comparators against which current performance can be measured and as "authority to spend" within which expenditure will be allowed. A budget is an effective planning and control tool for service based organisation.

Standards measure performance at a lower, operational, level. Standard costing is extensively used in manufacturing industries but can equally be applied to service based organisations e.g. in the insurance industry, a standard may be the time to process an insurance claim or key in a document.

Standard costing and budgetary control can be used effectively in both manufacturing and service organisation. They should however be used in combination because together they are more powerful and embrace the organisation more completely than either can do in isolation. It makes little sense to control, or plan, at operational level, without considering impacts at higher levels. Similarly, overall budgets cannot be realistically set without looking at the feasibility of setting operational standards.

Performance Pillar

P1 – Performance Operations

21 November 2012 – Wednesday Morning Session

Instructions to candidates

You are allowed three hours to answer this question paper.
You are allowed 20 minutes reading time **before the examination begins** during which you should read the question paper and, if you wish, highlight and/or make notes on the question paper. However, you will **not** be allowed, **under any circumstances**, to open the answer book and start writing or use your calculator during this reading time.
You are strongly advised to carefully read ALL the question requirements before attempting the question concerned (that is all parts and/or sub-questions).
ALL answers must be written in the answer book. Answers written on the question paper will **not** be submitted for marking.
You should show all workings as marks are available for the method you use.
ALL QUESTIONS ARE COMPULSORY.
Section A comprises 8 sub-questions and is on pages 2 to 5.
Section B comprises 6 sub-questions and is on pages 6 to 8.
Section C comprises 2 questions and is on pages 10 to 13.
Maths tables and formulae are provided on pages 15 to 18.
The list of verbs as published in the syllabus is given for reference on page 19.
Write your candidate number, the paper number and examination subject title in the spaces provided on the front of the answer book. Also write your contact ID and name in the space provided in the right hand margin and seal to close.
Tick the appropriate boxes on the front of the answer book to indicate which questions you have answered.

P1 – Performance Operations

TURN OVER

© The Chartered Institute of Management Accountants 2012

SECTION A – 20 MARKS

[You are advised to spend no longer than 36 minutes on this question.]

ANSWER *ALL* EIGHT SUB-QUESTIONS IN THIS SECTION

Instructions for answering Section A:

The answers to the eight sub-questions in Section A should ALL be written in your answer book.

Your answers should be clearly numbered with the sub-question number then ruled off, so that the markers know which sub-question you are answering. **For multiple choice questions, you need only write the sub-question number and the letter of the answer option you have chosen.** You do not need to start a new page for each sub-question.

For sub-questions **1.6** to **1.8** you should show your workings as marks are available for the method you use to answer these sub-questions.

Question One

1.1 A five year investment project has a positive net present value of $320,000 when discounted at the cost of capital of 10% per annum. The project includes annual net cash inflows of $100,000 which occur at the end of each of the five years.

The percentage reduction in the annual net cash inflow that would result in the project not being financially viable is:

A   31.25%

B   118.5%

C   84.4%

D   18.5%

(2 marks)

1.2 A company's working capital cycle can be calculated as:

A   Inventory days plus accounts receivable days less accounts payable days

B   Accounts receivable days plus accounts payable days less inventory days

C   Inventory days plus accounts payable days less accounts receivable days

D   Accounts payable days plus accounts receivable days plus inventory days

(2 marks)

The following data are given for sub-questions 1.3 and 1.4 below

XY can choose from four mutually exclusive projects. The projects will each last for one year and their net cash inflows will be determined by market conditions. The forecast net cash inflows for each of the possible outcomes are shown below.

Market Conditions	Poor	Average	Good
	$000	*$000*	*$000*
Project A	440	470	560
Project B	400	550	580
Project C	360	400	480
Project D	320	380	420

1.3   If the company applies the maximin criterion the project chosen would be:

A   Project A

B   Project B

C   Project C

D   Project D

(2 marks)

1.4   If the company applies the maximax criterion the project chosen would be:

A   Project A

B   Project B

C   Project C

D   Project D

(2 marks)

Section A continues on the next page

1.5 JK has budgeted sales for next year of 24,000 units and inventory levels are expected to remain constant throughout the year. Each unit produced will require 3 labour hours and the budgeted labour rate will be $15 per hour. It is estimated that 10% of units produced will be wasted.

It is expected that 15% of the total hours worked will be paid at overtime rates. 10% of the total hours will be paid at the basic rate plus an overtime premium of 50% of the basic rate. 5% of the total hours will be paid at the basic rate plus an overtime premium of 100% of the basic rate.

The labour cost budget for next year is:

A $ 1,350,000

B $ 1,306,800

C $ 1,188,000

D $ 1,320,000

(2 marks)

1.6 RS reviews the financial performance of potential customers before setting a credit limit. The summarised financial statements for PQ, a potential major customer operating in the retail industry, are shown below.

Summary Statement of Financial Position for PQ at year end

	2011	2010
	$000	$000
Non-current assets	6,400	5,600
Inventories	1,200	1,120
Trade receivables	800	840
Cash	200	40
Trade payables	(1,120)	(1,160)
Non-current liabilities	(3,600)	(3,200)
Net assets	3,880	3,240
Share capital	2,400	2,400
Retained earnings	1,480	840
	3,880	3,240

Summary Income Statement for PQ for the years

	2011	2010
	$000	$000
Sales	12,000	10,000
Cost of sales	6,400	5,200
Operating profit	2,400	1,800

Required:

Calculate the following ratios, to the nearest 0.1 days, for PQ for 2011

(i) Receivables days
(ii) Payables days
(iii) Inventory days

(3 marks)

1.7 KL has determined from past experience that the following equation provides a reliable estimate of its future sales volume:

y = 15,000 + 2,200x

where   y is the total sales units per quarter, and
         x is the time period

KL has also derived the following set of seasonal variation index values for each quarter using the multiplicative model:

Quarter 1	80
Quarter 2	110
Quarter 3	120
Quarter 4	90

Required:

Calculate the forecast sales units for the third quarter of year 6 using the above model and assuming that the first quarter of year 1 is time period 1.

(3 marks)

1.8 A $100 bond has a yield to maturity of 6% per annum and is due to mature in three years' time. The next interest payment is due in one year's time. Today's market value of the bond is $108.06.

Required:

Calculate the coupon rate on the bond.

(4 marks)

(Total for Section A = 20 marks)

Reminder

All answers to Section A must be written in your answer book.
Answers to Section A written on the question paper will **not** be submitted for marking.

End of Section A. Section B begins on page 6

TURN OVER

SECTION B – 30 MARKS

[You are advised to spend no longer than 9 minutes on each sub-question in this section.]

ANSWER ALL SIX SUB-QUESTIONS. YOU SHOULD SHOW YOUR WORKINGS AS MARKS ARE AVAILABLE FOR THE METHOD YOU USE.

Question Two

(a)   FG is concerned that the payment record of one of its customers is extremely poor. An extract from the trade receivable account for the customer, for the period 1 July to 31 October, is shown below:

Date	Narrative	Debit $	Credit $	Balance $
01/07/2011	Balance b/fwd			142
08/07/2011	Invoice No. 345	102		244
12/07/2011	Invoice No. 423	234		478
15/07/2011	Credit note No. C85 (Balance b/fwd)		78	400
23/07/2011	Receipt No. R69 (Balance b/fwd and Invoice No. 345)		166	234
04/08/2011	Invoice No. 460	156		390
11/08/2011	Invoice No. 489	87		477
14/08/2011	Invoice No. 558	34		511
05/09/2011	Receipt No. R92 (Invoice No. 558)		34	477
18/09/2011	Invoice No. 576	183		660
20/09/2011	Invoice No. 615	263		923
04/10/2011	Receipt No. R121 (Invoice No. 489)		87	836
16/10/2011	Invoice No. 678	128		964

Required:

(i)   **Prepare** an aged debt analysis showing the outstanding debt of the customer at 31 October analysed by month.

(3 marks)

The credit control department has been chasing the outstanding invoices by telephone, email and post.

(ii)   **State** TWO further actions that FG may take after reviewing the information shown in the aged debt analysis prepared in part (i).

(2 marks)

(Total for sub-question (a) = 5 marks)

(b) A company has recently sold part of its trading operations and is reviewing potential long term investment opportunities for the funds. Until a suitable opportunity is identified the funds are being held in a bank deposit account but the company is considering the following alternative short-term investments:

    (i)   Certificates of deposit
    (ii)   Bills of exchange

Required:

Describe the alternative short-term investments in terms of their risk, return and liquidity.

(5 marks)

(c) The following data are available for Products A, B and C:

	Budget			Actual		
	Product A	Product B	Product C	Product A	Product B	Product C
Sales units	6,000	8,400	9,600	6,400	9,200	8,700
Selling price per unit	$150	$160	$70	$142	$168	$77
Variable cost per unit	$75	$90	$45	$69	$92	$48

Required:

    (i)   **Calculate** the total sales mix contribution variance.

(3 marks)

    (ii)   **Calculate** the total sales quantity contribution variance.

(2 marks)

(Total for sub-question (c) = 5 marks)

(d) The managers of a hospital are in the process of preparing the annual budget for the next financial year using incremental budgeting. The hospital's directors are concerned that the approach used will result in a budget that does not reflect the aims and objectives of the hospital. They have requested that the budget should be produced using zero based budgeting.

Required:

Explain the potential difficulties that the hospital's managers may face when setting budgets using zero based budgeting.

(5 marks)

Section B continues on the next page

TURN OVER

(e) RS is a travel company providing daily tours of a major European capital city. The market is highly competitive and RS has commissioned some market research to help with the pricing decision for a new tour. The research identified the probability of three possible market conditions and the number of tickets that would be sold each day at three different price levels.

| | | Ticket Price | | |
| | | $80 | $90 | $100 |
Market	Probability	No. of tickets	No. of tickets	No. of tickets
Weak	0·3	80	60	30
Good	0·5	100	90	80
Excellent	0·2	150	150	120

Variable costs are expected to be $20 per ticket irrespective of market conditions.

Required:

Demonstrate, using a decision tree and based on expected value, which ticket price RS should choose.

(5 marks)

(f) **Explain** the meaning of expected value and the limitations of using expected values for decision making.

(5 marks)

(Total for Section B = 30 marks)

End of Section B. Section C begins on page 10

This page is blank

SECTION C – 50 MARKS

[You are advised to spend no longer than 45 minutes on each question in this section.]

ANSWER *BOTH* QUESTIONS IN THIS SECTION. EACH QUESTION IS WORTH 25 MARKS. YOU SHOULD SHOW YOUR WORKINGS AS MARKS ARE AVAILABLE FOR THE METHOD YOU USE.

Question Three

GH produces three models of speedboat for sale to the retail market. GH currently operates a standard absorption costing system. Budgeting information for next year is given below:

Model of speedboat	Superior	Deluxe	Ultra	Total
	$000	$000	$000	$000
Sales	54,000	86,400	102,000	242,400
Direct material	17,600	27,400	40,200	85,200
Direct labour	10,700	13,400	16,600	40,700
Production overhead				69,600
Gross profit				46,900

	Superior	Deluxe	Ultra
Production / sales (number of boats)	1,000	1,200	800
Machine hours per boat	100	200	300

The production overhead cost is absorbed using a machine hour rate.

GH is considering changing to an activity based costing system. The main activities and their associated cost drivers and overhead cost have been identified as follows:

Activity	Cost Driver	Production overhead cost
		$000
Machining	Machine hours	13,920
Set up	Number of set ups	23,920
Quality inspection	Number of quality inspections	14,140
Stores receiving	Number of component deliveries	6,840
Stores issue	Number of issues from stores	10,780
		69,600

The analysis also revealed the following information:

	Superior	Deluxe	Ultra
Budgeted production (number of boats)	1,000	1,200	800
Boats per production run	5	4	2
Quality inspections per production run	10	20	30
Number of component deliveries	500	600	800
Number of issues from stores	4,000	5,000	7,000

The machines are set up for each production run of each model.

Required:

(a)   **Calculate** the total gross profit for each model of speedboat:

    (i)   using the current absorption costing system;

                                                           (4 marks)

    (ii)   using the proposed activity based costing system.

                                                         (12 marks)

(b)   **Explain** why an activity based costing system may produce more accurate product costs than a traditional absorption costing system.

                                                           (3 marks)

(c)   **Explain** the possible other benefits to the company of introducing an activity based costing system. You should use the figures calculated in part (a) to illustrate your answer.

                                                           (6 marks)

                              (Total for Question Three = 25 marks)

Section C continues on the next page

TURN OVER

Question Four

JK is a profitable international pharmaceutical company that develops, produces and markets drugs that are licensed as medication. The pharmaceutical industry has grown rapidly and faces challenges in preventing and controlling environmental pollution. Over the past few years there has been growing pressure on the industry from government, shareholders and other stakeholders to improve its environmental management performance. JK has taken a proactive approach to environmental management and has invested significant resources introducing pollution prevention and clean manufacturing practices into its operation in order to reduce waste and minimise negative environmental impacts. The company has used marketing and advertising campaigns to develop an image as a company that is at the cutting edge of 'green' technology.

As part of its environmental management programme, JK is considering investing in a new system that will significantly reduce hazardous emissions and waste.

The estimates for the proposed investment are as follows:

Initial investment	$60 million
Useful life	6 years
Residual value	$12 million
Annual income from sale of recycled waste	$5 million
Annual savings in waste disposal costs	$5.5 million
Annual fixed maintenance costs per annum	$1.5 million
Other annual fixed operating costs per annum (including depreciation)	$10.6 million

JK has experienced a number of external environmental failures over the past few years which have resulted in total costs to JK, including government fines, of $20 million per annum. The environmental officer has estimated that, as a direct result of this investment, future external environmental failure costs that will be borne by JK and their associated probabilities are as follows:

Annual external environmental failure costs	Probability
$18 million	30%
$12 million	25%
$10 million	35%
$5 million	10%

The company uses expected value for this type of analysis.

Depreciation of the initial investment will be calculated using the straight line method and has been included in other fixed operating costs.

The company's financial director has provided the following taxation information:

- Tax depreciation: 25% per annum of the reducing balance, with a balancing adjustment in the year of disposal.
- Taxation rate: 30% of taxable profits. Half of the tax is payable in the year in which it arises, the balance is paid in the following year.

The company uses a cost of capital of 12% per annum to evaluate projects of this type. Ignore inflation.

Required:

(a) **Evaluate** the investment in the proposed system using net present value as the basis of your evaluation. Your workings should be shown in $m to one decimal place.

(13 marks)

(b)

(i) **Calculate** the payback period for the investment.

(3 marks)

(ii) **Discuss** the advantages and disadvantages of payback as a method of investment appraisal.

(5 marks)

(c) **Explain** TWO factors related to JK's approach to environmental issues that should be considered before making a final decision about the project.

(4 marks)

(Total for Question Four = 25 marks)

(Total for Section C = 50 marks)

End of question paper
Maths tables and formulae are on pages 15 to 18

This page is blank

PRESENT VALUE TABLE

Present value of $1, that is $(1+r)^{-n}$ where r = interest rate; n = number of periods until payment or receipt.

Periods (n)	Interest rates (r)									
	1%	2%	3%	4%	5%	6%	7%	8%	9%	10%
1	0.990	0.980	0.971	0.962	0.952	0.943	0.935	0.926	0.917	0.909
2	0.980	0.961	0.943	0.925	0.907	0.890	0.873	0.857	0.842	0.826
3	0.971	0.942	0.915	0.889	0.864	0.840	0.816	0.794	0.772	0.751
4	0.961	0.924	0.888	0.855	0.823	0.792	0.763	0.735	0.708	0.683
5	0.951	0.906	0.863	0.822	0.784	0.747	0.713	0.681	0.650	0.621
6	0.942	0.888	0.837	0.790	0.746	0.705	0.666	0.630	0.596	0.564
7	0.933	0.871	0.813	0.760	0.711	0.665	0.623	0.583	0.547	0.513
8	0.923	0.853	0.789	0.731	0.677	0.627	0.582	0.540	0.502	0.467
9	0.914	0.837	0.766	0.703	0.645	0.592	0.544	0.500	0.460	0.424
10	0.905	0.820	0.744	0.676	0.614	0.558	0.508	0.463	0.422	0.386
11	0.896	0.804	0.722	0.650	0.585	0.527	0.475	0.429	0.388	0.350
12	0.887	0.788	0.701	0.625	0.557	0.497	0.444	0.397	0.356	0.319
13	0.879	0.773	0.681	0.601	0.530	0.469	0.415	0.368	0.326	0.290
14	0.870	0.758	0.661	0.577	0.505	0.442	0.388	0.340	0.299	0.263
15	0.861	0.743	0.642	0.555	0.481	0.417	0.362	0.315	0.275	0.239
16	0.853	0.728	0.623	0.534	0.458	0.394	0.339	0.292	0.252	0.218
17	0.844	0.714	0.605	0.513	0.436	0.371	0.317	0.270	0.231	0.198
18	0.836	0.700	0.587	0.494	0.416	0.350	0.296	0.250	0.212	0.180
19	0.828	0.686	0.570	0.475	0.396	0.331	0.277	0.232	0.194	0.164
20	0.820	0.673	0.554	0.456	0.377	0.312	0.258	0.215	0.178	0.149

Periods (n)	Interest rates (r)									
	11%	12%	13%	14%	15%	16%	17%	18%	19%	20%
1	0.901	0.893	0.885	0.877	0.870	0.862	0.855	0.847	0.840	0.833
2	0.812	0.797	0.783	0.769	0.756	0.743	0.731	0.718	0.706	0.694
3	0.731	0.712	0.693	0.675	0.658	0.641	0.624	0.609	0.593	0.579
4	0.659	0.636	0.613	0.592	0.572	0.552	0.534	0.516	0.499	0.482
5	0.593	0.567	0.543	0.519	0.497	0.476	0.456	0.437	0.419	0.402
6	0.535	0.507	0.480	0.456	0.432	0.410	0.390	0.370	0.352	0.335
7	0.482	0.452	0.425	0.400	0.376	0.354	0.333	0.314	0.296	0.279
8	0.434	0.404	0.376	0.351	0.327	0.305	0.285	0.266	0.249	0.233
9	0.391	0.361	0.333	0.308	0.284	0.263	0.243	0.225	0.209	0.194
10	0.352	0.322	0.295	0.270	0.247	0.227	0.208	0.191	0.176	0.162
11	0.317	0.287	0.261	0.237	0.215	0.195	0.178	0.162	0.148	0.135
12	0.286	0.257	0.231	0.208	0.187	0.168	0.152	0.137	0.124	0.112
13	0.258	0.229	0.204	0.182	0.163	0.145	0.130	0.116	0.104	0.093
14	0.232	0.205	0.181	0.160	0.141	0.125	0.111	0.099	0.088	0.078
15	0.209	0.183	0.160	0.140	0.123	0.108	0.095	0.084	0.079	0.065
16	0.188	0.163	0.141	0.123	0.107	0.093	0.081	0.071	0.062	0.054
17	0.170	0.146	0.125	0.108	0.093	0.080	0.069	0.060	0.052	0.045
18	0.153	0.130	0.111	0.095	0.081	0.069	0.059	0.051	0.044	0.038
19	0.138	0.116	0.098	0.083	0.070	0.060	0.051	0.043	0.037	0.031
20	0.124	0.104	0.087	0.073	0.061	0.051	0.043	0.037	0.031	0.026

Cumulative present value of $1 per annum, Receivable or Payable at the end of each year for n years $\frac{1-(1+r)^{-n}}{r}$

Periods	Interest rates (r)									
(n)	1%	2%	3%	4%	5%	6%	7%	8%	9%	10%
1	0.990	0.980	0.971	0.962	0.952	0.943	0.935	0.926	0.917	0.909
2	1.970	1.942	1.913	1.886	1.859	1.833	1.808	1.783	1.759	1.736
3	2.941	2.884	2.829	2.775	2.723	2.673	2.624	2.577	2.531	2.487
4	3.902	3.808	3.717	3.630	3.546	3.465	3.387	3.312	3.240	3.170
5	4.853	4.713	4.580	4.452	4.329	4.212	4.100	3.993	3.890	3.791
6	5.795	5.601	5.417	5.242	5.076	4.917	4.767	4.623	4.486	4.355
7	6.728	6.472	6.230	6.002	5.786	5.582	5.389	5.206	5.033	4.868
8	7.652	7.325	7.020	6.733	6.463	6.210	5.971	5.747	5.535	5.335
9	8.566	8.162	7.786	7.435	7.108	6.802	6.515	6.247	5.995	5.759
10	9.471	8.983	8.530	8.111	7.722	7.360	7.024	6.710	6.418	6.145
11	10.368	9.787	9.253	8.760	8.306	7.887	7.499	7.139	6.805	6.495
12	11.255	10.575	9.954	9.385	8.863	8.384	7.943	7.536	7.161	6.814
13	12.134	11.348	10.635	9.986	9.394	8.853	8.358	7.904	7.487	7.103
14	13.004	12.106	11.296	10.563	9.899	9.295	8.745	8.244	7.786	7.367
15	13.865	12.849	11.938	11.118	10.380	9.712	9.108	8.559	8.061	7.606
16	14.718	13.578	12.561	11.652	10.838	10.106	9.447	8.851	8.313	7.824
17	15.562	14.292	13.166	12.166	11.274	10.477	9.763	9.122	8.544	8.022
18	16.398	14.992	13.754	12.659	11.690	10.828	10.059	9.372	8.756	8.201
19	17.226	15.679	14.324	13.134	12.085	11.158	10.336	9.604	8.950	8.365
20	18.046	16.351	14.878	13.590	12.462	11.470	10.594	9.818	9.129	8.514

Periods	Interest rates (r)									
(n)	11%	12%	13%	14%	15%	16%	17%	18%	19%	20%
1	0.901	0.893	0.885	0.877	0.870	0.862	0.855	0.847	0.840	0.833
2	1.713	1.690	1.668	1.647	1.626	1.605	1.585	1.566	1.547	1.528
3	2.444	2.402	2.361	2.322	2.283	2.246	2.210	2.174	2.140	2.106
4	3.102	3.037	2.974	2.914	2.855	2.798	2.743	2.690	2.639	2.589
5	3.696	3.605	3.517	3.433	3.352	3.274	3.199	3.127	3.058	2.991
6	4.231	4.111	3.998	3.889	3.784	3.685	3.589	3.498	3.410	3.326
7	4.712	4.564	4.423	4.288	4.160	4.039	3.922	3.812	3.706	3.605
8	5.146	4.968	4.799	4.639	4.487	4.344	4.207	4.078	3.954	3.837
9	5.537	5.328	5.132	4.946	4.772	4.607	4.451	4.303	4.163	4.031
10	5.889	5.650	5.426	5.216	5.019	4.833	4.659	4.494	4.339	4.192
11	6.207	5.938	5.687	5.453	5.234	5.029	4.836	4.656	4.486	4.327
12	6.492	6.194	5.918	5.660	5.421	5.197	4.988	7.793	4.611	4.439
13	6.750	6.424	6.122	5.842	5.583	5.342	5.118	4.910	4.715	4.533
14	6.982	6.628	6.302	6.002	5.724	5.468	5.229	5.008	4.802	4.611
15	7.191	6.811	6.462	6.142	5.847	5.575	5.324	5.092	4.876	4.675
16	7.379	6.974	6.604	6.265	5.954	5.668	5.405	5.162	4.938	4.730
17	7.549	7.120	6.729	6.373	6.047	5.749	5.475	5.222	4.990	4.775
18	7.702	7.250	6.840	6.467	6.128	5.818	5.534	5.273	5.033	4.812
19	7.839	7.366	6.938	6.550	6.198	5.877	5.584	5.316	5.070	4.843
20	7.963	7.469	7.025	6.623	6.259	5.929	5.628	5.353	5.101	4.870

FORMULAE

PROBABILITY

$A \cup B = \textbf{A or B}.$ $A \cap B = \textbf{A and B}$ (overlap).

$P(B \mid A)$ = probability of B, **given** A.

Rules of Addition

If A and B are mutually exclusive: $P(A \cup B) = P(A) + P(B)$

If A and B are not mutually exclusive: $P(A \cup B) = P(A) + P(B) - P(A \cap B)$

Rules of Multiplication

If A and B are *independent*:: $P(A \cap B) = P(A) * P(B)$

If A and B are **not** *independent*: $P(A \cap B) = P(A) * P(B \mid A)$

$E(X) = \sum$ (probability * payoff)

DESCRIPTIVE STATISTICS

Arithmetic Mean

$$\bar{x} = \frac{\sum x}{n} \qquad \bar{x} = \frac{\sum fx}{\sum f} \quad \text{(frequency distribution)}$$

Standard Deviation

$$SD = \sqrt{\frac{\sum (x - \bar{x})^2}{n}} \qquad SD = \sqrt{\frac{\sum fx^2}{\sum f} - \bar{x}^2} \quad \text{(frequency distribution)}$$

INDEX NUMBERS

Price relative = $100 * P_1/P_0$ Quantity relative = $100 * Q_1/Q_0$

Price: $$\frac{\sum w * \left(\dfrac{P_1}{P_o} \right)}{\sum w} \times 100$$

Quantity: $$\frac{\sum w * \left(\dfrac{Q_1}{Q_o} \right)}{\sum w} \times 100$$

TIME SERIES

Additive Model

Series = Trend + Seasonal + Random

Multiplicative Model

Series = Trend * Seasonal * Random

FINANCIAL MATHEMATICS

Compound Interest (Values and Sums)
Future Value S, of a sum of X, invested for n periods, compounded at $r\%$ interest

$$S = X[1 + r]^n$$

Annuity
Present value of an annuity of $1 per annum receivable or payable for n years, commencing in one year, discounted at $r\%$ per annum:

$$PV = \frac{1}{r}\left[1 - \frac{1}{[1+r]^n}\right]$$

Perpetuity
Present value of $1 per annum, payable or receivable in perpetuity, commencing in one year, discounted at $r\%$ per annum:

$$PV = \frac{1}{r}$$

LEARNING CURVE

$$Y_x = aX^b$$

where:
Y_x = the cumulative average time per unit to produce X units;
a = the time required to produce the first unit of output;
X = the cumulative number of units;
b = the index of learning.

The exponent b is defined as the log of the learning curve improvement rate divided by log 2.

INVENTORY MANAGEMENT

Economic Order Quantity

$$EOQ = \sqrt{\frac{2C_o D}{C_h}}$$

where: C_o = cost of placing an order
C_h = cost of holding one unit in inventory for one year
D = annual demand

LIST OF VERBS USED IN THE QUESTION REQUIREMENTS

A list of the learning objectives and verbs that appear in the syllabus and in the question requirements for each question in this paper.

It is important that you answer the question according to the definition of the verb.

LEARNING OBJECTIVE	VERBS USED	DEFINITION
Level 1 - KNOWLEDGE What you are expected to know.	List	Make a list of
	State	Express, fully or clearly, the details/facts of
	Define	Give the exact meaning of
Level 2 - COMPREHENSION What you are expected to understand.	Describe	Communicate the key features
	Distinguish	Highlight the differences between
	Explain	Make clear or intelligible/State the meaning or purpose of
	Identify	Recognise, establish or select after consideration
	Illustrate	Use an example to describe or explain something
Level 3 - APPLICATION How you are expected to apply your knowledge.	Apply	Put to practical use
	Calculate	Ascertain or reckon mathematically
	Demonstrate	Prove with certainty or to exhibit by practical means
	Prepare	Make or get ready for use
	Reconcile	Make or prove consistent/compatible
	Solve	Find an answer to
	Tabulate	Arrange in a table
Level 4 - ANALYSIS How are you expected to analyse the detail of what you have learned.	Analyse	Examine in detail the structure of
	Categorise	Place into a defined class or division
	Compare and contrast	Show the similarities and/or differences between
	Construct	Build up or compile
	Discuss	Examine in detail by argument
	Interpret	Translate into intelligible or familiar terms
	Prioritise	Place in order of priority or sequence for action
	Produce	Create or bring into existence
Level 5 - EVALUATION How are you expected to use your learning to evaluate, make decisions or recommendations.	Advise	Counsel, inform or notify
	Evaluate	Appraise or assess the value of
	Recommend	Advise on a course of action

Performance Pillar

Operational Level Paper

P1 – Performance Operations

November 2012

Wednesday Morning Session

Operational Level Paper

P1 – Performance Operations
November 2012 examination

Examiner's Answers

Note: *Some of the answers that follow are fuller and more comprehensive than would be expected from a well-prepared candidate. They have been written in this way to aid teaching, study and revision for tutors and candidates alike.*

These Examiner's answers should be reviewed alongside the question paper for this examination which is now available on the CIMA website at www.cimaglobal.com/p1papers

The Post Exam Guide for this examination, which includes the marking guide for each question, will be published on the CIMA website by early February at www.cimaglobal.com/P1PEGS

SECTION A

Answer to Question One

Rationale

Question One consists of 8 objective test sub-questions. These are drawn from all sections of the syllabus. They are designed to examine breadth across the syllabus and thus cover many learning outcomes.

1.1   Discounted value of cash inflow = $100k x 3.791 =$379.1k
Sensitivity = $320k / $379.1k = 84.4%

The correct answer is C.

1.2   **The correct answer is A.**

1.3 The minimum outcome for Project A is $440k
The minimum outcome for Project B is $400k
The minimum outcome for Project C is $360k
The minimum outcome for Project D is $320k

Therefore if the company wants to maximise the minimum it will choose Project A.

The correct answer is A.

1.4 The maximum that can be achieved is $580k for Project B.

The correct answer is B.

1.5 **The correct answer is D.**

1.6 Receivables days = (800/12,000) x 365 = 24.3 days
Payables days = (1,120/(6,400 +1,200 - 1,120) x 365 = 63.1 days
Inventory days = (1,200/6,400) x 365 = 68.4 days

Or alternatively

Receivables days = (((800+ 840)/2)/12,000) x 365 = 24.9 days
Payables days = (((1,120 + 1,160)/2)/(6,400 +1,200 - 1,120)) x 365 = 64.2 days
Inventory days = (((1,200+ 1,120)/2)/6,400) x 365 = 66.2 days

---

1.7 The third quarter of Year 6 is time period 23

Expected sales volume based on the trend equation

= 15,000 + (2,200 x 23) = 65,600 units

Forecast sales volume after allowing for seasonal variation

= 65,600 x 1.2 = 78,720 units

1.8 The yield to maturity is 6% therefore the net present value of the cash flow when discounted at 6% will be equal to zero.

Year(s)	Description	Cash flow	Discount factor (6%)	Present value $
0	Purchase	(108.06)	1.000	(108.06)
1-3	Interest	9	2.673	24.06
3	Redemption	100	0.840	84.00
NPV				0

To achieve a NPV of zero the present value of the total interest paid has to be $24.06 therefore the annual interest payments are $9 which is a coupon rate of 9%

SECTION B

Answer to Question Two

(a)

(a) (i)

	< 1 month $	1<2 months $	2<3 months $	3 months +	Balance
Invoice no.423				234	
Invoice no.460			156		
Invoice no.576		183			
Invoice no.615		263			
Invoice no.678	128				
	128	446	156	234	964

(ii)   *Examiner's note: the question asks for two further actions. Examples of actions that would be rewarded are given below.*

- They may decide to take legal action to collect the debt.
- They may decide to stop further supplies to the customer.
- They may decide to reduce the credit limit available to the customer.

(b)

Certificates of deposit

These are securities that are issued by a bank as an acknowledgement that funds have been deposited. Certificates of deposit are traded on the money market and so the holder can sell them to obtain immediate cash at any time. They are therefore a suitable option in terms of liquidity and have a low risk. Interest is paid on the deposit at a fixed rate based on current market interest rates at the date of issue but this will reflect the low risk involved. They are therefore subject to interest rate risk since if market rates increase they lose the opportunity for higher rates.

They normally have maturities from three months to five years. The lower end of this time range would be most appropriate for the company's circumstances however because of the marketability the upper end of this time range gives flexibility. The company however would also be exposed to capital risk as the value of the investment changes in response to market interest rate movements.

Bills of exchange

A bill of exchange is an unconditional order by one person/company to pay another a given sum of money at a specified future date. These are tradeable and have a short date normally within 180 days. There is a particularly active market in bills that are payable by top-quality banks although it is also possible to buy bills that have been accepted by trading companies. These would therefore be a suitable option in terms of liquidity. They are issued at a discount to the face value with the yield on the bill dependent on the credit worthiness of the drawee and market interest rates. They are therefore subject to interest rate risk since if market rates increase they lose the opportunity for higher rates. They are also subject to default risk depending on the credit worthiness of the drawee.

(c)

Rationale

The question assesses learning outcome A1(f) *interpret material, labour, variable overheads, fixed overheads and sales variances, distinguishing between planning and operational variances.* It examines candidates' ability to calculate a sales mix contribution variance and a sales quantity contribution variances.

Suggested Approach

In part (i) candidates should calculate the sales mix contribution variance by comparing the actual sales quantity at the budgeted mix with the actual sales quantity at the actual mix. The variance calculated in units for each of the products should then be multiplied the standard contribution per unit to calculate the variance for each product. These should then be added together to calculate the total mix variance. In part (ii) the budgeted sales quantity should be compared to the actual sales quantity at the budgeted mix. The resultant variance in units should be multiplied by the standard contribution per unit to calculate the sales quantity contribution variance for each product. These should then be added together to calculate the total sales quantity contribution variance.

(i) **Sales Mix Contribution Variance**

	Actual Sales Quantity	Actual Sales at budget mix	Difference	Contribution $	Variance $
Product A	6,400	6,075	325 F	75	24,375 F
Product B	9,200	8,505	695 F	70	48,650 F
Product C	8,700	9,720	1,020 A	25	25,500 A
	24,300	24,300			47,525 F

Or alternatively:-

	Actual Sales Quantity	Actual Sales at budget mix	Difference	Variance from weighted average contribution per unit	Variance $
Product A	6,400	6,075	325 F	($75 - $53.25)	7,068.75 F
Product B	9,200	8,505	695 F	($70 - $53.25)	11,641.25 F
Product C	8,700	9,720	1020 A	($25 - $53.25)	28,815 F
	24,300	24,300			47,525 F

(ii) **Sales Quantity Contribution Variance**

	Budget Sales Quantity	Actual Sales at budget mix	Difference	Contribution $	Variance $
Product A	6,000	6,075	75 F	75	5,625 F
Product B	8,400	8,505	105 F	70	7,350 F
Product C	9,600	9,720	120 F	25	3,000 F
	24,000	24,300	300 F		15,975 F

Or alternatively:-

	Budget Sales Quantity	Contribution $	Total Contribution $000
Product A	6,000	75	450
Product B	8,400	70	588
Product C	9,600	25	240
	24,000		1,278

Weighted average contribution = $1,278k / 24,000 = $53.25
Sales quantity contribution variance = (24,300 – 24,000) x $53.25 = $15,975 F

(d)

Rationale
The question assesses learning outcome B3(b) *apply alternative approaches to budgeting*. It examines the candidates' ability to explain the difficulties that a not-for-profit organisation may experience when using a zero based budgeting system.

Suggested Approach
Candidates should clearly explain why setting budgets using zero based budgeting may be difficult in a not-for-profit organisation.

The hospital has previously used an incremental budgeting system and therefore the potential difficulties with setting a budget using a zero based budgeting system are as follows:

Zero based budgeting is extremely time consuming; the work involved in the creation of decision packages and their ranking is considerable. The hospital may not have the resources available to enable a full zero based budget to be prepared within the timescale required. It may also require skills that the current management of the hospital do not possess as they are inexperienced in this type of budgeting. As this is the first time a zero based budgeting approach has been used it will mean that all activities carried out by the hospital will need to be reviewed and justified.

There may be difficulty in identifying the activities undertaken by the hospital particularly if the organisation structure is based on traditional functional departments. This may result in a tendency to try to cut costs rather than identifying the main drivers behind costs.

The ranking process can be very difficult as value judgements are required. Widely different activities cannot be compared on quantitative measurement alone.

(e)

Rationale

The question assesses learning outcome D1(f) *apply decision trees.* It examines candidates' ability to use decision trees to evaluate a decision where there is uncertainty regarding expected cash flows.

Suggested Approach

Candidates should firstly draw the decision tree and then using the various contribution levels for each branch of the tree work back to calculate the expected contribution at each node. They should then clearly indicate the most profitable decision.

Decision tree: See next page

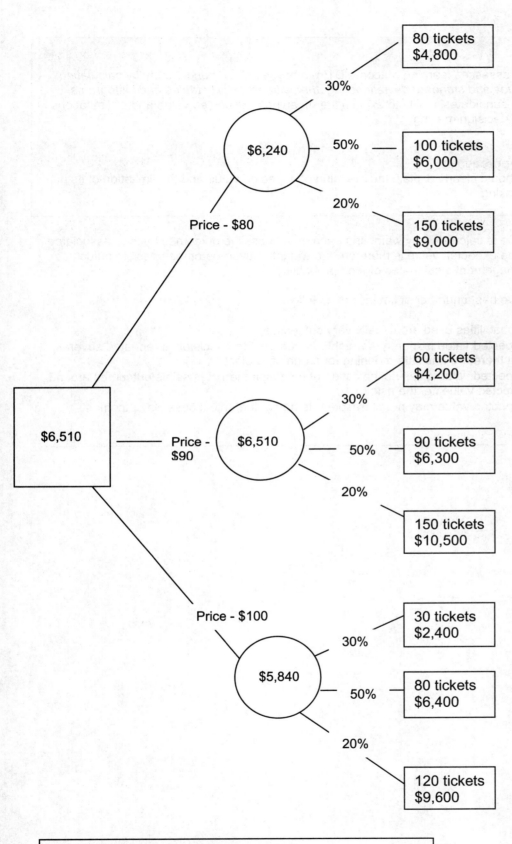

RS should charge a ticket price of $90.

(f)

Rationale

The question assesses learning outcome D1(c) *analyse risk and uncertainty by calculating expected values and standard deviations together with probability tables and histograms.* It examines the candidates' ability to explain the meaning of expected value and its limitations when used in decision making.

Suggested Approach

Candidates should clearly explain the meaning of expected value and the limitation of its use in decision making.

Expected value is calculated by weighting each of the possible outcomes by their associated probability. The expected value is therefore the weighted average of the possible outcomes based on management's estimates of their probability.

Expected value has a number of limitations as follows:

- The probabilities used are usually very subjective;
- The expected value is merely a weighted average if the decision is repeated several times. It therefore has little meaning for a one off project;
- The expected value gives no indication of the dispersion of possible outcomes around the expected value i.e. the risk;
- The expected value may not correspond to any of the actual possible outcomes.

SECTION C

Answer to Question Three

Rationale

Part (a)(i) of the question assesses learning outcome A1(a) *compare and contrast marginal (or variable), throughput and absorption accounting methods in respect of profit reporting and stock valuation.* It examines candidates' ability to calculate the cost of a product using a traditional method of overhead absorption. Part (a)(ii) assesses learning outcome A1(c) *discuss activity-based costing as compared with traditional marginal and absorption costing methods, including its relative advantages and disadvantages as a system of cost accounting.* It requires candidates to be able to apply activity based costing to the calculation of the cost of a product. Part (b) assesses learning outcome A1(c) *discuss activity-based costing as compared with traditional marginal and absorption costing methods, including its relative advantages and disadvantages as a system of cost accounting.* It examines candidates' ability to explain the why activity based costing would result in more accurate product costs compare to a traditional absorption costing system. Part (c) also assesses learning outcome A1(c) *discuss activity-based costing as compared with traditional marginal and absorption costing methods, including its relative advantages and disadvantages as a system of cost accounting.* It examines candidates' ability to explain other benefits to a company of introducing an activity based costing system.

Suggested Approach

In part (a)(i) candidates should identify the direct costs for each product and then calculate the overhead absorption rate. This rate can then be applied to each product and the gross profit calculated. In part (a)(ii) candidates need to calculate a cost driver rate for each of the activities and then apply this cost driver rate to calculate the overhead cost for each activity per product. The gross profit for each product can then be recalculated. In part (b) candidates need to clearly explain why activity based costing produces more accurate product costs. In part (c) the potential benefits to the company of the activity based costing in the areas of planning, decision making and control should be explained.

(a) (i)

Fixed production overheads = $69,600,000
Budgeted machine hours = (1,000 x 100) + (1,200 x 200) + (800 x 300) = 580,000
Fixed production overhead absorption rate = $69,600,000 / 580,000 = $120 per machine hour

	Superior $000	Deluxe $000	Ultra $000
Sales	54,000	86,400	102,000
Direct material	17,600	27,400	40,200
Direct labour	10,700	13,400	16,600
Production overhead	12,000	28,800	28,800
Gross profit	13,700	16,800	16,400

(a) (ii)

Cost Driver	Number of cost drivers
Machine hours	(1,000 x 100) + (1,200 x 200) + (800 x 300) = 580,000
Number of set ups	(1,000 / 5) + (1,200 /4) + (800 / 2) = 900
Number of quality inspections	(200 x 10) + (300 x 20) + (400 x 30) = 20,000
Number of component deliveries	500 + 600 + 800 = 1,900
Number of issues from stores	4,000 + 5,000 + 7,000 = 16,000

	Superior $000	Deluxe $000	Ultra $000
Sales	54,000	86,400	102,000
Direct material	17,600	27,400	40,200
Direct labour	10,700	13,400	16,600
Machining	2,400 (13,920 / 580 x 100)	5,760 (13,920 / 580 x 240)	5,760 (13,920 /580 x 240)
Set ups	5,316 (23,920 / 900 x 200)	7,973 (23,920 / 900 x 300)	10,631 (23,920 / 900 x 400)
Quality inspections	1,414 (14,140 / 20 x 2)	4,242 (14,140 / 20 x 6)	8,484 (14,140 / 20 x 12)
Stores receiving	1,800 (6,840 / 1,900 x 500)	2,160 (6,840 / 1,900 x 600)	2,880 (6,840 / 1,900 x 800)
Stores issuing	2,695 (10,780 / 16 x 4)	3,369 (10,780 / 16 x 5)	4,716 (10,780 / 16 x 7)
Gross profit	12,075	22,096	12,729

(b)

Under an activity based costing (ABC) system the various support activities that are involved in making products or providing services are identified. ABC recognises that there are many different drivers of cost not just production or sales volume. The cost drivers are identified in order to recognise a causal link between activities and costs. They are then used as the basis to attach activity costs to a particular product or service. Through the tracing of costs to cost objects in this way, ABC establishes more accurate costs for the product or service.

(c)

The cost drivers identified under an ABC system provide information to management to enable them to take actions to improve the overall profitability of the company. Cost driver analysis will provide information to management on how costs can be controlled and managed. Variance analysis will also be more useful as it is based on more accurate product costs. The establishment of more accurate product costs should also help managers to assess product profitability and make better decisions concerning pricing and product mix.

Based on the existing method of absorbing production overheads, the profitability for each model is as shown below:

	Superior	Deluxe	Ultra
Selling price per unit	$54,000	$72,000	$127,500
Gross profit per unit	$13,700	$14,000	$20,500
Gross margin	25.4%	19.4%	16.1%

Under the ABC system the profitability for each model is significantly different as shown below.

	Superior	Deluxe	Ultra
Selling price per unit	$54,000	$72,000	$127,500
Gross profit per unit	$12,075	$18,413	$15,911
Gross margin	22.4%	25.6%	12.5%

The Ultra model is even less profitable than originally thought and the company will need to look at ways that profitability can be improved. Cost driver analysis may give an indication of how this might be achieved. Alternatively, depending on market conditions, the company may have to consider increasing the price of this model. The Deluxe model under the ABC system is more profitable than the Superior model. The company may wish to direct its marketing efforts towards this model to increase the volume sold and the overall company profitability.

An ABC system can be extended beyond product costing to a range of cost management applications known as activity based management. These include the identification of value added and non value added activities and performance management in terms of measuring efficiency through cost driver rates.

Answer to Question Four

Rationale

Part (a) assesses learning outcomes C1(b) *apply the principles of relevant cash flow analysis to long-run projects that continue for several years* and learning outcome C2(a) *evaluate project proposals using the techniques of investment appraisal*. It examines candidates' ability to identify the relevant costs of a project and then apply discounted cash flow analysis to calculate the net present value of the project. Part (b)(i) assesses learning outcome assesses learning outcome C2(a) *evaluate project proposals using the techniques of investment appraisal*. It examines candidates' ability to calculate the payback period of a project. Part (b)(ii) assesses learning outcome C2(b) *compare and contrast the alternative techniques of investment appraisal*. It examines the candidates' ability to discuss the advantages and disadvantages of payback. Part (c) assesses learning outcome C1(g) *prepare decision support information for management, integrating financial and non-financial considerations*. It examines candidates' ability to explain two factors relating to environmental issues that the company should consider before making a decision regarding the project.

Suggested Approach

In part (a) candidates should firstly calculate the expected future environmental failure costs and compare this to the current level of costs to identify the future cost savings as a result of the investment. They should then identify the other relevant cash flows for each year of the project. The tax depreciation and tax payments should then be calculated. The net cash flows after tax should be discounted at the discount rate of 12% to calculate the NPV of the project. In part b)(i) the project cash flows before discounting from part a) should be used to calculate the payback period. In part (b)(ii) candidates should then discuss the advantages and disadvantages of payback. In part (c) candidates should clearly explain two environmental related factors that the company should consider.

(a)

Other fixed costs
Depreciation per annum = ($60m - $12m) / 6 = $8m

Other fixed costs (excluding depreciation) per annum
= $10.6m - $8m = $2.6m

External environmental failure cost savings:
Expected future cost
($18m x 0.3) + ($12m x 0.25) + ($10m x 0.35) +($5m x 0.1) = $12.4m

Expected Savings = $20m - $12.4m = $7.6m per annum

Cash flows years 1 – 6
Income / cost savings = $5.0m + $5.5m + $7.6m = $18.1m
Fixed maintenance costs = $1.5m
Other fixed costs = $2.6m
Net cash flows = $18.1m - $1.5m - $2.6m = $14.0m

Taxation

	Year 1 $m	Year 2 $m	Year 3 $m	Year 4 $m	Year 5 $m	Year 6 $m
Net cash flows	14	14	14	14	14	14
Tax Depreciation	(15)	(11.3)	(8.4)	(6.3)	(4.8)	(2.2)
Taxable profit	(1)	2.7	5.6	7.7	9.2	11.8
Taxation @ 30%	0.3	(0.8)	(1.7)	(2.3)	(2.8)	(3.5)

Net present value

	Year 0 $m	Year 1 $m	Year 2 $m	Year 3 $m	Year 4 $m	Year 5 $m	Year 6	Year 7
Investment / residual value	(60)						12	
Net cash flows		14	14	14	14	14	14	
Tax payment		0.2	(0.4)	(0.9)	(1.2)	(1.4)	(1.8)	
Tax payment			0.1	(0.4)	(0.8)	(1.1)	(1.4)	(1.7)
Net cash flow after tax	(60)	14.2	13.7	12.7	12.0	11.5	22.8	(1.7)
Discount factors @ 12%	1.000	0.893	0.797	0.712	0.636	0.567	0.507	0.452
Present value	(60)	12.7	10.9	9.0	7.6	6.5	11.6	(0.8)

Net present value = -$2.5m

The net present value is negative therefore on this basis the company should not go ahead with the project.

(b) (i)

Payback

Year	Cash flows $m	Cumulative cash flows $m
0	(60)	(60)
1	14.2	(45.8)
2	13.7	(32.1)
3	12.7	(19.4)
4	12.0	(7.4)
5	11.5	4.1
6	22.8	26.9
7	(1.7)	25.2

Payback period = 4 years + ((7.4 /11.5) x 12)
   = 4 year 8 months

(b) (ii)

- Payback is a simple evaluation method and is easy to understand. However its simplicity is also one of the main criticisms of payback in that it does not take account of the time value of money. This means that cash flows that occur in Year 1 are assumed to have the same money value as the same cash flows occurring in Year 2. This problem however can be overcome by calculating the payback using discounted cash flow.

- The method favours projects that pay back early thus recognising the importance of liquidity for a company. Early payback of cash flow means that the funds can be reinvested in other profitable projects sooner thus leading to increased company growth. It does however ignore cash flows, both positive and negative, after the payback point.

- The method recognises the uncertainty involved with forecasting future cash flows, particularly in a rapidly changing environment. It therefore minimises the risk associated with long time horizons as projects that pay back early are selected in preference to those projects that have a long payback period that may have been acceptable using net present value. However not all risks are related to time and payback may result in many profitable investment opportunities being overlooked because the payback period is too long. It therefore should not be used on its own but in combination with other investment appraisal methods such as NPV and IRR.

(c)

There are a number of environmental factors that are difficult to quantify as follows:

- The investment offers significant reduction in waste and external failure costs. The company may place a value on these above the quantifiable cost savings particularly in view of its commitment and previous proactive approach to minimising negative environmental impact.
- Potential impact on the company image and future sales from being seen as an environmentally friendly company.
- Potential savings in environmental costs relating to pollution and the consequential cost to health care and the global environment.
- Potential saving in future compliance costs if the government changes the compliance levels required.
- The pressure from government, shareholders and other stakeholders to improve environmental management.
